A LAWLESS BREED

John Wesley Hardin, Texas Reconstruction, and Violence in the Wild West

By
Chuck Parsons
and
Norman Wayne Brown
with a Foreword by Leon C. Metz

Number 14 in the A. C. Greene Series

UNT PRESS

University of North Texas Press
Denton, Texas

Printed in the United States of America.

10 9 8 7 6 5 4 3 2

Permissions:

University of North Texas Press
1155 Union Circle #311336
Denton, TX 76203-5017

The paper used in this book meets the minimum requirements of the American National Standard for Permanence of Paper for Printed Library Materials, z39.48.1984. Binding materials have been chosen for durability.

Library of Congress Cataloging-in-Publication Data

Parsons, Chuck.
    A lawless breed : John Wesley Hardin, Texas Reconstruction, and violence in the Wild West / by Chuck Parsons and Norman Wayne Brown.
    p. cm. -- (Number 14 in the A. C. Greene series)
    Includes bibliographical references and index.
    ISBN 978-1-57441-505-6 (cloth : alk. paper) -- ISBN 978-1-57441-515-5 (ebook)
    ISBN 978-1-57441-555-1 (paper : alk. paper)

1. Hardin, John Wesley, 1853-1895.   2. Outlaws--Texas--Biography.   3. Frontier and pioneer life--Texas.   4. Reconstruction (U.S. history, 1865-1877)--Texas.   5. Texas--History--1846-1950.   6. Violence--Texas--History--19th century.   I. Brown, Norman Wayne.   II. Title.   III. Series: A.C. Greene series ; 14.
    F391.H38P37 2013
    976.4'05092--dc23
    [B]
                                        2013009230

A Lawless Breed: John Wesley Hardin, Texas Reconstruction, and Violence in the Wild West is Number 14 in the A. C. Greene Series

The electronic edition of this book was made possible by the support of the Vick Family Foundation.

DEDICATION

For my wife Bettie and her constant support;
for Joe Arrington who loved reading the West;
for Mike Tower and Don Jay, friends to ride the
river with. Also for Connie and Tim Huddleston;
and in memory of my son Jason Wayne Brown
waiting with Joe at Fiddler's Green.
                              —Norman Wayne Brown

Again for Pat who continues to love and support
me in all my endeavors; and to the memory
of two friends of years ago: Ed Bartholomew
of Fort Davis, Texas and C. L. Sonnichsen of
Tucson, Arizona, who encouraged me from
the very first writing efforts–dealing with
the life and times of John Wesley Hardin.
                              —Chuck Parsons

CONTENTS

vi   Contents

MAPS AND ILLUSTRATIONS

FOREWORD

John Wesley Hardin is not a name that most readers today recognize, but as an Old West gunslinger he was the giant of his time. He was a man among men, a titan in Western gunfighter history. Granted that he was not a killer like Billy the Kid, but in his own way, he was better. Billy the Kid supposedly killed twenty-one men. Hardin most likely killed several dozen.

John Wesley Hardin was named for the founder of Methodism, his father a Methodist preacher. So what was it that pointed Hardin in the direction of death as well as history? In this respect, Hardin may have slain as few as fifteen or twenty, or as many as thirty or forty.

However, Chuck Parsons and Norman Wayne Brown made an excellent choice in choosing as their subject a man who would shoot first, pray quick, and ride harder than any outlaws or lawmen in western United States history. It would seem that killing people was what John Wesley Hardin was born for, and speaking of that he was born near Bonham, Texas, May 26, 1853.

As he grew up, his parents raised him in a religious tradition, one steeped in Christian virtues. But somewhere during this early period, he grew up not only occasionally virtuous, but a man on a mission. And for whatever reason this mission seemingly was death. Not his own, of course, but that of folks who opposed him.

Readers may of course wonder about the wicked brew of ideas that bathed and shaped the mind of the boy Hardin. He grew up with a fierce fire and a brimstone religiosity, but what turned him to killing, we really don't know. Did he lose his embedded religiosity, the answer apparently being yes . . . and no.

As a man who could have become a respected and accomplished preacher, he chose instead to become a defiant, murderous outlaw. So as a writer, I have lived most of my adult life in the town where Hardin was killed. I have many times visited his grave at El Paso's Concordia

Cemetery, in which John Wesley Hardin remains to this day. He continues to be the prime drawer of multi-hundreds—even thousands—of visitors each year. Inside this cemetery lie former city mayors, county judges, preachers, shady ladies, ordinary citizens, businessmen, soldiers, teachers, politicians, a large Chinese group, and finally other gunslingers such as John Selman—who ultimately killed John Wesley Hardin. John Selman himself rests under a shade tree perhaps a hundred yards from a foot of concrete covering Hardin's grave. The concrete and cage of course are there not to keep Hardin in, but to prevent screwballs, idiots and lunatics from digging Hardin up.

Leon C. Metz,
El Paso, 2012

PREFACE

In 1895 John Wesley Hardin was nearing the conclusion of his auto-biography. He had brought the story of his adventurous life up to the year of 1889, relating how he was beginning the study of law, deter-mining what books to obtain in order to pass the bar exam. He had just quoted a letter from the noted legislator A. T. McKinney, itemizing what volumes he should acquire. The list of recommended works may have seemed huge, the number totalling twenty-four volumes. It is difficult to picture Hardin seated in a law office (which he had in both Gonzales and El Paso) pondering the contents of those two dozen tomes. We know that in the latter years of his sentence at Huntsville he had the very best of intentions, but once pardoned the realities of the world of 1894 and 1895 altered those good intentions. His law practice, which never really was lucrative, was neglected. His drinking increased as did his gambling. His love affair with the widow no longer had the bloom—in short Hardin was nearing the bottom. When he set aside his pen that day there was one more score to settle, and that was with John Henry Selman Sr. On the evening of August 19, 1895, all the desires of respectability, the dreams of seeing his children lead honorable and respectable lives, the prob-ability of being recognized as an author, all ended. His challenge to Con-stable Selman ended with him being shot dead, collapsing to the floor of the Acme Saloon. He was forty-two years old. He left a modest estate which included nearly 200 handwritten pages telling of his life. That manuscript became the most important part of what he left for posterity.

An El Paso court determined the Hardin children would receive the estate, including the manuscript. The one-time Hardin lover who had probably actually written much of the manuscript while Hardin dic-tated received nothing. She left El Paso and moved on, only to sink into wretchedness.

The first publication dealing with the life of the premier gunfighter of Texas—and arguably the entire American west—appeared in 1896 in a small 144-page soft cover edition with illustrations by San Antonio artist R. J. Onderdonk. It has been kept in print through various editions, the first by the original publishers, Smith & Moore, who discovered that their portrait engraving labeled as John Wesley Hardin was in reality a portrait of his brother, Joseph G. Hardin. They subsequently inserted a smaller page with an authentic photograph of Hardin, a bust image of him wearing a string tie which he had made for his wedding. This image is among the most familiar of gunfighter images.

For years these two editions were all that were available on Hardin. Then in 1925 J. Marvin Hunter reprinted the work in larger format, again in soft covers, with an unsigned introduction by Hunter and four pages of articles from the *Galveston Daily News* relevant to Hardin's life. Curiously this edition is rarer than either of the 1896 editions.

In 1961 the University of Oklahoma Press brought out a new edition of the *Life* as number sixteen in their popular Western Frontier Library series. It included a new introduction by noted western authority Robert G. McCubbin. This hardcover edition was reissued in 1966, 1972, 1977, and in 1980 brought forth in soft cover.

Since the *Life* was first published, many writers have utilized it extensively to recount Hardin's life. Many magazine articles have appeared, generally by a writer who does no additional research and attempts to improve the work with invented conversation and creating incidents for dramatic effect.

Thomas Ripley placed Hardin with other Texas gunfighters in his popular work *They Died With Their Boots On*. This is a casual study of the three most notorious Texas gunfighters: Hardin, Ben Thompson and Bill Longley. It is based on Hardin's *Life* and other secondary works for the treatment of Thompson and Longley. Doubleday Doran & Co. first published it in 1935. Ripley's book received recognition when reviewed in *Time* magazine in its July 29, 1935, issue. In 1936, Ripley's work was published in Sydney, Australia, but without the numerous illustrations of the first edition. It appeared again in 1937 from Sun Dial Press of Garden City, New Jersey, then in 1949 by Pocket Books of New York.

Lewis Nordyke treated the story of Hardin with his biography *John Wesley Hardin Texas Gunman* published in 1957 by William Morrow Co. of New York. This edition, again based primarily on Hardin's *Life*, was reissued by Castle Books of Edison, New Jersey, in 2001. Neither had illustrations, but Nordyke did provide a map of the essential places of Hardin's life. Nordyke did attempt a serious biography, as he visited numerous places where Hardin lived, and interviewed people who had known him, such as F. M. Fly of Gonzales, or were relatives, such as Mr. and Mrs. E. D. Spellman who then owned the Hardin correspondence now archived in the Wittliff Collection at Texas State University in San Marcos. Nordyke could not refrain from inventing conversation, but it is a more reliable work than that of Thomas Ripley.

A totally different format for the life of Hardin appeared with the "graphic novel" of Jack Jackson in 1988: *Lost Cause: John Wesley Hardin, the Taylor-Sutton Feud, and Reconstruction Texas*. This highly respected Texas artist and historian produced a history of the violent post-Civil War period while following the factual aspects of Hardin's career. It was published by the Kitchen Sink Press of Northampton, Massachusetts.

Two highly respected writers produced outstanding biographies of Hardin in the 1990s. Richard C. Marohn's *The Last Gunfighter: John Wesley Hardin* appeared in August 1995, published by Creative Publishing Co. of College Station, Texas. Marohn researched his subject thoroughly and the publisher, James H. Earle, allowed many illustrations to increase the value of the work. Shortly thereafter another extremely well written biography appeared, *John Wesley Hardin: Dark Angel of Texas*, by Leon Metz, published in 1996 by Mangan Books of El Paso. This biography was illustrated with many of the same images as in Marohn's work. Both remain outstanding works of biography.

This is essentially the publishing background of works by and about John Wesley Hardin, although there are also editions which give no credit to the original publishers. Clearly, the life of John Wesley Hardin holds a fascination for many. This writer found the gunfighter fascinating and

for years considered writing the "definitive" biography of the man, but at
the same time other contemporaries of Hardin demanded attention, such
as John B. Armstrong, the Texas Ranger who captured Hardin in 1877.
Another "amateur historian"—Rick Miller—also found the lesser known
contemporaries of Hardin fascinating, and in 1988 his biography of John
Riley "Jack" Duncan appeared, *Bounty Hunter*, also from Creative Publishing Company of James Earle's press. Duncan also participated in the
capture of Hardin.

With this amount of biographical material on the man-killer Hardin
was there a need for another biography? Certainly. Compared to other
western icons such as Custer, Wyatt Earp, Billy the Kid or Jesse James,
the amount of literature on Hardin remained minimal. Chuck Parsons
has found Hardin and his contemporaries, especially his friends and
relatives, a fascinating subject for decades; Norm Brown, fewer years
perhaps, but by chance we met and discovered our common passion for
anything connected to John Wesley Hardin and his associates. A discussion on the feasibility of a biography not only of John Wesley but of his
siblings and friends as well as resulted in an agreement to work together.

From Norm Brown's viewpoint, the interest is relatively recent. "My
interest in John Wesley Hardin began only within the last two years.
My barber is directly related and told me the story of Hardin's brother,
Jefferson Davis Hardin, who was killed in a gunfight in Kent County,
Texas. I also met Don Jay, a Kent County historian and writer who has
authored an article on the death of Jeff Hardin, 'Bad Blood' published
in *Frontier Times* in 1967. His grandmother Fannie Hardin Fox, was
a second cousin of the Hardins. Don knew much about Jeff and the
gunfight and willingly shared his knowledge. This increased my interest, and I was fortunate to locate Jeff's grandson in Arizona who also
shared information and numerous family photographs. Some of my
findings were recently published in the Wild West History Association
Journal."

Chuck Parsons' interest in Hardin goes back to the book by Ed
Bartholomew, *Kill or Be Killed*, which relates the chain of killings from

Hardin killing Charles M. Webb, then John Selman killing Hardin, then George Scarborough killing Selman, then outlaws—possibly Will Carver—killing Scarborough and finally with the killing of Carver by E. S. Briant, ending the chain with Briant's death from natural causes. Through the years I corresponded often with Mr. Bartholomew, and at some point I decided the outlaws and lawmen of Texas would be my primary interest, and of all the hardcases of Texas my concentration centered on Hardin, and to a lesser degree his cousins the Clements brothers.

Through the many years prior to *A Lawless Breed* I was able to share information and photographs I had amassed with both Leon Metz and Richard Marohn. The latter's book appeared in August of 1995. Among my fondest memories is that of sitting alongside him, Leon Metz, and others at a book signing in El Paso at the book's premier as well as the premier of the little pamphlet prepared by Leon for the occasion, *Four Sixes to Beat*, which is now quite rare. It was the centennial of Hardin's death and as far as I was concerned being in El Paso on that occasion was *the* place to be. The day ended with several re-enactments of the shooting of Hardin by Selman in that same bar where the book signing had been, then later with the moon shining over the stones in Concordia we celebrated the event at Hardin's grave.

It may be presumptive on our parts to believe what we have produced is superior—or even equal to—the efforts of the two most recent biographers, Leon Metz and Richard Marohn. We have discovered new information as well as unpublished photographs. We felt we could provide a more complete biography of John Wesley Hardin than previous writers, and the new information would be justification for publication. We envisioned a new and complete biography of Hardin and associates who made such fascinating history.

In our research we paid close attention to the writings of Hardin himself, not only his autobiography but also the many letters preserved, mainly from 1877 until his death. We also went further than merely recording the events he alluded to in the *Life* or the letters: we rarely accepted what he wrote at face value, and frequently discovered information which reinforced statements he made. The events were generally accurately described, verifiable, but naturally presented in his favor. Often we found that an incident he described did occur, in essence, but he, after the years of being an outlaw and the years in prison, having contemplated his life, presented his version with his defending his life and liberty. Naturally the other man would have seen the incident differently. For example: Hardin recounts the run-in with three men he described as State Policemen, even identifying them as Smith, Jones, and Davis. The records of the Police fail to show that any Smith, Jones, or Davis died in the line of duty. Was it a complete fabrication of Hardin? Not necessarily, as we did discover there is solid evidence that Hardin did kill three men whom he *thought* may have been policemen, but were probably bounty hunters after the reward. We believe the incident did happen, not totally as Hardin described of course, and certainly he did not care about their names.

A number of photographs will be new in this book. Among the exciting finds was a photograph of one-time State Policeman Jeremiah Alexander Ferguson, who after a brief period in the State Police later assisted Hardin in his *escape* following a gunfight. In spite of our efforts to learn more about J. A. Ferguson, we did not discover the reason he helped the fugitive rather than assist in his capture. Another example of a new discovery concerns "Tip" Davis. Hardin, prior to leaving Texas in 1874, wrote of saying goodbye to two individuals, George C. Tennille and Davis. From the pages of the *Life* one must accept that these two figures were esteemed by Hardin, or otherwise why would he remember them after so many years. We were pleased to locate a photograph of Davis, when he was a deputy in Gonzales County.

Brother Jefferson Davis Hardin left no autobiography or letters, unfortunately. We did locate some additional information about him as well as his brother Gip. One important find was locating a photograph of one of the three wives of Jeff Davis Hardin, a lovely photograph of her and the children and a niece, a group of Hardins who later changed their name to Davis, apparently due to the "shame" of being related to a member of the

Hardin clan. There may not have been an official name change, but the death records give their name as Davis, not Hardin.

Since the life of John Wesley Hardin and his brothers and cousins has held our interest for so long, we presume it will continue to do so. In spite of once contemplating the definitive biography of Hardin, in our maturity we realize there is no such thing. Once the book is in print we anticipate someone, or several someones, coming forth with new and important information about the premier gunfighter of Texas.

ACKNOWLEDGMENTS

A ny biography worked on over years by two different authors requires the assistance of many, many people. The following are some of those people who provided information or encouragement through the years. If we have overlooked anyone, please accept our apologies.

Annie M. Allis, Special Collections, University of Texas at El Paso; Ronnie Atnip, Frontier Properties, Bonham, Texas; Karen Ileana Barraza, Special Collections, University of Texas at El Paso; El Paso; Melleta Bell, Special Collections, Sul Ross University, Alpine; Donaly E. Brice, Research Specialist, Texas State Archives; Donna Buchell, Chaves County Historical Museum, Roswell, New Mexico; Sarah E. Cleary, Dolph Briscoe Center for American History; Dorothy Elder, El Paso; Douglas W. Ellison, Medora, North Dakota; Elvis Fleming, Archivist, Chaves County Historical Museum, Roswell; David George, San Antonio; Charles D. Grear, Dept. of History, Prairie View University, Prairie View, Texas; Gail Hall, Reference Library, Lordsburg, Hidalgo County Library, Lordsburg, New Mexico; Jane Hoerster, Mason, Texas; Kurt House, San Antonio; Kenneth W. Howell, Dept. of History, Prairie View University; Norman Huppert Sr., Enterprise, Alabama; and Ken Kyser of Margate, Florida, for their assistance in researching John and Gussie Hardin Snowden. Bill C. James, Independent Historian, Carrollton, Texas; Harold D. Jobes, Cedar Park, Texas; Linda Kirkpatrick, Leakey, Texas; John Luckey, Whitehorse, Texas; Dennis McCown, Independent Historian, Austin; Robert G. McCubbin, Santa Fe; Lucy Mendoza, Chief Deputy Clerk Hidalgo County, Lordsburg; Rick Miller, Harker Heights, Texas; Pat Mosher, Director, Records Center and Archives, Gonzales, Texas; Mae Nielander, Del Rio, Texas; DPS Officer Tanner Purvis, for his obtaining court records on Gip Hardin in Junction, Texas; Larry and Paula Reck, Lone Star Ranch, Whitewright, Texas; Marlene Siepel, Director, Hidalgo Library, Lordsburg. Edward Southerland, Sherman,

Texas; Donna Tomlinson, Cypress, California; Rachel Vasquez, Hays County District Court, San Marcos, Texas; Margaret T. Waring, Director, Comanche Public Library, Comanche, Texas; Keith Wilden, Independent Historian, El Paso.

A special thanks to Morris "Mo" Hardin of Lubbock, Texas, historian of the Hardin family and good friend who shared with us much information; Don M. Jay, author and historian, Lubbock, for his assistance with events in Kent County and for the use of photographs from his extensive collection; to Jeff D. Hardin of Arizona, grandson of Jefferson Davis Hardin, for the rare photographs from his collection and his knowledge of the Hardin family; and to Doug Hitchcock and his wife Barbara Slade of Colorado, granddaughter of Jeff Hardin and his second wife Ida Mae Croussore for the information regarding the name change from Hardin to Davis. A special thanks to Dave Johnson of Zionsville, Indiana, who has for years encouraged, and sometimes, nagged to finish a project before starting another; and to Jim and Sarah Mundie of Kenner, Louisiana for their willingness to tramp through various cemeteries through the years to find a grave of someone who played a role in the saga of the Hardin family. A special thanks to Roy B. Young of Apache, Oklahoma, editor of the *Journal* of the Wild West History Association for his assistance in clarifying the relationships among various families of 19th century Texas. And a very special recognition to Bettie Brown and Pat Parsons for their patience, and their support, while we followed the occasionally dim trails of the career of various members of the Hardin family.

INTRODUCTION

*"[M]y father told me to keep in hiding until that good time
when the Yankee bayonet should cease to govern."*

—*John Wesley Hardin*

In November of 1868 young John Wesley Hardin, all of sixteen
years of age, shot to death a former slave who had belonged to his
uncle, Major Claiborne C. Holshousen. The black man was known
as "Maje," a nickname he either adopted or was given. This is the only
name history has preserved for him. It was Hardin's first killing, a killing which he claimed had to happen or else he himself would have been
killed by the overbearing black man. In his mind, this killing—like all
those killings that would follow—was a clear case of self-defense. In his
autobiography, *The Life of John Wesley Hardin, As Written by Himself,*
written years later after many more killings and published the year after
his death, he explained the justification of his violent acts. Some killings he barely mentioned, as if they were of no great importance. Others
received considerably more attention. Each killing, in the eyes of the
law, however, was significant, and John Wesley Hardin became the most
wanted man in Texas, at a time when chronologically he was not yet really a man, but still a boy, a wild and reckless youth. The lines justifying
his killings were written later after he had had ample time to reflect on
his life and career, he having been sentenced to serve twenty-five years
in the penitentiary at Huntsville for the killing of Brown County, Texas,
deputy Charles M. Webb. At the time of his capture he had a reward of
$4,000 on his head.

The Civil War had ended three years prior to the killing of the former
slave, but it was in the years of Reconstruction when Federal troops ruled
Texas. "Wes" Hardin and his father both believed there would be a "good
time," when the troops no longer patrolled, when he could stand trial and

1

come clear for the killing. But that good time never really came, as after the first killing many more followed; Hardin was not able to accurately determine the number of his victims. His many gun battles usually ended in hasty flight, for hanging around to determine if his adversary was dead—or merely wounded—was ordinarily not a wise decision.

John Wesley Hardin became a wanted man following the killing of Maje. Rewards increased from a few hundred dollars, to over $1,000, and finally to $4,000. On occasion he was captured but managed to escape. His final capture occurred on August 23, 1877, in Florida, when Texas Rangers and Florida law officers subdued the man-killer. During that dangerous but successful encounter a companion of Hardin's was killed, but he was now a prisoner and would remain a prisoner until his final release from prison through a pardon from Texas Governor Hogg in 1894. After his 1877 capture Hardin did not kill again, so far as known. The number of victims certainly was twenty, maybe thirty, maybe more. He was a violent man in a violent time of Texas' history. His parents were classic examples of enablers, as each time Hardin returned home to tell his parents of yet another killing, they invariably accepted his version of events and then either helped him find refuge among relatives or provided him with money for traveling expenses while he evaded the law. His father, Reverend Hardin, never informed the authorities where his man-killing son could be found. No doubt he too believed the killings were all done in self-defense. He too expected a "good time" in Texas when young John could stand trial and be found not guilty.

The name of John Wesley Hardin undoubtedly reminds one of another John Wesley: the founder of the Methodist Protestant denomination. Not surprisingly, his father, the Rev. James Gibson Hardin, held high hopes for his son, intending him to follow in the footsteps of the founder of Methodism. In spite of the shame the transgressions of his son brought upon the family name, Reverend and Mrs. Hardin, born Mary Elizabeth Dixon, could look back upon their ancestors and feel a degree of pride. They considered the violent acts of their second-born son a natural but unfortunate result of the times, the unrest following the end of the Civil

War causing him to become a fugitive. They certainly never considered him a narcissistic killer, who no doubt would have become a killer at any other time in the state's history.

John Wesley Hardin could easily boast of his heritage, if he was concerned about his ancestors. Colonel Joseph Hardin, a Revolutionary War veteran, with his wife Jane Gibson moved to Tennessee where they began their family. The couple gave twelve children to the world, of which the tenth child was a son named Benjamin, born February 28, 1782. On December 2, 1801, Benjamin P. Hardin married Martha Anne "Patsy" Barnett in Knox County, Tennessee. The last child born of this union, James Gibson, became a minister of the gospel, James Gibson Hardin.

Several of the children of Benjamin and Patsy Hardin appear as significant figures in John Wesley's autobiography. William Barnett Hardin, born April 20, 1806, in Tennessee, came to Texas in 1826 and established a plantation near Moscow, the site near where Hardin would kill his first man. W. B. Hardin was the first white settler in the area of today's Polk and Trinity counties. Uncle Barnett, as the Hardin boys called him, married Ann Holshousen on August 20, 1829; the couple lived out their lives near Livingston in Polk County. Barnett served in the Texas War for Independence, being wounded during the Battle of San Antonio in December 1835. For his service President Sam Houston granted him 640 acres of land, although in 1855 he moved to a plantation near Livingston where he farmed and helped survey the county roads. That William Barnett Hardin was a successful planter is borne out by the census of 1860. He is shown to be fifty-four years of age with real estate valued at $20,000, plus a personal estate valued at $10,850. But his success in part depended on his slaves who worked for him. The 1860 census enumerator recorded Hardin as owning six slaves, male and female, ranging in age from six years to forty years.

Another brother, Robert Echison Hardin, born April 11, 1808, married Nancy Brinson Dixon on April 27, 1833, she being a sister of Mary Elizabeth Dixon. They left Tennessee and settled in Washington County, Texas, not far from brother William B. Hardin. In 1870, by the time their

Benjamin P. Hardin, father of Rev. J.G. Hardin and grandfather of John Wesley
Hardin. *Courtesy Don Jay Collection.*

nephew John Wesley Hardin was a teenager roaming off to visit relatives
on his own, the census taker enumerated head of household Robert as
sixty-two and Nancy as fifty-two. They had four children: William G.,
age 29; Aaron B., age 23; Joseph, age 19, a daughter Martha, 16, and
one other whom the census taker assumed was also their child, whom
he counted simply as a male, 18-years-old, named John. In reality the
cousin was only visiting when the census taker came. Whoever provided

the information made no distinction between John Wesley Hardin not being brother to the other children in the household. All the boys gave their occupation as farmer. It was at Uncle Bob Hardin's farm that young Wes Hardin occasionally found temporary refuge from authorities. In respect for his aunt and uncle, he worked the land alongside his cousins, William, Aaron, and Joseph.

Tennessee native Joseph B. Hardin and his wife Anne Elizabeth Dixon were established in Hill County, Texas, prior to the Civil War. At age fifty-six Joseph B. operated a hotel, no doubt with the help of his wife and daughters: Margaret, Nancy G. and "Analiza" as the census taker spelled her name. Joseph B. Hardin's younger sister Martha Balch Hardin, born January 4, 1817, in Tennessee, married Emanuel Clements, born May 10, 1813. They married on July 20, 1836, in Marshall County, Mississippi, and after locating in Texas their children—first cousins of Wes Hardin—became close friends. The childhood years of the boys, the years of working cattle and the years of violence, were often times spent together. Of the eleven children of the Emanuel Clements family, three daughters died shortly after birth. Son William Barnett Clements died in the war; Emanuel Jr., known as "Mannen" or "Manning," John Gibson, known as "Gip," Joseph Hardin, known as "Joe," and James A. or "Jim" all worked, played and fought at times beside cousin Wes. Of the four Clements brothers, Mannen died violently: in a saloon brawl. James was killed by his brother-in-law in a personal difficulty.

But the sons of Rev. James Gibson Hardin attracted more violence not only during the period of Reconstruction following war's end, but until their own deaths. Joseph Gibson, born January 5, 1850, died at the hands of a lynch mob in June of 1874; John Wesley, born May 26, 1853, died in a personal argument with a man whose record was perhaps more violent than Hardin's in August of 1895; Benjamin died at the age of nine years of some unknown disease; Jefferson Davis, born September 7, 1861, died in a gunfight in October of 1901; Mary Elizabeth Hardin's last son, James Barnett Gibson, "Gip," born August 15, 1874, allegedly died following an accident on a ship off the coast of Florida in 1918. What double sorrow Reverend Hardin, along with his wife, endured, as a father who witnessed the errant ways of his sons, and as a minister of the gospel who witnessed the sinful life his sons were leading.

CHAPTER 1

FIRST BLOOD

*"To be tried at that time for the killing of a Negro meant certain
death at the hands of a court, backed by Northern bayonets. . . .
Thus, unwillingly I became a fugitive, not from justice, but from
the injustice and misrule of the people who had subjugated the
South."*

John Wesley Hardin

On May 19, 1847, the Rev. James Gibson Hardin (age twenty-five), and Mary Elizabeth Dixon (a year younger than he), were joined in holy matrimony in Navarro County, Texas. History has not preserved any details of the ceremony, however. Presumably, the groom wore his best suit of clothes, and the blushing bride her best dress, but no newspaper account has been found to verify the details of their wardrobe. Any information about the guests also remains undiscovered. The only record that has been preserved is a court document proving that Justice of the Peace Q. N. Anderson solemnized the ceremony.[1]

Mary Elizabeth Dixon, most often referred to by her middle name, was born December 7, 1826 in Sullivan County, Indiana. She was the daughter of Dr. William A. and Malinda McArthur Dixon.[2] There may have been other children who did not survive to adulthood. Several of Dr. Dixon's sons were to die violently, as did their cousins, the sons of Rev. J. G. Hardin. Other families closely related to the Hardin and Dixon families also experienced tragedy due to the post Civil War Reconstruction violence and the fact that they were associated with John Wesley Hardin.

7

Rev. James G. Hardin, father of John Wesley Hardin. *Courtesy the Robert G. McCubbin Collection.*

James Gibson Hardin, born March 2, 1823 in Wayne County, Tennessee, was a minister of the Methodist Episcopal Church, having been ordained at age twenty-two.[3] Hardin was among the early circuit-riding preachers in East Texas, which may be where he met Mary Elizabeth Dixon. Unfortunately, their son "Wes" (as he was frequently called) failed to mention any details about his parents when he wrote the story of his life years later. Their first-born was a son whom they named Joseph Gibson, born January 5, 1850. The name of Joseph for the first-born was a natural for them, as the reverend picked that name from the Bible. It was a common name, yes; but in choosing that name of his first-born, Reverend Hardin showed to all how he intended the boy to become like the father of his Lord. The name Gibson was a family name, repeated through several generations, ultimately reflecting the family's origins.[4]

At the time of the wedding in 1847, much of Texas was unsettled—more than half of it was a dangerous frontier. The Comanche, the fiercest of the southwest Indian tribes, ranged freely over the Panhandle and central and west Texas, as well as what was New Mexico Territory. To the south and west of capital city Austin was a vast area of dangerous territory reaching to the Rio Grande, a natural border which would be contested between the two countries and three races—the Mexicans, "Americans," and Comanche—for generations. Much of the state was a virtual No Man's Land.

The 1850 census reported the Texas population slightly over 212,000. Of these, 154,000 were white; just over 58,000 were slaves, and a very few were free blacks.[5] No one counted the Comanche and other warlike tribe members. So far as is known, circuit-riding preacher Hardin never had difficulty with anyone: whites, slaves, freedmen, or Comanche. He had, however, a singular characteristic as a parent which resulted in serious issues with his sons: he was what society terms an "enabler." When his son Wes told him he had killed a man, he didn't punish him. Instead he gave him money to find refuge among relatives or to leave the country. He often refused to believe what his son had done. If we could magically interview John Wesley Hardin today with our current understanding of

Elizabeth Dixon Hardin, mother of John Wesley Hardin. *Courtesy the Robert G. McCubbin Collection.*

why humans act as they do, we would find the reason for his dissocial behavior. We would also gain insight into the personality of the man-killer's father and mother.

John Wesley, "Wes" as we will call him, was almost a harbinger of things to come. In southeast Texas, Abner H. Cook was named superintendent of a newly constructed state prison in the town of Huntsville in Walker County. When baby Joseph was born, there were only a handful of prisoners. But by the time his brother, John Wesley, entered the world that number had increased to hundreds.[6] Hardin's sons would eventually become inmates of Huntsville State Penitentiary, although not at the same time. But envisioning their sons to be some day inmates of Huntsville prison was never contemplated by the Reverend and Elizabeth Hardin.

Little factual material has been preserved about Reverend Hardin. None of his sermons have survived, giving us insight into the quality of his writings or the themes of his sermons. Why he chose to locate in Fannin County (on the border of modern Oklahoma) is unknown, but by the early 1850s he selected land to purchase on which to establish his home, which also became a primitive school for neighborhood children. In a few years, Fannin County and the three counties bordering it—Hunt, Collin and Grayson—would become the scene of violence among survivors of the defeated Confederate army, as well as those who remained loyal to the Union. Typically of so many young men whose sympathies were pro-Confederate, they later resented the presence of occupation troops in their area. Members of the Hardin and Dixon family seemingly could not avoid participating in this post-Civil War conflict known as Reconstruction. There were numerous Dixon family members in Fannin County and that is, perhaps, the reason Reverend Hardin established his home there. Whatever the reason, the minister created his home. On August 7, 1852, for $200.00 he purchased 100 acres of land out of a 330-acre tract situated on Bois d'Arc Creek.[7]

On the same day, Reverend Hardin purchased, for $40.00, an additional twenty-nine acres situated on Bois d'Arc Creek. He planted four pecan trees to mark the boundaries of his home site. On the southwest corner of his farm, centered within the pecan trees, he built a Methodist church out of logs.[8] Although no remnants of the church or home remain, one can visit the site today and look out on the four pecan trees that mark the exact spot where the Hardins began their family and where John Wesley Hardin was born.

Wes was the only one of the Hardin family to leave a significant paper trail: numerous newspaper articles about him in Kansas, Texas, Florida, Alabama, and elsewhere; his own life story; and a great number of letters his family preserved. He wrote his autobiography after years in prison, but it is a selected and dramatic saga of his adventures, describing only some of the killings, and those are filled with half-truths. He wrote his *Life of John Wesley Hardin* in an effort to prove to the world—or at least his fellow Texans—that what he had done was purely justified in order to preserve his own life or to maintain his personal freedom. He relates how he was forced to engage in several dozen or more killings. Certainly there were others he intentionally ignored. Even the opening paragraph is misleading: "I was born in Bonham, Fannin County, on the 26th of May, 1853."[9] If he had been honest about his earliest years he would have written: "My father owned a piece of land between Blairs Springs Creek and Bois d'Arc Creek, less than two miles from where the town of Whitewright now stands. On this land he had built a home for my mother and the children who were born. Today the location can be easily recognized due to the impressive pecan trees which father planted to mark the boundaries of his homestead." But Hardin, for whatever reason, stated that he was born in the county seat town of Bonham, Fannin County.

Ministerial work demanded the Reverend Hardin's time and effort, as well as tilling the land and helping educate his children. The Methodist church he established on his land was not the first church he started. Five years before, in 1847, he and Rev. James E. Ferguson founded the first Methodist Church of Richland, Navarro County. Years later, the American Association of Methodist Historical Societies honored Richland as the oldest continuous congregation in central Texas. It was an honor indeed for the Hardin family legacy.

The Reverend Hardin's sermons were perhaps preached without notes; if he did write them out, none have survived. But he did leave an impression on one person who provided us with just a glimpse into the preacher's life. John W. Connelly, himself a minister, gathered newspaper clippings and preserved a grass-roots history of northeast Texas. Some of them are his own writings, undated, but the majority appeared as anecdotes in a column he entitled "Old Choc's Philosophy." In one column, he wrote:

> The first Methodist preacher I ever heard in the state was Rev. Hardin, father of the notorious John Wesley Hardin. He was living in that old school house at the time, and in it John Wesley Hardin first opened his eyes upon this world. Mr. Hardin was a good man and an average preacher, and his wife was a most elegant Christian woman. They furnish an illustration of the fact that very pious parents sometimes raise very wicked sons.[10]

To be described as a "good man" would perhaps have satisfied Reverend Hardin if he had known that was how one man remembered him.

Circuit-riding was anything but a secure life style as it required frequent absences from home and frequent moves—as Reverend Hardin spread the gospel he also found it necessary to relocate. In 1860, with war clouds growing darker every day, the Hardin family, now with five children— Joe (ten), John (seven), Elizabeth Ann (five), Martha Ann (three) and Benjamin (one)—moved to Trinity County to be closer to William Barnett Hardin and his household.[11] There were two small communities in the area—Sumpter and Moscow—which became important entities in the life of Joseph and his brother John Wesley, especially Wes. The town of Sumpter lay in Trinity County; Moscow was in neighboring Polk County.

Reverend Hardin intended to join the Confederate army to defend the principles of the South. He even organized a company and got elected captain, but men he knew and respected convinced him that he was more needed on the home front.[12] There may have also been a health issue involved: although he was only thirty-seven years of age he suffered from whooping cough occasionally which prevented him from his normal duties. This may have been the real factor in his not going to the front lines. He may have helped raise a company, but Howard H. Ballenger became the captain, commander of Company M, called the "Sumpter Light Infantry" organized in Trinity County. On May 5, 1862 it was mustered into the Confederate service at Sumpter.[13]

Many boys wanted to join to show their patriotism, but due to their young age they were prohibited from joining up. Wes was one of those boys who had to remain at home, fighting blue-coated Yankees in his imagination, but only for a while. At only nine years old, Hardin "conceived the idea of running off and going with a cousin to fight Yankees," but his father learned of the plan and ended it by giving him a "sound thrashing." This remains the sole punishment Hardin alludes to in his autobiography.[14]

Instead of shouldering a musket with which to kill Yankees, Wes could only observe Reverend Hardin's mustering in the company and observe his preaching. Wes must have observed his father studying law books (he passed the bar examination in 1861). He certainly thought of those years while he himself was in prison studying law. Reverend Hardin also established a Masonic school at Sumpter, fifteen miles northwest of Moscow. Then the family moved again, this time to Livingston, the seat of Polk County. But then in 1865 the war ended and the Hardins returned to Sumpter.

While conflicting armies bloodied the landscape of eastern states, Texas had remained relatively peaceful. Not so for young John Wesley Hardin. In 1861, when he was eight years old, he saw his first act of real violence (or at least the first act of violence he remembered)—the death of one man at the hands of another. The details of this incident remain sparse. Jesse Turner Evans, a virtual Texas pioneer, was born in Georgia in 1816. On April 30, 1855 he was appointed post master of Sumpter and served in that position until June 11, 1856.[15] Evans owned extensive acreage and in 1860 he owned forty-one slaves, blacks and mulattos, ranging in age from eleven months up to sixty-two years.[16] He thus was in a position to loan money to a less fortunate neighbor, John H. Ruff, a twenty-three-year-old farmer born in Alabama.[17]

As Hardin understood it, Ruff owed Evans money, and Evans continually browbeat Ruff to pay it back. Hardin recollected Evans as an overbearing man who "annoyed him [Ruff] greatly" and "being rich and influential, had a crowd of hangers-on around him." Under the influence of the whiskey of Sumpter saloons, Evans began searching for Ruff with the intention of beating him with his cane. When Evans found Ruff in a small grocery store, he "at once commenced to curse and abuse him." Ruff attempted to ward Evans off, but Evans persisted, going so far as to strike Ruff on the head with his cane. Ruff then pulled "a large bowie knife" to defend himself as Evans' friends joined in the assault, hitting Ruff with chairs, while Evans "used his stick freely." Ruff, now fighting for his life, slashed Evans severely in the neck. By this time, Sheriff John F. Moore had arrived on the scene, and he quickly arrested Ruff. Evans' friends carried him off where he could receive medical attention; Ruff was taken to jail. Evans bled to death, his "jugular vein being completely severed, and he soon died and left a large family" as Hardin recalled.[18]

John H. Ruff was from Alabama and, according to the 1860 census, had real estate valued at a mere $260, and no personal estate of note. Ruff may have been jailed initially but he did not remain in jail "for several years" as Hardin believed. He certainly claimed self-defense as his reason for the killing. At this point—in Hardin's recollections of events from his youth—he was inspired to moralize: "Readers, you see what drink and passion will do. If you wish to be successful in life, be temperate and control your passions; if you don't ruin and death is the inevitable result."[19] Why had he not followed his own advice through the years? Perhaps he had gained such insight only after having learned life's lessons the hard way.

John H. Ruff remained in the Trinity County area, probably out on bond and tending to his farm. On April 15, 1862, fourteen months after the creation of the Confederate States of America, Ruff enlisted as a volunteer in Capt. Walter C. Gibbs' Company C. Enlistment was at Sabine Pass, on the Texas coast, about 140 miles southeast of Trinity County where Ruff called home. He survived the war, returned home, and, on September 13, 1869, married Elizabeth M. Sweeney, a thirty-five-year-old widow who had lost her husband two years before. Ruff inherited four young children with this marriage. In July of 1869, he became a guard at the state penitentiary in Huntsville. Over the next seventeen months, he watched prisoners and, at times, worked as a prison steward. His last pay record was dated December 1870. Ironically, if he had remained a few more years, he could have welcomed and guarded his old neighbor from Trinity County—John Wesley Hardin, number 7109. But Ruff died before then, passing from an undisclosed cause on February 25, 1875. Elizabeth M. Ruff, widowed twice by the age of forty, never remarried. She later applied for a widow's pension as a family in indigent circumstances.[20]

Although Reverend Hardin had organized a company of Trinity County men to fight for the Confederacy, he never left the state at the head of those men. The "best citizens" had convinced him he would do more good on the home front. Neither the father nor the son saw action during the war years, but young John Wesley proved to be an irregular soldier during the Texas Reconstruction years, 1865–1874. He claimed to have seen Lincoln burned and "shot to pieces" in effigy so often that he "looked upon him as a very demon incarnate." Hardin learned early "the justice of the Southern cause." He grew up in the midst of the "peculiar institution" even though his father—unlike his Uncles William Barnett Hardin and Claiborne C. Holshousen—owned no slaves. Before the war, Uncle Barnett, as Wes knew him, owned six slaves and Holshousen owned a dozen.

On June 19, 1865, Union General Gordon Granger read the Emancipation Proclamation in Galveston, Texas. How quickly the news of this dramatic, cultural-changing event reached Hardin territory—Polk, Trinity, and Walker counties—is undetermined, but most freedmen found their lives did not improve a great deal as freed men. Most continued to work menial jobs: some joined the army, and some even became cowboys. The children of the slaves often played with the children of their masters before and after the proclamation. During his formative years Wes thought of himself as a "child of nature," explaining that "her ways and moods were my study." His greatest pleasure, he said, was to spend his days in the open fields, the forests and the swamps. Among his playmates he recalled years later were John Norton, Bill Gordon, Shiles and Hiram Frazier and Sol Adams, all of Sumpter. He enjoyed going out "among the big pines and oaks with my gun and the dogs and kill deer; coons, 'possums, or wild cats."[21]

"Constant association with Negroes in my young days," Hardin recalled, "had made me superstitious . . . and I was well versed in old folklore about ghosts, spirits, dead men's shadows, grave yards, etc., and many a time then did I honestly believe I had seen them." Years later, Hardin recalled an almost fatal incident in which he stabbed a classmate, a fellow white boy, identified by Hardin as Charles Sloter, but in truth the name was Slater, as identified by the 1860 census. His father, Georgia-born Samuel Slater was farming in Burleson County in 1850 with his wife, Sarah, and their four children: sons James and Frances and daughters Mary and Martha Ann.[22] Charles was born in 1851. Sometime between 1850 and 1860 the family moved to Trinity County where Samuel—widowed in 1855—continued to farm and raise his five children alone.[23] No contemporary record of the classroom fight between Charles Slater and Wes Hardin is known to exist, but according to Hardin, Slater intended to be the "boss" among the boys at school, and Hardin stood in his way. Slater wrote some "doggerel" on the schoolhouse wall about one of the girls in class and accused Hardin of being the culprit. Hardin denied Slater's accusation, and according to his version: "He came over to my seat in the school room, struck me and drew his knife. I stabbed him twice almost fatally in the breast and back." Hardin could have responded in kind by striking Slater, but his personality prevented an equal response and he drew his knife to stab instead of his fist to strike. He had to prove his way superior, as if others would consider him less of a man if he did not. In his mind, his honor was definitely at stake in this instance. Naturally, there were considerable hard feelings over this incident, and those who supported Slater insisted that Hardin be expelled. Fortunately the school trustees investigated the incident fully and took no action against Hardin, who was now, probably like most boys in those days, continually armed with a weapon. Wes further recalled that the court exonerated him of any wrongdoing; perhaps the same was true for Slater, who may have quit school at that time. Whatever he did after the near-fatal knife fight in the schoolroom is unknown, but by 1880 Slater was living in Collin County, Texas, with a wife and family.[24] His further career has been lost to history, but Hardin recalled he was lynched years later by a mob. We can't determine with finality whether Hardin's belief was true or not, but Charles Jefferson Slater died fairly young (at the age of thirty-six) of unknown causes.[25] What became of the wife and children is also unknown.

As Wes described it, the incident with Slater was definitely an act of self-defense. One cannot help but wonder if the aggressive Charles Slater was not a mirror image of young Hardin, having the same psychological issues as the boy he tried to stab. Unfortunately, we do not have Slater's version of the schoolhouse assault. Fortunately, we do have record of a similar incident of Hardin taking control and using a weapon in the classroom. William Baker Teagarden, born March 13, 1854, was almost a year younger than Wes and sat beside him in their early years of schooling. They were students of Reverend Hardin's school in Sumpter (est. 1859), having "entered in the same class in the study of the alphabet, and under succeeding teachers . . . continued in the same class and at the same desk until [they] passed through the highest classes of the Seminary ten or eleven years later." Teagarden claimed Hardin protected him from older boys, and even from one of the teachers. On at least one occasion, Hardin "stepped out into the aisle of the large school room, with open knife in his hands, and met the irate teacher coming with hickory in hand to whip [Teagarden] unjustly, and told him he would kill him if he struck [him] with that stick. The teacher retreated. . . . [E]verybody in the school room knew that John meant what he said."[26]

Violence and death seemingly were constant during the youthful lives of Wes and his older brother Joe, although Joe was less a "child of nature" than John. The first tragedy to strike Reverend Hardin's home was the death of son Benjamin on August 3, 1868. He was all of nine years old.[27] Typically, Hardin made no mention of this tragedy in his later writing; we are left with the impression that brother Benjamin's death meant virtually nothing at all to him. Was Benjamin simply forgotten? Hardin revealed no concern or even awareness for the sorrow his parents had to have experienced; no mention of seeing his mother weep, nor of his attempting to comfort her. Did seeing Benjamin die and his family grieve mean nothing to him?

Benjamin died in early August. Later that year, perhaps as late as November, Hardin went to visit Uncle William Barnett Hardin in Polk County, four miles north of county seat Livingston. He was—or at least he considered himself to be—a very capable adult then at the age of fifteen, and he often made the trip alone, on foot or on horseback. Wes probably went to make some money helping the family make sugar on the farm. On his way, close to Moscow, Wes met a solitary freedman— formerly a slave of Claiborne C. Holshousen ("Major" Holshousen as friends called him).[28] The name of the freedman is known today only as "Maje," short for the major who once owned him. He was "a large, powerful man," and for some reason Wes and cousin Barnett Jones arranged for a wrestling match against him. William Barnett Jones,[29] five years older than Wes and presumably quite capable of steering him into a wrestling match, made the arrangements for them to wrestle the adult exslave. We have no version of the subsequent events from Barnett Jones; thus we are left with Hardin's explanation.

His account borders on the unbelievable: the two young boys threw Maje twice, the second time drawing blood. It was certainly an accidental facial scratch. "Negro like," Hardin explained, "he got mad and said he could whip me and would do it." But Uncle Barnett and other witnesses drawn to the match ended it, preventing any further altercation that day. Maje threatened Wes and went to get a gun. Hardin went to Uncle Barnett's house, where he was staying, to get his pistol. Maje, then armed and angry, "went around cursing and abusing [him], saying that he would kill [him] or die himself; that no white boy could draw his blood and live; that a bird never flew so high not to come to the ground." At this point Barnett Hardin became involved—"took a hand" as Wes termed it—and ordered Maje off the plantation. This settled the conflict for that day.[30]

The next morning Wes began the journey home, but was to go out of his way to deliver a message to Capt. Samuel Rowe, a neighbor, for Uncle Barnett. After some miles, Hardin overtook Maje who had a "stout stick" in his hand. He was walking along on a path that occasionally ran parallel along a creek.[31] He wrote that it was Maje who now became the aggressor, although one might interpret his writing that as he was on horseback he saw Maje, then easily caught up with him as Maje was on foot, and then he himself initiated the contest. Wes recorded that Maje recognized him on his horse, "Old Paint," and accused Wes of being a coward for not "shooting it out" the previous day. Wes explained that he was "but playing with him," and the scratch was unintentional. Maje threatened to "get hold of him and throw him in the creek." Wes, trying to avoid further confrontation, "whipped Old Paint into a trot" to make a quick get-away. Maje ran along the path parallel to Hardin, and when their paths intersected, he stood, braced and armed, ready to face the white boy who had drawn his blood. Hardin had two choices: fight or run.

Wes stopped and Maje attacked with his "stout stick," which was probably nothing more than a solid walking stick. Maje struck at Wes, and as he did Hardin drew his Colt .44 and warned him to get back. Maje grabbed Old Paint's bridle, but then Wes, perhaps after receiving a few blows from Maje's stick, began shooting, causing him to release the bridle. "He kept coming back, and every time he would start I would shoot again and again until I shot him down." Hardin left the wounded man bleeding in the roadway and went to Uncle Holshousen, seeking help. Holshousen and Wes returned to the scene and found the dying Maje. He still showed fight, even though severely wounded, and called Wes a liar. Uncle Holshousen prevented the boy from shooting the man again. There must have been a brief conference as to what to do with Wes and what to do with the dying freedman; ultimately Uncle Holshousen gave Wes a twenty-dollar gold piece and told him to go home and explain to his father "all about the big fight" and that the wounded man was "bound to die." He also warned him about the "Yankee soldiers who were all over the country at that time." This is how Wes told the story, but there exists at least one other version. Freedmen Bureau Agent Lt. Charles Schmidt learned of the killing and reported it to his superior. His report differs substantially from Hardin's remembered account, stating that the killing happened near Sumpter. Hardin, described as "a mere lad," shot Maje "without cause as the latter did not like the abuse of Hardin." Schmidt reported that Hardin shot Maje "five times every wound dangerous."[32] This last comment suggests that Wes had practiced considerably with his handguns and was a dead shot.

Hardin, now a fugitive, did go home and tell his parents what had happened, and the news "nearly distracted" Reverend Hardin and his mother. Instead of keeping their son at home, the reverend advised him to go to his brother's place on the Nogalus Prairie, near the line of Trinity and Houston Counties, a distance of some twenty miles.[33] Before the war, Hardin would have had no difficulty with the authorities for killing a black man—the man would have been considered of no import, a piece of personal property. But now it was Reconstruction and the game had very different rules than before. Neither the military, nor the Freedmen's Bureau, (created to assist the former slaves adjust to their newfound freedom) could let it pass. Hardin, along with his father and other relatives, perceived that the courts were unwilling to give a white man a fair trial for injuring or killing a black man. He wrote: "All the courts were then conducted by bureau agents and renegades, who were the inveterate enemies of the South and administered a code of justice to suit every case that came before them and which invariably ended in gross injustice to Southern people, especially to those who still openly held onto the principles of the South." Reverend Hardin and other family members believed the boy could not possibly receive a fair trial. Believing his son would receive "certain death at the hands of a court, backed by Northern bayonets," the minister father advised him to "keep in hiding until that time when the Yankee bayonet should cease to govern."[34]

In John Wesley Hardin's mind, he had been forced to become a fugitive from *injustice*, not from justice. Killing Maje was the first serious act that placed him on the road to eventual prison, numerous other killings followed, all in the name of self-defense. Hardin always claimed that he only killed to preserve his own life or retain his freedom. Not surprisingly, Rev. Hardin and Mary Elizabeth had an especially difficult time accepting that their son, only fifteen-years-old, was a murderer. Could young John now have any hopes of becoming a minister like his father wanted him to become? Could John Wesley Hardin, now with blood on his hands, follow in the footsteps of John Wesley, the founder of Methodism?

Even though his killing Maje created considerable grief among Hardin's relatives, some individuals actually praised him, subtly if not openly, for his defiant act against a black man in post-Civil War Texas. Justice of the Peace Frank M. Fly later recorded that "[T]he reason that John Wesley Hardin had the sympathy of many prominent men in the South was that the negroes were afraid of him and he was a protection to the community from the freed slaves roaming the county. Carpetbaggers . . . from the North settled in Southern states and often incited the negroes to lord it over the southern whites."[35] Whether or not young Hardin was consciously aware of it, he had become a hero to some, fighting back against oppression. Others, of course, may have seen him a conscienceless bully. At this point the question of self-defense was all that mattered in his mind.

The military quickly learned, no doubt from friends of the late Maje, of the young white boy who killed a freedman. Unfortunately, no details of the investigation have been preserved. By year's end, only son Wes had gotten into trouble. Older brother Joseph, now eighteen in 1868, had

Frank M. Fly, friend of Hardin and later deputy sheriff in Gonzales County. Photograph by M. Hughes, Gonzales. *Gonzales County Records Center & Archives*

made his parents proud by teaching school at Nogalus Prairie. At the end of 1868 the Hardin family consisted of oldest son Joseph, who was teaching school; next in line John Wesley, who had stabbed a schoolmate and had killed a freedman and was now a fugitive; and the daughters

Elizabeth and Martha Ann, ages thirteen and eleven years respectively, who were helping around the house and growing into young womanhood. The family still mourned the loss of Benjamin, who had died on August 3, and now to add to their grief, they had to worry about Wes. What would happen to the second oldest?

While father and mother Hardin agonized over the path John Wesley was taking, Wes began his life as a fugitive. He joined Joseph, then teaching school at the little community of Nogalus Prairie. Whether Joseph hid his younger brother, or if Wes simply chose to hide elsewhere, is uncertain. He did find temporary refuge at "Old Man" Morgan's where he spent his days hunting wild cattle and game. This may have been J. O. Morgan, a farmer from Tennessee who lived in Navarro County with his wife, four daughters, and a younger son. If this is where teenaged Wes hid out for a while, he certainly must have noticed Morgan's teenage daughters, ages twelve, thirteen, sixteen, and seventeen years of age.[36]

As a hunted man, Wes had to rely on his self-training as a true "child of nature": constantly watching his back like an animal, always on the alert for Yankee soldiers or lawmen. Joseph communicated with him, and even left his teaching duties one day to alert Wes that there were soldiers in the area looking for him. Now, instead of being the hunted man, he became the hunter. Of this incident Wes later wrote: "In a little while the United States soldiers heard of my whereabouts and came after me. . . . I soon was after them instead of they after me. We met in the bed of a deep creek and after a sharp fight two white soldiers lay dead, while a Negro soldier was flying for his life. I ran up on him and demanded his surrender in the name of the Southern Confederacy. He answered me with a shot, when I brought him to the ground with a bullet from my Colt's .44."[37]

If we accept Hardin's version of this incident, it was a successful ambush with the teenager starting the fight with a double-barreled shotgun—killing the white soldiers each with a blast, and then finishing off the third with his pistol. He admitted as much: "I waylaid them, as I had no mercy on men whom I knew only wanted to get my body to torture and kill. It was war to the knife with me." The ambush was successful, but he received a wound in the arm—he failed to explain which soldier fired the lucky shot. Presumably, the two blasts from the shotgun ended the lives of the two white soldiers, who died while the black one fired at Hardin. Instead of leaving the three bodies along the road for the wolves, he, with the help of sympathizing friends, buried them in a creek bed some hundred yards from where they fell. Hardin and his helpers burned their personal effects and took their horses.[38]

This ambush has not yet been confirmed by contemporary documentation, but we accept Hardin's account due to an oral tradition in the area that supports it. Cliff Davis, as a young boy growing up at Nogalus Prairie some years later , found some bones while walking along a creek bed. Davis told his father, who told Cliff that his grandfather Alexander Davis had related the story to him that "a man shot three men and buried them near the creek bed." As an adult Cliff Davis forgot about the bones but recalled what Alexander Davis had passed on when he read Hardin's life story. The physical site was changed after a dam was built and a pond now covers the area where the bones had been originally found. A short distance from that site the old road bed that once crossed the creek is visible, where Cliff Davis believed Hardin shot the Union soldiers and where they were buried. Alexander Davis was a young farmer in 1880 with a wife and family living in Trinity County and could certainly have been aware of local lore such as the killing of three soldiers a decade before. He could easily have told the story to his children who passed it on to their children.[39]

That Hardin had killed one man in 1868 is certain; that he had killed three more before the end of 1868 is probable, but they may have been mere citizens hunting for him, perhaps soldiers only in Hardin's imagination. An ambush by one young man against three *soldiers* would certainly have greater reader appeal in the *Life* than merely shooting down three men. Instead of fleeing the state, which he would do in 1874 after killing a deputy sheriff, Wes returned home to his father and explained what had happened. Father and son then went to Navarro County where Mrs. Hardin had relatives. Reverend Hardin, in lieu of turning his son over to local authorities, now rewarded him, arranging for him to teach in a community school at Pisgah Ridge in Navarro County.

Some have questioned how teenager John Wesley Hardin could in reality have taught a roomful of children of varying ages. Amanda Trammell, born March 10, 1864, at Pisgah Ridge, was perhaps the youngest of his pupils.[40] Years later after her marriage to John Swink, she recalled that she was in a class of twenty-five, crowded in a one-room school house with no books. "Some folks may have made him out real bad, but John Wesley Hardin was a religious gentleman. Why, he prayed before class every morning." If Amanda's memory was correct, was all learning done by the teacher verbally instructing the children with slates, or hornbooks to teach them the ABCs? Was it rote memorization of certain facts? Although Amanda says they didn't have books in the school, the Bible was present in all schools and was no doubt a vital tool in his teaching. A strict teacher could devote every classroom minute to teaching the very basics: spelling, addition, basic writing. And if Hardin's classroom was typical of the day the older students certainly helped teach the younger ones. Certainly the value of learning basic reading was understood: learn to read to learn the Bible. Hardin taught moral values as well as the basic "Three Rs." He may have also emphasized the first law of nature, that of self-defense.

But teaching school was not exciting enough; he had other plans and he ended his teaching career. One may surmise that as a fugitive, albeit a teacher, he had a pistol in his waist band, or concealed somewhere on his person at all times. For a fugitive from justice, a weapon was a necessary tool to assist in teaching the basic lessons to children of the frontier, and perhaps the real frontier was not so far away in the Texas of the late 1860s. During this relatively peaceful time Hardin became acquainted with other relatives and neighbors, such as the Newmans, the Trammells, the Rushings, and kin folk such as the Andersons and the Dixons. At least part of the time John stayed with an aunt, Susanna Louise Dixon Anderson. On March 20, 1869, Reverend Hardin wrote a letter to Susanna, in which he also communicated with his son. "John, there are some dangers teaching school in Navarro [County]. How easy for the prairies to be full of soldiers all of a sudden. Then it is too late!" He advised John that his mother, Mary Elizabeth, sat there beside him with "a sorrowful heart," wishing she was with her son. The reverend advised John that he would try and see him in May or June but if he (John) could get a job driving cattle—perhaps with Uncle Alec Barekman or other "honorable persons"—he should go ahead. "The military" he advised, "may come upon many like a thief in the night! Let them watch the corners—be wide awake."[41]

Hardin ended his teaching duties and then drove cattle, but he spent little time working as a drover, apparently devoting his time to living a fast and carefree life. Besides doing some honest work he also learned various games of chance, such as poker, seven-up, euchre, and betting on fast horses. He soon began to bet on "any kind of horse race, a chicken fight, a dog fight, or any thing down to throwing 'crac-a-loo,' or spitting at a mark." In all likelihood along with learning games of chance he learned to like the taste of liquor, all elements of the life style which he embraced, and which would inevitably lead to more killings and more sorrow to the Hardin family.

Although there is no way to verify the incident, his *Life* claims that during this period he devoted some time to correcting a freedman who had the reputation of insulting white people. No name of an impudent freedman or even a county is given in his memoir, but Wes wrote that he exerted some effort to find him and punish him. Wes probably didn't bother to find out the man's name, only to learn where he could locate this "terror to the community." Disguised as an old and feeble ex-Confederate, he met the man on a country road. The "big burly Negro" began to pop his whip at Hardin and called him "vile names and low-down white trash." Enough was enough: Hardin shed his disguise, drew his six-shooter "told the man to say his prayers before he was killed" for his cruelty to white folks. Hardin fired one shot to scare him, and if we believe his story the "Negro afterwards became one of the best citizens of that county; became civil and polite and was never known to insult a white person, male or female, after that."[42] Those who consider Hardin as nothing more than a blood-thirsty killer must consider the fact that at least on this occasion he claimed he maintained self control. He could have easily shot this unknown man to death, but instead chose to allow him to alter his behavior. Was there an attitudinal change taking place within the heart of John Wesley Hardin then? Or were there other forces at play, such as a crowd of the "big burly Negro's" friends near by?

Among the various families and individuals whom he got to know at this time, Wes recalled in later years Frank Polk, a desperado much like Hardin himself, who had killed at least one man. Franklin Polk is how James A. Nelms, Navarro County sheriff, identified him. Sheriff Nelms prepared a list of crimes committed in Navarro County and a list of twenty names for which "no final Disposition has been Made." According to this list, Franklin Polk had killed Thomas Bandy, no date given, and was released on a bond of $10,000. After Polk had killed Bandy (Hardin misidentified him as "Tom Brady") a squad of soldiers came from Corsicana, Navarro County, to track him down. Hardin's name was also on their list. The soldiers captured Polk but failed to capture Hardin. Polk eventually was cleared of the killing; not so when he later got into a difficulty in Freestone County, and in a brawl on the streets of Wortham was killed by citizens of the town.[43] Two others who would figure in the Hardin tragedy and whose names were also on the list were cousins Hamilton Anderson and James Anderson, charged with the homicide of one Gibbons. At the time a warrant had been issued but no arrest had been made.[44]

Of much greater notoriety than Franklin Polk was John Simpson "Simp" Dixon, son of John H. Dixon, who was brother to Hardin's mother. Wes held a high regard for Simp, and was under the impression that Yankee soldiers had killed several members of his family—his mother, a brother and a sister—and thus Simp had "sworn to kill Yankee soldiers as long as he lived."[45] Hardin also believed he was a member of the Ku Klux Klan. Simp and Wes spent time together, and on one occasion a squad of soldiers challenged them near Richland Crossing. During the "pitched battle" Dixon and Hardin each killed a soldier, while the remaining members of the squad fled.[46] So was Dixon as notorious as some historians would have us believe? Possibly, although the number of his killings could not have been as great as some historians have written. Dr. James Smallwood wrote of the number of murders which had been committed in Reconstruction Texas: "For example," he wrote, "Simp Dixon killed at least thirty men and probably scores more for there was never any report about many of the blacks he murdered."[47] Later, in February 1870, soldiers under the command of Sergeant Adam Desch caught up with Simp Dixon, when he was alone. This time the result was far different, as the *McKinney Enquirer* reported, in part: "When he was ordered to surrender he drew his two six-shooters and commenced a rapid fire upon his assailants, until he had nearly exhausted his charges, and being rushed upon by the troops he stood his ground and fought desperately until he was killed." Simp Dixon was buried in what is today the historic Fort Parker Memorial Cemetery near Groesbeck, Limestone County. Wes wrote that Simp was nineteen years old at the time of his death, and "was undoubtedly one of the most dangerous men in Texas."[48]

At the end of 1869 brother Joe and his parents convinced Wes to leave Navarro County and go further west into Hill County. He stopped for a visit with Aunt Anne Hardin and her family, and also Uncle Barnett Hardin.[49] In Hill County, located midway between the counties of McLennan and Dallas, was Hillsboro and a smaller community known as Peoria. There were opportunities for a wild youth: places to explore, places of excitement and places to gamble, challenging fate. "Jim" Bradley was among the gambling fraternity whom Wes would meet, a man from Arkansas who had a reputation and who would challenge the young Wes. The pair would meet with deadly results.

CHAPTER 2

GUNFIRE IN HILL COUNTY

*"He commenced to fire on me, firing once, then snapping, and
then firing again. . . . I fired with a Remington .45 at his heart
and right after that at his head. As he staggered and fell, he
said, 'O, Lordy, don't shoot me any more.' I could not stop."*

John Wesley Hardin

Hill County lies in north Central Texas, a day's ride south of Fort Worth and two or three days' ride north of Austin in Hardin's time. The county was created in 1853—the year Wes Hardin was born—and an election was held to select county officials on May 14 of that same year, twelve days prior to Wes's birthday. James H. Dyer was elected county judge and Charles Davis the first sheriff. That the county strongly supported Secession was made obvious to any who may have doubted by the final vote: 376 for and only 63 against. Home Guards were established to protect the citizens from possible marauding parties; three cavalry units were created and left to fight during the war, mainly in Louisiana and Arkansas. Following the war's end great resistance was made against the occupation troops. Enough turmoil was reported that Gov. Edmund J. Davis deemed it necessary to declare martial law in January 1871 to re-establish order by sending in the State Police, although by then Hardin had moved on.[1] How much of this historical background Hardin was aware of cannot be determined, but he would become familiar with the character and purpose of Governor Davis' police force.

Hardin made enjoyable family visits to Aunt Anne Hardin at Hillsboro, or Hillsborough as it was then called, the county seat. She was the widow of Joseph B. Hardin who had been elected sheriff of the county

30

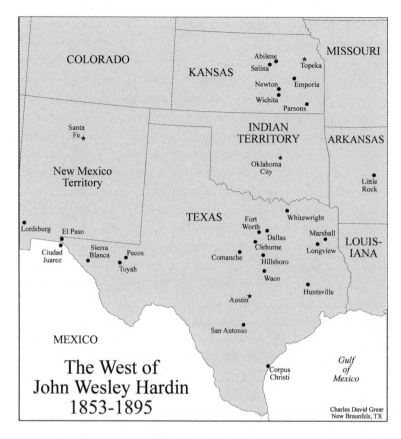

COLORADO

KANSAS

Abilene
Salina
Topeka
Newton
Emporia
Wichita
Parsons

MISSOURI

Santa
Fe ★

New Mexico
Territory

INDIAN
TERRITORY

Oklahoma
City

ARKANSAS

Little
Rock

Lordsburg
El Paso

Ciudad
Juarez

Sierra
Blanca
Toyah

Pecos

TEXAS

Comanche

Fort
Worth
Dallas
Cleburne
Hillsboro
Waco

Whitewright

Marshall
Longview

Huntsville

LOUIS-
IANA

Austin ★

San Antonio

MEXICO

The West of
John Wesley Hardin
1853-1895

Corpus
Christi

Gulf
of
Mexico

Charles David Grear
New Braunfels, TX

The West of John Wesley Hardin, 1853–1895. *Map courtesy Charles David Grear, Ph.D.*

on August 4, 1862. She also showed her business acumen by successfully operating a hotel. The 1860 census shows him as a fifty-six-year-old Tennessee native with wife Anne and children Margaret, twenty-six; Nancy G., seventeen; and Analiza, fifteen.[2] The next household the census taker visited was that of Barnett Hardin, a stock-raiser, and his wife Minerva, and their family. Needless to say a visit to Hill County provided ample opportunity for young Wes Hardin to lose himself among friendly relatives. But Hardin needed more excitement than his visits with family members could provide. Excitement with the element of danger and situations where he could challenge the laws of chance, such as the various types of card games he was becoming expert in, was what he craved most. Harsh words could easily become a reason for gunplay.

One such place offering that kind of excitement was the community of Towash, named after an Indian tribe that had called the area their home before the westward push of white settlers drove them away. When Wes arrived it was a thriving village situated on the mouth of Towash Creek, fifteen miles west of county seat Hillsboro. The basics of a frontier community were established there: the Dyer mill, operated originally by brothers James Harrison and Simpson Cash Dyer; several stores, a wagon yard, a blacksmith shop, a church, a ferry boat crossing over the Brazos River, and more importantly for young men looking for excitement, there was also a race track for men and boys to exercise their mounts as well as to place bets on the outcome of races. It was known as the Bowles track, probably named after Thomas Bowles, the man who carved it out of the good earth in the first place, and who by chance was the sheriff who followed Joseph B. Hardin after he died in office in December 1862.[3]

Once there, Hardin established a partnership with a man named John Collins, but perhaps his partner really was James B. Collins who resided there in 1870.[4] Hardin called him a relative but did not explain how he was related, nor did he identify what type of partnership the pair made. All he said was that he and Collins were partners, "until a tragedy occurred that forever dissolved our partnership."[5]

The tragedy, described by Hardin in terms reminiscent of a Greek tragedy, was another killing, one which in his version was simply a case of kill or be killed. Unlike the previous deaths attributed to this young gunfighter that remain with little corroboration by contemporary records—other than the killing of Maje—that of Benjamin B. Bradley is well documented. It was significant, significant as perceived by Hardin in that he devoted approximately 2,000 words to it in his autobiography, far more than any of the other killings with the exception of that of Charles Webb in 1874.

Perhaps the best known image of John Wesley Hardin, possibly his wedding portrait. *Courtesy the Robert G. McCubbin Collection.*

The Bradley killing occurred in mid-December 1869, although Hardin, writing years later, placed it just prior to Christmas day. He only had
a vague recollection that it was around Christmas, and that it occurred
at the little community of Towash; possibly he felt placing the killing
so close to Christmas Eve gave it a more tragic if not dramatic touch.
Fortunately a small item in *Flake's Semi-Weekly Bulletin* of Wednesday,

December 22, 1869, provides the date. It was reprinted from the *Waco Register* of December 18. Even though the two protagonists' names were reversed, it is a valuable clue to an early Hardin killing. "We learn that on last Saturday [December 11] at Williams' gin, below Towash, Hill county, a young man named Bradly, late from Rusk county, shot and killed a man named Hardin. We have none of the particulars, save that the affair grew out of card-playing."[6]

Towash had its grocery store next to the mill and both were operated by Simpson C. Dyer who was now in partnership with a man named Jenkins. We presume the introduction of Williams' gin is part of the confused report received initially by the *Waco Register* and repeated by the *Flake's* report, not knowing any different. Dyer was a sixty-year-old Georgian who perhaps left most of the mill operations to his son, also named Simpson, a nineteen-year-old and also Georgia-born. Dyer also had six black servants and laborers on his payroll. Elsewhere in the community was a twenty-year-old laborer named George Boles, as spelled by Hardin, but certainly correctly spelled Bowles. Bowles was also a Texan, and was perhaps of the same family who operated the race track.

In addition to these locals, others who would play a role in the tragedy included a Hamp Davis, a Judge Moore, and a man who had a reputation as a dangerous desperado who had killed at least one man thus making him a fugitive from justice in Arkansas—if we believe Hardin.[7] To Hardin the man was known as Jim Bradley, but his real name was Benjamin B. Bradley, and he was indeed from Arkansas, although a native of North Carolina.[8]

At the race track a number of men gathered to gamble; all seemed peaceful among the men until Bradley and Hardin disagreed on some point of racing etiquette. Their disagreement turned to anger, and their anger increased nearly to the point of drawing their weapons, it becoming almost "a shooting match" as Hardin recalled. Nearly all the other gamblers were armed, but by the end of the day, with horses tired and nerves relaxed, the men opted to play cards. The group chose a building separate from Dyer's grocery store and began playing poker. As Hardin recalled, the setting was "in a small box house . . . with a place open for a chimney in the north end. . . . about 13 × 14 feet [in size] and was situated about a quarter of a mile from the grocery." Not long after the game commenced tempers again flared, the pair nearly drawing their weapons. Once the game resumed Collins stood watch over the four players: Hardin, Bradley, Davis and Moore. Hardin related that he had removed his boots and set aside his pistol, an unwise choice to make for the sake of comfort.

By midnight Wes had won all the money, around $100 in coins, and chose to quit the game. But then the argument erupted, and now became violent. Naturally Wes placed the blame on his protagonist, Bradley, who "drew a big knife, [and] made a grab for me." Collins prevented Bradley from stabbing Hardin. Bradley wanted money and threatened to kill him if he did not give up all his winnings. Again Collins interfered, and Wes escaped from the building intact, although without boots or pistol. Collins urged him to go home, in spite of his embarrassing position of being bootless and weaponless. He refused, saying he could not and would not leave in that condition. Collins managed to persuade Bradley to allow Hardin his boots, while Wes borrowed a pistol from someone. Then, booted and suitably armed, he and Bradley confronted each other. As Wes recalled:

> [We] saw Bradley with six or seven others, including Hamp Davis, coming toward us, threatening to kill me, his crowd urging him on. . . . Bradley . . . commenced to fire on me firing once, then snapping, and then firing again. By this time we were within five or six feet of each other, and I fired with a Remington .45 at his heart and right after that at his head. As he staggered and fell, he said, "O, Lordy, don't shoot me any more."

But Wes could show no mercy, and he admitted it: "I could not stop. I was shooting because I did not want to take chances on a reaction. The crowd ran, and I stood there and cursed them long and loud as cowardly devils who had urged a man to fight and when he did and fell, to desert him like cowards and traitors."[9]

So said Hardin, after more than a decade of prison life pondering the events of his wild life. If Hardin had been honest with himself in relating the adventures of his life, he would have described what happened in the aftermath of the Bradley killing. That killing, for those who may be tabulating the number of dead men at his hand, is a definite kill. Several others immediately in the wake of Bradley's death are uncertain. Due to contemporary evidence we must increase the tally of Hardin's dead. While Hardin might have put the killing out of his mind, two years later, in 1872, an indictment was drawn up charging that he "feloniously, willfully, unlawfully and of his malice aforethought" did kill and murder Benjamin B. Bradley. The image Hardin wished to create in the mind of his readers was that this was yet another example of his being forced to kill to save his own life, that he was a victim of external events. But as demonstrated by the indictment, the good citizens of Hill County perceived the killing of Bradley in a totally different light.

The "tragedy" happened, according to "creditable sources" in the county, quite differently from what Wes described. The killing took place during the night of December 11, 1869, not Christmas Eve, following an argument during a card game. The other players managed to convince the pair to forget their differences, but

> Later Hardin missed some money and charged Bradley with taking it. Somebody put the lights out. The lights were lit again and Moore [one of the players, called "Judge Moore"] was missing. Hardin went out to look for him. Hardin and Collins left the house to go up to a saloon on the hill. On the way they met Bradley. He was on the ground holding his horse. He [Hardin] said: "Is that you Ben?" Bradley answered, "Yes," and he had no sooner spoken than Hardin fired. Mounting his horse he disappeared. Moore was never seen after that night.[10]

That Moore "was never seen after that night" gives credence to the belief that Moore was also killed, but Wes, writing years later, chose to overlook that. That Wes conveniently overlooked some killings in his writing is certain; it is suspected that the killing of Judge Moore was ignored. Lending credence to the account originating in Hill County was the statement that "old settlers" had been interviewed who knew of the Bradley killing as well as the killing of "a Negro in Leon County," and that Hardin had been in the county four or five months before the "difficulty" with Bradley. Wes claimed that a mob formed quickly against him, and that "the whole country, with the exception of a few friends and relatives" were hunting him. The relatives would include members of the Anne Hardin family, of the William Barnett Hardin family, and perhaps members of the James W. Page family, whom Hardin recalled as relatives. The truth will never be known for sure: did Bradley win the money from Hardin fairly and Hardin chose to kill him to regain it? Did he blame Bradley and Moore for his losses, and then killed both? What is curious and lends credence to the killing of both Bradley and Moore is that over two years later, on October 10, 1872, a George W. Taylor of Travis County, swore in an affidavit that Hardin "confessed in his presence that he killed two men in Peoria, Hill County, two years previously," or, in 1870. A week following Taylor's affidavit, on October 17, Adjutant General James Davidson wrote to the Hill County sheriff that Hardin, then under arrest, made a statement that he had killed two men in Peoria. Curiously Hardin makes no mention of any action in Peoria. With this information, on October 30, Davidson issued a *capias* against Hardin for the murder of Benjamin B. Bradley.[11] Wes Hardin left Hill County behind but it would not become peaceful with his absence. As if they had been waiting, within months of the Bradley killing Kincheloe "Kinch" West and a dozen or more ruffians caused additional turmoil in that county. Hardin had gone on by that time, and he and the notorious Kinch West never met so far as known.[12]

Due to the callous unconcern for others, whatever violent acts he committed at Towash and Peoria did not cause him any concern. The problem that had been raised over gambling had resulted in his killing again, but he would experience no feelings of guilt or remorse. In the mind of John

Wesley Hardin, the one or two or three men who were killed had brought about their own deaths. He was forced to defend himself once again.

With the blood of one or more behind him, Wes left the excitement and the relatives in Hill County, traveling east toward Navarro County where he spent a brief period with his "dear mother and my brothers and sisters." But soon Reverend Hardin alerted him that a mob—or perhaps in reality a legally organized posse—from Hill County was after him, headed for Pisgah believing he was hiding out there. Hardin and several of his "best friends" met the mob near Pinoak,[13] then a small community in eastern Milam County, several miles from Pisgah. He and one of the friends informed the mob, which had to be a relatively small number of Hill County citizens, that "if they loved their wives and children to go back to Hillsboro. They went." Then Hardin "fixed up" his affairs with cousin Alexander Henry "Alec" Barekman and the pair headed for Brenham, the county seat of Washington County, directly east of Austin.

Wes recalled that he headed for Brenham on January 20, 1870, intending to visit Uncle Robert Echison Hardin and family. On the way, however, he stopped at a place he recalled as Horn Hill where a traveling circus was in town; again Hardin erred in the community's name as it was in reality known as Union Hill. Wes claimed he found all the rooms at the local hotel filled with visitors. He did find space where some of the circus men had established a site for camping, and where there were campfires, there was welcome warmth. It was in this setting that another incident occurred that ended in gunfire. Hardin claimed he accidentally struck the arm of one of the circus workers who then testily challenged him, threatening to injure him. Hardin of course could not let well enough alone and responded in kind—after all, he had to defend himself. Harsh words ended in gunfire, with Hardin shooting the man. Surrounded by the man's friends, he and Barekman left immediately. Did the circus hand receive a mortal wound, or was he simply wounded and survived? Hardin did not stick around to find out, although he later boasted of shooting his victim between the eyes. In fact the man may have survived whatever wound he received.

That little community known as Union Hill was originally known as the Kerr Settlement, later named Union Hill due to the "harmonious disposition of the people" and due to it being situated on a high hill, located two miles north of present-day Burton, Washington County. By the time Hardin was there the population had reached 1,500 people with two Methodist ministers, four physicians, seven merchants, and teachers, pupils, lawyers, a stone mason, a blacksmith and other businesses. Later in 1870 the railroad entered nearby Burton, and the businesses moved there, leaving Union Hill to become only a memory soon after Hardin's visit.[14]

Hardin could not have imagined that what really happened would become news in an eastern newspaper. The *New York Clipper* carried news of circuses and although Hardin was not named as a participant, the time and place certainly indicate his recollection was based on reality. The *Clipper* reported in its "Circuses" column:

The Orton Brothers Circus had a "cleaning" match on Jan. 21st at Union Hill, Texas. Some roughs tried to pass into the show without paying, but the canvas boys went for the crowd and "cleaned" them. After the concert at eight three roughs returned and commenced firing on the canvas men. None of the circus boys were hurt, but one of the roughs was reported to have died the following day.[15]

This description obviously was quite different from how Hardin wished it to be known by his readers, and certainly more accurate.

Shortly after this incident Wes and Alec separated, at least for a while, but later would be together again. Now Hardin again headed for Brenham, but found himself in Kosse, not far from present-day Calvert and Bryan in Brazos County. Here Wes fell to the charms of a pretty girl. In his dramatic version of the incident he was invited to her house where they soon began demonstrating their mutual affection; but then there was a knock on the door. Actually it was a set-up and the girl's paramour, or pimp, entered and demanded money from Wes to ignore what he had found. In spite of his relative inexperience, or perhaps because of his experience, Hardin pretended to surrender his money to the man. He claimed he had a little money on him but had more in his saddlebags on his horse. The man, identified as Alan Comstock by historian Charles Askins, first wanted the money he had on him.[16] Wes pulled some coins from his pocket and managed to purposely drop a few on the floor, at which point the naïve man stooped to pick them up. That was his fatal mistake, as when he looked up it was into the barrel of Hardin's six-shooter, perhaps the same Remington .45 with which he had dispatched Bradley. Wes fired. He ignored the girl and did not stick around long enough to find out if his bullet was fatal or not. Fired at such close range it probably was. Although no contemporary document has been located to substantiate Hardin's claim, local lore indicates that the man did die from Hardin's bullet, and the incident happened in the Dillon Hotel.[17]

Robert E. and Nancy Brinson Hardin, aunt and uncle of the gunfighter. *Author's Collection.*

With the troubles at Union Hill and Kosse behind him, Hardin again was on his way to visit family in Washington County. Here was Uncle Robert E. Hardin and Aunt Nancy, and their children. Uncle Bob was sixty-eight years of age and still considered himself a farmer, while Aunt Nancy, fifty-three, kept house. Their oldest two boys, Benjamin and John, were grown and had left home although William, Aaron and Joe were there still, along with sister Martha. Now Wes Hardin could settle down to a more peaceful life style and do honest labor. But whether doing the hard work of farming or the easier work of teaching, Wes had to have his revolver with him at all times. During the day Wes helped with farm work, and whatever money he earned he gave to Aunt Nancy. He recalled it was a relative peaceful time: "I thus became a farmer and made a good plough boy and hoer."[18] Not having any reason to discredit such a statement one must accept it at face value. He was considered a member of the family, literally, as on July 20 census taker B. J. Arnold visited the Robert Hardin farm and noted the head of household claimed $6,740.00 worth of real estate and $1,000 worth of personal estate. Wife Nancy kept house and their four children still at home were listed as William G., 29; Aaron B., 23; Joseph, 19; and Martha, 16, but without occupation. The 18-year-old enumerated as family was listed simply as John Hardin, and one wonders if B. J. Arnold had any inkling that this teenager was the already noted John Wesley Hardin. The boys' occupation was listed as farming.

Although Hardin may have prided himself on his ability to operate a plow and a hoe, and generously gave his money to Aunt Nancy to keep, he was less than honest with her. "I would often want to go to Brenham and did go with William or Aaron or Joe. I used to find it hard to get my money from my good aunt. I used to tell her I had to go to town to get me a pair of shoes or a hat and that she could not suit me if she went."[19]

Of course going to Brenham meant finding a place to challenge fate, by shaking dice or betting on the fleetness of a horse or the turn of a card. On one occasion Wes said he won $60 at the popular game of roulette, and then gave the winnings to Aunt Nancy to keep. She wanted to know the source of the money and Wes told her "with a laugh that I had the money all the time." On one occasion the tables were literally turned on the boys. Will and Wes rode their "best horses" to town and hitched their mounts to the courthouse fence. While they were "sporting," however, those best horses disappeared. Not daring to go to the Brenham authorities, the luckless boys "rode a hundred miles or more, we never laid eyes on those horses again."[20] One wonders how they explained this incident to good Aunt Nancy and hard-working Uncle Bob and if Aunt Nancy could possibly be as naive about the source of Wes's money as he believed.

Census taker B. J. Arnold's visit to the Hardin home was only one event during that summer of 1870. The government in Austin was wrestling with the amount of lawlessness in the state. The legislative concern now was not the marauding Comanches or Kiowas raiding eastern settlements, but desperados waging war against law and order. Republican Gov. Edmund J. Davis now established a force to combat lawlessness, the State Police.

> I have always said we must have peace and quiet in Texas—that lawlessness must be suppressed. . . . I do not purpose [sic, propose] to impose upon you a military government, and maintain it over you by force. I will establish order without regard to politics. I do not attribute lawlessness altogether to politics. A large class are not politicians. But, my friends, we have always been lawless in Texas. . . . We are the most lawless people on the face of the earth.[21]

Whether or not Texans were the most lawless people on earth was not further discussed openly, but Governor Davis did receive credit for whatever good the State Police did, and blame for whatever bad happened because of the State Police. The police bill did pass in the legislature. The force was composed of one chief of police, the duties falling on Adjutant General James Davidson, four captains, eight lieutenants, twenty sergeants and 225 privates. The men would have no uniforms, but each—on paper at least—would be issued a silver badge with the wording, "State Police" on it with a number. All sheriffs, deputies, constables, marshals, police and their deputies would become a part of the force. The primary responsibility of each member was "to see that the laws of the State are observed and enforced, and use their utmost endeavor to prevent and repress crime of all kinds."[22]

The force never reached full strength, but of the four initial captains—Leander H. McNelly, John Jackson Marshall "Jack" Helm, M. P. Hunnicutt and E. M. Alexander—two would have a definite influence on the young fugitive living with the Robert Hardin family. After all, the police bill provided that any member of the force who captured a fugitive for whom there was a reward offered would receive that reward. While Wes Hardin plowed and tilled his uncle's fields in the Brenham neighborhood, when not gambling or sporting with one of his cousins, L. H. McNelly was preparing himself for his new position as one of the captains of the State Police. His home was near Burton, a mere ten miles west of Brenham. No evidence suggests that McNelly and Hardin ever met, as Hardin respected the man sufficiently to purposely avoid him. In contrast McNelly desperately wanted Hardin, but never caught up with him.

Wes Hardin may have found some tranquility working with Uncle Bob and his cousins, but one wonders if he gave much thought to his parents and siblings. The Robert Hardins certainly were aware of their guest's growing notoriety and must have experienced some concern. But what stress they felt, John's parents had more. Besides the grave concerns for son Wes, Reverend Hardin had health problems, which only added to the family's stress. He suffered from a type of pneumonia leading to fits of coughing: it certainly interfered with his preaching. In August 1870 he hired some workers to cut timber and at times was with them. On August 26 it rained and due to the dampness he became ill and suffered from a fever. When he reached home Mrs. Hardin gave him medicine, but the next day he was still very sick. On the following day she wrote he had "come home yesterday Still very Sick [and] took medicine. Last knight [*sic*] very Sick to day vomiging [*sic*]. He is So Sick[.] I do feel so uneasy."

Besides worrying about her husband, she also had cause for concern for her son Wes. They had just received a letter from their son Joseph, who shared with them news of family members he had visited. He "was treated very kindly" by them all, he wrote. Joe had intended to meet brother Wes in Round Rock, north of Austin, but Wes had left a week before and now his whereabouts were unknown. Joe wrote that Wes "Said that he was going on to meet us and that is the last we have herd [*sic*]" of him. Joe explained that he thought his brother was at Mount Pisgah. With such stress Mrs. Hardin could not conceal her anguish in her reply to Joe: "if my Sweet Johnny is there tell him to come to us a mediatly [*sic*] his Pa Says So. We want to see him So bad tell him to come quickly." The letter's salutation was to "dear brother" but much of the letter was intended for her other son Wes, whom the family called John, to read as well. She concluded: "I hope to see you face to face ear [*sic*] long. The children wants [*sic*] to see you so bad. Come home Sweet John." The children then at home, who grew up without really knowing their brothers Joseph or John Wesley, were Elizabeth Ann, Martha Ann, and Jefferson Davis, born September 7, 1861, and the youngest Nancy D., born May 31, 1866. At the time she explained that they were three miles above Mt. Calm at the widow Rushing's house.[23] A last request was that if they were not at home when he came to visit "we will be in the neighborhood [please do] come Johney."

Further lines reveal a statement that presumably only the immediate family members would understand—if the letter should fall into the wrong hands. "John," she added, "if you are at Pisgah come home to us your Ant [*sic*] Prude[24] would not come to see us. Start and do not stay with them. I could tell you a great many things though."[25] The reference almost certainly alludes to the hatreds between the Anderson family and the Love family, now in its second decade of bitterness. This was one dispute that Wes and Joe Hardin would avoid participating in.

At about this time, Hardin claims to have encountered the famous gunfighter William Preston Longley. In 1870, Longley was the subject of a $500 reward offered by the commander of the Fifth Military District. Longley and partner John Wilson each bore the $500 reward, dead or alive. The pair had committed a number of crimes, but what drew the attention of the military resulting in such a large reward was their alleged slaying of a freedwoman near Evergreen during that year of 1870. Many consider Hardin and Longley the two deadliest gunfighters of post-Civil War Texas. The question naturally arises: did they ever meet? Years later Wes described a meeting with Longley and others in a gambling game at Evergreen. His version not only depicts him as taking no sass from the older Longley but describes Longley as an overbearing man who upon realizing Hardin was not afraid of him offered his apologies. Hardin recalled Longley "as a dark-looking man [who] came to me and said, 'My name is Bill Longley and I believe you are a spy for [Police Captain Mc-Nelly]. If you don't watch out, you will be shot all to pieces before you know it.'" Hardin was not about to back down and replied, "You believe a darned lie, and all I ask is that those who are going to do the shooting will get in front of me. All I ask is a fair fight, and if your name is Bill Longley I want you to understand that you can't bulldoze or scare me." Then Longley apologized: "I see I have made a mistake." Wes then provided a detailed description of a card game during which he won $300. "Some way or another they all got on to my identity, and they all treated me with a good deal of respect at the races the next day."[26]

Unfortunately the Hardin-Longley confrontation happened only in Hardin's imagination, although he did very likely gamble in Evergreen. Among others, he did meet up with Philip H. Coe, a professional gambler who was afterwards killed in Abilene, Kansas, by the noted marshal James Butler "Wild Bill" Hickok. He also met a lesser known gambler, Benjamin J. Hinds. He claimed it was Phil Coe who gave him the nickname of "Young Seven-Up," which no doubt revealed Hardin was proficient at the popular card game of Seven-up.

Hardin remained with Uncle Bob Hardin until the crops were in. Then, after consulting with friends he decided to move on, no doubt due to McNelly's success in hunting fugitives. He left the Hardin family and went to Round Rock in Williamson County, a town that eight years later would become famous as the site of the gun battle between outlaw Sam Bass and the Texas Rangers. At Round Rock he visited Julius C. Landrum, his teacher from back in the 1860s. Round Rock today is proud of its "outlaw heritage" based on the stories of Sam Bass dying there and John Wesley Hardin spending a day or so at Landrum's higher institute of learning. Local history places this in 1872 but certainly the year was 1870.

Following his visit with Professor Landrum, Wes headed to Navarro and Limestone counties, visiting unidentified friends and relatives. "I naturally wanted to see them," he recalled, "even if I had to take risks in doing so." He claimed that he still cherished the hope that the day would come when he "could stand my trial and come clear. My father always told me that when the Democrats regained power, I could get a fair trial, but I would never expect that under carpet-bag rule. Of course I had long ago concluded not to surrender for the present, and whenever force was unlawfully employed to make me do so, I met it with force, or else got out of the way."[27] Hardin here reveals his father's influence, that even after killing freedmen and whites he could be acquitted of the numerous killings with a plea of self-defense. Writing in 1894, with years to reflect on his father's teachings, as well as his own beliefs, he obviously was not being realistic. He had conflicted with society from the late 1860s to 1874, and yet he still believed it was society that was at fault.

After spending some time at Pisgah where he gambled for a while, he then went on to Mount Calm where Reverend Hardin taught school. There he earned some money peddling in hides, but was it honest labor or was it the business of stealing cattle and selling the hides? Brother Joe sent him a letter advising him to come to Round Rock again, and Wes recalled he received a letter from Professor Landrum also, asking him to return to school so he and his brother could graduate together. "I went up

Brother Joseph G. Hardin, lynched by a mob in 1874. *Courtesy the Robert G. McCubbin Collection.*

there but only went to school for one day. The rewards that were offered for me made the country too dangerous a place for me to stop. I passed my diploma examination, however, satisfactorily, so Joe and I graduated together."[28] Whereas brother Joseph is forgotten about, being innocently classed as among "other graduates [who] followed more illustrious professions," John Wesley is recalled "as the most notorious graduate of the Greenwood Masonic Institute."[29] Following graduation, Wes went on the run again while Joe went to Mount Calm to help Reverend Hardin teach school. Of Hardin's siblings, brother Joe is the only one really mentioned in his autobiography, either because he was simply the older brother or because John Wesley actually admired him. After helping his father with the school, Wes recalled Joe "became a lawyer. He afterwards moved out to Comanche in 1872 and there lived until he met his death at the hands of a howling midnight mob of assassins in June, 1874."[30]

Hardin then "concluded" to head further east to Shreveport, Louisiana, as unidentified relatives lived there. But while stopping at Longview, only some forty miles from the border, he was arrested by members of the State Police, "on a charge of which I was innocent." He was arrested for the murder of Laban J. Hoffman, a former private in the State Police but at the time of his death City Marshal of Waco, the county seat of McLennan County. Reportedly Hoffman was in a Waco barber shop when a man rode up, dismounted and entered the shop from the rear. He looked closely at the lathered face of Hoffman, stood behind the chair and then shot him in the back of the head. The man quickly mounted his horse and fled across the bridge spanning the Brazos. By then Waco police were approaching the man. He threw a dollar at the ferryman and shouted, "Haven't time to wait for the change."[31] Now Wes Hardin was to be delivered to Waco to stand trial for a murder he had not committed.

CHAPTER 3

MEXICO OR KANSAS?

*"As he was only a boy they did not watch him closely, and at
night lay down to sleep. Hardin arose in the night and killed
every one of them."*

Dallas Herald, August 25, 1877

With the advent of the Texas State Police many men, some former
slaves, applied for a commission. Those who were accepted
were sworn in for a period of not less than four years—"unless
sooner removed." Policemen also would earn what some considered an
inordinate amount for services: a private would receive $60 per month,
each sergeant $75, each lieutenant $100, and each captain would receive
$125. In addition, if a policeman captured a fugitive for whom there was
a reward offered, he could claim the reward as well as draw his regular
salary.[1]

Although Hardin had a sizable reputation, his image had not yet appeared on any wanted posters, and his physical description could have fit
many young Texans. But the work of the police would make his existence
more dangerous. Each police captain was to inspect the criminal dockets
of the various counties in their assigned district, and in addition, was to
"use every means in their power to arrest all parties who may have committed offenses and who have not been arrested." Then captains were "to
ascertain the whereabouts of all persons evading arrest, and should it be
found that such persons are out of the district, a copy of indictment will
be forwarded to the Chief of Police, and the necessary information given
of the whereabouts of the accused, to the end that measures may be taken
to secure the arrest."[2]

By July 1870 the officers had been appointed and recruitment started, although the number of privates never reached the allotted 225. The fugitives would not be aware of that fact, however. As Wes Hardin evaded patrols and lawmen of all types at this stage of his life, his brother Joe reacted differently to the changing political realities. He became a Texas State Policeman, plainly ignoring the oath that he took, by knowing where his brother the fugitive was. During this time Joe was studying for a law degree, which he would soon obtain. By 1872 he had established a practice in Comanche County. The Reverend and Mrs. Hardin with the other children would locate there as well. After serving a decade and a half in Huntsville, Wes also studied for the law, and was interviewed and allowed to practice, ironically.

In spite of all Wes's watchfulness and his attempts to get out of the jurisdiction of the State Police, he was again in the hands of law officers. Perhaps he had acted suspiciously; perhaps he had had an inordinate amount of money for a seventeen-year-old "boy"; or perhaps he could not give an adequate account of the horse he was riding. It was January 1871, only a year after the Bradley killing in Hill County. He was charged with not only theft of a horse, but also for the killing of Waco's city marshal, Laban J. Hoffman,. Hardin of course denied the killing, and this was one of which he was innocent. The police took him to Marshall and placed him in the Harrison County jail. "I was put in an old iron cell in the middle of the log jail, and nobody was allowed to see me. There were three older prisoners in there, and together we planned our escape." The plan was to wait until the food was brought to them, then make the break. In spite of his youth, Hardin "had money with me to buy whisky and tobacco for us all."[3]

The three other prisoners backed out of the escape plan, as they were incarcerated for relatively minor offenses. Hardin's plan was to kill the jailer "if he did not obey orders." This was too reckless for them and the trio "weakened," but were willing to sell what would be useful for the young Hardin if he did escape. He bought a ".45 Colt with four barrels loaded" for $10 in gold and, as he recalled, an overcoat. Hardin had no idea when he would be taken, nor could he make any arrangements to get his horse still left at Longview.

It was a cold Friday night that January 20, 1871. Although there had been no communication as to what his fate would be, Wes knew what was up "when the Negro cook only brought supper plates for three, and there were four prisoners." Wes figured he was the one who was going to leave the jail that night, and he was prepared for a miserable, cold journey. "I had a very heavy fur coat, a medium sack coat, two undershirts, and two white shirts. I hid the pistol, tied with a good stout cord, under my left arm and over it my top shirt. I put on the rest of my clothes to see how it looked. It looked all right, so I took off my coat and vest and went to bed."[4]

Hardin recalled that he had prepared himself for any emergency. He lay down on the cot feeling confident that the other prisoners would not reveal his intent. The guards came and Wes "pretended to be awakened out of a sound sleep and to be very much surprised." They now told him they were to deliver him to Waco for the killing of city marshal Hoffman. Wes acted "very much frightened" and asked if there was any danger of a mob. The jailer and Lieutenant E. T. Stakes[5] assured him there was none (Hardin remembered him as Captain Stokes).

After a careless search Hardin must have been relieved that the lieutenant had not discovered his pistol. It was at that point that he also realized that his guards were not as careful as they should be. The comfort of their prisoner was of no concern: he had only blankets folded up to serve as a saddle. The officers tied him "hard and fast." There were but two policemen, and "if you had met our party that day, you would have seen a small white man about 45 years old who was a captain of police named Stokes, a middle-weight dark-looking man, one-fourth Negro, one-fourth Mexican, and one-half white, the former riding a large bay horse, the latter a fine sorrel mare and leading a small black pony with a boy 17 years old tied thereon and shivering with cold."[6] Lieutenant Stakes tried to frighten the prisoner, threatening to shoot him if he tried to escape, and if he told Smalley, the "middle-weight dark-looking man" to shoot him he would obey orders.[7] Hardin naturally "talked very humbly, was full of morality and religion and was strictly down on lawlessness of all kinds."

If Hardin's chronology is correct they left Marshall late, and may have traveled much of the night as Hardin wrote "when daylight came" his legs were untied so as to guide the pony. That first full day they reached the Sabine River. The town of Longview was behind them, although Hardin gave no indication as to whether they rode through it or around it. The Sabine River was "booming"; there was no ferry so it had to be crossed in the water. They tied the prisoner on and put a rope around the pony's neck with Stakes in the lead, then Hardin, and then policeman Smalley. "The little black pony could swim like a duck," Hardin recalled, "and with the exception of getting thoroughly wet and cold, we got over all right."[8]

That night, the party stopped but nothing happened, except Hardin was silently contemplating how to escape. A big fire made by Smalley permitted all to stay warm. With morning light it was time to head out; there was the Trinity River to cross. Fortunately a ferry was available, and the rest of the day was spent traveling until nightfall. Again it was time to build a fire to prepare a meal and get warm. Hardin recalled it was the lieutenant who went to gather fodder for the horses, leaving Smalley alone to guard the prisoner. This in itself suggests Hardin's memory was failing, or that he was ready to embellish his narrative. Fortunately a newspaper account is extant which provides us with what in all likelihood did happen. It first appeared in the Freestone County newspaper, the *Fairfield Ledger* of January 28, 1871. The report later appeared in the *Daily Bulletin* printed by Ferdinand Flake of Galveston in the issue of February 4. It began:

On last Sunday morning [January 22] Lieutenant E. T. Stakes of the State Police, with one private, James Smalley, and a citizen named L. B. Anderson, came to this place [Fairfield, some 125 miles southeast of Marshall], having in charge a prisoner named John R. Hardin [*sic*], who they had arrested at Marshall for alleged murder in Hill county, and theft of a horse from S. C.

Clinton, of McLennan county, and were taking him to Waco for trial. When they arrived here the man Smalley passed through with the prisoner without halting, while the other two stopped. After getting some two miles west of town they halted and sat down, the prisoner behind the policeman. Almost instantly the prisoner drew a repeater and shot Smalley through the back, and as Smalley turned and attempted to draw his own pistol, he was again shot in the abdomen and fell, whereupon Hardin got on Smalley's horse and fled, no one being nigh but an old black woman, who fled on seeing Hardin's approach.

Why did the report state he was arrested for an "alleged murder in Hill county" when it was clearly for the Hoffman killing in McLennan County? Apparently the Fairfield authorities, or reporter, was aware of the Hill County killing, but inadvertently wrote Hill instead of McLennan.

Why Hardin failed to mention the third party, L. B. Anderson, is unknown; why he failed to mention the "old black woman" is equally mysterious. The *Fairfield* account continues:

Lieut. Stakes and Anderson had nearly overtaken their party when the shooting took place, and upon hurrying to the spot saw Hardin galloping off. Lieut. Stakes did not attempt to follow, for the reason, as he alleges, that his horse was much faded, and greatly inferior to the horse Hardin was on. Anderson followed some few miles, but as his horse was very lame—being the one Hardin had stolen—had to give up the chase, and so the murderer made good his escape. There is a reward of $1100 offered for the apprehension of Hardin to the authorities of Hill county.[9]

The *Austin State Journal* was conscious of any criticism of Governor Davis and his State Police force, and this incident had the potential of providing considerable negative publicity. For a lieutenant of the force to allow a private to be murdered, and the prisoner to escape, indicated reckless management. To counter the negative publicity it became common to see in the columns of the *Daily State Journal*—the official mouthpiece of the governor—lists of the arrests made by the police. In the issue of Sunday, February 12, a listing appeared that shows "John R. Hardin, horse stealing and four cases of murder." Why this notice of the arrest is nearly a month after the fact is not explained, nor the incorrect middle initial. Whoever provided the *Journal* with the press release may have been simply late in so doing. The authorities obviously did not have their suspect's name correct. One also wonders who were the four *known* men murdered by this "John R. Hardin?" Was one the freedman known as Maje? Certainly Benjamin B. Bradley of Hill County, and possibly the two men murdered in Peoria, which Hardin conveniently overlooked in writing his memoir. Apparently the *Journal* reporter was as yet unaware of the death of Private Smalley, or else he would have been listed as the fifth victim of this young fugitive.

Following the killing of State Policeman James Smalley, Hardin believed his best course was to head for Mexico and remain there until the political situation changed in Texas so he could—in his mind at least and the mind of his father—receive a fair trial. Once Republican Governor E. J. Davis was out of office and the State Police force no more he could then return. He headed for San Antonio, intending to reach Laredo and there cross the Rio Grande.

But he was again arrested before he could proceed very far. In his version he was taken "by men calling themselves" members of the State Police. Perhaps they were simply bounty hunters; Hardin called them Smith, Jones and Davis, and although there were State Policemen by those names, they did not suffer the fate Hardin described: killed in action. What did John Wesley Hardin have to say about this supposed triple killing? Wes gave no details as to how this arrest occurred; only saying that after the arrest the three men stopped for the night somewhere between Belton and Temple, south of Waco. They divided the responsibility of guarding their single prisoner so that "Smith" had first watch. The trio "had a good deal of whisky with them, and they all got about half drunk," so explained Hardin. Sleep soon followed for all but the prisoner who had observed where they had placed their weapons. "I picked up Davis' shotgun and Jones' six-shooter. I fired at Smith's head and then turned the other barrel on Jones at once. As Davis began to arise and inquire what was the matter, I began to work on him with the six-shooter. He begged and hollered, but I kept on shooting until I was satisfied he was dead." This is how Wes "got back" his liberty and his weapons. Right there he took an oath "never to surrender at the muzzle of a gun."[10] If asked, Hardin would have explained that he was a young freedom fighter, a rebel acting against tyranny.

Some historians doubt that this incident even occurred, citing the fact that there were no policemen with those names who were killed in the line of duty. Curiously, historian Charles Askins transformed these three into Smith, Jones and Ellis, with no explanation of the difference in the third man's name, nor did he cite any source. The only printed sources of the story are Wes's *Life* and an interview in the *Dallas Daily Herald.* After Hardin's capture in 1877 and on the return trip to Texas, he was interviewed by a reporter of that paper, who wrote the following lines: "As he was only a boy [after the arrest for the Smalley killing] they did not watch him very close, and at night lay down to sleep. Harding [*sic*] arose in the night and killed every one of them."[11]

After he told his father of the killing, Reverend Hardin advised Wes "never tell this to mortal man." Certainly as early as 1877, long before he contemplated writing his life story, however, Hardin was willing to relate his version of the incident to the reporter. The only fiction about it is that he did not know the real names of those who had captured him, hence the fictitious names of Smith, Jones and Davis. Hardin certainly did kill three men at this point in his career; he had nothing to gain in telling of this triple homicide to a newspaper reporter. He already was notorious, so creating an additional killing would have brought nothing to him. Amazingly the reporter stressed that the reward for Hardin amounted to $20,000, five times what the actual reward offered for him.

After killing his captors and on the run through Belton in Bell County, through Georgetown in Williamson County, and on to Austin in Travis County and Lockhart in Caldwell County, Hardin changed his plans and decided to go a few miles out of his way to visit the Clements family, his first cousins whom he had never met. He only knew that they lived in Gonzales County. He hired Jim Cone, whom he recalled as "an old and honored citizen" to show him the way to the Clements' ranch. He recalled the four boys and the two girls: Emanuel, called Mannen or Manning for short; James A., called Jim; John Gibson called Gip; Joseph Hardin, called Joe, and the two girls, Mary Jane and Minerva. James Cone, who must have had positive feelings about the Clements family, was one of the five sons of Archibald Greene Cone. All had served in the Confederate army, although one had served as the Confederate post master at Rancho in Gonzales County. It was James B. Cone whom Hardin had met at Rancho. Cone actually lived in Wilson County, but Rancho was very close to the line.[12]

The Clements family[13] lived "almost directly" between Gonzales and Helena, then the county seat of Karnes County, but today only a historical museum in the old court house surrounded by a few houses and a cemetery. Hardin and his cousins became close immediately. Wes must have explained why he was on his own, so far away from his home country, and may have also told his cousins of some of the killings. Or possibly the Clements family already knew of their cousin's difficulties through correspondence with other family members. We don't know how much he told of his past adventures, but a common bond was forged, a bond making them as close as if they were brothers. The trip to Mexico was quickly forgotten as the Clements men were preparing to drive cattle to Kansas markets. Mannen, always the leader of the clan, simply told Wes to join up and be a cowboy. He could easily forget about his troubles with the law; during a trail drive the State Police would not bother him, no matter how much they may have wanted him. Wes chose the trail drive to Kansas over flight to Mexico. Being with his cousins, the hazards of the trail probably seemed inconsequential: the crossing of dangerous rivers; the threat of Indian raiding parties; the drudgery or monotony of driving cattle north; the probable stampedes; the potential accident with a horse or a wild steer; lightning in a storm . . . it all added up to 677 miles from

Emanuel "Mannen" Clements. A tintype which Hardin preserved in his photo album. *Courtesy the Robert G. McCubbin Collection.*

Gonzales, Texas, to Abilene, Kansas.[14] Almost seven hundred miles with only one responsibility: protect the herd and get it to Abilene. The law could simply wait until he returned to Texas; and if he did not, so much the better. There were the Clements boys to watch his back as well—just in case. From various sources we know the names of some who were on this trail drive to Abilene with Wes Hardin: the four Clements brothers;

Columbus Carroll; brothers John and William M. Cohron; Jim Rodgers; a man named Pain; Hugh Anderson; Ephraim Baker; George Johnson; and brothers John and Fred Duderstadt.[15]

In contrast to the adventuresome and dangerous life Wes Hardin was living and was about to face, brother Joe Hardin was living in comparable luxury, teaching school and studying law. Born January 5, 1850, he was all of twenty-one and so far as known had never killed a man nor gotten into any difficulty with the law, quite the opposite of his younger brother. After all, his thoughts were to become a member of the State Police, a lawman. He had met and fallen in love with Tennessee-born Arabelle

Joseph Hardin Clements and cowboy friends, probably in Abilene in 1871. Clements is seated center. Standing left is James Monroe "Doc" Bockius; to his left is John Gibson "Gip" Clements and two men unidentified; seated left is James Clements [?] and at right Frank Smith. Partial identification by Ed Bartholomew. *Courtesy the Jack Caffall Collection.*

Adams, and they were married in September 1871. "Belle" Adams was born August 31, 1850, the daughter of S. H. and Sallie P. Adams, and was thus less than a year younger than her husband.[16]

Working cattle was certainly not new to John Wesley Hardin, and it would not be long before he was also known as "Wes Clements," a tactic to keep bounty hunters and others from knowing his true identity. Not long after joining the Clements family he became involved in a difficulty. He recalled how one night "the boys" took him to a Mexican camp to gamble, *monte* being the game of choice. In spite of previous experiences with gambling he wrote as if he was unaware of how it was played. "I soon learned the rudiments of the game," he recalled, "and began to bet with the rest." Maybe he hadn't learned the rudiments of the game well enough as he and the dealer disagreed on the turn of a card. When the dealer refused to pay, Wes struck him on the head with his pistol "as he was drawing a knife." Hardin also shot another as he too was drawing a knife. Apparently one of the Clements boys joined in, as the "total casualties" consisted of one Mexican with a broken arm, another shot through the lung and yet another "with a very sore head." The Clements party all returned to camp and with some refreshing drinks, "laughed about the matter."[17] Hardin claimed that the "best people of the vicinity said I did a good thing" in breaking up that Mexican *monte* game. Wes placed the incident as happening in February 1871.

There were times when for some unknown reason—certainly unknown to Wes himself—when instead of shooting a man, he "buffaloed" him, striking him on the head with a pistol. The herd boss, Mannen Clements, had given Wes "strict orders to let no one go into the herd" and Hardin intended to follow orders to the letter. Clements may have explained to young Hardin why, or perhaps Wes already knew the reason, as some of those longhorns may have carried brands other than that of the Clements herd. Hardin makes no mention of Clements driving for anyone else, nor does he mention road branding the herd. For whatever reason, a black cowboy identified as Bob King[18] rode in brazenly intending to cut out certain cattle. Wes approached, told him to keep away, that

James Clements, who participated in the fight on the Newton Prairie in 1871. *Courtesy the Jack Caffall Collection.*

he needed Clements' permission to cut the herd, and that Clements would be along directly. King ignored the warning and "cut out a big beef steer." Hardin then rode up and struck King on the head with his six-shooter and told him to "get out of my herd." King was armed as well as Wes, but he chose not to make an issue out of it, and asked for Hardin's pardon. Did Wes avoid shooting King because the sharp blast of a gun might have

Joseph Hardin Clements, brother of Mannen, Gip and Jim Clements. *Courtesy the John Wesley Hardin Papers, The Wittliff Collection, Texas State University.*

startled the herd, causing it to stampede? Or did he earnestly attempt to avoid trouble now with the responsibility of watching Clements' herd?

All was ready for the drive north by the first of March 1871. Wes and James Clements were in charge of 1,200 head of longhorns belonging to Columbus Carroll,[19] while Mannen Clements was in charge of a herd belonging to the noted cattleman Crawford "Doc" Burnett. Burnett had in the spring of 1871 contracted with P. R. Armour & Company to "road-brand and put on the trail ten thousand big steers, four years old and up" according to the recollection of cowman R. T. Mellard when he wrote his reminiscences of the trail for J. Marvin Hunter.[20] Hardin claimed that he and Jim were earning $150 a month, which seems like an extraordinary amount, especially for Wes who had never driven cattle on the trail to Kansas before. Presumably brothers Joe and Gip were close at hand with the herds.

The drovers herded the cattle from Gonzales County north through Caldwell County, driving them across Plum Creek where early settlers thirty years before had battled Comanche warriors returning from a raid into deep South Texas. Then they drove the herds through Travis and Williamson counties. This was an area Wes certainly was acquainted with, as he had attended school in Round Rock and later in Georgetown. There, in Williamson County, all the hands "caught the measles except Jim [Clements] and myself." This delayed the drive considerably, but all hands rested up while the cattle grazed; Wes wrote that he spent his time doctoring his sick companions, cooking and branding cattle. The measles outbreak caused a ten-day delay. By the time the hands were well again the cattle and horses were "improved so much in flesh, we again started north."[21] North meant heading for the Red River, the natural border between Texas and the Indian Territory, or what is now Oklahoma, and then into Kansas.

Hardin's cattle driving experience proved uneventful even working through counties where the State Police presence was real, as was the possibility of Indian raiding parties. After several weeks they reached the Red River. Crossing it could be dangerous, and once crossed they would be entering Indian Territory. The drovers became more aware of Indians as two weeks before crossing the Red River they had heard of two men being killed. But in spite of the possible Indian threat there was game of all kinds: buffalo, antelope, and wolves. The day they crossed the Red River they were not alone: fifteen herds crossed as well, meaning thousands of hooves were stirring up dust and making a trail easy to follow. The herds were kept close together as the cowboys provided mutual protection from any and all potential troubles. "The trail was thus one line of cattle," Wes wrote, "and you were never out of sight of a herd."

Apparently John Wesley Hardin, living in East Texas much of his life, had never encountered an Indian. "I was just about as much afraid of an Indian as I was of a coon," he claimed. On one occasion he roped a wolf, and later killed an Indian who had shot an arrow at him. Wes buried him with his bow and arrows, concealing the grave as best he could. On one occasion the herders refused to pay the toll some Indians wanted for driving cattle across their lands.[22] Apparently nothing came of this refusal, although some cattlemen routinely paid the toll. On another occasion some warriors rode into the herd and cut out a few head for their own use. Wes was not about to bow down to what he called "straight-out robbery." When an Indian did ride into the herd to take a "big beef steer" Hardin, apparently managing to communicate with the Indian through sign language, warned him to desist. The Indian responded that if could not have the animal he would kill it. Naturally Hardin responded in kind, warning him that if he killed the steer he would kill him. "Well, he killed the beef, and I killed him," Hardin recalled, adding that "the other Indians promptly vanished." He mounted the dead Indian on the dead steer as a warning to others.[23]

One of the hands working with Wes during this 1871 trail drive was Frederick Christoph "Fred" Duderstadt, a young man three years older than Wes, and a native of Germany. In his later years a *Kerrville Mountain Sun* reporter interviewed Duderstadt, revealing incidents of his youth, but providing a glimpse into various happenings on the trail to Kansas as well. When Fred was five years old the family emigrated to

Fred Duderstadt, a lifelong friend of John Wesley Hardin. *Courtesy the Robert G. McCubbin Collection.*

America and settled in DeWitt County, just south of Gonzales County. Duderstadt "spent his young manhood in DeWitt County and that portion of the State, learning the art of wild steers and other tricks of early day cowboys." Of Indians, the reporter wrote: "Having no fear of Indians and desperadoes, who were numerous at that time, he joined the trail drives and for nine years followed the herds from Texas to points in Kansas." Duderstadt was described as "quiet and peaceable and shunned trouble [but] even a peaceable man often found himself involved in trouble without looking for it." Duderstadt may have been the direct opposite of Hardin in personality. As a fellow drover he "accompanied Hardin along the cattle trails for many miles and felt positive Hardin was a much better man than he was given credit for being. He was falsely accused of being a blood-thirsty outlaw and being guilty of countless crimes committed by other men."[24]

Whereas the drovers had relatively little trouble crossing Indian Territory, once in Kansas life-and-death situations began. Maybe the herders felt better as there was now little chance of a raid by Indians, although security was really an illusion on the Kansas plains in 1871. Any real security was dependent on how well a man could defend himself against any perceived threat—with his fists, his knife, his rifle or six-shooter.

CHAPTER 4

SHEDDING BLOOD IN KANSAS

"I have seen many fast towns, but I think Abilene beat them all. The town was filled with sporting men and women, gamblers, cowboys, desperadoes, and the like. It was well supplied with bar rooms, hotels, barber shops, and gambling houses, and everything was open."

John Wesley Hardin

Twenty miles south of Wichita was a crossing over Cowskin Creek, although Hardin mistakenly remembered it as Cow House. There a group of men met the Texans. They were not to cause trouble for the drovers but wanted the herd to be driven west of Wichita, opening a trail to their community to build up "a new town on the north bank of the Arkansas River." They furnished a guide, and the group followed a plow furrow. On the north bank of the Arkansas was the new town with the imposing name of Park City, some fourteen miles northwest of Wichita. Then, it was not yet much of a town; today it is part of ever-expanding Wichita. Once there, having the river behind them, "a delegation from the new town came out to meet us and invited all those that could leave the cattle to enjoy the hospitality of the new town."[1]

Who were these entrepreneurs who met the drovers just in from Indian Territory, eager to convince them to change their course northward, hoping to provide a sense of permanence to fledging Park City? No roster is extant but based on the plats, perhaps the group meeting Hardin and the others included C. A. Nichols, J. A. McIlvain, F. C. Hawkins, D. A. Bright, and D. M. V. Stewart. Stewart had intended Park City to become the county seat of Sedgwick County. He was a gambler like all

66

the others, but all was lost when the railroad tracked at Wichita fourteen miles southeast. Then Wichita, with the railroad, became the county seat and the people of Park City simply moved there, leaving the nascent Park City to become part of the prairie.[2]

Hardin of course paid no mind as to who composed this delegation, but he did remember that about sixty cowboys went to the new town and, "it is needless to say filled up on wine, whiskey, etc., some getting rather full." Of course Hardin did not claim to be one of those who got "rather full," but certainly he did. After frolicking they all returned to the herds, although one wonders how many cowboys remained with the cattle while *sixty* went off to frolic.

Wes now—at least in his memoir—claimed to be the trail boss, stating, "We were now on the Newton prairie, and my herd was right in front of a herd driven by Mexicans." He explained the resulting trouble originated when the Mexican herders crowded the Hardin herd. The boss, whom Hardin identified as "Hosea" (but Hardin, with his prejudice against Mexicans, considered every Hispanic male was named Hosea, or his version of José), expressed his anger at Hardin for not moving his herd faster. To Hardin the solution was simple: he should simply move his herd around Hardin's if he wanted to proceed at a faster rate; he did not have to stay behind. *El jefe* Hosea then considered the time to talk was over and went to get a rifle. Without Hosea present, his cattle began to merge with Hardin's herd, causing him unnecessary work to keep the cattle separated.

Thus while Wes was engaged with separating cattle, Hosea arrived armed with a rifle. Unbelievably, if we believe Hardin's account, he "rode up to within about 100 yards of me, got down off his horse, took deliberate aim at me, and fired." But his aim was poor and the bullet simply knocked Hardin's hat off. Then his rifle jammed. With the rifle useless he then jerked his pistol and began to advance on Hardin, who was armed with "an old cap and ball," worn to the extent that he had to hold the cylinder with one hand and squeeze the trigger with the other. What followed seems almost like a scene from a western comedy, with the Mexican covering the hundred yards, firing his pistol, while Hardin, forced to hold the pistol together with both hands while shooting, and both men missing their mark. At this point Jim Clements rode up, told Hardin to turn his horse loose and hold the cylinder and shoot straighter. Wes, certainly with Hosea now much closer, managed to hit his opponent in the thigh. By now a group of cowboys, having heard the gunfire, gathered around Hardin and Clements, as well as some *vaqueros*, were ready to fight for their wounded boss. Clements prevented further violence then by declaring both Hardin and Hosea were drunk. In reality Clements realized the disadvantage his cousin was in and convinced everyone a truce was necessary for both groups. It was only a ruse of course, as once back in camp the two checked their weapons, Hardin now getting a much better pistol to work with. A messenger from the Mexican camp alerted the Texans that the truce was over, and some *vaqueros* were coming, apparently intending to kill this Hotspur of a Texas cowboy.

"Presently the boss, Hosea," Hardin continued, "my old foe, with three men, came around [and] I rode to meet him. He fired at me . . . but missed me. I concluded to charge him and turn my horse loose at him, firing as I rode. The first ball did the work. I shot him through the heart and he fell over the horn of his saddle, pistol in hand and one in the scabbard, the blood pouring from his mouth."

But killing the boss herder did not stop the battle. The Mexican herders chose to continue the fight, dividing into two separate groups. Hardin described the battle, and from his confusing description one would think dozens of men were engaged in the bloody contest, but the number was far fewer. Hardin concludes his narrative:

A crowd of cowmen from all around had now gathered. I suppose there were twenty-five of them around the two Mexicans we had first rounded up. We thus had good interpreters, and once we thought the matter was settled with them, when suddenly the Mexicans, believing they "had the drop," pulled their pistols and fired point blank at me. I don't know how they missed me. In an instant I fired first at one, then at the other. The first I shot through the heart and he dropped dead. The second I shot through the lungs and Jim shot him too. He fell off his horse, and I was going to shoot him again when he begged and held up both hands. I could not shoot a man, not even a treacherous Mexican, begging and down. I knew he would die anyway. In comparing notes after the fight, we agreed that I had killed five out of the six dead Mexicans.[3]

The narrative as Hardin presented is almost too exciting, too dramatic to be accepted as factual. Certainly Hardin did have a difficulty on the trail in 1871, just after crossing into Kansas. But more than two decades had passed from the experience to the telling of it, and his glorified remembered exploit perhaps can be best understood by keeping in mind he had many other exciting adventures, and years in prison to ponder each one. Further, to exhibit his honor and sense of fair play, Wes reminded his readers that he had a high degree of character, as he *could not shoot a man, not even a treacherous Mexican, begging and down.* Apparently to Hardin's way of relating to his fellow man, every Mexican was treacherous.

The *Wichita Tribune* learned of the battle and recorded its version for the readers. At that time the *Tribune* was a weekly publication, probably the only newspaper in Sedgewick County. The article attempted to explain why the cattle trail had been diverted from Wichita to run farther west. "Only a few herds, however, have as yet passed the new trail. The first, as we are informed, arrived at Park City, last Sunday, and as near as we can learn, both joy and bad whiskey was unconfined, and all joined in the jubilee." This obviously corroborates Hardin's tale of the cowboys' filling up on wine and whiskey, "some getting rather full." It was at this point however that the unknown correspondent changed the tone of his report, as at "this stage of the game, matters assumed a different phase." Keep in mind Hardin gave the number of cowboys participating in the drunken revelry at Park City as sixty, which left the cattle essentially on their own.

> The cattle left almost unguarded roamed at will, and their will led them into a cornfield, and a boy was sent to drive them off, and while in the act of driving them away, one of the herders came up and threatened to kill the boy. His threat was heard by another herder who had just come up, and by a single shot brought him to the ground. This act was witnessed by a third party, who soon dispatched him to the spirit world. Another man coming up in time to witness the effects of the last shot, done likewise, and another saddle was emptied. The whole matter ended in two men being killed and one mortally wounded.[4]

The *Tribune* report indicated that the first herd of the season had arrived at Park City "last Sunday," providing us with a date for the multiple killing—it being Sunday, May 28—two days after Hardin turned eighteen. Apparently anxious about the reputation of Wichita, the reporter concluded: "We hope that our exchanges in reference to the matter, will bear in mind that these murders were not committed in Wichita."

Fred Duderstadt, who rode up the trail with Hardin that year, witnessed the gun battle. It proved to be a thrilling conversation piece on the trail, and the news of the killing probably reached Abilene before Hardin and the herds did. Years later rancher Duderstadt gave an interview to K. C. White, which appeared in the *Kerrville Mountain Sun* and corroborates Hardin's version in his memoir.

> [Duderstadt] said the Mexicans were driving cattle just behind a herd in charge of Hardin, and kept crowding the two herds together. Hardin spoke to the Mexican boss about keeping a little more distance between them, but the Mexican began to curse him and said he would kill him as soon as he could find a gun. The Mexican rode away and in a short time returned and opened fire on Hardin.

Hardin's pistol was an old cap-and-ball, and "would not fire because of bad repair," Duderstadt said. If it had been in good working order the confrontation would have ended there. The Mexican's gun also failed him, and then both the Mexican and Hardin went "into a fist fight and the Mexican called for his companions to come to his rescue. In the melee they tried to get in a shot at Hardin but were afraid to fire at him for fear of hitting their boss." Now, another Mexican rode up and took two shots at Hardin, but missed. Jim Clements then entered upon the scene and the fighting stopped. Both sides agreed to return to their respective camps to obtain better weapons. "After a brief interval of time the Mexican boss approached Hardin's camp on horseback. Hardin went out and told him to go back to his herd, that he wanted no more trouble." However, the Mexican told Hardin that they were ready to fight and to "come on." Hardin and Clements accepted the invitation. "Soon the fight was on, bullets flying from the guns of six Mexicans and the two Texas cowboys." Hardin had requested his companions take no part in the fight, "as he considered two Texas cowboys were equal to six Mexicans." Duderstadt summed up the result of the fight: "The Mexicans started the fight; they forced it. Hardin tried to do the right thing but it took gun powder to make the Mexicans believe he meant it when he said, 'keep your cattle away from my herd.'"[5]

Today it is impossible to say whether what Fred Duderstadt told K. C. White was only what he remembered, assuming he was an actual eyewitness, or if he had possibly read Hardin's *Life* and had mixed what he read and what he saw. The Wichita *Tribune*'s account, or tally of the dead, is much lower than Hardin's and the number recalled by Duderstadt. Perhaps the *Tribune* reporter lowered the number, thinking such a number as six men killed in a prairie gun battle would not be believed by his readers.

The site of the gun battle perhaps covered several hundred square yards, so trying to pinpoint a precise spot for such a bloody encounter would be futile. Its location can be generally placed just north of the confluence of the Little Arkansas River and Jester Creek, both waterways flowing into the Arkansas River, which runs through Wichita today.

THE FIGHT WITH THE MEXICAN HERDERS.

Artist R.J. Onderdonk's depiction of the fight on the Newton Prairie which appeared in Hardin's memoir *Life of John Wesley Hardin.*

Kansas historian Waldo E. Koop best determined the question of where the fight took place. In 1973 he interviewed J. N. Hoefgen of neighboring Valley Center, Kansas. Hoefgen's uncle, James Thompson, had homesteaded in the area in 1869. He had told his nephew Hoefgen of laying track for the railroad in the spring of 1872, and he had heard talk about the fight and even knew where the six victims were buried. The site is now lost due to extensive earth moving for the Wichita-Valley Center Flood Control Project.[6]

Perhaps the Texans gave the six dead Mexicans a hasty burial, only deep enough to discourage ravaging by wolves. Hoefgen believed they had been buried.[7] Hardin made no mention of burying the dead in this instance, which is quite different from the time shortly before when he had killed an Indian and took the pains to bury the warrior with his bow and arrows. At any rate, Hardin was thinking of what lay ahead; he and Jim Clements, Fred Duderstadt and the others would not be bothered by the ghosts of the dead left on the banks of the Little Arkansas River. The name of that smooth-flowing stream would soon become a nickname for the young drover when he met up with the city marshal of Abilene, James Butler "Wild Bill" Hickok. He would be addressed as "Little

Arkansas," indicating word of the killing had reached the town before he did. Abilene was only a few more days' drive north, and it had all the characteristics of a town that Hardin reveled in.

Did John Wesley Hardin and other cowboys go into nearby Wichita at all? He made no mention of Wichita in his autobiography, but curiously Stuart N. Lake, who made the name of Wyatt Earp a virtual household word with his fictionalized biography of the Kansas-Tombstone lawman Earp, wrote in his lurid prose,

> Among the hired gunmen in the cowskin camps were . . . that notorious quartet of gunthrowing brothers, Mannen, Gyp, Joe and Jim Clements [who] were up with a gang of Texas men that included Tom, Bud, and Simp Dixon . . . Brown Bowen, and, for a short time, John Wesley Hardin—who had opened the shooting season by killing a buffalo hunter who appeared on Douglas Avenue wearing a silk hat—every last one noted for six-shooter proficiency and almost every one of whom had his boots on at his finish.[8]

We know that Simp Dixon was already dead, but the others were very much alive and they could have accompanied Hardin into Wichita, but certainly if Hardin had shot a buffalo hunter there would have been some mention of it in the *Tribune*.

On the banks of the North Cottonwood, south of Abilene, the drovers went into camp, waiting for the sale of the cattle to be completed. Hardin said it was about thirty-five miles south of Abilene. About the first of June they received word to come into town, draw their pay and be discharged of responsibility for the herd. The wildness of Abilene was no surprise to the young cowboy, as it already had a reputation and Wes himself had, or so he claimed, encountered "many fast towns." He was eager to experience what Abilene had to offer in the way of the gambling and dance halls, where an individual could wear his pistols openly, play any type of card game, pay for any type of female companionship, live and survive by his wits alone. Since the *Abilene Chronicle* noted the first herd of cattle had arrived on May 10, some 1,600 head driven by Columbus Carroll,[9] perhaps Hardin only recalled the date of June 1 as approximate. At that time there was no reason to pay much attention as to what day it was, having spent weeks on the trail when one day was the same as another.

Hardin recalled the town was filled with "sporting men and women, gamblers, cowboys, desperadoes, and the like," in other words he would be among men he would be very comfortable with. Everything was open as he described it, and the law was Wild Bill Hickok, who had only a few deputies. In April of 1871 the city had hired Hickok as city marshal. Thus he was relatively new for the position, although he had had experience as a lawman elsewhere. He was in his early thirties, and by some was considered a very handsome man. George C. Anderson, who in early June of that year, saw Hickok and described him as "tall, slender with long, black hair hanging to his shoulders. From a belt around his waist, hung two navy revolvers and a large bowie knife; being marshal of the town, he moved around with an air of authority; a terror to all evil doers."[10] Hardin at this time feared no man—Hickok was no terror to him. In 1867, when Abilene wasn't much more than an idea, Joseph G. McCoy described it as "a very small, dead place." McCoy noted that the purchase and sale of cattle, "was conducted in two small rooms, mere log huts, and of course the inevitable saloon also in a log hut, was to be found."[11] The Abilene patrolled by Hickok and visited by Hardin four years later was much different. Typically once the cowboys had been paid it was time for cleaning up, as they had been months on the trail, living in the clothes they wore, sleeping on the ground, their only bathing facilities being an occasional river. If the cowboys had had enough of sleeping on the ground, perhaps they now took rooms at the Drovers Cottage, and met the landlady Mrs. Lou Gore, who had been in Abilene since the spring of 1868.[12] She was described as "a true sympathetic friend . . . a true guardian and nurse, one whose kind, motherly heart was ever ready to provide for every proper want, be they [cowboys] hungry, tired, thirsty or sick, it mattered not, she

Joseph Hardin Clements, center, with two unidentified trail driving friends. This reveals their working clothes, prior to getting dressed up in Abilene. *Courtesy the Robert G. McCubbin Collection.*

Author Joseph G. McCoy included this engraving of the early cattle town, entitled "Abilene in its glory", to illustrate his history of the southwestern cattle trade. From *Historic Sketches of the Cattle Trade of the West and Southwest*, first published in 1874.

was the Florence Nightingale to relieve them."[13] After a needed shave and a haircut and perhaps a new set of clothes many cowboys visited a photographer.

In 1870 Abilene had three photographers and perhaps Hardin visited the studio of one of them there, as in his album he identified his image as "Abaline 1871."[14] Or perhaps he rode over to Junction where he posed for photographer Andrew P. Trott. One of the best-known images of Hardin, used on the jacket of this book, shows him standing, his hand resting on a pedestal, wearing a dark suit, vest, and white shirt, but no revolvers visible, although they were certainly there. The hard look on his face may have been due to the requirements of early day photography, which forced an individual to hold a pose for nearly a minute to avoid blurring. Others also dressed up for the photographer, and they may have all visited the studio at the same time. Two different poses remain of cowboys

John G. "Gip" Clements, Fred Duderstadt and Ephraim Baker. They had their image preserved for posterity in what appears to be new suits, but again no revolvers visible. Brother Joe Clements and two friends, their identity lost, also had their image made, but are dressed as they must have been on the trail, apparently deciding to be photographed in their "range clothes" rather than fancy duds.

Whether the saloons and the gambling houses were all in a row is probable, thus allowing a person to go from one to another with ease. We know the names of a few: The Alamo and the Bull's Head were the most prominent, both in name alone appealing to the Texans for their business. The latter was operated by a pair of Texans, Benjamin Thompson and Philip H. Coe, both professional gamblers whose permanent dwelling place was in Austin. There is no evidence they knew each other well, but Hardin and Coe certainly had met in Texas. What is perhaps not unusual is that Hardin claimed that although there was a reward for him, the Kansas authorities paid little attention to rewards offered for Texans. He claimed that the owners of his herd, Columbus Carroll and Jake Johnson, had "squared" him with Abilene's law. If this was true, Hickok was well aware of Hardin, not only for offenses he may have committed in Texas, but for his deadly battle on the Newton Prairie, close to the Little Arkansas River. In fact Hickok, considerably older and certainly wiser than Hardin, addressed him as "Little Arkansaw" as Hardin spelled the nickname. Hickok made it a point to let Hardin know that he was aware of what had happened out on the Newton Prairie.

Hardin may have been "squared" by Carroll and Johnson, but if he intended to wear his guns in Abilene—at least openly—he knew he was violating city ordinance. Around the first of June Hickok, or his deputies, had posted notices around Abilene that there was a "no-gun" ordinance and it must be obeyed. Commented M. B. George, the *Chronicle* editor: "That's right. There's no bravery in carrying revolvers in a civilized community. Such a practice is well enough and perhaps necessary when among Indians or other barbarians," he intoned, "but among white people it ought to be discountenanced."[15]

John Wesley Hardin in Abilene, Kansas in 1871. *Courtesy the Robert G. McCubbin Collection.*

M. B. George's agreement with the city ordinance was reasonable, but it was not long before a shooting affray took place on First Street, which Hardin may have witnessed, but did not participate in. Both men shot at each other, and both were wounded, but not seriously. Editor George

Three cowboys dressed up at the end of the cattle trail in Kansas, 1871. From left: John Gibson "Gip" Clements; Fred Duderstadt and Ephraim Baker. *Courtesy the Jack Caffall Collection.*

recalled his advice of a few issues before, and pointed out to his readers that while he was ignorant of which man was to blame, nevertheless "the slight value some men place upon human life is a sad commentary upon the custom of carrying fire-arms among people who claim to be civilized." He was not through, as one of the men supposedly had drawn a concealed Derringer and fired. George commented this was "far from being in accordance with the 'code of honor,' observed by all men who lay claim to bravery or chivalry. To stand up and shoot at a man, who has an equal chance with you, indicates that you are not a coward, but to fire at a man when you know that he is defenseless and can't return the compliment, is next to the lowest species of cowardice known among men." George concluded his editorial pointing out that "life is sweet to all—and ought to be held sacred by people who are not completely buried in moral darkness."[16] John Wesley Hardin would have certainly agreed with the editor on the question of what constituted honor—recall that he claimed he could not even shoot a treacherous Mexican begging for his life, and down—but he certainly carried a concealed weapon even if he did outwardly respect the "No Firearms" ordinance of Abilene. John Wesley Hardin was quite capable of keeping that moral darkness at bay.

Marshal Hickok earned $150 per month, plus 25 percent of all fines assessed for violating city ordinances against those arrested by him. The potential was there to bring in several hundred dollars per month, plus whatever he made at the gambling tables. He also had the responsibility of street commissioner, which amounted to the less glamorous task of getting dead animals removed, shooting stray dogs, and so forth. There was no additional compensation for those duties. Section 7 of the ordinance could have been directed at such a man as John Wesley Hardin: "That any person who shall carry within the corporate limits of the city of Abilene or commons, a pistol, revolver, gun, musket, dirk, bowie knife, or other dangerous weapon upon his person, either openly or concealed except to bring the same and forthwith deposit it or them at their house, store, room, or residence, shall be fined in a sum not more than seventy-five dollars." Section 8 provided the punishment for whoever chose to

James Butler "Wild Bill" Hickok, Abilene, Kansas's City Marshal in 1871. *Courtesy Joseph G. Rosa Collection.*

"shoot-up the town" or disturb the peace by firing their weapons: not less than ten nor more than three hundred dollars.[17] These were ordinances approved not only for the benefit of the city marshal and his deputies, but as a warning to all Texas cowboys who celebrated too wildly upon reaching the end of the trail. Or, for that matter, to recklessly announce with gunfire their departure from Abilene.

Once in Abilene, Hardin chose to stay indefinitely. Cousin Jim Clements decided to return to Texas, in spite of being offered $140 per month to stay. Hardin claimed he was offered $150 to remain and look for strays in the area, an offer he accepted. Perhaps he did spend his days out on the range looking for stray longhorns, as he then could spend the evenings in Abilene's saloons. The Alamo was a popular establishment. An unidentified correspondent contributed a description of it for posterity, stressing the fact that the name alone would appeal to the Texans. "Crowds swarm within and about its doors. At night it is brilliantly illuminated. There are tables covered with 'the green cloth.' On them are piled the checks of ivory, the gold and silver. About the bar costly mirrors, pyramids of sparkling glasses, and vases of the choicest flowers give the place an air of elegance." One wonders how many Texas cowboys appreciated the apparent opulence provided by the Alamo's proprietor, George Burt.[18]

But did young Wes Hardin actually remain in Abilene and hunt for strays during the day and enjoy the night life of Abilene in the evenings? That is the impression he left in his autobiography, but he may have in reality returned to Texas to participate in a revenge killing that he chose to ignore in writing his memoir. During the troubles between the Lee and Peacock factions in the Grayson-Hunt-Collins-Fannin corners area of northeast Texas, his cousins Billy and Simp Dixon had been slain. Unionist Lewis Peacock had been credited with killing Billy Dixon, and thus Peacock was marked for death by those sympathetic to the Lee faction. On June 13, 1871, three men ambushed Lewis Peacock. He had risen in the morning and gone outside to get stove wood for the morning fire when shots disturbed the morning air. To the followers of Bob Lee, those who had slain Peacock had avenged his death and the deaths of the Dixons. Two of the slayers were readily identified: Dick Johnson, half brother of Simp Dixon, and Joe Parker.[19] But who was the third? Gladys B. Ray in her study of the feud, an early work on the violence of Reconstruction Texas, identified the three as Johnson, Parker and "an unknown man."[20] Others have suggested, however, that the the third man was Hardin. James M. Smallwood, Barry A. Crouch and Larry Peacock, in *Murder and Mayhem: The War of Reconstruction in Texas*, stated that "after Unionists killed Billy and Simp, John Wesley swore revenge."[21] Although beyond proving it today, John Wesley Hardin could have been the mysterious third man participating in the group killing of Lewis Peacock. The first documentation of Hardin in Kansas was the gunfight on the Newton Prairie on May 28. The next is his acting to avenge the death of herder Billy Cohron, after July 5. If in truth he was not spending his days searching for stray longhorns, he easily could have returned to Grayson County, Texas, joined up with Johnson and Parker, and laid their plan to avenge the death of their friends. With a span of good horses, the distance could have been covered within a few days. Or he could have returned home with Jim Clements, the pair splitting after crossing the Red River, Jim going on home to Gonzales and John Wesley going to meet with Johnson and Parker. Peacock was killed by shotgun blasts, plus balls from pistols. It is known that Hardin on occasion used a shotgun to kill, and with two others he may have used such a deadly weapon on the thirteenth of June to rid the Four Corners of Peacock. The killing of Lewis Peacock should be added to the list of Hardin's victims.

While Hardin was possibly spending his days searching the prairies for lost strays and his nights in the Alamo, or Bull's Head, or at any of the numerous saloons and gambling houses, or rushing back to Grayson County to kill Peacock, herds were still heading north. William M. "Billy" Cohron was a young drover working for Colonel O. W. Wheeler.[22] Forty miles south of Abilene, on the Cottonwood River, he told a Mexican to go to a different herd. The Mexican, identified by Hardin as Juan Bideno, "took umbrage at this order, and watching a favorable opportunity assassin-like," approached Cohron from the rear and shot him in the back, inflicting a wound from which he died within a few hours. Bideno then mounted "a fleet pony and made for Texas." The *Abilene Chronicle* reported that the "most heartless murder" took place on the Cottonwood, and accepting the feeling expressed about Billy Cohron, described him as "a young man of excellent morals, honorable and trustworthy [with] many friends and acquaintances who sincerely mourn his untimely end." His body was delivered to Abilene, the funeral being held in the Drovers Cottage, a large, three-story hotel. It was the largest funeral ever held in Abilene, with twenty-four carriages and thirty-eight horsemen in the procession. Editor George could not resist the opportunity for another comment on the practice of every man going armed: "Peace to his ashes, and may the time speedily come when the carrying of firearms and

Ben Thompson, noted gambler and gunfighter, and associate of Hardin in Abilene. This image was probably made in Ellsworth, Kansas in 1873. *Courtesy the Western History Collections, University of Oklahoma Libraries.*

reckless regard of human life will only be remembered, with feelings of regret, as dark spots upon the civilization of our country."[23]

Although Hardin's memory was at times inaccurate, and at times he simply lied, at other times an historian must cautiously accept what he claimed as basically true, unless there is contemporary evidence to the contrary. Much of what appears in his autobiography remains only his claim. One such instance is a story he relates about Marshal Hickok. In his *Life* he tells of the dislike Ben Thompson and Phil Coe, who owned the Bull's Head Saloon, had for Hickok, claiming that Thompson even asked Hardin to kill Hickok for him, because Hickok objected to the saloon's advertisement of a longhorn bull with an inordinate emphasis on its masculinity. Hardin refused to do the favor for Thompson, claiming, "I am not doing anybody's fighting just now except my own, but I know how to stick to a friend. If Bill needs killing, why don't you kill him yourself?"

Shortly after this exchange, if it indeed happened, Hardin and Hickok were introduced by George Johnson. Hickok and Hardin drank several glasses of wine together. Hickok supposedly showed Hardin proclamations from Texas offering a reward for him and asked all about the fight on the Newton Prairie. Hardin recalled Hickok advising him: "Young man, I am favorably impressed with you, but don't let Ben Thompson influence you; you are in enough trouble now, and if I can do you a favor, I will do it." Hardin was "charmed by his liberal views," and told him so. They departed as friends.[24] This is what Hardin claimed, but we have only his version of his meeting with the city marshal. Was not Hickok's allowing Hardin to wear his guns in Abilene part of his "liberal views"?

Being "charmed" apparently caused Hardin to forget about rounding up strays, so he spent more time in the saloons and gambling halls of Abilene. One day, when he was playing ten pins with other Texans and wearing two six-shooters—which he admitted was against the city ordinance of Abilene—he admitted: "I suppose we were pretty noisy." Hickok entered and informed the players that they were making too much noise, and, on this occasion, decided to enforce the ordinance.

Hardin responded by saying he was ready to leave town then, saying he "did not propose to put up my pistols, go or no go." Hickok exited with Hardin behind him. At that point someone shouted, "Set up. All down but nine." Hickok then "whirled around" and faced Hardin.

"What are you howling about, and what are you doing with those pistols on?" Hickok demanded. To this Hardin answered, "I am just taking in the town." At this point Marshal Hickok forgot about any previous "squaring" Hardin may have enjoyed and demanded he remove his pistols and that he was under arrest. As Hardin recalled:

> I said all right and pulled them out of the scabbard, but while he was reaching for them, I reversed them and whirled them over on him with the muzzles in his face, springing back at the same time. I told him to put his pistols up, which he did. I cursed him for a long-haired scoundrel that would shoot a boy with his back to him (as I had been told he intended to do me). He said, "Little Arkansaw, you have been wrongly informed."

This is how Wes recalled the action, pulling a stunt on Hickok who had his own pistols pointing at him. But it is certainly a creation of Hardin's, safely made long after Hickok's death in 1876. There are a number of reasons to suspect it did not happen at all as he described. According to Hardin, Hickok had his own pistols covering him. If so, and Hardin had tried what was known as the "border roll" or "road-agent's spin"—the trick of whirling the pistol on the trigger finger—Hickok could have easily shot him during the act. Hickok's known victims by mid-1871 included three men killed, all in a face-to-face situation, while he acted in his capacity as sheriff or deputy U.S. Marshal. Prior to his initial experience as a lawman he had killed a fellow gambler, and may have killed one or more men in the famous fight at Rock Creek in Nebraska. Historians can count only four known victims prior to meeting Hardin, all in face to face encounters. If Hardin had pulled his pistol on Hickok—while Hickok had him "covered"—why would he not have shot in self-defense?

Certainly Hickok, an experienced law officer, scout, and former Union soldier during the late war, was well aware of the various tricks that could be performed with a six-gun, and he was far too wise to fall for such a thing as the "border-roll." Furthermore, if Hardin indeed performed this trick on the unsuspecting Hickok, one who he supposedly believed would shoot him in the back, why did *he* not shoot? He never experienced any qualms about killing freedmen, soldiers, civilians, why would he not have shot in this instance? So in all likelihood what did happen was what Albert Iverson "Babe" Moye, one of the cowboys who had come up the trail, observed and later recorded. His description of the peaceful "confrontation" between Hardin and Hickok is more reasonable and must be accepted as closer to the truth. As Moye tells it, the incident happened one night in the Black Bull Saloon. Hardin was standing at the bar with some friends drinking, and had his pistol out toying with it, and Hickok walked in and said: "Arkansaw, you had better put that pistol up before you let it go off and hurt somebody." Hardin complied with Hickok's order, and "didn't seem to get mad about it."[25]

If additional evidence is needed that the Hardin-Hickok confrontation did not occur as he described it in his autobiography, it appears in a letter written in 1888 from prison. Hardin wrote his wife Jane regarding some of his experiences. In this personal and honest letter, in which he had no concerns about impressing anyone, he noted, with his misspellings retained, that:

> It has been Said of me before I reached my majority that I had vanquished E. J. Davis's police from the red river to the rio grand[,] from matamoris to Sabine Pass that I had defeated the diabolical Burero agents and U S Soldiers in many contests and that I had invaded a foreign State [Kansas] and released from prison a relative a dear a true friend [Mannen Clements] whoose custodian was Wild Bill the Notorious the redoubtable Bill Heycoc of Abaline of whoom no braver man ever drew breath[.][26]

Alfred Iverson "Babe" Moye, 1871, who witnessed the confrontation between Hardin and City Marshal Hickok. *Courtesy the Gonzales County Records Center & Archives.*

Coming from John Wesley Hardin, that compliment—"no braver man ever drew breath"—spoke volumes and should put to rest the legend that Hardin "bested" the City Marshal of Abilene with a gun trick everyone already knew about.

Following the non-episode with Hickok, Hardin related how he and a one-armed friend named Pain were drinking in a bar when some drunken fellows came in cursing Texans. He interpreted this as a challenge, a personal insult, and informed the unsuspecting drunk "I'm a Texan." Of course this led to gunplay. The drunk jumped behind Pain and Hardin—who was probably far from sober—fired, the ball entering his friend Pain's only arm, while the unidentified Texan-hater tried to flee. Another shot brought him down with a bullet that passed through his mouth and out by his left ear, a dangerous and probably fatal wound. Hardin now was the one to flee, apparently not wanting to face Hickok so soon after he had been told to put his guns away. Flight to where was the question, and Hardin chose to head for the Cottonwood River, which he placed some thirty-five miles north of Abilene, but was in reality south, "to await results."

While Wes was awaiting results, Juan Bideno refused to follow orders and shot and killed young Billy Cohron, a cowboy who had gone up the trail with Hardin. Hardin claimed that Cohron's murder "was a most foul and treacherous one" and numerous groups had gone in search of Bideno, but failed to find him. Hardin did not use the words "mob" but probably that was the situation, and now he was asked to get Bideno. In order to act with a semblance of legality, Hardin had his friends obtain a warrant for Bideno's arrest and he was made a deputy and given letters of introduction to explain his purpose to those he met on the trail. One wonders what Marshal Hickok thought of the situation when he learned that "Little Arkansaw" was made a deputy. For a young eighteen-year-old man-killer with rewards posted for him all across Texas, this seems unbelievable, but Hardin, along with friend Jim Rodgers, took up the trail after Bideno. He knew the Mexican would head south; he sent word to the dead man's brother, John Cohron, who joined the Hardin "posse" with another Texan, Hugh Anderson.[27] The four-man posse headed out intending to catch up with Bideno before he reached the Indian Territory. Hardin relates a lengthy description of the chase, how they changed horses frequently, inquiring about a Mexican who wore a big sombrero, and, as he recalled, the chase finally ended at a place called Bluff, which "was a town of about 50 houses [with] some bar rooms and restaurants in a line." Ultimately Hardin and Anderson found the unsuspecting quarry in a saloon with a restaurant in the back room. Hardin demonstrated his awareness of the code of honor that *Chronicle* editor George was so intent on returning to the streets of Abilene. Had Hardin been reading the columns of the *Chronicle*? Hardin wrote that he warned Bideno he was under arrest and to surrender. He also said that he would be safe in Hardin's custody, meaning that he would not be turned over to a blood-thirsty mob of Anglo Texas cowboys. Bideno knew better than to surrender to a mere youth, and "shook his head and frowned. He then dropped his knife and fork and grabbed his pistol. As he did it, I told him to throw up his hands." Hardin, showing just how far his code of honor could go, allowed Bideno to get his pistol out after he ordered him to surrender. Only then did he draw his own. "When he got his pistol out," Hardin explained, "I fired at him across the table and he fell over a dead man, the ball hitting him squarely in the center of the forehead."[28]

Other descriptions of the Bideno chase agree with Hardin's version, although others, not surprisingly, diverge. Thanks to a contemporary account of the killing we have a more acceptable version of the incident. A man identified as Captain Folks apparently was on the scene and spoke with an eye-witness and reported what he learned to the *Oxford Times,* the sole newspaper of a community roughly thirty miles from Wichita. The headline certainly drew attention: "A Man Killed at a Table," followed by a lengthy two-paragraph dissertation on the need for law and order, and for the laws to be rigidly enforced. A sub-headline read "Terrible Murder." This is the information Captain Folks provided and the *Oxford Times* reported:

> A man was shot dead while sitting at the table in the dining room of the Southwestern hotel, at Sumner City, at noon last Friday [July 7], by a man who called himself Conway, from Cottonwood river. Conway claimed that the man he shot without warning killed his brother a short time before, and that he

(Conway) had followed him until he overtook him at Sumner, where he had stopped to take dinner. The murdered man was supposed to be a Mexican. His name was not ascertained by those who witnessed the tragedy, nor but few of the particulars of the incentives Conway had in thus taking the law into his own hands—if indeed, he had any other motive than the obtaining a fine horse ridden by the murdered man, which he asserted belonged to his brother. The Mexican being instantly killed, of course could not give his side of the story.

Hardin described the chase as taking at least several days, and since Cohron was killed on July 5, perhaps it did take that long for the avengers to catch up with him. The *Oxford Times* account corroborates some aspects of what Hardin remembered.

The shot took effect in the forehead, passing through the head and the partition, barely missing a girl in the next room, and was flattened against the stove. The so-called Mexican was totally unconscious of danger seemingly, and though facing the door fairly in which the assassin stood, was struck down while drinking coffee, with his cup to his lips.

At least Hardin recalled the accuracy of his shooting, although the warning he gave Bideno apparently was not heard by any of the onlookers with whom Captain Folks may have spoken. Certainly Hardin was unaware of a little girl in the next room who almost became an innocent victim of his shooting. But there is more to the *Oxford Times* account:

Conway apologized for the confusion the shooting occasioned, handed the proprietors of the hotel five dollars, remarking that that would pay for cleaning up, and left, taking with him the horse before mentioned. No arrest.[29]

How Hardin's memory failed him during the years between 1871 and his taking up the pen to record his adventures is striking. He recalled given the restaurant proprietor $25 to clean up the mess, but apparently it was only $5 for that purpose. Instead of Hardin's claim that four men were in the chase, the *Times* recorded but two, and a brief article in the same issue suggested the main purpose was to obtain the good horse. Did not Hardin show to the various witnesses his warrant for the arrest of Bideno? Apparently not. It is apparent that Hardin had no qualms about using another man's name to assure his protection, as he identified himself as "Conway" which was a misunderstanding of the name Cohron. It is known that he also used the name Wesley Clements. Or in this instance did Hardin allow Cohron to shoot Bideno to satisfy his need for vengeance, but later claimed the kill as his own?

With Juan Bideno's blood staining the floor of the Southwestern Hotel in Sumner City, Hardin, either alone or with his one, two or three companions, had to decide to return to Abilene, or do what? Go home to Texas? Hardin explained to his companions about his troubles in Abilene, suggesting he actually had misgivings about returning. Cousin Jim Clements had already left for Texas, and he perhaps considered doing the same at this point. But instead, he chose to go back to Abilene and if Hickok gave him any trouble, he would kill him. Before Abilene the group stopped in Newton, taking in "that town in good style. The policemen tried to hold us down, but they all resigned—I reckon. We certainly shut up that town."[30] Perhaps Hardin's chronology is misplaced at this point, and their "celebration" at Newton actually had been part of celebrating the Fourth of July, before the Bideno killing. The taking-in of Newton became news, as a report reached Topeka.

> A party of Texas Rangers visited Perry Tuttle's *maison de joie*, in Newton, on the Fourth, and compelled the demireps to stretch themselves at full length, upon the prairie. Perry escaped through the back door. The house was riddled with bullets.[31]

Hardin, after emptying his pistols in Tuttle's *maison de joie*, returned to Abilene with his companions, no doubt laughing at how they had convinced the Newtonians that he and his companions were Texas Rangers.[32]

By killing Bideno, John Wesley became something of a town hero, an Abilene celebrity, to the extent that besides whatever official reward may have been offered, the citizens who appreciated swift justice presented him with "substantial compliments in the shape of $20, $50, and $100 bills." Initially he didn't want to accept this blood money, but "finally concluded there was nothing wrong about it, so took it as a proof of their friendship and gratitude for what I had done." Hardin recalled receiving about $1000 in all as his reward, including a purse of $600 given by several wealthy cowmen, probably a large amount coming from Colonel Wheeler for whom Billy Cohron worked.[33] It is possible the cowmen did gather up a purse, but more likely the amount was considerably less than six hundred dollars. In fact the total amount probably was far less than the thousand dollars Hardin recalled. What activities Hardin engaged in the rest of the time in Abilene is difficult to determine, other than that he probably spent considerable time in the various saloons and gambling halls. After returning to Abilene he parted company with his companions. Shortly thereafter cousins Mannen and Gip arrived in Abilene. Mannen had his own violent incident to relate, and found Hardin with cowmen Jake Johnson and Frank Bell. After several celebratory drinks, the Clementses and Hardin retired to his private room.

There, Mannen explained that the night before he had slain two cowboy brothers, Joseph and Adolph Shadden, who had been with the herd. Supposedly the Shadden brothers had been hired in Gonzales County to work for Clements all the way to Abilene. Once they had crossed the Red River however, they "commenced playing off and refused to go on night duty." From then on they did do night duty, but by the time they had crossed the Arkansas River, it became known among the herders that the Shaddens had threatened Clements and intended to kill him. Hardin described the gunfight in dramatic terms: Mannen facing the two brothers, with three shots fired. Clements received a bullet through his slicker and vest, but shot Joseph Shadden dead with a bullet through his heart and Adolph dead with a bullet through his breast, living just long enough to utter the words that he was killed. The bodies were left where they fell, or possibly the other cow hands gave them a decent burial. Mannen and Gip then went on to Abilene after turning the herd over to other responsible hands.

Hardin's memory was hazy at this point. Two different newspaper accounts referred to the Clements-Shadden confrontation. The *Wichita Vidette* reported that "a herdsman named Lee was killed by another herdsman named Clemens [*sic*], on the 9th inst., at Slate Creek, Sedgwick county."[34] The *Kansas State Record* of Topeka reported that J. H. Lee was killed at Burnes' Ranch on Slate Creek, pointing out that the difficulty "grew out of a drunk among cattle drovers."[35] This may have been the report of a separate incident involving Clements, or the killing of Lee may have been only part of the Shadden fight. Hardin made no mention of a herdsman Lee in his *Life*.

But certainly two Shaddens were killed. Some years later, during the troubles known as the Sutton-Taylor feud, Richard McCoy, a Gonzales County resident, defended his honor in correspondence to the *Gonzales Inquirer*. Apparently Clements had accused McCoy of mistreating certain members of his family. McCoy denied that any member of his posse hunting Mannen Clements mistreated the Clements women in any fashion, but did infer that Clements himself was a cold-blooded murderer. His denial included this intriguing line: "Has he forgotten that he assassinated Dolph and Joe Shadden while asleep?"[36] How did McCoy learn Clements killed them in such a callous fashion, if he did? And did Clements actually explain the fight to Hardin truthfully, or, when Hardin was writing later, did he choose to falsify the killing to preserve the honor of his cousin Mannen Clements? We only wish Richard McCoy had provided more details, especially how he became aware of the incident on the trail.

In Abilene, according to Hardin, Hickok had a warrant for Clements' arrest for the Shadden killing. This is impossible to verify due to the loss of some early Abilene records, so we only have Hardin's version. This described how Clements calmly submitted to arrest, allowing himself to be jailed by deputy James H. McDonald. Hardin had convinced Clements to submit because he had an arrangement with Hickok—and Clements was released that same night. Clements had had enough of Abilene, and after making arrangements for Hardin to "take care of his younger brother" Gip, who was only one year younger than Hardin and quite capable of caring for himself, Mannen returned to Texas. He agreed to meet Hardin in Hill County, an unusual meeting place because Hardin could not have forgotten about his serious troubles there—in Towash—over the killing of Bradley and perhaps one or two others he failed to recall later in his autobiography.

Hardin had a poor memory for dates, as the next incident he placed on July 7, now attempting to "justify" his killings by claiming to be continually a potential victim of assassination. "In those days," he explained, "my life was constantly in danger from secret or hired assassins, and I was always on the lookout." He did not explain who these secret or hired assassins might have been, as he was in Kansas, far from those possible avengers in Texas. His only possible enemies in Kansas may have been friends of "Hosea" from the Newton Prairie battle, but presumably any of Hosea's friends had learned their lesson not to tangle with Hardin. Or did Hardin consider Marshal Hickok a potential assassin? Consequently we must reject Hardin's claim that he was forced to kill an intruder breaking into his room at the American House, someone he described as "attempting to burglarize his room." Hardin explained that he and Gip had retired for the night, when "I heard a man cautiously unlock my door and slip in with a dirk in his hand. I halted him with a shot and he ran; I fired at him again and again, and he fell dead with four bullets in his body." Hardin with Gip then unceremoniously jumped out of the window into a hack which was conveniently below their window. He managed to get Gip to a friend to hide him out, then left Abilene for good.[37]

This was Hardin's version. The *Chronicle* however reported the killing quite differently. The killing took place during the night of August 6, the victim identified as Charles Couger. But the "murderer" was identified as "Wesley Clemons, *alias* Arkansas." Reported the *Chronicle*:

> A most fiendish murder was perpetrated at the American House, in this city . . . Couger was a boss cattle herder, and said to be a gentleman [.] Couger was in his room sitting upon the bed reading a newspaper. Four shots were fired at him, through a board partition, one of which struck him in the fleshy part of the left arm, passing through the third rib and entering the heart, cutting a piece of it entirely off, and killing Couger almost instantly. The murderer escaped, and has thus far eluded his pursuers. If caught he will probably be killed on sight.

Coroner J. M. Shephard with a jury examined the body, determining the man's identity and the probable murderer.[38] Shephard offered no reason for the killing, but some Abilene citizens concluded "there is not much use in taking murderers before [Dickinson] county burlesque juries, and we fear that summary justice will hereafter be meted out to murderers in this neck of the woods."[39] Apparently mob justice was as common in Kansas as in Texas.

The *Weekly Journal* of the neighboring community of Salina also commented on the killing. Without identifying the victim, this source reported the man was killed "by a desperado called 'Arkansas.' The murderer fled. This was his sixth murder."[40] Apparently the Salina correspondent had not been well informed; with the five dead on the Newton Prairie, and Bideno, the Couger killing would raise the count to number seven in Kansas, not six.

Were the citizens of Abilene relieved that Hardin and Clements were on their way out of town? Hickok may have performed some type of investigation of the dead man in the room at the American House, and probably was there when Shephard conducted his investigation. With two fewer Texans in town he may have felt relieved. The August 17 issue of the *Chronicle,* however, brought the name before the readers again, at least those who may have forgotten the Couger killing. The tombstone to be placed at the grave of Billy Cohron had arrived at the Abilene depot. It was described as "about four feet high, and very neatly lettered." The inscription read:

W. M. Cohron.
Born April 4, 1848.
Died
July 5, 1871.
A native of
Belton Bell County
Texas.

Commented the *Chronicle*, "To make this item more interesting, the man who killed Charles Couger on the 6th inst., in this place, also shot and instantly killed the Mexican who killed young Cohron."[41]

Eighteen-year-old Hardin left Abilene and soon met up with Gip Clements on the Cottonwood, then headed home. Instead of traveling in a straight south line which seemingly would be quicker, they traveled south-eastward, on horseback, "well armed and equipped in every way. We went by Emporia and Parsons and thence into the Nation."[42] Two significant incidents occurred after they left the Cottonwood. Hardin recalled only one in his autobiography; the other he ignored. One was a shooting contest which could easily have resulted in another killing. Not knowing the individual by name, only referring to him as "a trader who had a wagon drawn by a horse and a mule. . . . a rough-looking fellow, heavy set, and weighing about 180 pounds. He professed to be an expert shot." Hardin and the trader arranged a contest whereby they would each shoot at a target, the loser paying the winner a dollar. Hardin claimed to be a crack shot and won from the trader several dollars. The trader was not satisfied so they bet and shot again. He continued to lose, and then became "wrathy" and wanted to fight. Bloodletting was narrowly avoided when Wes stuck his pistol in the man's face and Gip took his pistol. Finally the two cousins rode off, laughing, richer by about $200, but "glad we did not have to kill him" as Hardin summarized their meeting.[43]

The other incident Hardin avoided mentioning, either through forgetfulness or through design, was their narrow escape from the "cabin of death," a restaurant-hotel operated by the Bender family. The Bender building was not far from Parsons in Labette County in the southeast corner of the state. The family consisted of John Bender and his wife, a son John and an attractive daughter named Kate. They had appeared in Labette County in late October 1870. The family lived in a frame dwelling, actually a shell of a house about sixteen by twenty-four feet in size, facing the main road. There was a large room separated into two smaller rooms by an old wagon cover and a quilt hanging from the joists. Above the front door was a sign reading "Groceries." The traveler could enjoy a meal and a night's lodging. What any traveler was unaware of however was that a number of people had been killed in this cabin and their bodies buried in the acreage surrounding the Bender homestead.[44]

Fortunately we know of this incident thanks to Gip Clements. He left no written record of this, but he did tell brother Joseph Hardin Clements, who related the incident during an interview with historian Robert N. Mullin in El Paso in 1963. Joe told about brother Gip and cousin Wes "coming back from a cattle drive and while traveling through Kansas they stopped over one night with the family who killed so many [individuals]." They stopped at this Bender Hotel, but they did not spend the night. Joe and Gip were unaware of the identity of the Benders at this early date, as the truth about them was unrealized. The discovery of their victims would come later. But in August 1871

> John Wesley Hardin was suspicious. He had seen a pile of saddle blankets in a corner, and he thought there was blood on some of them. They sat down for supper with their backs to a curtain, and that made John Wesley Hardin still more uneasy. This broke up the plans of his hosts to knock him in the head, but they did not give up easy. Gip and John Wesley Hardin had to keep their guns on to make him get out their horses and saddle them.[45]

Hardin and Clements continued, not realizing how close they had come to being victims of the Bender murder family.[46] Their destination was Hill County where they planned to meet with Mannen Clements. Then they would all head for Gonzales County.

While Hardin and Clements loped on toward home, the Benders continued with their evil ways. Ultimately authorities realized that the real purpose of the Benders was to murder and rob travelers. When authorities became suspicious in early 1873 the Benders fled the area. Upon investigation of the premises the graves of thirteen victims were uncovered. Posses went out looking for them but there was no official report they had been found. It is believed one posse did catch up with them and dealt them prairie justice, vigilante style. If so their bodies were never found. The $2,000 reward offered for them was never collected.[47]

Meanwhile, two myths have endured about Hardin and his time in Kansas. That he performed a sleight-of-hand trick on an experienced professional lawman, James Butler Hickok, is a myth he created in his autobiography. The second is the myth that he killed a man just for snoring which was widely touted as part of an effective advertising campaign of Time-Life Books. This publishing firm in 1974 provided a series of books on the Old West, all handsomely designed and heavily illustrated, one of which was entitled *The Gunfighters*, which has a section on Hardin. Part of their television campaign stated that Hardin was so mean he once killed a man for snoring. The textual line was slightly softened: "Hardin shot a snoring hotel guest for disturbing his rest and had to leave town." Actually the story of the snoring man as victim may have started with Gip Clements and it became something of an immediate folk tale. In 1878, after Hardin was imprisoned in the Travis County jail, a reporter visited the jail, met Hardin and described him as "pert and saucy as ever." He conversed with the reporter, stating: "They tell lots of lies about me. They say I killed six or seven men for snoring, but it isn't true. I only killed one man for snoring."[48]

CHAPTER 5

THE TEXAS STATE POLICE

"It has been Said of me before I reached my majority that I had vanquished E. J. Davis's police force from the red river to the rio grand from matamoris to Sabine Pass that I had defeated the diabolical Burero agents and U S soldiers in many contests."

John W. Hardin

Hardin and cousin John Gibson "Gip" Clements arrived at Uncle Barnett Hardin's in Hill County where they met Mannen Clements, Gip's older brother, as planned. Hardin recalled the date as July 30, but it was closer to the end of August. After visiting a week with relatives the trio then started for home in Gonzales County, some 200 miles south. Although a fugitive, Hardin did not purposely avoid entering the various towns along the way; in fact, with his aggressive attitude toward State Policemen, his irresponsibility and his disregard for societal mores he may have been reckless enough to welcome a confrontation with a figure of authority.

Assuming that Mannen Clements had indeed killed two of the Shadden brothers on the trail to Kansas, the three may have anticipated trouble from the remaining brother and brother-in-law. But apparently the remaining Shaddens left. As Hardin expressed it, "soon after our arrival they concluded to move out."[1]

Two significant movements were operating in Texas while Hardin was out of state. Governor E. J. Davis's State Police continued to operate and had developed a presence in Gonzales County. A roster of "special policemen" does exist and reveals, in its aggregate, the names of several who would figure prominently in upcoming events: Green Paramore,

John Lackey, and George Tennille, who served as specials and William E. Jones who served as regular police. Each one, when accepted into the force, received a commission and a badge with a number embossed as a symbol of his authority. In neighboring DeWitt County, special policemen Martin V. King and Pitkin B. Taylor and regular policeman Joseph Tumlinson were commissioned. In neighboring Karnes County John M. Taylor was accepted as a special policeman. Not surprisingly, men serving as special or regular police were engaged in the Taylor-Sutton feud, then raging in DeWitt, Karnes and Gonzales counties and the surrounding area. Members of each faction considered the other a mob, lawless, and worthy of being shot down.[2]

In the weeks following the return of the fugitive to Texas the police intensified their efforts to capture him. As a hunted man in the middle of two feuding parties, he had to make a decision whether to join the Taylors or the Suttons if he intended to remain in the country.[3] In spite of what some authors have written, he was not related to the Taylors, but he chose to align himself with them. Ironically, brother Joe was a member of the police force, but he was in far off Comanche County.

Just how many of Governor Davis's policemen were stationed in Gonzales County in October 1871 is unknown, but two privates—Green Paramore and John Lackey—were there and they began to hunt for John Wesley Hardin. Even though they were special police they were at a terrible disadvantage, as they were inexperienced and they did not know Hardin by sight, only by reputation. Lackey was a Tennessee-born mulatto about thirty-four years of age, and by occupation a blacksmith. He was also a family man with a wife—Eliza—an Indian five years his junior, and five children. Green Paramore was classified simply as a laborer on the 1870 Gonzales Census. He was then twenty-five years old, born in Georgia, classed as a black man, and also a family man. He and his wife Lucinda had three children.[4] These two inexperienced men now chose to arrest the most dangerous man in Texas.

Special policemen Lackey and Paramore somehow learned that Hardin could be found in the small community of Smiley, also known as

Smiley Lake, located about twenty miles southwest of Gonzales. Hardin made no distinction between regular or special policemen; each represented a man who would take his liberty or his life. He placed them all in that class of men he described as "carpet-baggers, scalawags from the North, with ignorant Negroes frequently on the force." "Further," as he recalled years later, still feeling bitter hatred towards them, the police "frequently destroyed" life, liberty, and property. In fact, he may have considered the State Police Force and the members of William E. Sutton's faction all in the same bag. "We all knew," he wrote, placing himself with the Clements cousins, that the policemen "were members of some secret vigilant band, especially in DeWitt and Gonzales counties." He and his friends were "all opposed to mob law"; thus they and the police "soon became enemies."

Hardin gave an example of police abuse that very well could have happened. On one occasion a "lot" of police made a raid looking for him, going from house to house threatening his life when found. As he had no permanent home at this time he probably stayed with the Clements family on their ranch. He claimed these raiders frightened the women and children "to death."[5]

On October 19, 1871, Privates Paramore and Lackey stopped to investigate who was in the general store in the small community of Smiley Lake. Smiley Lake, barely a few years old, had originated when trader John Smiley settled there by a then-existing lake.[6] The store provided a place for men to gather, cattlemen driving their herds to market could water them there; they could obtain supplies at the general store, and could relax with friends. The police may have stopped there on an irregular basis as part of patrolling their county. As Hardin recalled, he was innocently minding his own business when someone yelled, "throw up your hands." He turned, arms raised, and saw "a big black Negro with his pistol cocked and presented." Hardin, intending to gain the advantage even though the policeman had the "drop," responded: "Look out, you will let that pistol go off, and I don't want to be killed accidently." Private Paramore demanded his prisoner surrender his weapons. Hardin then carefully offered up his pistols, butts forward. Then something happened that Paramore never could have expected, as he was unfamiliar with the tricks that could be performed with a pistol. "One of the pistols turned a somerset in my hand and went off. Down came the Negro, with his pistol cocked," as Hardin described his demonstration of what has been called the "Road Agent's spin" of the "Border Roll."

Private Lackey had remained outside, seated on his white mule, but now realized his partner was in trouble and began firing into the store. Hardin naturally returned fire and, as he recalled, knocked Lackey off his mule with the first shot, not knowing his bullet had hit Lackey in the mouth. He turned and saw Paramore sprawled "on the floor with a bullet through his head, quivering in blood." Having determined that man was no longer a threat, he now determined to kill John Lackey, who was galloping away.

Lackey escaped from Hardin that day, although severely wounded. He reached the waters of Smiley Lake and dove in. In spite of his condition being worsened by the impure waters of the lake, he hid from the man-killer—and survived. After searching for some time, Hardin grew tired and gave up the hunt. Lackey, years later, could look back upon this experience and boast how he had been in a gunfight with John Wesley Hardin and lived to talk about it, no doubt embellishing the event considerably, depending on his audience.[7]

The killing of another policeman by this young desperado, and the wounding of another, resulted in swift action in Austin. Governor Davis announced a reward of $400 for the capture of "Wesley Clements, alias Wesley Hardin," now wanted for another murder. Davis also contemplated a more serious declaration: martial law, but he decided against it. The *San Antonio Herald* reported the county had "narrowly escaped martial law" due to the amount of lawlessness. This same report declared that Hardin was in company of "an armed body of men" (which he failed to mention in his autobiography). Friends of the two special policemen, believing both were slain, "assembled in numbers, armed, and wanted to go after the bodies of their comrades." Wiser heads prevailed, primarily Sheriff James T. Mathieu and Gonzales Mayor Ezra Keyser, who "interfered and prevented the proceeding." A final comment was encouraging: "Every effort is being made by the good people of the county to bring the murderers to justice."[8]

A number of Negroes in Gonzales County gathered together to determine what could be done against this young Hardin. He wrote that many were threatening to join together "and with torch and knife depopulate the entire country [of white citizens]." In response to this perceived threat Hardin—again using the vague "we"—gathered some two dozen men "good and true" and sent word to the mob that they were ready for a fight, and that "we would not leave enough of them to tell the tale."[9] Citizens in Gonzales, certainly the sheriff and the mayor were among them, convinced the angry black mob to go back to their homes, and nothing more was done. Who went to the store in Smiley Lake and gathered up the corpse of policeman Paramore is unknown as is the place where he was laid to rest.

Hardin then left the country for a while to visit the Robert E. Hardin family in Washington County, although he soon returned to Gonzales County and claimed that a "posse of Negroes from Austin" now came after him. Someone warned him of their coming; he met them, and in the battle killed three. Again, this could not have happened as no contemporary source mentions such a battle, not even a hint in the official reports. Hardin, as well as other desperadoes in the seventies, made good headlines. The counties of Central Texas had numerous newspapers that would have relished a report of one man fighting off a posse, killing three of them. If the *Gonzales Inquirer* had reported such a story, the exchanges would have reprinted it all over the state. Hardin placed this event in September 1871, but his chronology is inaccurate as it supposedly happened after the gunfight with Paramour and Lackey, which took place in October.

However, according to his own account, Hardin did leave the area for some time, going to visit his parents, who were "well and glad to see me again." He stayed there until after Christmas, and for an unknown reason then went to Dallas and back to Gonzales.[10]

It is difficult to picture Wes Hardin enjoying Christmas with his family. At this time, December 1871, his family—if we assume older brother Joe also joined in the celebration—consisted of Reverend and Mrs. Hardin, Joe and his bride Arabelle, sometimes known as Alie or Allie, who were married on September 22 of that year in McLennan County. Daughter Elizabeth was about sixteen; Martha Ann "Matt" was fourteen. Jefferson Davis was ten and Nancy Brinson, "Nannie," the youngest, was six. It could have been an enjoyable family gathering. But Wes had a reward for his capture; and certainly the parents had not forgotten the death of little Benjamin. With the family together it must have been a time of mixed emotions for the Hardins: a joyous period as the children were home, but also a worrisome time. As a mother, Mary Elizabeth—always referred to by her middle name—was happy that her roaming son was with her, but for the minister father, it must have been troubling: giving shelter to the most wanted man in Texas, even though celebrating Christ's birth, could result in charges against him for harboring a fugitive. Worst of all, that fugitive son could be captured and strung up to a tree or simply shot to death wherever he was captured, depending on who managed to corral him.

But Hardin did not remain with the family; instead he returned to Gonzales County, perhaps intentionally arriving there the same night that cousin James Clements, with whom he had battled Mexican herders on the Newton Prairie the preceding summer, married Anne C. Tennille, the daughter of George Culver and Amanda Jane Billings Tennille.[11] Jim had obtained the license on January 8, 1872, and the marriage was solemnized three days later. (Wes incorrectly remembered—and wrote—that it was Gip Clements who was married that night.) The marriage record shows not only the date of their marriage but identifies some who were present, noting the marriage was performed in the presence of Gipson Clements, Miss Elizabeth Burnett, Fred Duderstadt and Miss Martelia Billings. Elizabeth Burnett was the fourteen-year-old daughter of cattleman Crawford "Doc" Burnett, for whom Hardin had worked; Martelia Billings was the daughter of Jasper Billings. There were certainly others, probably members of

Jim Clements and family. Seated beside him is his wife Anne, daughter of George C. Tennille. Children from left are Viola, born in 1877; Emma, James and Virginia, born in 1875. *Courtesy the Jack Caffall Collection.*

the Burnett, Bowen, Billings, and Tennille families. This may have been the first time Hardin met the bride's father, George Culver Tennille, born in 1825. In fact from reading Hardin's *Life* one easily gets the impression that George Tennille was a father figure to many of the young feudists who aligned themselves with the Taylor cause. The Tennilles and the Clementses became kin by marriage several times over. Daughter Sarah Tennille, known as "Sallie," was already married to James' brother, Joseph Hardin Clements, having married July 29, 1870.[12]

The combination of Hardin, the Clementses, Bowens, and Tennilles and others proved to be a formidable group of men. On this special occasion they may have all been on their best behavior, at least until they celebrated the wedding with whatever beverages they had. They soon would be deeply involved in the troubles with William E. Sutton and his followers, however. At a typical frontier wedding the celebration lasted more than just the day of the ceremony. This was no exception, for Wes later wrote of the Clements-Tennille union:

> Nothing of interest happened until I married Jane Bowen, though we were expecting the police to come any time. They would have met with a warm reception in those times, when the marriage bells were ringing all around.[13]

In his *Life,* Hardin gave little attention to his own marriage to Jane Bowen shortly after that of Jim Clements and Anne Tennille. The daughter of Neill and Mary Weston Bowen, Jane was born early in 1857; thus when marrying the wanted fugitive she was all of fifteen years of age. He was eighteen years old and perhaps to Jane he appeared to be the knight errant on a white stallion who would take her away from the boring existence of a rancher's daughter in rural Gonzales County. Hardin obtained the license and became her husband on the same day, February 27, 1872. Strangely, clerk R. L. Miller recording this vital record spelled his name "W. Handen" although he certainly knew better. The bride's name was spelled correctly.[14]

Although not positively identified, this is believed to be a young Jane Bowen, some years before her marriage to John Wesley Hardin. *Author's Collection.*

Later, when "nothing of interest happened," an incident occurred which remains mysterious. Hardin offered no clue as to why he traveled down to Corpus Christi, in far-off Nueces County, and then on to the huge Santa Gertrudis Ranch operated by Capt. Richard King. Hardin claimed that after leaving Corpus Christi he was followed by two Mexicans who he believed intended to rob him. Instead of becoming the victim, he

Jane Bowen, at the time of her marriage to John Wesley Hardin. *Courtesy the Robert G. McCubbin Collection.*

attacked. He fired, dropping one, while the other scurried away, possibly wounded. Concluded Hardin: "Being in a strange country I put as much space between myself and the robbers as possible." For once he admitted not staying around to investigate the results, writing, "I never did know whether I killed both Mexicans or not."[15]

Hardin arrived at the King Ranch later that day, riding on a "splendid horse" as he recalled. What he could not have known was that the pair he identified as robbers may not have been robbers at all, but hired men of Richard King, perhaps acting as "range detectives" to guard King's interests. They may have been trying to determine why this lone stranger was on the King range. It is unknown what business he had with Richard King, but he transacted that business and then in company with James W. "Jim" Cox—who also was at the King Ranch on an unknown mission—traveled to San Diego and then to Banquete where they remained a few days. The question arises: what was the infamous Hardin doing on the King Ranch, and also why was he now in company with Jim Cox, a one-time special policeman whose jurisdiction was DeWitt County?

This is the first time the name of James W. Cox appears in the Hardin saga, but it would appear again. Cox was a native of Kentucky, born there about 1823. When he arrived in Texas is unknown, but by 1860 he had a wife and five children residing in DeWitt County, although during the next decade he lost his wife.[16] When the State Police force was organized he became a private, commissioned on July 13, 1870. But he did not remain in that force long as he was removed on February 13, 1871, no reason provided.[17] During those years he resided in DeWitt County, so what took him down to the King Ranch, over a hundred miles south? Hardin made no explanation, but possibly he intended to work for King as a range detective, a "hired gun" protecting King's interests. Could that have been the reason Cox was there as well? Perhaps both men had gone there to offer their gunfighting services, and King rejecting them, decided to return to the Gonzales-DeWitt county area together for mutual protection. Possibly Hardin was unaware of Cox's previous service in the State Police, or if he was aware, he chose to overlook that since he was no longer a policeman, and he was also white. Cox was a close associate of Joseph Tumlinson, John Jackson Marshall "Jack" Helm and William E. Sutton, three men who soon would become hated enemies of John Wesley Hardin. They were considered leaders of the vigilante forces that Hardin had condemned operating in the DeWitt-Karnes-Gonzales counties area.

But Hardin and Jim Cox were together, the former with a significant reward offered for his capture, the latter a former State Policeman, and soon-to-be an avowed enemy. The pair spent a few days in Banquete, only a few miles west of Corpus Christi. At that time Banquete was a very small community with little more than a post office, a few dwelling places and perhaps a saloon.[18] After their visit there Hardin returned home to his bride, while Cox returned home to his wife and family.

Hardin provided no real information about Jane Bowen, other than describing her as "one of the prettiest and sweetest girls in the country."

He remembered he had "promised" to be gone on this King Ranch venture no more than twelve days, and "the more I thought of her the more I wanted to see her." Whether he had been gone the twelve days or less we do not know, but he wanted her then and headed home as fast as the horse could take him. From Banquete to Gonzales is nearly 100 miles, if galloping in a straight line. How many hours it took him to get back to the arms of the prettiest girl in Gonzales County he did not say, but she was well worth the cost of his "good horse worth $50," which he ruined in covering those many miles so fast. Seeing Jane "recompensed" him for the loss of his horse, however.[19] So much for the romance of being married to gunfighter Hardin.

Hardin placed his return to Jane in May of 1872. Unable to settle down and enjoy the comforts of home, he promptly began to gather a herd of horses to drive east and sell in Louisiana. By early June he was ready to go, and again bid his "angel wife good-bye" which "nearly broke my heart" but nevertheless Jane had "implicit confidence" in him and "her hope and prayer" was for his safe return.[20] The departure occurred on the fifth day of June, as he recalled.

Although Hardin had gathered the herd together, he chose not to do the actual driving but instead hired two brothers named Jesse and John Harper while he went on ahead, intending to meet them in Hemphill, county seat of Sabine County, nearly 300 miles east. Here again an interesting question is raised by Hardin's choice to retain the Harpers. He knew they were from Sabine County, in east Texas, and he also knew their father, Elmer (or Elmore) Harper, then county sheriff. As county sheriff, Harper, by the requirements of his office and being officially a member of the State Police, should arrest fugitive Hardin if the opportunity arose. Did he remain unaware of who his sons were working for? Did Hardin intentionally hire the sons of the sheriff, creating a conflict of interest, intending Sheriff Harper to overlook Hardin's presence when he arrived in his jurisdiction? One also wonders how Hardin managed to hire the Harper boys: did they happen to be in Gonzales County when he needed them?

Elmer Harper was a respected man of the county. He farmed, but on March 29, 1871, he was appointed sheriff and later was elected sheriff on November 8, 1872. He served until October 6, 1874.[21] One wonders why Wes didn't accompany the Harpers, rather than going on alone. Perhaps Hardin went on ahead of his horse herd in order to have the time to "square" himself with Sheriff Harper. It would be convenient if he knew the sheriff would leave him alone, as long as he behaved himself in Sabine County. On the way to Hemphill, nothing "unusual" took place except at Willis, in Montgomery County, where "some fellows tried to arrest me for carrying a pistol, but they got the contents thereof instead."[22] A week spent with Uncle Barnett and Aunt Anne Hardin and cousins allowed Wes to have a "splendid time" and by the first of June, according to his reckoning, John Wesley Hardin was in Hemphill. His reckoning was about a month off, however, as he earlier stated he had left Jane about the fifth of June. His *Life* is full of inaccurate dates, as Wes's wandering life style didn't require strict time keeping. Probably the visit was around the first of July instead of June. In Hemphill, he would await the arrival of the Harper brothers with his herd, and then go on across the border into Louisiana for the sale, proving he was making an honest living.

Arriving in Hemphill before the Harper brothers left him with time on his hands. He did join up with their younger brother, William "Billy" Harper, and the pair entered neighboring San Augustine County where Wes placed his horse in a race, a mount which he described as "hard to catch on a quarter of a mile." His horse won and Wes was richer by $250, and experienced no trouble in San Augustine County. They then returned to Hemphill for the herd's arrival; there Hardin spent the time gambling, "as much for past time as for money."[23]

But trouble was never far away, and during this time of idleness, Wes "got into a difficulty." He recalled it was on July 26, but as frequently seen his memory for accurate dates tended to be about one month off. As Hardin recalled, State Policeman "Sonny" Spites arrested a man named O'Conner for carrying a pistol. He learned that the man was traveling from Louisiana to his home in Austin when he was arrested. O'Conner was taken before a magistrate who fined him $25.00 and costs and confiscated the pistol. To Hardin this was an "outrage" and explained the situation to the justice, who then granted the man a new trial. He was now acquitted. To add to the "outrage," the policeman had taken his horse and saddle and was attempting to sell them to pay for the fine and costs. The policeman's real name was John Henry Hopkins Speights, although he may have been known as "Sonny" to distinguish him from his father who was also a State Policeman. The man arrested was William Conner, not O'Conner. Hardin wrote:

> I was on the front of the courthouse talking the matter over with O'Conner [*sic*] and some others when a small boy about ten years old began abusing Spites [*sic*] for arresting O'Conner at his father's house. Spites came up and listened to him and finally told the boy if he did not shut up he would arrest him, too. The boy ridiculed him and defied him to do it, telling him that no one but a coward would arrest a poor traveler.[24]

At this point the policeman actually "got up to slap the boy" and Hardin decided it was time to interfere. He challenged Speights, who in turn threatened to arrest Hardin for interfering with an officer. Hardin now had Speights where he wanted him to be, in a position such that he could claim self-defense if additional trouble arose. "I told him he could not arrest one side of me," Hardin sassed, "and the boy laughed." Obviously, Speights could not have appreciated how dangerous the situation had become, and in response to Hardin's challenge and the boy's mockery, he started to draw his weapon to make the arrest. Hardin drew a derringer with his left hand and a six-shooter with his right and squeezed the trigger of the derringer. Even with this inferior weapon his aim was true. Speights took a ball in the shoulder. He ran into the courthouse where he appealed to Judge Oran M. Roberts—later a Texas governor—for help.[25] Hardin "would not shoot a fleeing man, not even a policeman," so he gave up on Speights, mounted a convenient horse and rode to where his own was kept at Dr. D. M. Cooper's place. There Billy Harper brought him his horse, "Old Joe," while Mrs. Cooper, Billy's older sister,[26] brought him his saddlebags. Mrs. Cooper cried out, "Wes, yonder comes pa [Sheriff Harper] with some men, for God's sake, don't shoot." He did not, but he galloped away after a hasty good-bye, not knowing if a mob would be forming or what the situation might become. The urgency was to flee, not stay around to see how badly he had wounded Speights. In the race to catch the fleeing man the hastily formed posse fired at him, but only hit the horse. A few miles out of town Hardin pulled up at a friend's house and sent for Billy Harper.

Young Harper conferred with Hardin, then returned to Hemphill and learned that the policeman was not seriously wounded, merely shot in the shoulder, but "scared to death." He further learned that everyone approved of what Hardin had done, not necessarily for shooting the policeman but for asserting the feeling of the community that the arrest of Conner had been unnecessary. Fortunately he also learned that Jesse and John Harper had arrived with the horse herd, and they all could now go on to Louisiana to make the sale.

The next day Hardin went to Frank Lewis's place where the horses were being held. Instead of continuing with his original plan, he sold the horses to the Harper brothers, then started back to Gonzales, there no longer being any reason to go to Louisiana. After all, he had the prettiest and sweetest girl in Gonzales waiting for him.[27]

This is essentially what Hardin recalled and presented to his readers concerning the Hemphill difficulty. Because his aim was poor that day, or because the derringer did not carry the firepower of the six-shooter, or possibly because it was his intention—Speights was white, whereas Green Paramore was black—he only wounded Speights rather than killed him that day. He probably fairly quickly dismissed the whole matter from his mind.

Fortunately Policeman Speights reported to his superior in Austin, Adjutant General Davidson. He offered fewer details than what we would have preferred, but did include some comments which were not offered by Hardin. Speights stated that he had arrested William Conner for carrying a pistol, then turned him over to the civil authorities. Further, he was shot at and wounded by Wesley Hardin, who was then "still at large." Indeed he was at large, and no doubt Sheriff Harper intentionally did not catch up with him, knowing perhaps that Hardin would soon be out of his county and that his sons were friends of the man. He may have resented the presence of the state police in his county anyway, as, different forces of society refrained from cooperating at times then even as today. Speights also stated that William Harper and a *discharged policeman* named Ferguson had assisted Hardin to escape.[28] Hardin did not mention this, probably because he was unaware of Ferguson's former occupation.

Jeremiah Alexander Ferguson, who had aided and abetted Hardin in his escape, had indeed been a policeman for a short time, from September 19, 1871, to October 31, 1871.[29] He had served during the late war, enlisting in Company F, 11th Texas Infantry, the same regiment in which Sheriff Harper had served. No reason was given for Ferguson's exit from the State Police force. Ferguson moved on to Sterling County in West Texas where he ranched and raised cattle. He died on February 12, 1912, leaving a wife and a number of children and step-children.[30] Did he know, or ever realize, who the young man was whom he had helped escape from Policeman Speights?

Of further interest in Speights's report, and not mentioned in Hardin's, is that Hardin "boasted" that Speights was the *eighth* policeman he had shot, and that he—Speights—"was the only one he did not kill." Speights certainly did not embellish his report with this final comment. But how to reconcile the numbers? Hardin obviously forgot about John Lackey, whom he shot but did not kill, but at the time possibly did believe he had killed the man, learning years later that he survived by hiding out in Smiley Lake. He certainly knew he had killed policemen Jim Smalley and Green Paramore; perhaps he thought he had killed Lackey as well. He may have believed he killed the three policemen he identified as Smith, Jones and Davis, but no official record of that incident has been located. This does add up to seven, but only if we accept Lackey and the Smith,

Jeremiah Alexander Ferguson, one time Texas State Policeman who later aided a badly wounded Hardin to escape. *Courtesy Charlotte Pool.*

Jones and Davis trio as policemen being killed. Or instead of that trio, did he believe he had killed three members of a "posse of Negroes from Austin," which also is impossible to confirm from the available records? Speights may have simply misunderstood Hardin's boast at the time, as he was bleeding from a shoulder wound and running for safety in the courthouse. At that point he may not have even realized whom he had faced and attempted to arrest; he only knew then that he was going to survive.

Speights was not alone in reporting the Hemphill gunfight. Later, after Hardin was safely a prisoner in the Travis County jail in 1877, two justices of the peace in Sabine County, S. A. Alford and Solomon Arthur, wrote to then-Adjutant Gen. William Steele (Davidson had absconded in late 1872 with state funds and was now a fugitive himself) that on September 12, 1872, Hardin "shot and wounded J. H. H. Speight[s], State policeman, in the arm, and then made his escape."[31]

Although wounded, John Speights continued to serve as a policeman until the force was disbanded in April 1873. His last pay voucher was for service during the April 1–22 pay period. It shows he had earned $58 for his services. Apparently any medical treatment he received for his wound was paid for out of that $58. On July 17, 1883, Speights married Emily Jane Mashburn Bourland, a widow with one child. The new Mr. and Mrs. Speights would give eight children to the world.[32]

Organized with the best of intentions in July of 1870, the State Police organization experienced controversy throughout its existence. The Republicans who favored Gov. E. J. Davis praised its successes, and there were some successes; but the Democrats who opposed any plan of Governor Davis to reduce lawlessness in the state condemned it. One editor of a frontier newspaper, proud of his linguistic skills and fearing nothing with his insulting accusations, penned the following: "We may be mistaken, but it is our opinion that governor e.j. Despot (who is to our mind a cowardly cold blooded murderer, and instigator of lawlessness and crime; who stands convicted of perjury in the hearts of the people; who is a consummate ignoramus, a detestable villain, a theif [sic], a knave and robber) . . . "and further vitriol.[33] Others felt the same way, but considered the State Police a worthy organization which did much to combat lawlessness in post-Civil War Texas. Perhaps most important of all is to ask how John Wesley Hardin felt about the matter, after he had killed and wounded policemen but then had spent years in prison to contemplate his back trails. On June 24, 1888, in a letter to his beloved wife Jane, he wrote:

> I belong to no man or Set of men[.] I belong to my Self and god. for all my acts I am reSponsible to my Self to my God. his laws are right. It has been Said of me before I reached my majority that I had vanquished E. J. Davis's police force from the red river to the rio grand from matamoros to Sabine Pass that I had defeated the diabolical Burero [*sic*] agents and U S Soldiers in many contests . . . as to the truth or falsity of these assertions I have nothing to Say, except that I have ever been ready to Stand trial on any or all of these charges when a fair and impartial investigation was vouchsafed. but never willing to place my life my liberty in the hands of a mob even if they wore the eupaulets [*sic*] of the State.[34]

Indeed, in the mind of many, Hardin had, before he reached the age of twenty-one, "vanquished" the State Police. After the gunfight with J. H. H. Speights he had no further difficulties with State Policemen, Bureau agents or US soldiers. By the end of April 1873 the State Police no longer existed, and Reconstruction in Texas ended the following year. When E. J. Davis was voted out and Richard Coke became the new governor of Texas, he created a force to protect honest Texans. It was called the Frontier Battalion, a larger force whose initial purpose was to solve the "Indian problem" and reduce lawlessness. Much of what they did was no different from what the State Police tried to do, but they gained the respect of most Texans, law-abiding or lawless, and continue to serve the state to the present day.

CHAPTER 6

CAPTURE AND ESCAPE

"I am either killed or shot. If all the gold in the world belonged to me, I would freely give it to kill him. I have one consolation, however, I made the coward run."

John Wesley Hardin

ugitive Hardin did not leave Sabine County in a gallop as one might expect him to do after wounding a state policeman. He intended to return to Gonzales County—to Jane—but on the way he stopped in Polk and Trinity counties to visit relatives. At a store not far from Livingston he and a man identified only as Hickman engaged in a horse race. The winner would walk away with a purse of $250. There were several Hickman families living there at the time: Bartley, Asa, Hezekiah, Morton S. and James as heads of households. They were all from Louisiana with the exception of Morton S. Hickman who was a native Texan. These all constituted a group who were related.

What is most interesting is that an acquaintance named Richard B. "Dick" Hudson now informed Hardin that the Hickmans intended to take the $250 winning purse whether they won or lost the horse race. It was set for noon on a certain day. Each party put up an initial sum of $100 "as a forfeit." Hardin informed Hudson that he was aware of what the Hickmans intended to do, and that he was ready to fight them, as "I wanted [them] to understand that no man or set of men could take my money without killing me unless they won it," and if they wished to fight, "they would not commence any too soon to suit me."[1] No race occurred, nor did a fight occur, as the "Hickman Bros." learned of Hardin's response—carried to them by Hudson certainly—and they backed off, surrendering

119

the $100 forfeit money as well as the $250, totaling $350 for the non-race. Hardin, in relating this incident, acknowledged that Hudson and he had been boys together in Polk County. At this point in time the two were trusted friends, but that would soon change.

Although Hardin had ruined a good horse in his efforts to get back to Jane not long before, he now felt it more important to spend time with relatives. He stopped at Uncle Barnett Hardin's place and spent a relaxing week hunting and fishing with his cousins. While he enjoyed this time with them one wonders how often he thought of Jane. Along with cousin Barnett Jones, the same one who had arranged the "wrestling match" with Maje resulting in his first kill, Wes Hardin went to Trinity to be with more relatives and friends. Here he met a man named Philip Allen Sublett, the son of a wealthy planter, who also enjoyed gambling and perhaps was not a great deal different in character from John Wesley Hardin. The pair met at the saloon and bowling alley of proprietor John Gates.

Gates operated a combination drinking establishment and gambling hall and it was there that Hardin chose to relax, drink and bet on a game of pins. Cousin Barnett Jones remained a bystander, perhaps to watch Hardin's back while he enjoyed himself. Sublett remains a mysterious figure essentially, one whose life begs for disclosure. He was born about 1842, the son of Philip A. Sr. and Easter J. Sublett. In 1850, when the family resided in San Augustine County, the twenty-one-year-old first-born son Franklin B. Sublett was an attorney; Philip Allen was eight years old, and younger brother Henry but four years. The family had located in Texas at least by the 1830s, before Phil Jr. was born. By 1860 Easter J. Sublett was a widow but remained in San Augustine County. As head of household, she had her sons to help as well as forty-three slaves among her chattel.

When Hardin and Phil Sublett met they of course found reason to have a drink or two prior to any gambling. Wesley apparently lost shaking dice to see who would pay for drinks, perhaps purposely, intending to lure Sublett into a higher stakes game. Hardin now was not yet twenty years old; Sublett was thirty-five, and judging from his background was flush enough to spend a great deal of time carousing and gambling. He and Hardin bowled at $5.00 a ball. Hardin beat Sublett six times straight, winning $30. Then they argued about ending the game, as Sublett now realized he was overmatched and put his hand on his pistol and cursed Hardin. "I slapped him," Hardin recalled, and "shoved a bull-dog pistol at his head."[2] Friends then interfered and "peace" was restored. Then, with Hardin's derringer back into his pocket or stuck in his belt, it was time for a round of drinks. Then Sublett exited from the scene.

After a while Hardin realized that Sublett was probably getting a weapon, so he went to his saddlebags behind the bar and removed his six-shooters. If necessary he would be ready to defend himself adequately as the bull-dog was good only at very close range. John Gates informed Hardin that the difficulty was over, and that he should go into the alley where the bowling took place. Sublett was there, and one wonders if Gates purposely sent Hardin into that situation. Hardin then heard a shout, "Clear the way. I will shoot anyone that interferes with me." It was Sublett, and he continued with the challenge: "Come out, you g—d—s— of a b—." There was no exhibition of fair play here, no stand-up face-to-face showdown, as Sublett fired one barrel of his shotgun at Hardin—and missed. Then a drunken man appeared and pulled Wes into the doorway, providing Sublett with a good target. He fired again, "and as we darkened it, he fired the other barrel of his shotgun at me. I knew I was shot, so I instantly took after him with my six-shooter, but he threw down his gun and broke for his life."

Sublett ran, but Hardin could not keep up with him due to his wounds from the shotgun blast; further his pistol was malfunctioning. He gave up the chase, informing those within hearing: "I am either killed or shot. If all the gold in the world belonged to me, I would freely give it to kill him. I have one consolation, however, I made the coward run."[3] Hardin realized he was in a dangerous situation. Fortunately Barnett Jones was there to help him, holding him up. He had Jones get his saddlebags from behind the bar, and with them and what he had in his money belt he had altogether $2,250 in gold and silver. He told Jones to take it to Jane in Gonzales, and to tell her that he had "honestly tried to avoid the trouble." No doubt the expression of this concern suggests that Jane was seriously working with him to adjust his life style, that there were ways and means to avoid trouble, to avoid the difficulties and especially the killings.

But before Jones left with money for Jane, he arranged to deliver the bleeding Hardin to get medical attention. Virginia-born Dr. Paul Carrington was there to provide help. He was a forty-two-year-old doctor who probably knew Hardin's family. Carrington, with his wife Mary F. and servants, could take good care of this badly wounded man.[4] Carrington however called in an associate and together they removed the shotgun pellets. Hardin stated that two balls had struck him to the left of his navel and had passed through the right kidney, lodging between his backbone and ribs. Two others had struck his belt buckle, the big silver buckle probably preventing a mortal wound. He remained conscious throughout the ordeal, refusing opiates, wanting to stay alert. His friends placed him in a hotel with a clear head but in extreme pain.

His wounds, "ordinarily speaking" would have proved fatal according to Dr. Carrington. He spent days in that hotel where he received "the best of treatment" but then around mid-August he had to be moved. Friends took him to a place east of Sulphur Springs, then within a few days moved him again to Old Sumpter to Dr. Teagarden's. The doctor's son, Billy,[5] was an old friend. They were both the same age and Billy helped his wounded friend move from location to location. Unless he kept moving the posse would find his hiding place. With the help of Teagarden he was moved into Angelina County where friend Dave Harrel lived. Here Hardin found safety but in a few days Harrel warned him that a party of police was coming to arrest him. Hardin acquired a double-barreled shotgun and "resolved to sell my life dearly if they did come."

Three men, believed by Hardin to be state policemen, did come to Harrel's and attempt the arrest, but in the ensuing gun battle Hardin claimed to have killed one and wounded another. However, he himself received an additional wound in the thigh. Harrel now moved him to Till Watson's place, a sanctuary for only a short time as yet another posse—or mob—would soon locate him. We do not accept the gunfighter's statement of killing a member of this group, believing the claim was just another example of Hardin's literary creativity. There was some gunfire however, as there is evidence of shots fired before Hardin's actual capture by Cherokee County Sheriff Richard B. Reagan in an extant letter. W. M. Waddell and five other citizens sent a letter to Governor Davis, dated September 30, 1872, advising him that Reagan had captured Hardin "after a sure and bloody encounter."[6] Certainly if Hardin had actually killed a posse member the outcome would have been different.

Hardin now chose to surrender in order to obtain medical attention, plus protection from whatever groups were after him. In his mind anyone hunting him constituted an illegal mob. He sent Dave Harrel to Sheriff Reagan, an old acquaintance of Reverend Hardin. Hardin felt he could trust Sheriff Reagan to protect him as well as provide help for his wounds. He described the conditions of his surrender: Reagan would provide medical attention; he would receive half of the reward Reagan earned; he would not be put in jail; he would be protected from any mob; and he would be taken to Austin as quickly as possible and then to Gonzales. This is what Hardin wrote, and it may have been what he wanted, but he must have realized he was in no position to bargain for much of anything. He was suffering from several wounds, which could turn to infection which could cause death. What he needed badly was good medical attention.

Sheriff Reagan did come to Hardin's location at Till Watson's place, with a four-man posse, as Hardin recalled. He gave the date as September 4, 1872. Curiously, as Hardin was surrendering his pistols, one of the posse members thought he was going to shoot the sheriff and shot Hardin, giving him yet another wound, "on the right knee." Hardin's first reaction was "I would kill the sheriff, but it flashed across me at once that it was a mistake and that in him was my only protection."[7] Reagan did protect Hardin, and although Hardin's version of laying down the

Sheriff Richard B. Reagan, the sheriff who accepted Hardin's 1872 surrender. *Author's Collection.*

rules for his surrender is preposterous, he was taken to Austin as he had wished.

Possibly Sheriff Reagan and Reverend Hardin were old friends, but the W. M. Waddell letter provides a different version, which may be closer to the truth: "[Reagan] followed and caught him in Nacogdoches County [.] Reagan was fired on by Hardin and ran a great risk of his life [.]"[8] According-ing to another version, Reverend Hardin told the sheriff where his wounded son could be located, and only then did the sheriff make the arrest. If this was true it is the only instance where the father did not act as an enabler to his wayward son. Yet another version is provided by the granddaughter of the sheriff, who described the arrest in this manner: "A man found out that Harden [sic] was in a house out from Rusk and Grandfather went out and brought him in—he was wounded. He kept him in a room at the hotel, and my father—Dood Reagan—nursed him back to health. Grandmother cooked his meals while he was there, and when he was able to leave Grandfather carried him to Huntsville prison [sic]. He Harden told Grandfather he had been told to look out for Reagan for he would get him. He told my Grandmother when he left for her not to worry for he would not give Grandfather any trouble. He thanked them and was very greatful [sic] for the treatment he received while here."[9] Did the accidental shooting by a posse member actually occur? That is doubtful. Never before had Hardin reflected before shooting an adversary; previously he shot first and then, possibly, he took time to reflect. The additional wound may have been only added drama to the memoir. Sheriff Reagan, Mrs. Reagan, and their son, William Rider "Dood," cared for Hardin at the family's hotel in Rusk. While there Hardin received numerous curious visitors wanting to meet the famous desperado. He was by now a celebrity indeed, and they asked him many questions; someone even asked him if he had ever killed a woman. He did his best to be polite to all, no doubt even enjoying the attention he received. Although there are differing versions of how Reagan came to have John Wesley Hardin in his custody, the bottom line is that Hardin was now a prisoner.

Now he had ample time to reflect on his life, and even more time to think about Jane, although he wrote that he never mentioned her name at this time, but gave no reason for this. He also realized that even though he would be charged with killing Paramore and wounding Lackey, he had friends in Gonzales and a friendly jury might find his actions to have been in self defense. He felt he could "come clear if I had a fair trial there." He even claimed that in "putting down Negro rule there, I had made many friends and sympathizers and had made it a thing of the past for a Negro to hold an office in that county."[10]

Dr. Thomas Young Jameson[11] now became Hardin's physician, having replaced Dr. Carrington. He determined it would be safe to move him, and the party began the slow trek to Austin as Hardin had desired. He gave the date as September 22, the party consisting of Sheriff Reagan, deputy John Taylor, and himself. Hardin was now placed in the miserable Travis County jail, notorious in those days for the unsanitary and unhealthy conditions. At best it was considered a "nuisance," but also a "disgrace to civilization." A reporter from the *Daily Democratic Statesman*, Austin's leading newspaper, visited the jail and described it as "a single room without air or ventilation, infested with vermin, reeking with abominable stench and crowded with a sweltering mass of suffocating human beings, who strip themselves naked because of the intolerable heat and closeness [which] should bring a blush of shame to the cheek of every citizen in our county. It is a disgrace to the age and a crime against humanity."[12] Travis County Sheriff George B. Zimpelman[13] took custody of Hardin and placed him in a cell like any other prisoner. It was a drastic change from the Reagan Hotel.

The news of Hardin's arrest created headlines across the state. Reports reached Austin and editors emphasized the number of victims Hardin claimed. The *Lone Star Ranger* reported him as "less than 21 [years] of age, has been arrested in Cherokee county, in this state. He is said to have killed 24 men in Texas, and four in Kansas—making 28 in all. He is the most bloody desperado we ever heard of. His father is a Methodist minister, and is said to stand quite high in the estimation of the public."[14] A briefer report appeared in the *San Antonio Herald*.[15] In none of the reports yet found is there mention of Hardin being wounded by a posse member under Sheriff Reagan.

With Sheriff Reagan on the road back to Cherokee County, Hardin obtained the services of an attorney who secured an order for him to be delivered to the Gonzales County jail. A squad of police led by Capt. Thomas Williams left Austin and journeyed through Caldwell County and then on to Gonzales. Williams was a resident of county seat Lockhart

Sheriff George B. Zimpelman, Travis County sheriff who took custody of the wounded Hardin after the 1872 Trinity gun battle. From L.E. Daniell's *Personnel of the Texas State Government.*

so that may be the reason the police with their prisoner took that particular route. The State Police force by now had a reputation for murdering prisoners in their custody, with the excuse that they had "attempted to escape," but apparently Hardin had no fear with Captain Williams.[16]

A humorous incident occurred at the county seat of Lockhart. Hardin's horse had "played out" and he was ordered to ride a mule instead.

Hardin, still suffering from his wounds, refused, for he "did not like the looks of that mule." One of the guards, having some compassion for him, allowed the prisoner to ride his horse while he would ride the mule. Then a "regular circus" took place, as "the mule threw the policeman so high and hard that everybody made fun of him."[17] The bruised and embarrassed policeman then found a suitable horse for himself and the party continued to Gonzales.

Nothing more of interest happened until the party reached Gonzales where citizens "denounced" the treatment Hardin had received from the police. He was shackled and chained, which only demonstrated the caution the police used in guarding such a notorious prisoner. Those complaining citizens said he had "done more for the peace and welfare of the county than any other man in it." That was a special group of citizens, however, as they appreciated the fact that Hardin had killed at least one policeman and wounded another in that county. Captain Williams left no account of the delivery of Hardin; when the prisoner was delivered to Gonzales County sheriff William E. Jones[18] he returned to his home, feeling relieved that he had followed orders without incident. He did advise Sheriff Jones that the sympathy for Hardin was so strong that he might as well be released, as the prisoner would escape anyway. Sheriff Jones quickly sent for a blacksmith who cut the irons off.

Sheriff Jones informed the adjutant general that he had received the prisoner, but as court had recently adjourned "nothing can be done until the next term which will be in February 1873." He also recommended that Hardin be removed to a stronger jail.[19] Acting Assistant Adjutant General Henry Orsay responded to Jones' letter ten days later informing him that he needed a court order before he could deliver Hardin elsewhere.[20] Upon receiving such order, he was to inform Capt. Thomas G. Martin—stationed in neighboring Hays County—to send a strong escort of police to move the prisoner. All this was to result in nothing as on November 19 Hardin escaped from the insecure Gonzales jail, doing so possibly with Sheriff Jones' secret blessing. Hardin wrote that Jones told him his friends would soon be in to see him and "to keep quiet and patient." Someone, probably Mannen Clements, provided him with a strong saw. The guards "posted" him when to work on the bars as "the saw made a big fuss." Once the bars were cut sufficiently he was able to squeeze through and leave his cell window and go where friends Nathan "Bud" McFadden and Barry G. "Benny" Anderson awaited with a horse. The $400 prisoner was now on the loose.

Jones may or may not have been party to the escape. His offer of a $100 reward may have been only a token gesture, as it was not sufficient to attract anyone to attempt arresting him. Jones did inform his superior that Hardin had escaped; Adjutant General Britton now informed Jones that the order for the Hays County escort to be ready "for the conveyance to another jail is not now necessary."[21] The State Police now were aware that the notorious John Wesley Hardin had escaped. Even the governor did not act quickly on this information, as he waited until March 7, 1873, before he offered a proclamation of a $1000 reward for Hardin's arrest and conviction. Hardin now became not only a much more "valuable" fugitive to the state, but his reputation increased significantly. He continued to see himself as a man continually fighting against tyranny and for his liberty, never as a common criminal.

Hardin was now free and at home, thanks to the loan of Benny Anderson's "iron gray horse." He now could relax in the arms of Jane, his "darling and beloved wife" from whose charms he had been absent since leaving her to sell the horse herd in Louisiana, five months earlier. He recalled friends and relatives coming to see him and congratulating him for his "safe return." He stayed at home and recuperated, but he could not remain quiet for long, for on December 17 a number of men gathered to drink and carouse at Billings' general store in rural Gonzales County. Hardin was one of them, as was Jane's brother, Joshua Robert "Brown" Bowen, store proprietor William MacDonald Billings, Jim and Gip Clements, Thomas Haldeman, Rockwood "Jim" Birtsell, George C. Tennille, and the son of the proprietor, John MacDonald "Mac" Billings, fourteen years of age, was there also. What happened that day would have serious consequences for many of those present.

The cause of this gathering is not known, but Thomas J. Haldeman celebrated so much that he became drunk. Instead of becoming belligerent as some drunken individuals do, Haldeman became sleepy and went to a nearby tree, wrapped a blanket around himself and promptly dozed off under its branches. With Haldeman asleep, someone—Brown Bowen was later accused—approached him, placed a pistol to his head and fired once, killing him instantly. In contrast to some of the law's lengthy delays, Gonzales County authorities now acted. Someone notified State Police Sergeant Thomas G. Patton, stationed at nearby Helena in Karnes County, of the crime. On January 12, 1873, he and deputy sheriff David J. Blair with some citizens arrested Bowen, although a different report gives the credit for Bowen's arrest to Sheriff Green DeWitt and his deputy Richard B. Hudson. Apparently Bowen offered no resistance, and he was turned over to civil authorities.[22] An examining trial followed, allowing Bowen to be released on payment of a $2,500 bond which he could not pay, hence he remained in jail. The question remains to this day: did Brown Bowen really slay Haldeman?

Purely by chance teenager Mac Billings, son of the proprietor, was a witness to the Haldeman killing. He was at the store and when he saw Bowen's horse begin to wander he went to get it to secure it. According to his later testimony, on returning with the horse he saw Bowen approach the sleeping Haldeman and shoot one time into his head. Bowen then returned to the store, and Mac informed him, "Mr. Bowen, here is your horse." Hardin then asked him who had shot "out there" and the boy answered, "Mr. Bowen shot." And why? "He shot at Mr. Haldeman." This was the exchange between young Mac Billings and Wes Hardin within moments of the killing. Hardin told Mac to keep quiet and say nothing about it, or Bowen would shoot him, the only witness, as well. Proprietor Billings was not afraid to question Bowen as to why he had shot Haldeman. Bowen replied that he had "a right" to kill him. This did not anger Billings so much but the fact that he had shot him in the presence of his son did. Bowen replied: "I did not see Mac until my finger was on the trigger, and it was too late to stop then."[23]

On February 10, 1873, Bowen was indicted in Gonzales District Court for the murder of Thomas Haldeman. He was placed in the same jail from which his brother-in-law had only recently escaped. Nine days later Bowen, his uncle Joshua Bowen, Thomas Caffall and Brown's father, Neill, signed a promissory note for $500 in gold to attorney Horatio S. Parker of the firm of Parker & Cade to defend Brown.

As the Bowens were determining how best to defend their son, the conflict in DeWitt County between the Taylors and the Suttons had a brief respite, although it was rumored that Haldeman had been killed because he was a "spy" for the Sutton force. On August 12, 1873, eighty-seven men from both factions signed a treaty of peace that they hoped would end their feud. They signed a pledge "to keep the peace" before Judge Oliver K. Tuton, which was then publicized in the newly established *Cuero Weekly Star*. William E. Sutton and his seemingly constant companion Gabriel Webster Slaughter signed. On the opposing side Jim and Joe Clements, Jim Taylor and cousin Bill Taylor, and brothers John and Fred Duderstadt signed. But Mannen Clements did not, nor did John Wesley Hardin.[24]

Things were not idle in the governor's office while this turmoil was taking place south of Austin. Gov. E. J. Davis, on March 7, 1873, signed his name and "caused the Great Seal of the State to be affixed" on a proclamation offering $1,000 reward for the arrest and conviction of Hardin. The proclamation required that the fugitive had "to be delivered to the Sheriff of any of the Counties whose indictment for murder is pending against him," which included Hill, Gonzales, Polk, "and other counties."[25]

Brown Bowen and his brother-in-law now chose to do more for his defense than his attorneys could. On March 26 Hardin "with a squad of twelve men, all armed with Winchester guns and six-shooters, rode into the town of Gonzales, and delivered the county jail of all its prisoners, threatening the guard with death if he made any alarm." William E. Jones, who may indeed have had a single person guarding the jail then, let it be known that "he has made no effort to arrest any of these parties;

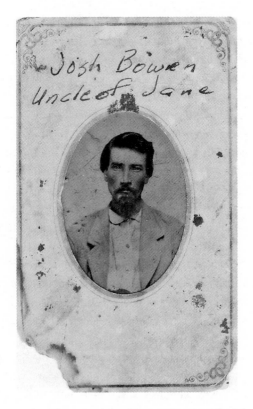

Joshua Bowen, uncle of Brown and Jane Bowen. *Courtesy The John Wesley Hardin Papers, The Wittliff Collections, Texas State University.*

that the citizens will not answer his summons, and that the outlaws would be released, even if caught and placed in Gonzales jail."[26] Was Sheriff Jones acting cowardly or was he simply being pragmatic?

Brown Bowen was now a liberated man. Wes Hardin—liberated from the same jail—was certainly among those defying Sheriff Jones. Probably young Jane Bowen Hardin had convinced her husband to rescue her brother. Others in the rescuing party were probably the Clements brothers; George C. Tennille, Joshua and Neill Bowen, may have been with them, and Jim and cousin Bill Taylor as well. No one was careless enough to accuse anyone. Now both men became notorious not only in Texas but elsewhere. The *New York Times* even noted Bowen in a brief article discussing rewards offered for fugitives from justice. The article stressed the inadequacy of Governor Davis' policies, underscoring the fact that "life is not yet hardly safe in Texas." Among the ten rewards itemized was the $500 reward offered for Brown Bowen "who has escaped from jail in Gonzales while awaiting trial on the charge of murder, and has committed another murder since his escape." The article was headlined "Murder Record in Texas."[27]

CHAPTER 7

THE END OF JACK HELM

*"They [Jack Helm and Jim Cox] said there were but two sides—
for them or against them. I talked as if I would join them, and
they told me of a dozen or more of my friends whom they wished
to kill, and who were the best men in the community, their sin
lying in the fact that they did not endorse the vigilant committee's murdering."*

John Wesley Hardin

Why did Brown Bowen kill Thomas Haldeman? Bowen later stated that Hardin killed him, because "he was afraid of him being a spy" for Joe Tumlinson, Jack Helm and W. W. Davis of the Sutton faction. Tumlinson, Helm and Davis had all been members of the State Police force, which Hardin so despised. Tumlinson had served as a private from July 13, 1870, until April 30, 1871. Helm had been chosen one of the first four captains, serving from July 13, 1870, until his resignation on November 30, 1870. William W. Davis began as a sergeant on April 6, 1872, and served until October 31, 1872, when he resigned.[1] These three men were now leading figures of the Sutton faction, feuding with the Taylors and their followers. Bowen claimed that he was a friend of Haldeman and therefore would not have had any motive to kill him. "[Hardin] told me himself that these men had sent Holderman [*sic*] to watch him. . . . I went one time and took Holderman away from Hardin; in fact, several times. . . . Hardin and Gyp Clements went into the [Billings] store and commenced drinking, after which [Hardin] told me he was going to show me how to kill a man. . . . Hardin told [Clements] it was equal to our Kansas trip." Bowen claimed Hardin then said to him

134

that if anything was said of the killing that he—Bowen—was to say that he himself did the killing. Hardin supposedly went to David Haldeman, Thomas' father, and told him that Brown Bowen had killed his son.[2]

At the end of 1872 Hardin made no visit to his family as he had at the end of 1871, or at least made no mention of one in his memoir. The reason was probably that he was still recuperating from the wounds he had recently received in Sabine County. Perhaps the Christmas revelry was at the home of Jane's parents—Neill and Mary Weston Bowen— instead. He did stay at the Bowen home in January 1873, then was able

Neill Bowen, father of Jane and Brown Bowen. *Courtesy The John Wesley Hardin Papers, The Wittliff Collections, Texas State University.*

to ride again and began putting together a herd to drive to Indianola, an important port in Calhoun County, to then be shipped to New Orleans.

For one who had been on his own for years, and had traveled to the Corpus Christi area and the King Ranch, and living in Gonzales County, he was surprisingly ignorant of the country surrounding him. He gave the date as April 9, 1873, when he learned of a new road being built from Cuero, DeWitt County, to San Antonio, which would go by way of Rancho, a small community in western Gonzales County. He was at Mannen Clements' place, preparing to depart, when John Gay informed him that if he followed that road, which he called a furrow, he would be able to get to Cuero much quicker. According to his memoir, when he approached a point near Mustang Motte in DeWitt County he saw a man "armed with a Winchester" who, in addition, "had two six-shooters on the horn of his saddle." Hardin suspected the stranger was either a lawman or someone on the dodge like himself.[3] The pair rode toward each other; after a few pleasantries the stranger introduced himself as the sheriff of the county. Hardin responded that he must be Dick Hudson then, the acting sheriff. No, the man answered, and introduced himself as Jack Helm. They knew of each other by reputation, although they had never met. Helm offered his hand, which Hardin refused. Hardin, realizing that this officer undoubtedly had papers for his arrest, dared Helm to try and arrest him, pointing out to Helm that he had accused him of being "a murderer and a coward" and had had his deputies searching for him. Helm denied this accusation, saying that if the deputies were looking for him, then they were doing that on their own account and not by his orders. By now Hardin had drawn his pistol; Helm begged him not to shoot and promised that he would ignore the papers for his arrest that he had in his possession if he would allow him to live. Hardin snarled: "You are armed, defend yourself. You have been going round killing men long enough, and I know you belong to a legalized mob of murdering cowards and have hung and murdered better men than yourself." According to Hardin, Helm refused to fight, which if indeed Hardin had his pistol pointed at him would have been suicide. He offered to be Hardin's friend. Strangely enough, the pair then rode toward Cuero, separating about two miles from the outskirts. They agreed to meet again the next day in Cuero to "come to an understanding." [4]

This is a most curious encounter, and if indeed Hardin and Helm met as Hardin described for the first time it suggests that at this point in his career, early 1873, he had ambivalent feelings about becoming involved in the Sutton-Taylor difficulties. Also it appears Hardin had forgotten that he had recently met with Dick Hudson back in Polk County where he and the Hickman brothers had nearly had a serious difficulty, which Hudson prevented. Hardin and Hudson supposedly knew each other from their boyhood days in school together, but now Hardin is writing that he met a man to whom he stated, "I suppose your name is Dick Hudson." Certainly Hardin ought to have known the man was not Dick Hudson, unless he was only pretending to be unaware of who the man was, and chose this way to express his caginess.

But in meeting with Jack Helm the following day, all that was accomplished was that Helm asked Hardin to join his "vigilant committee, of which he was captain." Hardin declined, as Helm was "waging war" against his friends. Hardin claimed that he only wanted to be considered a neutral in the animosity, and that he and his "immediate friends" would also remain neutral. The pair agreed to meet yet again, but this time Helm would bring along someone, and Hardin would be accompanied by Mannen Clements and George Tennille. If this indeed happened it was the first of an unwritten agreement that they would honor the position of neutrality between two groups intent on killing each other.

Hardin did not provide any background of the difficulties which he himself was closely involved in. In late October or early November 1872 Pitkin B. Taylor had been seriously shot, but was still alive. On December 17 as described above, someone killed Thomas Haldeman. Brown Bowen was arrested for the killing and on March 22 he escaped from jail, and Pitkin Taylor died sometime that month. Hardin failed to explain the cause of these feuding matters, but certainly was aware that Pitkin B. Taylor had lost his life to either William E. "Bill" Sutton directly or else to Sutton's friends. Pitkin was the father of his friend James Creed

"Jim" Taylor. Following these meetings between Hardin and Helm—if they indeed occurred as Hardin described—the killing of Pitkin Taylor and his sons-in-law Henry and Will Kelly must have been touched upon.

On April 4, 1873, as Hardin relaxed in a Cuero saloon, a man named J. B. Morgan, never a state policeman but a deputy of Sheriff Helm, sidled up to him and demanded he buy him a bottle of champagne. Hardin refused, and this refusal inflamed Morgan. Hardin wisely left the premises, obviously attempting to avoid a difficulty, but Morgan followed him out on the street, still angry at Hardin's refusal. As Morgan began to draw his weapon, Hardin realized he had to defend himself. He drew and fired, the ball "striking him just above the left eye." [5]

This was Hardin's version. The sheriff wrote out a report which landed on the desk of Adj. Gen. Frank L. Britton in Austin. He in turn reported that "John Morgan was killed in Cuero, April 4, 1873, by Fred. Johnson." Either Hardin was acting under an alias or the sheriff was unsure who had committed the killing. Immediately above Morgan's name in the listing of DeWitt County victims appears: "A man named Cooper was shot in Cuero, March 30, 1873, by Jack Slade." Was this not yet another killing Hardin conveniently omitted from his memoir, or was there a real Jack Slade who killed Cooper?[6] Further in the report is included news from Gonzales County, pointing out that "Wesley Hardin killed a man, name unknown, March, 1873."[7] Was this a reference to Cooper?

Hardin by 1873 had developed a sizeable reputation. Britton did more than list killings by Hardin—or someone using his name—as he further explained in his report to Governor Davis:

> In Gonzales county there is a strong band of thieves and murderers, headed by John Hardin, alias Wesley Hardin, *alias* Wesley Clements, who is reported to have committed sixteen different murders, and has threatened to kill a member of the Legislature, Hon S. T. Robb. One thousand dollars has been offered by your Excellency for Hardin, and one thousand by the State of Missouri.[8]

No evidence has been found that Hardin threatened Robb, or that he had ever been in Missouri. His reputation, however, was so great that he was accused of crimes he couldn't have committed.

Britton then reminded the governor that it was Hardin who "delivered the [Gonzales] jail of all the prisoners, threatening the guard with death if they made any alarm." There were other counties where mob law was acting in full force. In this same report Britton stated that since the beginning of 1873, the chaos in fourteen counties was so great that "county officers were unable to suppress the existing violence or give the citizens protection, and requested detachments of State police, to assist the county officers in the execution of the laws." The fourteen counties were Austin, Burnet, Comanche, Duval, Erath, Gonzales, Hill, Kerr, Kinney, Lampasas, Madison, McCulloch, Refugio and San Saba.[9] Very soon DeWitt County would also ask for assistance. Britton concluded his narrative report, he feeling justified by saying that: "[F]rom the information before me in stating that to-day not less than one hundred men, many of whom are charged with the highest crimes known to our law, are prowling about the State in gangs of twelve to twenty, murdering and robbing almost without restraint." [10]

Certainly if asked, Frank L. Britton would have itemized the John Wesley Hardin "gang" as among those acting against the law "without restraint." But to Hardin and his associates, in that year of 1873, "there existed in Gonzales and DeWitt counties a vigilant committee that made life, liberty, and property uncertain. This vigilant band was headed by Jack Helm, the sheriff of DeWitt, and his most able lieutenants were his deputies, Jim Cox, Joe Tomlinson [sic], and Bill Sutton. Some of the best men in the county had been murdered by this mob." Hardin mentioned the killing of Pitkin Taylor, Taylor's sons-in-law Henry and Will Kelly, killed "by this brutal Helms' [sic] mob. Anyone who did not indorse their foul deeds or go with them on their raids incurred their hatred, and it meant certain death at their hands." Hardin estimated the number in the mob was about 200, "and were waging a war with the Taylors and their friends." [11] All that remained for Hardin to cite in his memoir was that he was now ready to become a leader in the troubles known to history as the Sutton-Taylor Feud.

No one today can say with certainty when the feud began or what specific incident started it. Various newspaper accounts offered fragmentary explanations, until Victor M. Rose's seminal study of the feud published in 1880. William Steele, the adjutant general under Gov. Richard Coke, investigated in 1874, as the feud was still smoldering and apparently then drawing the attention of the governor's office, and interviewed numerous citizens in DeWitt, Gonzales, Karnes and Victoria counties. He determined the most recent cause of the feud continuing was because of Capt. Jack Helm. He wrote that the "present state of violence had its origin in the operations of Jack Helm, a sheriff appointed by Gen'l. J. J. Reynolds, and afterward made Capt. of State Police under Gov. Davis." Steele was keenly aware of numerous prisoners killed while in the custody of an officer, but who were murdered with the excuse that they were "attempting to escape." [12]

John Wesley Hardin had many issues to ponder before deciding which side to join. He was a first cousin of the Clements brothers, and must have known they favored the Taylor side over the Sutton side. The advantage of aligning himself with the Suttons, on the other hand, was that the charges against him could be dropped. But then he would be acting against his friends who were clearly anti-Sutton. Leaving the country was more or less out of the question.

While mulling over his decision, events were taking place that would force him to act. Shortly after the funeral of Pitkin Taylor in March, someone attempted to kill Bill Sutton. He was seriously wounded, but survived. Sprawled out bleeding on a Cuero saloon floor he recognized—or thought he recognized—Rufus P. "Scrap" Taylor and Alford Creed Day as his would-be assassins.[13] On June 16, 1873, Sutton, Horace French, J. P. "Doc" White, John Meador and Addison Patterson were going to Clinton—then the county seat of DeWitt County—to attend the examining trial of "Scrap" Taylor, accused of the Sutton shooting. They were ambushed, but the only casualties were French's horse killed, two other horses wounded, and Meador being wounded in the leg. There were no casualties in the ambushing party.[14]

Hardin would have us believe that during this violent period of 1873 he had remained neutral. Then he had killed J. B. Morgan, a deputy of Sheriff Jack Helm. Following the Morgan killing (Hardin incorrectly gave the date as April 23, when it was April 4) Helm and a posse approached the Hardin home looking for him, Mannen Clements and George Tennille. As the men were out hunting cattle the Helm posse insulted the women, according to Hardin. Jane and the others refused to give them any helpful information. Hardin believed they were especially abusive toward Jane, and this may have been the final act that drove him to join the Taylors, not to be simply a member of their force, but to join them and fight aggressively against the followers of William E. Sutton and Jack Helm. Upon their return he "found out what had happened, [and] we determined to stop this way of doing, and sent word to the Taylors to meet us."

The rendezvous occurred at Mustang Motte; the purpose being to develop "a plan of campaign." One can only imagine Hardin—not yet twenty-one—calling together other angry young men to discuss strategy. But he claimed the gathering brought in two cousins, Jim Taylor and Scrap Taylor (evidently out of jail after being arrested for attempting to kill Bill Sutton) their uncle John M. Taylor, cousin Mannen Clements, George Tennille and himself. Did the others realize that Hardin now was clearly the leader of the Taylor party? The final decision was that they "agreed to fight mob law to the bitter end, as our lives and families were in danger." [15] With Hardin clearly filling the leadership role, although no vote had been taken to determine this, the violence of the struggle between the opposing forces now intensified. Hardin's strong leadership ability as well as his reputation for killing certainly was the reason for his new position. Although Jack Helm had been removed from the State Police, he remained the DeWitt County sheriff, thus he had power in the county. A number of former policemen had signed his bond for the position, including Bill Sutton, Jim Cox, Joe Tumlinson and Richard B. "Dick" Hudson, among others.

In mid-July Hardin planned on doing away with two of those men
who had backed Jack Helm: Jim Cox and Joe Tumlinson. Instead of a
courageous challenge from Hardin to meet in the middle of the street
for a fair fight, however, the plan called for an ambush. Cox and Tumlinson were with several others, identified variously as John W. S. "Jake"
Christman, W. C. "Curry" Wallace, Henry Ragland and J. L. Griffin. Men
concealed alongside the road included Jim and Scrap Taylor, Alford Day
and Patrick Hays "Bud" Dowlearn. According to Jack Hays Day, who
almost certainly was also there, Jim Taylor opened fire first, followed
by the others. Two men "toppled dead from their horses" and the others
fled. Jim Taylor wanted to kill Joe Tumlinson most of all, but this time
he escaped.[16] Hardin was probably there as well, for he had planned the
entire ambush. He later wrote—perhaps with a smirk on his face—that
it "was currently reported that I led the fight, but as I have never pleaded
to that case, I will at this time have little to say." He merely admitted that
Cox and Christman were killed by the Taylor party.[17] What Hardin failed
to mention was that Cox was found with "nineteen buckshot in his body,
and his throat cut from ear to ear." This was an important addition to the
report appearing in the *Advocate* of Victoria, Victoria County, the leading newspaper of the area adjacent to DeWitt County. The report added
that Cox had been with Helm in his "Regulator depredations, and no
doubt he was killed to avenge some injury inflicted then." This double
assassination garnered considerable attention from the press. Different
victim names reflected the confusion, one report stating that the "unfortunate" Christman "was a stranger in this section, and not a party to
the feud." [18] Actually he was far from being a stranger in the area, as
six years prior to his death he had been a witness to the marriage of Jim
Cox and Mary E. Prather.[19] Justice of the Peace L. B. Wright of DeWitt
County reported on local affairs to Governor Davis, explaining he had
seen the bodies of Cox and Christman and "was pained" to inform him
that there "is a very bad State of affairs in our County[.]"As justice he
had conducted an inquest on their bodies, "a few Days Since they were
ambushed by 10 or 12 men and killed [.] ther bodes [their bodies] ware

mutaleated [*sic*]." L. B. Wright had good reason to be concerned not only as a DeWitt County citizen but also because one of the targets of the ambush was his father-in-law, Joe Tumlinson.[20] Tumlinson and Sutton were two figures on the top of the Taylors' list of enemies to be killed. Jim Taylor had let it be known that he wanted to kill Bill Sutton himself for Sutton's having killed his father. Jack Helm was also at the top of the list. Tumlinson and Sutton had both survived an ambush; now it was time for a more direct approach.

John Jackson Marshall Helm (who was always known as "Jack"), who dropped the "s" from his name when in South Texas, had led a career far from honorable. He was the son of George M. Helms, a Virginian, who had moved to Missouri by the time Jackson was born in 1838. As an adult, Jack joined Capt. J. D. King's Company, the 9th Texas Cavalry. In February 1862 George and son Jack were part of a vigilante group who "tried" five men for their Union sympathies. The trial resulted in the quintet being found guilty and hanged. A further act of reported violence in Jack Helm's background was the killing of his first wife, when she committed adultery with a neighbor.

Following the war, Helm journeyed to South Texas where he became better known. He worked for a while for cattleman Abel Head "Shanghai" Pierce in Matagorda County, where he was involved in vigilante justice against suspected cattle thieves. He then located to DeWitt County and was elected sheriff on December 3, 1869, and was later appointed to the position by Reconstruction's General J. J. Reynolds on March 23, 1870. As the top lawman in DeWitt County he became the leader of a group who became notorious for frequently killing their prisoners who "attempted to escape." By reputation he determined who were members of alleged horse or cattle theft gangs and took it upon himself to administer swift justice. Frequently he became judge, jury and executioner. Several members of the extended Taylor family had been killed while in the custody of Helm or his deputies. Later, as a captain of the State Police, he ultimately abused his power to the extent that he was dismissed from the force. Helm, on a more personal note, had insulted Hardin's wife. For this reason he became a natural enemy of her husband, a man marked for death.

Reports describing the death of Jack Helm were contradictory. The earliest appeared in the *San Antonio Daily Express* of July 25. It reported that "a desperado by the name of Hardin with several others of the same stripe rode up to the blacksmith shop of Jack Helm, while he was engaged at his work and riddled him with bullets." As a closing note to this report, the *Express* added that "a ruffian" named Bowen "committed rape on a colored woman and afterwards shot and killed one of the best Colored men in the County, Bob Thomas, by name." [21] This is an important addition as it reveals that Bowen was brave enough, or foolish enough, to remain in the area after having been freed from the Gonzales County jail by his brother-in-law.

A more detailed version of the Helm killing appeared in the *Gonzales Index,* and was then reprinted in the *Bastrop Advertiser* of August 2. The initial information was apparently first given verbally to Samuel McCracken, one of the leading citizens of the community of Albuquerque, then believed to be in Wilson County but actually just across the line in Gonzales County. He then provided the information to a reporter working for the *Index.* Reportedly McCracken, Helm and Hardin "were sitting engaged in friendly conversation, when a stranger come up, and walking up behind Helm attempted to shoot him. His pistol missed fire. As Helm turned, this stranger fired, shooting him in the breast. Helm at the same time rushed at him attempting to grapple with him." At this point, Hardin fired his shotgun at him, "shattering his arm." Helm, struggling with a pistol wound as well as the shotgun blast in his arm, attempted to get into the blacksmith shop, but "the stranger" followed, shooting him again and again. Helm fell dead in the blacksmith shop, amidst the tools he used to invent his cotton worm destroyer. Hardin and "the stranger," really Jim Taylor who may have been a stranger to McCracken and others in Albuquerque, rode away, "remarking that they had accomplished what they had come to do." [22]

If this was accurately reported, and there is no reason to doubt it, it appears that Hardin, although clearly an enemy of Helm, may have settled down in "friendly conversation" with him and McCracken only as a ruse to get Helm to relax his guard, thus allowing Jim Taylor easier access to him. Hardin may have even been talking about the possibility of his joining the Helm vigilante committee. Then James Creed Taylor arrived, and Helm unknowingly became the target of "the stranger."

Years later Hardin recalled essentially the same as what Samuel McCracken reported. He noted that he was "to meet" Helm at Albuquerque. "I went there according to agreement, a trusty friend accompanying me in the person of Jim Taylor. We talked matters over together and failed to agree, he seriously threatening Jim Taylor's life, and so I went and told Jim to look out, that Jack Helms [sic] had sworn to shoot him on sight

THE KILLING OF JACK HELMS.

The killing of Jack Helm by Hardin and Jim Taylor as depicted by artist R.J. Onderdonk in Hardin's memoir *The Life of John Wesley Hardin*.

because he had shot Bill Sutton and because he was a Taylor." This much agrees with the McCracken version. Hardin then continued by saying that Jim Taylor asked to be introduced to Helm, or at least have him pointed out, which seems odd as one would think Taylor by now knew Helm by sight. Hardin then went to the blacksmith shop to get his horse shod. After his horse was taken care of he paid the man and as he was preparing to leave, he heard someone shout: "Hands up, you d—s—of a b—." Hardin turned and saw Helm advancing on Taylor "with a large knife in his hands." Someone else hollered "Shoot the d—d scoundrel." Hardin perhaps looked back on this from twenty years distance (if it occurred as he described) and wrote that he thought Helm was the scoundrel and fired his shotgun at Jack Helm, "as he was closing with Jim Taylor." Hardin then covered Helm's friends with the shotgun while Taylor emptied his pistol into the head and breast of the dying Helm. What was remarkable to Hardin and to history is that this leader of the Sutton forces was not brought down in ambush, but by a carefully planned engagement in a community where Helm had "friends and advisors" who "stood by utterly amazed." Hardin received "many letters of thanks from the widows of the men whom he had cruelly put to death." Unfortunately none of the letters congratulating him have survived. Further, many "of the best citizens of Gonzales and DeWitt counties patted me on the back and told me that was the best act of my life." [23]

Although Hardin had avoided claiming participation in the ambush killing of Cox and Christman, the former being brought down by a shotgun blast, he now did use a shotgun, certainly a more reliable weapon than a six-shooter which might misfire, as apparently had happened when Taylor first attempted to shoot Helm. There is not enough evidence that Hardin preferred to use a shotgun in his battles, but Cox was killed by a shotgun blast, as was Lewis Peacock, back in 1871. And now Helm was killed by a shotgun blast. The weapon Hardin used to kill Helm was an English-made W. & C. Scott & Son 12-gauge side-by-side currently on display in the Buckhorn Saloon in San Antonio.[24] Helm's mutilated body was examined not by the angst ridden L. B. Wright, but by Wilson

County Justice of the Peace James W. Dicky. While Wright mourned over the loss of two friends of his father-in-law, the writer in the offices of the Gonzales newspaper provided a sort of *apologia* for Jack Helm.

> Jack Helm had many charges laid at his door while in command of the Police, and no doubt had incurred the mortal hatred of many surviving friends of men said to be hunted down and killed by him and his party. He was nominally sheriff of DeWitt County but had for a long time left its duties to be performed by efficient deputies, and turned his attention to improved farming implements. He was engaged at the time of his death in manufacturing a cultivator of his own invention.

And more remarkable is the concluding statement: "We heard of no cause of quarrel between Helm and the parties who killed him."

The shotgun that Hardin used in the killing of Jack Helm. *Courtesy The Buckhorn Saloon and Museum, San Antonio.*

Justice L. B. Wright now penned another letter to Governor Davis, pointing out—as if Davis was unaware of the volatile situation in counties southeast of Austin—that DeWitt County was in a "verry [*sic*] bad State of affairs," and that "our Sheriff Capt. Jack Helm was killed a few days Since." He continued, pointing out that freedman Robert Taylor had been killed, adding "the information that Brown Bowen Did the Deed [.] he was Broken out of Jaile [*sic*] in Gonzales county—Charged of murder [.]"Clearly the civil authorities were totally inadequate to bring the guilty parties to justice. Wright believed that if the State Police force were restored then things would be different. He concluded his sad communication, surrendering himself to hyperbole and grief: "I am wholey [*sic*] destitute of Power to inforce [*sic*] the Law. I have done all that I can[.] our best Citizens ar[e] being killed Evary [*sic*] few Days." [25]

CHAPTER 8

KILLING INTENSIFIES

"The feud between the Sutton and Taylor parties, which had likely to have provided a bloody encounter lately, at Cuero, has been happily adjusted."

Austin Daily Democratic Statesman, January 22, 1874

The killing of Jack Helm certainly caused members of the Sutton party great concern as it was obvious that with Hardin's leadership, the lay of the battlefields had changed in favor of the Taylors. Hardin's unbridled and psychopathic aggressiveness was now openly shown. He may have seen himself as a freedom fighter, killing the enemies who would kill him and his friends or deny his liberty. Sutton had been wounded in an ambush and he and Capt. Joe Tumlinson both now may have pondered their next moves in the wake of the killing machine that Wesley Hardin was. As Jim Taylor had made it clear to all, he wanted the chance to kill Bill Sutton, and he would if he could get to him before any of the others did. Now the obvious target was Joe Tumlinson.

That Tumlinson was considered a fervent member of the Sutton party, but had been married to a Taylor, underscores the fact that the troubles of South Central Texas were indeed a family feud, and not an exaggerated series of criminals acting against peaceful law-abiding citizens, although there were criminals on both sides. "Captain Joe," as he was frequently called, had married Johanna Taylor on April 2, 1832. She was a sister of William Riley Taylor, a brother of Pitkin who had lost his life due to Sutton's bullets in early 1873. Perhaps to bring the families closer together, William Riley Taylor had married Joe's sister, Elizabeth Tumlinson. Johanna died in 1858, leaving Joe a widower with no children. Joe then married Elizabeth Newman, their union producing three children, who created the link with the other group in the feud, that aligned with Bill Sutton. Daughter Ann married L. B. Wright, who became a justice of the peace in DeWitt County. Son John J. "Peg Leg" married Isabelle Cresap, a sister of Sam H. Cresap who joined the Sutton side during the feud. The third child, Martha E. "Matt," married William W. Wells, who also joined the Sutton side.

Joe Tumlinson had had extensive experience fighting prior to the outbreak of the feud. He had fought Indians and Mexicans prior to fighting Anglos, mainly the Taylors. He had served as a ranger under Capt. Robert M. Coleman in 1835 and 1836. He was at San Jacinto on April 21, 1836. After his marriage to Elizabeth Newman he settled down permanently in DeWitt County. When Governor Davis created the State Police force, Joe Tumlinson became a private to work in DeWitt County. But he was apparently too independent, and was dismissed on April 17, 1871, for refusing to obey orders.[1] He continued to raise stock, and worked with Bill Sutton in his feud with the Taylor party.[2]

As if killing their enemies one or two at a time was terribly inefficient, Hardin and the Taylor following now conceived a plan to lay siege to the Tumlinson home and force them out with fire—the nineteenth-century equivalent of the Molotov cocktail—and then shoot them down as they fled the flames. If it succeeded the way Hardin intended, it would be a dramatic engagement with the enemy, and rid the countryside of the vigilantes. In a move typical of his thinking, Hardin recalled his plan of laying siege as a *defensive* maneuver rather than an act of aggression. The inspiration for the plan was Hardin learning "of a mob of fifty men" led by Tumlinson "coming into our neighborhood to kill and raid us in revenge" for the death of Helm.[3] Hardin with a dozen or so vengeful combatants concluded to "go and meet them" where they were making their headquarters at Joe Tumlinson's place, only several miles west of Yorktown in DeWitt County. Hardin's group learned there were about fifty men together "and that at night most of them slept on the galleries." The initial plan, was to "slip up to the gallery and if we did this undiscovered, to fire upon the sleeping mob," when the Hardin party arrived at Tumlinson's at 2:00 a.m. This improbable plan had to be aborted when the Tumlinson dogs heard noises and awakened the sleeping men with their barking. In response, Hardin's group sent three couriers to get help while the remaining stayed and surrounded the house. Two hours later reinforcements arrived, but before any further action could be taken deputy sheriff David Blair[4] arrived "to relieve" the besieged Tumlinson party. Hardin bragged about capturing Blair and his posse "right in front of his friends." Hardin and Blair had words, but before the shooting could begin "some of the best citizens of the county came out to where we were preparing for battle." [5] Hardin's group numbered about seventy-five while the Tumlinson force numbered fifty. Good citizens convinced both parties it was time to stop the killing and accompanied both groups to Clinton where a treaty of peace was prepared and signed. County Clerk H. B. Boston prepared the document, and following a lengthy preamble, perhaps read aloud by clerk Boston, men from both sides signed. In simplest terms the preamble stated that "disputes and controversies of a nature likely to result in blood shed have existed between the undersigned" and those signing promised to "abstain from all hostile acts," and that all who signed would do all in their power to keep the peace. The two groups certainly kept their weapons close as they lined up to sign. In all, thirty-nine feudists signed this document: Joseph Tumlinson, with an "X"; his son Peter Creed Tumlinson;[6] C. C. Simmons[7] who had been involved in the killing of the Kelly brothers in 1870; and Reuben H. Brown, who later would become city marshal of Cuero and lose his life in the feud which only temporarily ended with this treaty. The most noted figures on the other side, twenty-one in all, were Lazarus Nichols, George C. Tennille, Edward J. Glover, Mannen Clements and his brothers Gyp, Joe, and James, John M. Taylor, P. H. "Bud" Dowlearn, Alford C. Day, and of course John Wesley Hardin. It is significant that William E. Sutton's name does not appear, either because he refused to sign or else he was simply not present. Nor is there the signature of Jim or Bill Taylor, cousins who would become notorious for their later acts in the feud. The peace treaty was an important document: if both sides kept their pledge, the bloodshed would cease.

The *Gonzales Inquirer* provided a comprehensive coverage of the siege and the subsequent treaty signing. With "no little gratification" the *Inquirer* reported a "cessation of hostilities between the belligerents." From a "responsible party" whose identification was not disclosed, it was learned that on August 11, Hardin with some thirty-five or forty men "well armed, marched to the residence of [Tumlinson and] surrounded his house and held him in siege for two nights and one day." Meanwhile, according to the *Inquirer's* informant, Tumlinson and his party—numbering a mere fifteen—managed to get a courier to Clinton asking for the sheriff "to hasten to his assistance." The sheriff summoned about fifty men and headed for the "seat of war." When he arrived on August 13, he found Hardin's men "formed in line of battle." A conference was held, which "revealed the unexpected but agreeable intelligence that a compromise had been effected" between the Hardin and Tumlinson forces. The two parties then headed for Clinton to sign the documents of peace. Hardin's men led the column, followed by the sheriff and his citizens, with Tumlinson and his men "bringing up the rear." At Clinton the Hardin party stopped on one side of town while Tumlinson and his men stopped on the other. Sheriff Blair marched directly into town, remaining between the two groups. Following the signing, both parties "quietly dispersed to the intense gratification of the law-abiding and peace-loving citizens." The *Inquirer* concluded that it was "the general belief that the conditions of the treaty will be rigidly observed" and noted further, the "relentless war so long waged between the two parties is at an end." [8]

Hardin's memory of the siege and temporary peaceful conclusion was essentially correct, although the contemporary reporting offered none of the drama that appeared in Hardin's account. But the "relentless war so long waged" was not at an end. Both sides still had scores to settle: Bill Sutton was still alive, and Jim Taylor had vowed to avenge the death of his father by killing him. Some believed that the difficulties in DeWitt

County could be ended permanently if the State Police were brought back. The *San Antonio Express* editor wrote that he knew nothing "of the merits or demerits of the parties to the guerilla warfare" but "the state of affairs existing in DeWitt county never was heard of until the State Police was abolished." What remained unsaid was that the editor expected the violence would only continue.

The feuding parties thus kept the peace for several months. What remains uncertain is whether both sides avoided each other to prevent a renewal of hostilities, or were they all seriously just remaining peaceful. Then there was another incident of violence. Bolivar J. Pridgen had been a severe critic of Jack Helm and the State Police and had been targeted for death. Just after Christmas, on December 30, 1873, a group found his brother, Wiley Washington Pridgen, and shot him to death. Was it a case of mistaken identity? Wiley was standing in the doorway of his brother's store in Thomaston, a small community south of Cuero, when several men rode up, shot him, and then rode away. He lived but a few minutes, but was unable to explain why he had been shot, or to identify his slayers. Jack Hays Day, a member of the Taylor family, identified the slayers as John Goens, Jim Mason, Bill Sutton, Jeff White and "Doc" White.[9] None had signed the August peace treaty and thus may have felt it did not pertain to them. Hardin believed the "murderers belonged to the Sutton gang," which belief was no doubt the general opinion of the times. Hardin offered no particulars of the killing, simply stating that it "stirred up" the war between the "two parties again."[10] It was Hardin's belief that since Pridgen "was a Taylor man" and his murderers had belonged to the Sutton side, there was ample reason for the feud to continue.

Hardin had avoided trouble during the months between August and December, gathering cattle, working "without anything tragical happening" until the killing of Pridgen. How did this wanted fugitive with a large reward manage to avoid further difficulties? He remained in the area of Gonzales, DeWitt and Karnes counties, perhaps working cattle, but did he avoid the saloons and gambling places at which he so often had entered into which frequently resulted in a difficulty leading to gunfire?

Was Jane exerting that much influence on this antisocial individual? It's an intriquing question, but one that we cannot answer for certain.

In revenge for the Pridgen killing, some of the Taylors ambushed a number of Suttons on a DeWitt County road, but inflicted no casualties, suggesting Hardin was not involved. The two groups nevertheless traded shots, then entered the town of Cuero. The Sutton party took over the Gulf House while the Taylors found refuge in the lumber yard. Then what had begun as an ambush—leading to a skirmish—became a siege lasting two days and nights. Some residents even abandoned their homes for the sake of safety. On January 3, 1874, the two forces left town, perhaps having been convinced by brave citizens to take their hostilities out in the country to prevent innocent loss of life.

Robert J. Kleberg, editor of the *Cuero Weekly Star*, observed what was happening firsthand. He headlined one report: "War at Home" and described how a "formal war reigned for two or three days in and about our town last week," identifying the warriors as "known respectively as the Sutton and Taylor parties [who] were arrayed against each other for some old feud." Kleberg noted that the sheriff "was powerless." With the sheriff unable to accomplish anything some citizens banded together, and vowed to protect themselves with the organization of a Home Protection Club.[11] Kleberg was not alone in observing what was happening in Cuero. Another business man, Robert J. Clow, an outsider with no connection to any of the feudists, happened to be in DeWitt County at this time. Recently he had obtained a leather-bound notebook in Port Lavaca in which he recorded various notes about business matters as well as family concerns. He separated his sentences by dashes instead of periods, suggesting his notes would be useful in later writing his memoirs or other reports. On New Year's Day 1874 he wrote of the skirmish in Cuero: "The hostile forces had a skirmish in suburbs of the town—no one hurt—both parties Stopped all night—One at B & Bro's Hotel [Brown Brothers, more commonly known as the Gulf Hotel] & the other in Lumber Yard[.]"That Clow was well aware of the celebrity status of John Wesley Hardin is confirmed in the entry dated January 2 in which he described the potential volatile situation: "Night *very quiet*—both parties still in town—The Forces Mustering—Hardin has arrived—Expect fight this evening—Very warm[.]" Later Clow added that the "hostile forces are still in town—Took possession of Brown's Hotel— . . . Dark—No fighting yet—Things look gloomy—Every body complaining—Don't know what will be the result[.]"[12]

How long Clow remained in Cuero is unknown, but one result of the skirmish was that several citizens again managed to get the two groups to sign another treaty of peace. This treaty had a much briefer preamble than the one of August 1873:

> We the undersigned, individually and collectively, do pledge ourselves, and solemnly swear to keep the peace between each other, and obey the laws of the country, now, henceforth and forever: furthermore, we pledge ourselves nevermore to engage in any organization against any of the signers of this agreement.

Justice of the Peace Oliver K. Tuton provided a copy to *Star* editor Kleberg, who placed the treaty on page one, column one.

The treaty provides an interesting grouping of names, and one wonders if some may have had their fingers crossed behind their backs when they signed. Jim Taylor and cousin Bill Taylor both signed, as did Uncle John Milam Taylor. Jim and Joe Clements also signed as did Bolivar J. Pridgen and his son Oscar, and John Duderstadt who had driven cattle up the trail to Abilene in 1871. George C. Tennille signed as well as Alford Creed Day and Jack Hays Day. But John Wesley Hardin did not sign.

From the other side of the feuding parties, the first name was William Sutton, followed by that of David J. Blair, a deputy. Frank Cox, a son of the ambushed James W. Cox signed, as it was now obvious that he intended to avenge his father's death. Several men who signed later would become well known for their participation in the feud during 1874 and 1875: Joseph I. Sitterle, brothers John J. and William L. Meador, Christopher T. "Kit" Hunter, Nicholas J. "Jake" Ryan, Addison "Add"

Kilgore, W. C. "Curry" Wallace, and Gabriel Webster "Gabe" Slaughter, although most merely used their initials. The most interesting signature of all perhaps, other than that of Sutton's, is that of John Gyns, who was one of the men accused of killing Wiley W. Pridgen back in December. The name of D. W. Mason also appears, who was perhaps the mysterious "Jim Mason" who was also accused of participating in the Pridgen killing.

This treaty of January 1874 listed the names of eighty-seven men who sided with the Sutton side or the Taylors. It appeared in the *Star* of Friday, January 9. In the following issue, that of January 16, in the "Local

Jane Bowen Hardin and Mollie, her first child. *Courtesy The John Wesley Hardin Papers, The Wittliff Collection, Texas State University.*

Matters" column, editor Kleberg reported that "Order and peace" had been restored, and the "spirit of security and firmness prevails. . . ." A week later, in the issue of January 23, Kleberg noted that "All is quite on the Guadalupe," the river which runs between Cuero and (then) county seat Clinton. He also reported that "up to the present" the week had been "exceptionally quiet, and a wholesome difference is already felt in business. One thing is certain, Cuero has a much worse name abroad than she in fact deserves." News of the peace treaty was publicized in numerous other newspapers, as the *Daily Democratic Statesman* of Austin reported that "the feud between the Sutton and Taylor parties, which had likely to have provided a bloody encounter lately, at Cuero, has been happily adjusted."[13]

During that winter the name John Wesley Hardin received no attention in the press. Editor Kleberg made no mention of him in his reporting on the troubles or the treaty of peace. Hardin had thought of his family. He had sent Jane and baby "Molly" (birth name Mary Elizabeth), to Comanche in far off Comanche County for the holidays. Molly had been born on February 6, 1873. Reverend Hardin and Elizabeth, living in Comanche, probably had never seen their granddaughter. Now Hardin decided to join his family, leaving his cattle business in charge of father-in-law Neill Bowen. Wes left the feud behind him, taking good friend James Monroe "Doc" Bockius and cousin Gip Clements with him. In Austin Hardin became ill, but was soon well enough to continue and enjoy the family gathering, albeit the remaining 170 some miles were covered in a buggy. There in Comanche the Hardins and friends had a belated Christmas gathering. Then Hardin, Jane and Molly along with Doc Bockius and Gip Clements, headed back to Gonzales. He could not avoid gambling however, as he wrote that while in Comanche he had purchased a horse for racing purposes. At Llano he bought a herd of steers for market, and also put his horse, Rondo, to the test and won a race with a prize of $500, a race which he claimed he "easily won."

By mid-February Hardin commenced organizing his cattle for another drive north. Abilene, Kansas, however, no longer wanted the cattle trade, claiming it brought too much violence to the community. In 1874 the drive would perhaps head for Wichita, an area Hardin knew from the adventures in 1871, or else a new cattle town named Ellsworth, north-west of Wichita. Many of his contemporaries had already driven herds to Ellsworth, including cattleman George W. Littlefield in May, Crawford "Doc" Burnett, Gonzales County sheriff William E. Jones, James G. McVea, who would later be killed by Cuero City Marshal Reuben H. Brown, W. W. Davis, a Sutton supporter, brothers John and Fred

James C. Taylor, who, along with Hardin, killed former Police Captain Jack Helm. *Courtesy Robert G. McCubbin Collection.*

Duderstadt, who had gone up the trail in 1871 with Hardin, William W. Meador, and most interesting of all William E. Sutton, who had signed in at the Grand Central Hotel in Ellsworth with his wife on August 15, 1873.[14]

But John Wesley Hardin never made his drive north to Kansas markets in 1874. Early that year he and brother Joe of Comanche were considering ways of getting to William E. Sutton. Jim and Bill Taylor had tried unsuccessfully, and perhaps a stranger in South Texas could accomplish what the men who Sutton knew could not.

In neighboring Brown County, to the immediate west, a Texas Ranger company was organized to protect the frontier from Indian raiding parties. The men elected J. G. Connell captain and Charles M. Webb as the first lieutenant.[15] Webb and Hardin would meet in 1874. Meanwhile, in Comanche, a man named Davis attempted to hoorah the town and was shot to death by the marshal.[16]

Brother Joseph G. Hardin had been in Comanche County for over a year and as far as is known had taken no part in the feud violence in which his brother had become dominant. Even with two peace treaties gathering dust in Clinton's courthouse, Jim Taylor was making plans to carry out the vow he had made to kill Bill Sutton and the plan would involve Wes's brother Joseph G. Hardin.

CHAPTER 9

A "BULLY FROM CANADA"

"But the lynx eyes of the Taylors never lost sight of him. Jim and Bill Taylor, implacable as fate, followed him to Indianola. Sutton's noble little wife suspicioned their intentions, and so assiduous was her solicitude for her husband that she remained at his side, and thus shielded him from the murderous lead already molded and consecrated for his destruction."

Victor M. Rose, *The Texas Vendetta*

It was common knowledge that the Taylors had attempted to kill Sutton several times. Jim Taylor had shot him in a Cuero saloon, breaking his arm; he had had a horse killed under him on the prairie in another assassination attempt, and another horse killed under him while crossing the Guadalupe River. Hardin complained that Sutton "was looked upon as hard to catch, and I had made futile efforts to get him myself. I had even gone down to his home at Victoria, but did not get him." The fact that Sutton was "so wiley that he always eluded us," explains why the Taylors had found it expedient to bring in an outsider, a man whom Sutton would not know. Joe Hardin and cousin Alec Barekman now entered into the feuding country, but whether Wes requested them for the specific purpose of setting up Sutton, or if it was simply a visit to him that took on this deadly addition is uncertain. But Joe did go to Indianola where Sutton's cattle were to be shipped from to investigate: "I told Joe that Bill Sutton was my deadly enemy," Wes recalled, "and that he was soon going to Kansas by way of New Orleans. Further instructions were that he was to find out when Sutton would be there to leave Indianola, in order that word could get to Jim Taylor in time." Joe Hardin and Alec

160

Barekman actually "got acquainted" with Sutton and learned when Sutton planned to leave.

When Joe Hardin learned of Sutton's plans he informed Jim Taylor, who, with his cousin Bill Taylor, went to Indianola for the sole purpose of killing Bill Sutton. The two Taylors remained out of sight until Joe Hardin learned the exact date and time of his departure. In addition two good horses were hired for their escape following the killing. It would take place aboard the steamer *Clinton*. Just in case Jim and Bill needed any back up, "there were six or eight brave men there who stood in with the play." Wes may have expected a regular battle, as he wrote that the plan was to allow "Sutton and his crowd go aboard and then for Jim and Billy to follow and commence shooting as soon as they saw him."[1]

Hardin does not explain who he meant as the "crowd" he believed would be accompanying Sutton. Apparently Sutton did not suspect he would be in any danger leaving the state, or that his actions would be known by his enemies. His wife was pregnant and he may have given unusual care for her and during this time let his guard down. Whatever the circumstances, on March 11, 1874, Bill Sutton and his wife were together with his friend Gabriel Webster "Gabe" Slaughter, whose only known participation in the feud with the Taylors was that he had signed one of the peace treaties. This is Hardin's version of the background and the "play" that resulted in the killing of Sutton and Slaughter.

Following an early lunch Mr. and Mrs. Sutton and Slaughter took a hack from the train depot to the wharf where the *Clinton* was docked. Stockman John N. Keeran and Ed McDonough rode in the same hack. McDonough and Slaughter got out first and walked up the gang plank, followed by Keeran and the Suttons. The *Clinton* was scheduled to depart at 2:00 p.m. While the Sutton party was getting onto the deck, "the utmost peace and quiet reigned all around," in the words of the *Austin Daily Democratic Statesman*, one of several stories about the incident.[3] But then the two Taylors appeared, shattering the day's tranquility. Their watching and waiting now had paid off as their prey was there before them only paces away. One witness observed that Jim Taylor drew a brace of pistols, Sutton "gasped" and uttered "Hell is in the door, Gabe. Yonder comes Jim Taylor." He drew his Smith & Wesson revolver but was instantly shot down. Meanwhile Slaughter had drawn his weapon but managed to fire only once before Bill Taylor shot him down. At the first shots the other passengers scattered, frightened, and made no attempt to interfere. Laura Sutton screamed and knelt down to hold her husband's head in her lap. She must have been concerned about her baby as well— to be born in August—as she was horrified at what she had just seen. She recognized the men who had shot her husband and his friend. Did she cry out at them when Jim Taylor picked up her husband's pistol?[3] Bill Taylor may have already been urging cousin Jim to quickly get away, as he left Slaughter's pistol on the deck. John Keeran picked it up and noted it was half-cocked, one barrel having just been fired. Strangely he handed it to Laura Sutton. By now any witnesses who remained on the deck approached her as she screamed and wept over her husband's corpse. The efforts she had made to shield him from the Taylors had failed.

While confusion reigned on the *Clinton,* Jim and Bill Taylor calmly rode away "in a short gallop." Austin's *Statesman* correspondent concluded his letter succinctly, stating that the "two young men [were] the Taylor boys, and the motive of their foul deed, revenge."[4]

Jim Taylor had now accomplished his purpose of blood vengeance. It was an eye taken for an eye, a tooth taken for a tooth; but with that double killing, both Taylors became fugitives. Mrs. Sutton, after arranging for her husband and his friend to be buried side by side in Victoria's Evergreen Cemetery, pondered offering a reward. Governor Coke first offered a reward of $500 for the arrest and confinement of each of the Taylors, and now, still in her mourning period, Laura Sutton arranged for a $1,000 reward to be offered as well. The public notice stated that she had seen Jim Taylor "shooting my husband in the back with two six-shooters" while Bill Taylor shot Slaughter. She made it clear that her reward would be paid to anyone who could "arrest and deliver" Taylor inside the Calhoun County jail. The word "alleged" did not appear in Laura Sutton's reward notice.[5]

The Taylors left Indianola and then went to Gonzales where Hardin and others were gathering cattle to drive north to Kansas. Joe Hardin and Alec Barekman, their mission accomplished, returned to Comanche. Wes sent his wife and child with them, planning to join them soon and spend time there before going up the trail again. But after sending them on their way he decided to stay in Gonzales and gather another herd, working now with cousin Joe Clements. Clements with his hands and the herd would be in Wichita, Kansas, by June, and he, Wes, would join them there. Perhaps this year they would sell the herd in Wichita instead of going on further north to Ellsworth.

Following the double killing of Sutton and Slaughter both Taylors ought to have left the area. Jim remained with Wes and left with him for Comanche, although Bill foolishly returned to his home territory in DeWitt County. Reuben H. Brown, who had assumed the leadership role after Sutton's death, and was city marshal of Cuero, arrested Bill Taylor and delivered him promptly to the Galveston jail, a secure facility. Wes certainly wanted to rescue him, but he could only complain that after Brown arrested Taylor, he "sent him at once to Galveston, so we never had a chance to rescue him."[6]

With their herd in charge of Doc Bockius, Wes Hardin and Jim Taylor now appeared in Comanche. The herds were to be gathered in a certain place in neighboring Hamilton County, and following that, Hardin and Taylor would join them all to go on to Wichita.[7] Therefore, his plans made for the next several months, surrounded by family and friends, John Wesley Hardin must have felt secure.

There was one problem in this situation that Wesley may have been ignorant of: the dishonest dealings of his brother Joe. Although he craved respectability outwardly, he was no more a model of civility than his younger brother. He had indeed for a short time been a member of the state police, and also had served as postmaster of Comanche for a year until Nathan Yarbrough took over the duties.[8] Now he was a father: his first child was a daughter named Dora Dean, born on October 15, 1872, and on May 24, 1874, a son would be born whom they named Joseph

Gibson Hardin Jr.[9] With his position as an attorney, Joseph G. Hardin managed to acquire considerable land holdings through fraud. Various land transactions were made out to him with his wife as witness. By mid-1874, Joe Hardin claimed a worth of $25,000, having thousands of acres of land.

When Wes "came home" to spend time with his family he may not have known the details of his brother's fraudulent activity. It could have been a wonderful time for the Reverend and Elizabeth Hardin family, as sons Joe and Wes were there with their children. Several cousins were present, two of the Dixon boys, William A. "Bud" and Thomas K. "Tom," Alexander H. "Alec" Barekman and Alexander H. "Ham" Anderson, and friend Jim Taylor. And as May 26 was to be son John's twenty-first birthday there would be reason to celebrate that milestone, even though he was a wanted fugitive. As always, the Hardin parents overlooked the fact that their Methodist namesake was a fugitive from justice with a large reward offered for his capture. When the "good times" came to Texas maybe he could stand trial and get his name cleared of all charges. After all the troubles with the law his son had had, did Reverence Hardin still believe that was possible?

But Wesley himself prevented that from ever happening. He could not stay at home and enjoy a peaceful family gathering. His personality did not allow that for any significant length of time. Instead, he preferred the reckless and dangerous life of a sporting man, betting on horse races, taking chances of winning big or losing big, the casual life of a saloon man. Instead of spending time with his wife and daughter, he answered the appeal of the race track. He arranged for several races as part of a local celebration. He had his horse Rondo to run against a mare which had earlier beaten his horse, and now he also matched one of Joe's horses named Shiloh; cousin Bud Dixon also matched horses. There were other attractions as well. The town was filled with men from other communities, as well as some from neighboring Brown County, one of whom was Brown County deputy sheriff Charles M. Webb.

What was the occasion for this celebration in Comanche? That is uncertain. All Hardin tells us is there was "a big crowd at the races, the
news of which had been published all over the county."[10] Certainly there
was more than Hardin merely turning twenty-one years of age. To young
Wesley of course it provided a "reason" for drinking and celebrating in
the saloons, but the motivations of others are uncertain. Why would the
deputy sheriff of the neighboring county leave his territory? We don't
know. The young man named Charles M. Webb remains today a man of
mystery.

Charles M. Webb was five years older than Hardin; his tombstone,
provided by the Masonic Order of Brownwood, gives his birthday as August 2, 1848, and his death date of May 26, 1874. He was possibly born
in Tennessee. A man with that name appears in the Dallas County, Texas,
census, which may be the same person; no occupation given for him.[11]
In 1873 Charles M. Webb was a member of Lt. James G. Connell's company of Brown and San Saba County Rangers, and after this service he
may have decided to continue in "lawing" and became a deputy under
Brown County Sheriff J. H. Gideon.[12] Why Webb went to Comanche
that day is uncertain, but Hardin believed he brought fifteen men "to kill
me and capture Jim Taylor for the reward." This is absurd, as no account
verifies that Webb had any others with him when he entered Comanche
County where he no longer had any authority to make arrests. Hardin
further suggests that Webb complained because the Comanche County
officers did not arrest him. John Carnes was the Comanche County sheriff then, and he was aware that fugitives Hardin and Taylor were in his
area of responsibility. Had he chosen to allow them free access out of
fear?[13] Another possible reason for Webb's presence was that he came to
visit his lady friend, and foolishly allowed himself to become involved
with Hardin. Whatever Hardin had heard from friends, or from rumors,
he honestly believed that Charles M. Webb had come to Comanche to
kill him. Others believed it also, such as J. P. Lipscomb who later wrote
to Hardin: "We can show that Webb came to Comanche for the express

purpose of arresting you without a warrant & that he said he was going to do it or kill you." And surprisingly, even then Lipscomb had ideas of writing Hardin's biography, adding: "Don't let any one write your life[.] I want that Job myself."[14] Hardin obviously even at this young age was a celebrity.

Webb and Hardin had never met prior to May 26, but they knew of each other by reputation. Hardin was aware of him because earlier that month, he recalled it was the fifth of May, John and Joe Hardin, Jim Taylor, "and the sheriff's party" had entered Brown County to retrieve cattle belonging to brother Joe. The cattle were in possession of the Gouldstones [sic, Gholsons][15] and after acquiring them, they returned to Comanche County. As night overtook them, the party stopped at the house of a Mrs. Waldrip where they penned the cattle and had supper. Here Mrs. Waldrip described how Charles Webb had entered her home and arrested her son Jim Buck Waldrip, then "cursed and abused her." This was the first time Hardin had ever heard of Webb. Bill Cunningham, Bud and Tom Dixon, brothers Jim and Ham Anderson, Alec Barekman, two deputy sheriffs named Jim Taylor and Jim Milligan, partner Jim Taylor, Joe Hardin and himself were present that night. He stated that they were all first cousins except Jim Taylor of DeWitt County notoriety. Hardin of course trusted all these men, but something was said at the dinner table, which later came to cause him considerable trouble. Cunningham later testified that Joe Hardin said about Webb, "We will get away with him at the proper time." This Hardin later denied; the accusation was made at a time when neither Joe Hardin nor Jim Taylor of DeWitt could verify or deny as they were both dead.

Another incident contributing to the tragedy commenced with Comanche County's Henry J. Ware. He was, as Hardin recalled correctly, a Canadian, and "from some cause or other" Ware disliked his brother Joe. When remembering these events two decades later Hardin described Ware as "a bully from Canada," which begs the question as to what had happened to give that impression to Hardin. One incident he described was that Ware rode to the Hardin herd one day and claimed a cow; Joe

Henry J. Ware, the "bully from Canada", with his wife. Photograph by D.P. Barr, San Antonio. *Courtesy the Whitehead Memorial Museum, Del Rio, Texas.*

denied it, claiming it was his. Ware persisted and put his hand on his Winchester. Joe Hardin now drew his six-shooter and Ware decided the cow was not worth killing over or possibly getting killed. Possibly a cow belonging to Ware had strayed into the Hardin herd, but Joe was not about to release it.[16] Was this the only cause of the animosity between Ware and Joe Hardin? What else happened to cause Wes to label Henry Ware a bully?[17]

Following the races, Hardin, flush from his winnings, went with his friends from bar to bar, drinking and treating. At one establishment he tossed some $20 gold pieces on the bar and called for drinks on the house. He was drinking "too freely" and his friends tried to persuade him to go home and avoid any trouble. They were fearful of his becoming intoxicated to the point that he would not be able to defend himself. This time he listened to his friends, at least agreeing with them and "at last thought I had better go home to avoid any possible trouble." He now had little brother Jefferson Davis, a thirteen-year-old, go to their brother Joe's stable and get a buggy. He purchased some supplies and told Jeff to get them in the buggy and then meet him at Jack Wright's saloon. Hardin and Jim Taylor would then deliver the supplies to Reverend Hardin's home, some miles outside of Comanche. Then it was time for one last drink. By Hardin's own account, he was dangerously intoxicated. Frank Wilson, one of Sheriff Carnes' deputies, realizing this, came to him and locking his arm in Hardin's told him he wanted to see him. Hardin agreed and the pair walked a little ways. Wilson told him that he should not drink any more, and that he should go home. Hardin replied that he was going to do just that as soon as Jeff brought the buggy. Wilson now pointed out that Hardin was in violation of carrying a pistol while in town, but Hardin lied to him and said his pistol was behind the bar, although from the subsequent events he had "a good one" under his vest. Then Hardin saw a man, "a stranger to me, with two six-shooters on coming towards us." Hardin told Wilson he now wanted to go into the saloon, pay his bar bill, and go home. Younger brother Jeff Hardin now came up with the buggy, and Jim Taylor also urged Wes to leave and go home. But

Earliest known image of Jefferson Davis Hardin. Image dates from circa 1877. Original from the photo album of Mary Bundrant whose family forbid their marriage. *Courtesy Donna Tomlinson*

Mary Lucinda (left) and her younger sister Sarah E. Bundrant, from a tintype dated 1880-1885. As a young woman Mary Lucinda was in love with Jeff Davis Hardin. She kept his image in her tintype album. *Courtesy Donna Tomlinson.*

Hardin responded, "Let us go in and get a cigar, then we will go home." Then Deputy Dave Carnes (a relative of Sheriff John Carnes) mentioned someone was coming, stating: "Here comes that damned Brown County sheriff," although he obviously meant Deputy Charles M. Webb.

Hardin turned and saw Webb approaching, noting the two six-shooters, about fifteen steps away, "advancing." Within five steps Webb stopped and "scrutinized me closely, with his hands behind him." Hardin asked if he had any papers for his arrest, to which Webb replied that he did not know him, which statement was probably true. Hardin then introduced himself, at which Webb responded that he had no papers for him. Now Hardin began to provoke him, saying: "Well, I have been informed that the sheriff of Brown County has said that Sheriff Karnes [*sic*] of this county was no sheriff or he would not allow me to stay around Comanche with my murdering pals." Webb fell for the provocation, responding, "I am not responsible for what the sheriff of Brown County says. I am only a deputy." Carnes then attempted to mollify the situation, now spiraling out of control. "Men, there can be no difference between you about John Karnes [*sic*]. Mr. Webb, let me introduce you to Mr. Hardin." Hardin, instead of holding out his hand to shake Webb's, asked him what he held behind his back. Webb displayed a cigar. Hardin, probably somewhat confused that Webb had held his hand behind his back anyway, now appeared to be polite and asked him to join him and Wilson inside to have a cigar. "Certainly," was the reply, and Hardin turned his back to enter the Jack Wright Saloon. He then heard Bud Dixon shout, "Look out, Jack." It was a warning shout, and as Hardin turned he saw Webb drawing one of those two six-shooters, "in the act of presenting it when I jumped to one side, drew my pistol, and fired."

Webb fired first, his shot hitting Hardin in the left side, "inflicting an ugly and painful wound." But Hardin's aim was better and his bullet tore through Webb's left cheek, which "did the work." Leaning against the wall, the dying Webb fired a second shot, but it went wild. At the same time Dixon and Taylor "pulled their pistols and fired on him as he was falling, not knowing that I had killed him. Each shot hit him in the side and breast."[18]

When Hardin later wrote of the Webb killing, there were few men still around to challenge his version. No one would of course, as he had served his time for the killing, but who could have? The Dixon brothers, brother Joe, Rev. J. G. and cousins Barekman and Anderson and Jim Taylor were all dead, all having died violently with the exception of his father. Others who may or may not have witnessed some or all of the exchange between Webb and Hardin saw it quite differently. One early report from "a gentleman from Brown county, who is also an official of that county" provided a lengthy report to the Comanche newspaper, which appeared in the *Houston Daily Telegraph*. This report termed the shooting a "cold-blooded murder" and then "a retributive uprising of the people of Comanche and Brown counties" followed. Webb's "murder," reported the *Telegraph*, "took place in front of a saloon on the public square of the village of Comanche . . . the victim being Charles M. Webb, a deputy sheriff, and the murderers were John Hardin, Budd [*sic*] Dixon, or Dickson, and two others whose names were unknown." Why and how did it happen? According to this report Webb had earlier arrested three of the Hardin "gang," two of whom had been released on bond while the other remained in jail at Georgetown, Williamson County. This report made no mention of a big celebration in Comanche, stating simply that Hardin and his friends "rode into town and laid in wait for Webb in a saloon. He soon entered it, whereupon they engaged in a quarrel with him, and soon showed a disposition to do him some harm. They paired off, two in front to defend against him, and two at one side to do the killing. Seeing this, he retreated to the outside of the house, and they followed, again pairing off as before, and drawing their six-shooters. Seeing this, Webb drew and fired with rapid movement, but his shots went wild. Hardin now fired, followed by Dickson [*sic*], and Webb fell mortally wounded in the neck, the hand, the abdomen, and soon expired."

Now "the Sheriff of the county" attempted to take control of the situation, certainly the last thing he wanted to happen on his watch. Wes handed over his pistol, saying, "Take that and then take me, if you can!" Sheriff Carnes then told several citizens to watch Hardin while he disarmed the others, which they allowed him to do. But at the same time Hardin, obviously showing no respect for Sheriff Carnes' efforts to control the situation, mounted a horse and rode off, "but barely escaped death in the act. Henry Ware fired four shots at him as he fled."[19] Henry Ware now appears in Hardin's account of the shooting. Hardin and Taylor realized the danger they were in when they saw Jane and Hardin's sister Matt "in the crowd crying" and also saw his father and brother Joe coming to the scene "with shotguns"—certainly a dangerous situation for his family members—all who knew full well the dangers of men shooting at each other. Taylor and Hardin rode away from Comanche, but Taylor wanted to "charge the mob" as he wanted to kill Henry Ware. This was the man who brother Joe had had the altercation with earlier, when a Ware animal was found in Hardin's herd. As Hardin and Taylor fled Comanche, shots were fired, "the mob firing on us and the sheriff's party trying to protect us." Later Hardin and Taylor met the Dixons and Anderson at Reverend Hardin's house, along with brother Joe. Possibly the sheriff was there also, as Hardin claimed he was willing to surrender, but the sheriff informed him that "the mob was too strong, and Charley Webb had been their leader." His advice was to remain in the area until the excitement decreased and only then surrender.[20]

How Hardin determined that the sheriff was in a position to advise him to surrender after the excitement had died down can be determined only by his attempt to make the episode another example of his being the victim of persecution, this time by a glory-hunting Webb, with himself being forced to kill to defend his own life. Whereas he considered the people of Comanche a "mob," others saw things differently. Perhaps the sheriff was weak, and thus the citizens chose to handle the situation in their own way. "The people," according to a Brown County official, "arose as by one impulse, and assumed in their sovereign capacity the functions of judge, jury and executioner. Vigilance committees were organized and sent in search of the desperadoes, with instructions to shoot all who refused to surrender and hang all who did submit."[21]

That may have been the intent and the instructions given to these men who chose to seek out all those alleged desperadoes; those self-styled posses were to Hardin nothing more than illegal mobs. But what Hardin soon learned was that besides the mobs, he had to avoid a company of the newly formed Frontier Battalion, Texas Rangers. The Rangers, a creation of Gov. Richard Coke, had replaced the State Police force. The six companies were initially placed on the edges of the frontier, that line having been pushed slowly eastward during the Civil War by an increase of raiding parties of various tribes, primarily Kiowa and Comanche. In Erath County—whose western border edged the eastern border line of Comanche County—John R. Waller was named Captain of Company A, Frontier Battalion. He mustered in on May 5, took the oath seven days later, and began enlisting men in his company. Once organized, the company began the hunt for outlaws in the counties of Brown, Comanche and Erath. Waller had command of not only his Rangers, but according to George A. Beeman, editor of the *Comanche Chief*, Waller also took command of the various vigilante groups. Beeman downplayed the amount of violence, denying the rumors of *eleven men having been caught and lynched* as a falsehood, but did clarify that "the people" had "caught and put in irons and imprisoned, under a strong guard, five of the Hardin gang, and that not less than 150 citizens of Brown, Comanche and Erath counties" had driven several members of the Hardin associates into a large thicket of about forty acres and intended to hold them until captured or they had surrendered. Beeman concluded his report by stating that Captain Waller was engineering the entire affair, "and with his known pluck and energy, there can be but little doubt how it will end with the desperadoes." Beeman reported that "he never saw the people more in earnest. . . . [T]he best citizens of his town seized their double-barreled guns and six-shooters, and boldly proclaimed that the power of the thieves should now be broken."[22]

CHAPTER 10

FICHTING WALLER'S
TEXAS RANGERS

"[Captain Waller] aroused the whole country and had about 500
men scouting for me, whose avowed purpose was to hang me."

John Wesley Hardin

harles M. Webb, deputy sheriff of Brown County, lay dead on the
street in Comanche. This victim was different from Hardin's previous ones: he was not a member of the unpopular State Police; he
was not a soldier wearing the uniform of an occupation army; this man
was a former Texas Ranger and a white lawman, respected by the popu-
lace and apparently with many friends. Hardin, the Dixon brothers, Jim
Taylor and other family and friends now faced the wrath of the Comanche citizenry. Wes and some of his friends galloped to "some mountains"
four miles from town. On the twenty-seventh brother Joe and some other
friends found him. He then sent back with Joe the horses they had used
to make their escape from town. Hardin did not want people to think him
a horse thief, which notion was admirable in this extreme case of emergency, but neither he nor his friends appreciated the anger of the Comanche County citizens. Hardin and Taylor and the Dixons no doubt felt that
within a week or so the anger would pass, and this violent incident would
be forgotten. They could not have been more wrong.

Hardin now became aware of Captain Waller and his company of
Frontier Battalion Rangers. In his mind they "were organized to keep
the peace and protect the frontier from Indians," which was correct, and
that they were taking the place of the "infamous State Police" which

Gravestone of Charles M. Webb, whose killing cost Hardin so very much. *Author's Collection.*

was only partly correct. Much of the work the Rangers did was formerly done by Governor Davis' police force, but at this point Hardin disrespected the new Ranger force, as he considered them no different from the police force. Part of Hardin's disrespect for the State Police grew from the fact that the force was not made up of white southern men. He may not have known that Waller's force was entirely white men, hence the same prejudicial attitude was transferred. Further, Hardin had no idea of the background and experience John R. Waller brought with him as a commander of an entire company of young men ready and willing to follow orders. Prior to his service in the Civil War he had served as sheriff of Erath County for two years and was certainly respected by Major John B. Jones, who selected him to captain Company A when he was about fifty years old. Waller farmed near Duffau in Erath County and was no doubt familiar with the geographical areas of his assigned territory. Hardin, who only knew him as leader of men who wanted to kill or capture him, wrote that Waller "wished to make himself famous at once." However, Waller had a farm and a family to support and no doubt merely wanted to do his job as best he could. The idea of working as a captain to gain fame was an idea that never entered his mind.[1]

Waller may have met with Comanche County Sheriff John Carnes and inquired why Wes Hardin, who had been there some time, had not been arrested. Carnes responded that he could and would arrest Hardin but only when he was confident he could protect him from mob violence. This appears to be a poor excuse for inaction on the sheriff's part. Waller may also have felt it was impossible to protect anyone from mob action if the mob was determined to take a prisoner from lawful authorities, but Waller had some seventy men under his command. If he did capture Hardin, and if a mob did come to lynch the prisoner, certainly Waller's men could hold it off .

But Waller "persisted" in "hunting" him with his mob, "composed of the enemies of all law and order." Hardin blamed Waller for having "aroused the whole country and had about 500 men scouting for me, whose avowed purpose was to hang me." Waller never did capture Hardin, but he did arrest his father and mother, wife and child, as well as Barekman's family, and the Dixon brothers, in order to prevent them from giving him any aid or comfort. Joe Hardin and the Dixons were taken to the courthouse under guard. This placed Jim Taylor and Hardin alone, continually hiding in the brush.

James Monroe "Doc" Bockius, survivor of the lynch mob which claimed three lives in 1874. *Courtesy the Jack Caffall Collection.*

Doc Bockius now came to Comanche to inform Hardin the herd was there and they could begin the long drive to Kansas. In the wake of the Webb killing Hardin may have actually forgotten about the cattle, and puny Bockius, away from any type of communication with Hardin, was totally unaware of the dangerous situation in Comanche that he had walked into. As part of Hardin's entourage Bockius was arrested as well. His sudden presence may have actually aroused the Comanche citizens to further anger, as instead of the excitement subsiding, the "heat" was becoming more intense. Waller divided his large company of men into small groups to scout the area; Hardin wrote that on one occasion two detachments accidentally fired on each other. If this did happen Captain Waller was kept ignorant of it, as there is no mention in his reports of such a confrontation. Perhaps the two groups were not Waller's Rangers but citizens acting on their own.

Captain Waller's scouting report unfortunately provides only meager details of the manhunt. On May 30, four days after Webb's death, he wrote to Major Jones that he had not yet had time to prepare his muster rolls, but he would as soon as possible. He referred to the petition the Comanche citizens had prepared requesting help from the state, and that there was "a great deal more danger from [the desperadoes] than from the Indians." He added in a post script: "While in pursuit of John Wesley Hardin and Jim Taylor yesterday we exchanged shots with them. They are still here but their horses were too quick for us."[2] A few days later, still being pursued some ten miles from Comanche, Hardin's horse was shot dead under him. A Brown County man who must have been there to witness, described Hardin as "a fearless man, and I expect he will kill some more before he is taken."

Hardin and Taylor were torn between leaving the Comanche troubles behind to lose themselves elsewhere, and their hesitation to leave their family. Hardin especially must have felt anguished, as his wife Jane was in custody as well as his baby daughter. Alie, or Belle, brother Joe's wife, had delivered a baby boy the twenty-fourth of May, named Joseph G. Hardin Jr.[3] Taylor had no real family ties to anyone in Comanche, but he and Hardin were close friends. The pair "had agreed to die together," preferring death over capture.[4]

From Hardin's account, Waller's brief reports and various newspaper articles, we learn additional details of the Webb killing and its deadly aftermath. In addition, two of Waller's Rangers also provided detailed first-hand accounts of the hunt. The two Rangers were John L. Taylor and William M. Green. Taylor in later years wrote two letters to Texas

State Library Archivist Harriet Smither describing his experiences. His brother Andrew L. also served with him in the company.[5] (These Taylor brothers were no kin to Jim Taylor the fugitive.) William M. Green's memoir was published in the popular periodical *Frontier Times* in 1924.[6] Although reminiscences written so long after the fact are commonly subject to error, the narratives of both Taylor and Green are remarkably consistent and are basically in agreement with other contemporary accounts.

Cousins Alex Barekman and Ham Anderson had eluded capture and were temporarily staying at a settler's place twelve miles east of Comanche. They believed the settler, identified by Hardin as Bill Stone,[7] was sympathetic to them and would protect them. Hardin however was not so gullible, and he warned them of the danger in trusting the man. The pair naively asked Stone to go to Comanche and find out what the Rangers were doing. Stone did go as requested, but instead of acting as a spy for the fugitives, he told Captain Waller where the pair could be found. Private John Taylor explained how the two "got in with the settler & they thought he was all right" but were betrayed to the Rangers. Knowing the pair was hiding in a certain thicket, he selected thirty of his men who had the best horses, divided them into two groups and surrounded the thicket. One group was led by Sgt. C. Y. Pool and the other by Lieut. James Millican. A small creek meandered through this thicket, and Lieutenant Millican ordered his men to spread out, following the meanderings of the creek and staying on the creek banks. The lieutenant also ordered them to keep absolute silence, and if a shot was heard then each man was to go to it as quickly as possible. This the Rangers did, and all was silent until "a horse snorted & the two outlaws Jumped up from their Pallets & shot (they were asleep & the horse woke them) [.] They shot two shots but they was shot to death immediately by the Boys [.] They made Their words good [as] They said they would not be taken alive."[8] Green's account has less of the drama, merely reporting that "they were found in the eastern part of the county and killed."[9]

Hardin remembered having numerous close calls in his fight against the Rangers. With another horse, the closeness of the fight resulted in it receiving a slight wound. Hardin wrote of being in close pursuit by Waller, taking the attack to the Rangers, "charging up hill" right among Waller's men, who were afraid to fire for fear of hitting each other—even nearly shot-gunning Waller. Hardin had a handkerchief that he placed over his shotgun to keep it dry. Just as he pulled the trigger to shoot Waller the wind blew this handkerchief on the hammers, preventing the

Alexander Hamilton "Ham" Anderson, victim of Texas Rangers in 1874. *Courtesy the Robert G. McCubbin Collection.*

gun from firing. This act of nature saved Waller's life. How much of this portion of Hardin's autobiography is accurate is speculative; Waller made no mention of such a narrow escape in his reports. Maybe he simply ignored it if it was true, or maybe he was unaware of how close he was to becoming another victim of John Wesley Hardin.

Captain Waller also commented on the deaths of Berekman and Anderson. "The Sheriff of Comanche County while trying to arrest Barekman & Anderson the murderers of Col[.] Love of Navarro County were compelled to kill them [.] His posse was composed of Citizens and some of the members of Company 'A'."[10] Captain Waller prepared his monthly scouting report on the thirtieth of June in Comanche. He wrote:

> Had commenced Scouting at Comanche, Comanche Co. Tex the 28th day of May, with the 1st Lieut 2nd & 3rd Sergts and three-fourths of my Command [.] was kept in Constant Service until the 12th of June [.] during that time I made over Twenty five arrests. Seven of the Parties arrested I sent to Dewitt [*sic*] County Supposed to belong to John Wesley Hardins gang of outlaws, the other Parties arrested I turned over to Sheriffs of different Counties. Berekman [*sic*] & Anderson two [of] Hardins gang fired on Some of my men and Several Cittazens [*sic*] men returned the fire Killing both Berekman & Anderson.

Captain Waller may have felt some satisfaction in ending the lives of two of the fugitives. He could only regret that his aim was not more accurate, as he concluded his report on his work in the month of June to capture Hardin: "I exchanged Several Shots with John Wesley Hardin & Jim Taylor wounding Hardin in the Shoulder but he made his escape being well mounted."[11]

Hardin and Taylor had little opportunity to determine what was happening in the town of Comanche itself, which was what Captain Waller and the authorities in Comanche wanted. One citizen wrote of the action, suggesting he was either a Comanche citizen with the Rangers or interviewed them when they returned to town. "[Hardin] and his party of seven or eight fought forty men all day," he wrote. "Last Tuesday ten miles from Comanche on Leon [River] bottom, he had his horse killed from under him. He is a fearless man, and I expect he will kill some more before he is taken. The authorities have his wife and child with his father, the preacher, in jail in Comanche." This anonymous writer also reiterated the news that on Tuesday the citizens had shot Anderson and Barekman "all to pieces" and the following day "seven men were hung at Waldrop's ranche, and old Mrs. Waldrop given seven days to leave the country with her family."[12]

These were rumors. Maybe Mrs. Waldrop [*sic*] was ordered out of the country but it was later determined the hanging of seven men was not true. But what did happen in Comanche to Joseph G. Hardin, and cousins William A. and Thomas K. Dixon, was true. The guards were overpowered and a mob took the three prisoners about two miles west of town and hung them. Comanche's newspaper editor George A. Beeman may have investigated this incident personally. In his report he wanted it clearly understood that no citizen of Comanche was involved, but men from elsewhere. He may have known better, but he did not want John Wesley Hardin to come back and take revenge on the whole town. "The citizens of our town," Beeman wrote, "we are confident, had nothing to do with this affair, nor do we think any one living in the country took part in it." He pointed out that the men making up the mob were disguised, and none of the guard nor any others present recognized any one. The man who provided Beeman with this information claimed to have been arrested himself, that the jail was guarded by "but few men" and after the prisoners had been removed he remained under guard. There were four others under arrest, "under suspicion": Doctor James Anderson, brother of the dead Ham Anderson; Thomas Jefferson Waldrip; William Green; and "Doc" Bockius. These four were hands from the herd at Hamilton who came into Comanche unaware of what had happened.[13]

Alford Creed Day as he appeared during the 1870s. *Courtesy the Western History Collections, University of Oklahoma Libraries.*

Hardin had to have known the dangers his brothers and cousins and friends were in but he could neither offer nor could he receive any help. He and Jim Taylor fled the country and within days were in Travis County, at relative "Fancy Jim" Taylor's place northeast of Austin on the fifth of June. They stayed there over a week, and on June 17 Alf Day and Charley, Hardin's cook for the Hamilton herd, arrived as well. They had managed to escape as Waller's Rangers had gone to the herd, arrested all hands, and confiscated the cattle. Alford Creed "Alf" Day, a relative of Jim Taylor, informed Hardin at this point what he may have already feared: that his brother and cousins were dead and his family was in house arrest.[14]

CHAPTER 11

LEAVING THE LONE STAR STATE

"The pursuing party [was] fixing to surround us again, [so] we got on our horses and ran off from them. It seemed to me as if their horses stood still. . . . Good horseflesh is a good thing in a tight."

John Wesley Hardin

he herd in Hamilton County was no longer in control of any of Hardin's hands, but confiscated by the Rangers. Waller's men had arrested the cowboys, or most of them, including James M. "Doc" Bockius, Rufus P. "Scrap" Taylor, Alf "Kute" Tuggle, Thomas Bass, James White, G. W. Parkes, and John Elder. Alf Day and Charley the cook were also taken in, but Day and Charley had somehow managed to get away. Whether the seven cowboys were placed in the inadequate Comanche jail or remained prisoners in the Ranger camp is unknown. Attorney at Law John D. Stephens wanted them out of the country as quickly as possible and started arrangements to have them delivered to DeWitt County.

The authorities had no real control over the volatile situation either. Major Jones ordered Captain Waller to remain in the Comanche County area as Hardin and Taylor's whereabouts were uncertain. As late as June 3 he ordered Waller "with a sufficient detachment of his company, say fifteen or twenty men" to proceed without delay to Comanche and procure from the authorities "necessary processes" and then if possible arrest those for whom he had papers and turn them over to the civil officers. Further, he was to "take such other steps" he judged to be necessary to protect the lives and property of the peaceable and law-abiding Comanche County citizens.[1] Major Jones could not have been ignorant of the mob violence and he wanted, as much as possible, to reduce the amount of lynch law, which was becoming more and more prevalent in Texas. Deep down however he may not have been concerned with the lives and property of such men as John Wesley Hardin and James Creed Taylor.

On June 10 John D. Stephens wrote Governor Coke that Sgt. J. V. Atkinson of Waller's command was on his way to Austin with seven prisoners, identified as Hardin's "gang of murderers or robbers," charged with "driving cattle without legal authority etc." Stephens concluded his rather vague communication to the state's leading law official that all was quiet in Comanche right then, "but expect Hardin to try for revenge." [2]

Captain Waller's Company A was not the only Ranger company making its presence felt in the area of Comanche, Brown and Erath counties. Capt. William J. Maltby, recently named commander of Company E, camped in Brown County, was also actively looking for outlaws.[3] He reported that the condition of affairs where he was headquartered prohibited him from leaving the county as "the lives of all the responsible Citizens" were threatened by "the notorious out Law John Hardin and a band of Desperadoes that he has enlisted under his Banner." He claimed to have "reliable information" that "Hardin & band" were in that county and had threatened the lives "of the best Citizens." [4] Captain Maltby would have been proud to have captured Hardin, but right then he was in no position to do so. His men were poorly armed, either without a good weapon or having only weapons which Maltby considered "worthless." [5]

Maltby's report suggests that somehow Hardin had learned the identity of some of the Brown County mob who had lynched his brother and cousins and was planning revenge. Hardin makes no mention of such a logical but dangerous intention in his memoir, however. He does hint that after sneaking into Comanche and visiting his brother's grave, he vowed vengeance. Companion Dick Wade, who only makes this one brief appearance in the Hardin saga, "showed me where he lay buried near two live oaks. I stayed there by my brother's grave. . . . Right there . . . I swore to avenge my brother's death, and could I but tell you what I have done in that way without laying myself liable, you would think I have kept my pledge well." Who Hardin may have found to kill in June 1874 is unknown, but he was not satisfied: "While I write this, [in 1894 or 1895] I say from the deepest depths of my heart that my desire for revenge is not satisfied, and if I live another year, I promise my friends and my God to make another one of my brother's murderers bite the dust. Just as long as I can find one of them and know for certain that he participated in the murder of my brother, just that and nothing more, right there, be the consequences what they may, I propose to take life." [6]

There is little evidence that Hardin kept his threat to avenge his brother's death, and it is believed that this was a statement of what he *wished* he had accomplished before his capture and prison sentence, rather than what he may have actually accomplished. In order for him to determine just who was in the mob he would have had to perform some very capable detective work, as the mob's members had certainly vowed to keep their identities secret. And certainly taking revenge would have been extremely difficult. It was not a situation of Hardin tracking down only one or two men and killing them; the mob that lynched the three prisoners numbered perhaps forty or more, although Hardin estimated it numbered 150 men.[7] Those men who killed Anderson and Barekman numbered perhaps thirty citizens as well as Rangers. The first step to accomplish his vow of revenge would have been to learn their names; did anyone give Hardin a single name? He no doubt knew enough of the character of the citizens of Comanche that he could have made some intelligent guesses, but another unknown was whether the mob was composed of men from Comanche or from citizens of Brown County, or men from both counties, intending to avenge the death of Webb. The idea may have entered his mind to simply burn the town, as that was one of the rumors swirling about in the days and weeks following the death of Charles M. Webb. If Reverend Hardin or anyone else gave a name, it amounted only to rumor, however.

What was best for Hardin and Taylor was to join up with a trail drive heading for Kansas. This would allow them to leave the area and state in relative safety. They could have taken the identity of Jones and Davis, experienced drovers, and become just two more cowboys on the trail. But that is not what they did. As mentioned earlier, they left the area and headed for Travis County where a cousin, "Fancy Jim" Taylor, lived. What they were not aware of was that Major Jones, the commander of all six companies of the Frontier Battalion, himself visited Comanche to investigate personally the situation. He found what Captain Waller had accomplished quite satisfactory. At the end of June he wrote Adj. Gen. William Steele:

> The company has been engaged patroling [sic] this county for the last month and has done good service in breaking up bands of outlaws which have been scourging the frontier for several years past, having arrested a number of them and driven others to points unknown. The people here are very much gratified by the work done by this company and are now in a state of peace, quietude and confidence.[8]

If Hardin indeed had managed to secretly discover who had made up the mob and had managed to kill a few, certainly Major Jones would not have found the citizens "in a state of peace, quietude and confidence." Rather, he would have reported the country was in a state of fear and dread.

Hardin recounted a number of meetings with various individuals as he was getting out of the Comanche County area. The more unbelievable deals with the Nix family, where he managed to obtain a good horse. He had offered $250 for the horse, and the man, Mr. Nix, accepted, and Hardin told him to give it to "the old lady." He counted out thirteen $20 gold pieces, but Mrs. Nix did not want to accept it, for, as she explained: "John I nursed you when you were a baby; take back this gold piece. I sympathize with you and want you never to stop killing those Comanche devils who hung Joe." Hardin told her he had plenty of money and thanked her for her kindness. Mr. Nix now had gotten the horse up to the house where Hardin was having breakfast. While he was eating, Mrs. Nix placed the $250 in gold into his saddlebags which he discovered later. But now before he could make an exit a "squad of men" rode up. Before any preliminaries Hardin began firing his Winchester from inside the house. The "squad," whether they were citizens or a legal posse or Rangers, Hardin did not identify, but he did say one of them was killed by his shooting.[9] The killing of this unidentified individual probably did not happen. The Ranger reports do not identify any Ranger killed at this time. And the Nix couple? The most likely couple he may have met during this stage of his flight was L. E. and B. S. Nix, whose names are found on the 1880 Comanche County census. In 1880 they had a family of seven children living at home, but in 1874 only three were born. L. E. Nix was a fifty-six-year-old Georgia-born farmer.[10]

Jim Taylor had gone on ahead to Gonzales, and supposedly was staying at the residence of Sheriff William E. Jones. If so, the question arises as to why the Gonzales County sheriff knowingly gave shelter to a fugitive from justice with a large reward for his capture. Charley, the cook who now had no cowboys to cook for, accompanied Hardin to Gonzales where he met up with George Tennille and others. They assured Hardin "of their lasting friendship and devotion." In spite of this he was not safe in Gonzales County, as he learned that Reuben H. Brown and "Captain Joe" Tumlinson had gathered a mob of seventy-five men and were now hunting him. Brown had assumed leadership of the Sutton party after the death of William E. Sutton, and Joe Tumlinson was considered a capable leader as well who had managed to avoid death in one of the Hardin-planned ambushes. Most of Hardin's remaining friends were in Kansas, or on the trail to Kansas, including the Clements brothers, and those few who remained were scared. So wrote Hardin.

While yet in Gonzales County Hardin stated he received a letter from Captain Waller, which at first may seem ludicrous but it was possible the Ranger captain may have sent him a note, perhaps addressed simply to "J. W. Hardin, Gonzales, Tex." to inform him that he was sending prisoners to Gonzales. He may have threatened that if the guard was molested in any way, or the prisoners were released, then he (Waller) would kill Reverend Hardin and little brother Jefferson Davis, and probably Jane and baby Molly as well. They were all then held in what amounted to house arrest, or "held as hostages" as Hardin expressed it. Hardin of course wanted to rescue his family but left them to their fate as he was fearful that what Captain Waller had threatened, he might actually do. Hardin now "did not know exactly what to do." He realized he could not attack the Ranger guard; he concluded to go to father-in-law Neill Bowen's and "keep quiet for a few days." He now had time to reflect and decided to somehow get more money from the sale of a herd which had previously gone on to Kansas. He learned Bowen was in Kansas but had not yet sold any of the cattle. Hardin thus sent cousin John Dixon Hardin of Brenham to meet with Bowen and convince him to sell as quickly as he could, rather than wait for maybe a better price. Bowen realized the situation his son-in-law was in and sold, providing Hardin with good traveling money.[11] He had the $250 that Mrs. Nix had given back to him, but he realized that would not suffice if he intended to leave the state. Always before, when in such a perilous situation, he could return to his father for money or advice, but now he was cut off from him.

While he was desperate for funds, what of his friends who had been guarding the herd in Hamilton County? The hands were in charge of a Ranger escort, being delivered to DeWitt County, and on arriving in Austin on June 16, a reporter from the *Statesman* managed to have an interview. The reporter stated that a total of thirteen men belonging to Capt. Waller's "frontier company" had arrived in Austin from Comanche, having in charge seven prisoners, charged with cattle-stealing. "The prisoners are from Comanche and DeWitt counties, and are to be turned over to the State authorities. Some of them are supposed to belong to the Hardin-Taylor gang of cattle thieves." [12] The reporter was allowed to interview Dr. Bockius, who was reportedly a graduate of a medical school in Philadelphia. "He appears to be well educated, and is gentlemanly in his manner and deportment. He says that the supposed connection with the cattle thieves is all a mistake." Bockius may not have been a cattle thief, but he had been with the Hardin herd, and after the Webb killing, many were accused of theft because of their association with Hardin. "His captors," the reporter continued, "say they can prove his partnership with J. W. Hardin, who is now flying to Kansas. The prisoners will be sent to DeWitt county, where they are under indictment." [13]

Hardin did not dare attempt a rescue of his hands. But another tragedy now occurred, and he could do nothing except vow more vengeance. The Rangers, as Hardin learned, arrived in Clinton, DeWitt County, without incident, and were informed there were no charges against their prisoners. Instead of releasing them they placed them in the Clinton "jail," however, in order that the Tumlinson mob could take them out and lynch them.[14] This is what did happen, although whether Tumlinson was involved was never made clear. Hardin understood that the Rangers on the night of June 30 "turned over to the Tomlinson [sic] mob Scrap Taylor, Tuggle, and White, who put them to death by hanging, Dr. J. B. Brosius [sic] escaping." Then the next day "these eighteen Rangers, whose hands were still bloody with the blood of my friends, made a raid on me." After this skirmish "they got frightened and left on short order, leaving a dead Ranger behind them." [15]

This incident did not happen. Captain Waller's muster and pay roll, showing a roster of eighty-seven names including Waller, and with comments added later in the year, do not show that any one of his command was killed. On June 24 Sergeant Atkinson and his Rangers were back in Austin and now, although he was ill, Atkinson wrote a brief report to Adj. Gen. William Steele:

> according to written orders from you to me to report at this place on my return from Dewitt [sic] I am now in Austin for that purpose but ill Health detains [me] at the place & doing this writing I was scarcely able to [word illegible] I carried the prisoners Safe and delivered them into the custody of the Shariff [sic] of that [place] at his Solicitations I remained in Clinton thirty six hours for the purpose of guarding his prisoners on Saturday night last [.][16]

According to Sergeant Atkinson's report, meager as it is, he turned the seven prisoners over to the sheriff of DeWitt County, William J. Weisiger, and remained through Saturday, June 18, and then headed for Austin to report. He made no mention of any attempt at rescuing the prisoners or once arriving in Clinton of any mob activity.

But there was a raid on the Clinton jail, or courthouse as the jail was reported full, and prisoners were taken out. The mob wanted four: Taylor, Tuggle, White and Bockius. The three remaining prisoners were apparently left alone, probably because they were strangers and the mob had no reason to suspect them of any real association with Hardin. Historian C. L. Sonnichsen described the night as "black as the bottom of a cellar—a perfect time for a deed of darkness." Guard Jim Wofford was in charge at the jail and threatened to shoot the first man who came up the steps, but there was a man behind him who told him he would fire only once. Then the mob threatened to burn the courthouse if the prisoners were not turned over to them, and no further resistance was made.[17] Doc Bockius was the lucky one, as Joseph Sunday, a very large man and a friend of Bockius and fellow Mason, happened to be there or perhaps chose to be there, and managed to save the life of little Doc Bockius. The trio of Tuggle, Taylor and White, who had no Masonic friends to help them, was taken to a pasture close to the Clinton cemetery. They were strung up from the branches of a tree and left hanging. The remains of Tuggle and White, if they were buried in the Clinton Cemetery, have no marker to establish where they were buried. The family of Rufus P. "Scrap" Taylor managed to cut his body down and haul it to the family cemetery on the other side of the Guadalupe River, or else dug it up and delivered it to the family cemetery. Of the three only Scrap Taylor has a marker. It had not been a full year before the body of Pitkin Taylor had been laid to rest there; and it would be only a little more than a year when the body of Pitkin's son, James Creed Taylor, would be added to the family plot. Those who buried Scrap Taylor could have gazed across the close by Guadalupe River and remembered the scene when the friends of Bill Sutton celebrated at the funeral of old Pitkin Taylor. If there was a celebration now because another Taylor was being laid to rest there is no record that the Sutton followers celebrated so openly. Perhaps if there was a celebration it occurred at the Joe Tumlinson ranch, not far from the outskirts of Yorktown.

This triple hanging did not receive as much press coverage as the lynching of Joseph G. Hardin and the Dixon brothers had. One initial report however leaves a question unanswered, as it stated that there were five men taken from the Clinton courthouse and lynched; then it clarified that of the five only three were hanged, while the "remaining two were shot in the woods." The correspondent added that the Sutton-Taylor feud "is more rancorous than ever." [18] A headline of another newspaper read: "Three Men Hung at Clinton," with a sub-headline identifying the victims. "On Sunday night last, about 1 o'clock A.M." it began, giving the date as June 19–20, "a large body of disguised men" took the prisoners from the sheriff's guard and hung them near the Clinton cemetery. This report further confirmed that because the jail was already full they were being held in the courthouse by the sheriff and a citizen's guard. There was to be an examining trial Monday morning, but on that morning, June 20, Justice O. K. Tuton released the others as there were no complaints made against them. This article concluded: "It is said that the parties who were lynched, were accused of theft and of having been accomplices in the murder of Webb, in Comanche county, and while public opinion condemns the manner of their execution, it does not deplore their fate." [19]

The mob's work of late June did result in action in the governor's office. Reportedly there was criminal activity all over the state. The *Daily Express* of San Antonio printed a horrible picture of crime, reporting that "murder, lynch law, and civil war seem about to over-run Comanche, Brown, Bell, San Saba, and other counties." The *Express* briefly reviewed the Webb killing, saying he was killed supposedly because he had "caused the arrest of three of a gang of cattle thieves"; Webb "was surrounded and murdered in cold blood in Comanche town, by four of their friends." The report continued with rumors, stating that eighteen persons "are said to have been killed in Bell county" including "nine killed in Belton jail." It was as if a civil war, a conflict between good and evil, was raging in Texas, as "Vigilance committees are forming rapidly, and the thieves and murderers will all be killed or driven off before the war ceases." According to this report the frontier counties were over-run by organized bands of cattle-thieves. Besides rampant lawlessness seemingly everywhere in the state, and the continued threat of Indian raiding parties on the western frontier, the Sutton-Taylor Feud which had flared up off and on since the Civil War was now raging again. If anyone doubted the existence of a genuine feud, rather than just a group of criminals acting against peaceful citizens, the killing of William E. Sutton

George Culver Tennille, a close friend of Hardin and victim during the Sutton-Taylor feud. *Courtesy the Jack Caffall Collection.*

and G. W. Slaughter in March by two Taylors, then the lynching of a Taylor and two companions in June, not to mention the killing of deputy sheriff Webb by Hardin and Taylor, certainly underscored the fact that a feud between two groups was taking place south of Austin, and the two groups had been feuding for some time. It was now time to send Adjutant General Steele into DeWitt County to examine the situation first hand. Was it a real feud, or just careless reporting by overzealous individuals?

During this latest mob action Hardin was concluding his plans to leave the state. He safely hid from lawmen for two days at the home of Stephen Tippet "Tip" Davis; the mysterious companion Mac Young was still with him, and after two days they bid Davis good-bye. Davis appears this first and last time in Hardin's autobiography. He was a son of San Jacinto veteran Jesse Kincheloe and Eliza Davis, born July 13, 1844, in Gonzales County. Whereas Hardin was too young to have served in the Civil War,

Stephen Tipet "Tip" Davis as a Gonzales County deputy sheriff on horseback in front of the old Gonzales jail. *Courtesy Juanita Davis Woods.*

Davis had served in the 23rd Texas Cavalry until the war's end. Two years later, on December 25, 1867, he married Miss Sarah J. Hodges in Gonzales. During the following years he resided in Gonzales, and perhaps in 1871, Hardin's first visit to Gonzales County it is believed, the two met and became friends. Davis was about a decade older and Hardin may have looked upon him as an older brother, or even a father figure. Davis may have even joined that 1871 trail drive to Abilene, Kansas. From 1871 to 1874 there was a three-year window for Hardin and Tip Davis to become acquainted, and most likely it was nearer 1871 than 1874.

Following that brief farewell in Gonzales, Hardin and Young headed for Waller County, and George C. Tennille went part of the way with them, and "when we bid him good-bye it was for the last time." [20]

The only further incident Hardin experienced prior to leaving the state was in Austin County where the sheriff, Charles Langhammer, attempted to arrest him and Young for carrying weapons. Hardin demurred, refusing to surrender his weapon, justifying his action because he was a traveler and travelers were allowed to carry arms. Hardin carried on but Young was arrested and later paid a fine. Langhammer had been elected December 2, 1873, and was thus relatively inexperienced, as his main profession was as a merchant in Cat Spring.[21] If this incident happened as Hardin described it—Langhammer unable to show a warrant and Hardin in turn threatening to kill the sheriff then taking his horse and pistol—it ought to have made some type of news report, but as yet nothing has been located verifying Hardin's claim. Hardin later learned Young had to pay a $100 fine, which seems inordinately high for the charge. Once Young joined Hardin the pair traveled to Uncle Robert Hardin's place in Washington County.

By now cousin John Dixon Hardin had returned with $500 from the sale of the cattle that Bowen had been holding in Kansas. With this extra money Hardin was truly ready to leave the state. In the meantime he had managed to have Jane and baby Molly arrive in Brenham. He described her as his "loving wife . . . true to me as the magnet to steel" and settled all his business affairs and said goodbye to "all my friends once more." Hardin does not explain why the authorities released those family members from "house arrest," nor how they traveled from Comanche to Brenham. Hardin was convinced he was forced to leave the state, "not because I was an outlaw, but because mob law had become supreme in Texas, as the hanging of my relatives and friends amply proved." [22]

Why the Hardin family did not continue on their way out of the state together is not revealed. Instead he and Young went ahead on horseback, going through New Iberia, Louisiana, before reaching New Orleans, while Jane and Molly went separately accompanied by one of the Swain men, probably Theodore S. Swain, a relative by marriage. Perhaps Uncle Robert of Brenham engineered the plan to get Jane and Molly out of the state and back into Wes's arms. Hardin recalled that "Harry Swain and wife of Brenham (of which town he was marshal) accompanied them there [to New Orleans]." In an effort to explain the relationship, he wrote that Harry C. Swain had married "Jenny" Parks, and his cousin J. D., meaning John Dixon Hardin, had married Molly Parks, "hence the friendship." [23] The Parks girls were daughters of Duley (or Dudley) Parks, who resided in Brenham, Washington County.[24] When husband H. C. Swain died, Elvira Jennie located in El Paso where she had other relatives. She died September 13, 1925, and is buried in El Paso's historic Concordia Cemetery.

The record however does not show Harry Swain ever was city marshal of Brenham as Hardin claimed years later. Did Hardin's memory fail him again, or was he purposely misleading his readers to protect the real city marshal's memory? According to the 1880 Washington County census, the city lawman was not Harry Swain but Theodore Swain, identified as the city marshal by census taker J. W. Hackworth.[25] T. S. Swain was born in New Orleans November 1, 1847, the second son of Robert and Maria Moor Swain. Henry Clay Swain, born in 1836, who would later become the husband of Elvira Jennie Parks, was T. S.' s older brother. No details on T. S. Swain's career or death have been learned, but the *Brenham Weekly Banner* carried occasional mentions of him in his official capacity as late as 1891. Perhaps it was Theodore S. Swain and not Harry

Swain who accompanied Jane and Molly Hardin from Brenham to New Orleans in 1874 where they joined John Wesley and Mac Young. Once together they spent at least a week in the Crescent City, perhaps playing the role of tourists, or perhaps merely relaxing after a stressful journey. Rested up, John and Jane and Molly continued on, taking a steamboat through the Gulf to Cedar Keys, Florida.

If during Hardin's preparations to leave Texas he read Austin's *Daily Democratic Statesman*—which he probably did—he was aware of the formation of another Ranger group, which was commanded by former State Police Captain Leander H. McNelly. This company, formed to deal with the state's interior problems, was to be sent into the midst of the feuding Sutton and Taylor parties in DeWitt County. The peace treaties were no longer in effect: the jail delivery and lynching of three prisoners in June was proof enough of that. William Sutton was dead, but now Reuben H. Brown and Joe Tumlinson were the leaders of the men feuding against the Taylors.

Captain McNelly arrived in Clinton the first day of August and found "a perfect reign of terror" existing there in DeWitt and adjoining counties. He reported how the peaceful citizens were terrified, as "armed bands of men were making predatory excursions through the country, overawing the lawabiding Citizens, while the civil authorities were unable, or unwilling to enforce the laws framed for their protection." He was aware of the peace treaties, one of which Hardin had signed and one which Jim Taylor had signed, but wrote "From the facility with which treaties of peace and compromise has been broken, confidence in each other's respective promises, was a thing un Known." Although mentioning Joe Tumlinson and ex-Senator B. J. Pridgen by name as leaders of the Taylor party, McNelly believed Hardin and Taylor were still there, and if they were captured the conflict would diminish.[26]

One of McNelly's men, T. C. Robinson, from Virginia, contributed numerous letters to the *Statesman* writing under the pseudonym of "Pidge." He wrote of the troubles in DeWitt County and of the principal characters of the feud. Of Hardin he wrote, after being ordered to lead a party to search for him: "I had heard of him before I ever came to Texas. He kills men just to see them kick, and on one occasion charged Cuero alone with a yell of 'rats to your holes!' . . . He can take two six-shooters and turn them like wheels in his hands and fire a shot from each at every revolution." And Pidge was well aware of the reward offered for this man so dexterous with pistols: "There is a reward of eighteen hundred dollars for him, and it will be well earned when he is captured. He is said to have killed thirty men and is a dead shot." [27] But in spite of McNelly's desire to capture or kill Hardin and Taylor, he never caught up with either one. By the end of 1874 there were worse problems on the southern Texas border and he and his company were sent into the Nueces Strip to fight the banditry along the Rio Grande.

CHAPTER 12

TROUBLES IN FLORIDA

"[W]hiskey is the cause of many troubles in this life. . . . may the God of mercies have mercy on us all [and] Remember the advice of your dear departed Father."

Robert E. Hardin to John Wesley Hardin, May 9, 1877

Why Hardin, traveling under the name of Walker, chose to visit Cedar Keys, Florida, is unknown. Incorporated in 1869 as the "Town of Cedar Keys"[1] the population by the time of its first census was 400. It scarcely increased through the years, not even doubling by the year 2000. The Keys had been a base for Seminoles, then the Spanish and later for such pirates as Jean Lafitte and Captain Kidd. This was the initial land stop for Mr. and Mrs. Walker and child. Apparently the family's stay there was very brief. Leaving Cedar Keys they then went to Gainesville, county seat of Alachua County, some forty-five miles inland.

Gainesville in 1874 was in some ways similar to the wild cow town of Abilene of 1871 and conceivably because Hardin was aware of this he chose this community for the next stage of his Florida escape. It was a rough and wild town; whites as well as blacks went armed outside of their homes, and the sound of gunfire was not uncommon. Naturally much of the violence was caused by racial animosities. There was a Young Men's Democratic Club which was in reality a cover for the Ku Klux Klan. Strangely there was but one police officer, and it was impossible for him to have much influence over anything. There was no fire department in an era of common wooden buildings.

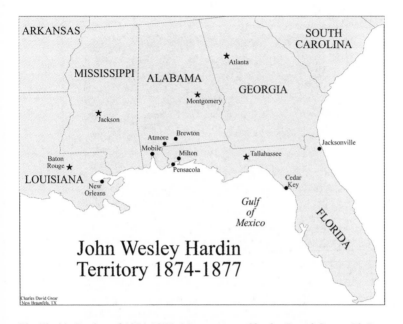

ARKANSAS

MISSISSIPPI

ALABAMA

★ Atlanta

GEORGIA

SOUTH
CAROLINA

★ Montgomery

★ Jackson

Atmore ● Brewton
●
Mobile ●
Milton ●
Pensacola

★ Tallahassee

Jacksonville ●

Baton
Rouge ★

LOUISIANA ●
New
Orleans

Cedar
● Key

Gulf
of
Mexico

FLORIDA

John Wesley Hardin
Territory 1874-1877

Charles David Grear
New Braunfels, TX

The Florida Region of 1874-1877. *Map courtesy Charles David Grear, Ph.D.*

Although he was only twenty-one, Hardin had a wife and child, whom he claimed to love deeply, and with her influence he may have felt it was time to "settle down." The thought of sailing on to England did enter his mind, and if the Hardin family had gone on across the Atlantic the change would have drastically altered history. Jane may have discouraged such a move, as she had family in Florida as well as in Texas. In England there would be no such network, so the voyage did not happen. Hardin made no comment regarding the possible voyage to England in his autobiography, but he did share that with an Austin reporter several years later.

Instead Hardin now considered becoming a Florida businessman,. In Gainesville he bought a saloon, which would allow him to engage in his gambling pursuits as well. Samuel W. Burnett had his saloon for sale and

John W. Hardin in Florida as he appeared in 1875. *Courtesy the Robert G. Mc-Cubbin Collection.*

Hardin bought it. The Burnetts were solid members of the community, as in 1870 Samuel W. was the town mayor, and ten years later his son Samuel J. was elected to the same position. When Hardin arrived, Sam the elder was about sixty-four years of age and probably intended to reduce his responsibilities. His son Samuel was four years older than Hardin.[2]

All did not go smoothly for the young saloon owner, as on the first day he opened for business, probably after a week or so of advertising and refurbishing, two men walked in who recognized that "Mr. Swain" was really John Wesley Hardin. Hardin identified them as Frank Harper and Bill McCulloch, "stockmen from Texas . . . . both men recognized me, for I had punched cows with them both."[3] Frank Harper was probably the mulatto from Washington County, born there about 1850. In 1874 Harper had a wife but no children. His partner, William M. McCullough as he spelled his name, had a much different background. In 1870 Mc-Cullough was residing in DeWitt County raising stock; like Samuel W. Burnett, he was a native of Georgia. He then had a wife and three young children. As a DeWitt County resident there were many opportunities for McCullough and Hardin not only to have met, but also to actually work together driving stock. In fact he may have gone up the trail to Abilene in 1871 with Hardin.[4]

A few days later one of the frequent street disturbances attracted Hardin's attention. Gainesville's only peace officer, Lemuel Wilson, had arrested a black man for an unidentified offense and was taking him to the town's wooden building, which served as the jail.[5] Policeman Wilson was in the dangerous position of losing his prisoner to a mob of the man's friends. Who Lewis had in his custody is unknown, but a friend of the prisoner—identified by Hardin as "a big black Negro"—interfered and Hardin knocked him down. This brought about a retaliatory move from the knocked-down man's friend. In typical Hardin fashion Hardin shot him, possibly mortally. In spite of Jane's efforts to quiet him down, Hardin could not refrain from reacting violently. Amidst the turmoil, Dr. James D. Cromwell arrived on the scene to offer his assistance, carrying a double-barreled shotgun.[6] Why this young dentist managed to appear on the scene with such a weapon Hardin made no comment, but Wilson, Hardin and Cromwell now managed to get "the whole mob" into the jail, although they left the two men lying on the street Hardin had knocked down and shot. Hardin dated this incident as happening on May 1, 1874, but it had to have occurred much later, perhaps about the first of August.

A few days later the same man who had the narrow brush with the law, identified by Hardin as Eli, probably Eli Williams, "attempted to rape a respectable white lady" and was again arrested and jailed. A black man assaulting a "respectable" white lady was reason enough for the members of the Young Men's Democratic Club, or local KKK, to take action. "Some of us went to the jail at midnight," Hardin wrote, "set it on fire, and burned Eli with it." The friends of Eli became "very much excited over the burning," but as the county coroner (a member of the mob), "set everything all right by declaring that Eli had burned himself up in setting the jail on fire" there were no further legal ramifications.[7] It was as if Hardin had two compartments in his personality: he was quite capable of participating in mob action to burn a black man, but if a "mob" attempted to arrest him he was justified in killing to save his life. He regarded defending himself as the first law of nature.

For reasons not explained Hardin now sold his business and went to another small community, Micanopy, less than twenty miles south of Gainesville. Again he "set up another bar" and also bought and sold horses. This was a business in which he could succeed, as he knew so very well what a good horse was worth, especially "in a tight."

Hardin's stay in Micanopy was brief, just as it had been in Gainesville and Cedar Keys. Trading horses and running a saloon proved to be not to his liking, and now the family moved to Jacksonville, nearly one hundred miles northeast of Micanopy. He entered into a contract with the Haddock Company of butchers to furnish 150 head of beef cattle to the firm. No details were offered on how he rounded up such a sizable herd, but he did and had them to sell to Haddock & Company, but the firm refused to take them. Hardin explained that William Haddock had just died, thus the company was not willing to accept the cattle. Instead of merely turning 150 head of cattle loose out of frustration, Hardin now went into the butcher and liquor business. He dated this activity as happening in May 1875, and noted that he eliminated the liquor aspect of the business, "finding that butchering and shipping cattle would consume all my time."[8]

John Wesley Hardin, Jr. *Courtesy the Robert G. McCubbin Collection.*

If that was the real reason for the refusal to accept the 150 head of cattle—that William Haddock had "just died"—the firm that remained consisted of Joseph H. Haddock, E. H. Hull, T. R. Hoyle, J. C. Thrasher and Philip Leonardy according to the 1876–1877 Jacksonville City Directory.[9] Elsewhere in the same directory appears this listing: "Swaine, John H., meat, City Market, h. 127 Pine."[10] This entry is most important as it confirms Hardin's claim that he was in the butcher business at this period of his career. The veracity of Hardin's autobiography has occasionally been challenged. Some statements are certainly untrue, but this single directory entry confirms the butchering claim. It would appear from this evidence that Hardin was making a sincere effort to become a businessman and intended to lead a respectable life in the community.

Circumstances may have been the leading cause of his outward change of life style. First-born Mary Elizabeth, called Mollie, born February 6, 1873, had gone through the "terrible twos" and was around three years old. The matter of the butchering business was in early 1875, and now Jane was pregnant, carrying her second child. John Wesley Hardin Jr. would be born on August 3, 1875. Presumably the dwelling at 217 Pine Street in Jacksonville was becoming a pleasant home, one that the head of household had not previously really experienced.

Hardin dated the year of his failed business with the Haddock firm as in May 1875. It may have been earlier, or perhaps this date is substantially correct, as it was a year since the Comanche tragedy, certainly an event that Hardin could not forget. We know Hardin kept informed of events happening in Texas by subscribing to the *Galveston Daily News*. He learned there of the death of George Culver Tennille, who was shot to death July 8, 1874, while resisting arrest, Tennille alone against Sheriff Green DeWitt and his men. The twenty-man posse found Tennille at John Runnel's ranch and ordered him to surrender. Knowing what had happened to others who were taken from a jail cell to a lynching tree or simply shot to death after surrender, Tennille chose to fight it out—even though the odds were twenty to one against him. After several shots his rifle jammed. He was trying to extract a shell when the fatal bullets struck him down. Sheriff DeWitt had intended to arrest Tennille on a charge of theft of a gelding. Whether this was a recent charge or one dating back to 1871 is unknown. In August 1871 special policeman Joe Tumlinson had arrested Tennille for theft of a horse, but the outcome is not known.[11] He appeared in district court on September 28 of that year and was released on bond of $800.[12] Why the sheriff took such a large posse to assist him in the arrest suggests he did not intend to bring Tennille in alive. Or perhaps the sheriff and posse now intended to eradicate one more member of the Taylor faction, and used the excuse of the horse theft charge to justify their action. If Hardin had not learned of his friend's death from the newspapers, then certainly he learned of it from correspondence from friends in Texas.

How long butcher "Swain" remained in the business is unknown for certain, but he claimed that in April 1875—although it could have been much later—two Pinkerton agents ventured into Florida and discovered

Swain was in reality the notorious—and badly wanted—John Wesley Hardin. Hardin had during his stay in Jacksonville made acquaintance with the county sheriff and town marshal—so he claimed—and these officials informed Hardin who the agents were. This is the reason Hardin gave for his relatively quick departure from Jacksonville. He and a policeman identified by Hardin as Gus Kenedy[13] together went to New Orleans, intending to go on to Mexico, but the Pinkertons were on their trail and caught up with them near the Florida-Georgia state line. "A fight was the natural result," recalled Hardin, "and two of the Pinkerton agents were killed. I escaped without a scratch." Hardin had made arrangements for Jane and children to meet him in Pollard, Alabama, but the alleged confrontation with the two detectives had cost him time. He found "that my beloved wife had fulfilled her part of the engagement" for they had registered as "Mrs. J. H. Swain and children" on the hotel register. She then found hospitality with relatives. Hardin "took the night train" for Pollard and finally rejoined his little family, his wife, Mollie and John Wesley Jr.[14]

Hardin may have actually believed the two men were agents of the Pinkerton Detective Agency. More than one historian has communicated with the firm and according to their archives there is nothing to substantiate Hardin's claim. This means that Hardin may have killed two men who were aware of his true identity, although they were not the professional detectives he claimed them to be. In his mind any professional detective could be called a Pinkerton. At this time in the firm's history the "Pinks" had been in operation since 1850, founded by Allan Pinkerton. The firm gained national publicity when it discovered and prevented an assassination plot against Abraham Lincoln and America never lost faith in them. They were not successful in tracking down members of the James and Younger Gangs of the 1870s, nor the Dalton gang members of the early 1890s.

What is fascinating however is that there is a contemporary reference to two men being killed by Hardin and Kenedy. Never one to shun a newspaper reporter, Hardin revealed that he "was forced to leave by detectives having found me out." He recalled that "Jacksonville was a big place. It was a resort for people from the North, who go down there to spend money. I found out the detectives at the same time they found me out, and escaped before they could get papers from the Governor."[15] In another interview, in answer to a question or comment from professional detective John R. "Jack" Duncan, who inquired of Hardin if he knew of two men who had been sent to Florida but who had never returned, Hardin replied that he knew of the pair, and added that he knew they would never return to Texas.[16] This definitely corroborates the story later described in his autobiography, that Hardin, and perhaps Gus Kenedy as well, did have a run-in with two men claiming to be detectives, and they were both killed. The discrepancy is that the two were not members of the Pinkerton organization.

Following a week-long visit in Pollard the family went to a community Hardin called Tuxpan, but most likely he misremembered the town of Tocoi in Clay County, Florida, today a ghost town. Hardin complained of being held in quarantine, as they had stopped in New Orleans during a yellow fever epidemic. Following their enforced stay there they went on to East Pascagoula. Then he and Kenedy went to Mobile to play poker and cards, and thanks to their ability to gamble, or more likely due to marked cards, they won $3,500. They began a circuit of going back and forth from Pascagoula and Mobile, a trip of about fifty miles between the two cities.[17]

Hardin knew full well Texas had not forgotten him. He was aware that the $1,800 reward offered on July 3, 1874—his body to be delivered inside the jail door—was outdated. Senator John D. Stephens, from Comanche, was then working on legislation to allow the governor to offer a reward of $4,000 for his capture. Rumors spread that because of this action, and his actions after the Webb shooting, Stephens became a marked man. Stephens had arranged for Hardin's cowboys working the herd in Hamilton County (arrested after the Webb killing) to be sent to DeWitt County, where Joe Tumlinson and his mob took them from custody and lynched three of them. Hardin later denied ever threatening

Senator Stephens, explaining that, "When Stephens had the bill passed offering a reward for me, and was so scared of his life, I was not here in Austin, and would not have hurt him, for I did not know anything against him in particular. If I had wanted to kill him I could have managed some plan to get at him."[18] Naturally such a large amount of money attracted all types of man-hunters, amateur and professional alike. In November 1875 a man in Dallas was shot to death by lawmen when convinced the man was Hardin. He was not.[19]

In spite of J. W. Hardin becoming J. H. Swain, Hardin's personality did not change. On November 7, 1876, during the excitement of the Hayes-Tilden presidential election contest, Hardin, Gus Kenedy and another companion identified as Cliff Lewis were in a gambling house in Mobile when an argument erupted, probably an irate player accusing Hardin or Kenedy of cheating at cards. The police did quiet things down and Hardin and Kenedy were both arrested, charged with disorderly conduct, and fined $5.00 for their troubles.[20] In writing his life story Hardin recalled this unpleasant incident but chose to add considerable drama and danger in the telling. In his version "all the gambling fraternity [of Mobile] got on a high lonesome and took in the town. One of our party got into a row, and of course I took a hand." The row escalated from the gambling hall into the street, with those who remained inside—many city policemen—starting to shoot at those outside. Hardin claimed he and Kenedy each shot a policeman and wounded a third. Then in their flight they threw away their weapons, at least Hardin did.

But we cannot accept this version of the incidents of that November night in Mobile as described by Hardin. There was a saloon row, and there was gunfire, but there were no mortally wounded policemen as a result of the fight. If that had been the case the *Mobile Register* would have had banner headlines and Hardin and Kenedy would have faced charges much more serious than disorderly conduct. Sergeant Ryan[21] of the police force, "while in discharge of his duty was shot in the arm Tuesday night by one of three parties whom he and Officer Spencer tried to put out of a house up town." Two of the three revelers were arrested and were told to leave Mobile on the first train out.[22] Swain and Kenedy did leave town but they failed to take the marked cards with them. With those cards they had been able to cheat—and win—at the gambling tables of Mobile and elsewhere.[23]

Hardin now moved to Pollard, Alabama, and stayed at the home of one of Jane's uncles, Neill McMillan Sr. So far Hardin, known generally as J. H. Swain, had been successful in hiding his true identity. A few people were aware of who he really was, and undoubtedly Uncle Neill was aware of whom his niece was married to. What Hardin was not aware of was the troubles of brother-in-law Joshua Robert "Brown" Bowen. David Haldeman of the Sutton side of the DeWitt County feud, which Hardin had now conveniently left behind, had not forgotten the man who had murdered his son Thomas. Mr. Haldeman went to a Clinton attorney, William R. Friend, and shared with him what he knew, or at least what he believed to be true. Haldeman explained to attorney Friend that he wanted a requisition to be sent to the governors of Florida and Alabama for the arrest of Bowen for the Gonzales County murder. Attorney Friend in turn communicated with Governor Coke.[24] Somehow David Haldeman had learned that Bowen was somewhere in the area of Pollard, Escambia County, Alabama. At this time Bowen still had a reward of $500 offered for his capture, and Hardin of course had a much higher reward for his capture.

If Haldeman and now Friend knew where Bowen was, they would have made the logical assumption that brother-in-law Hardin was probably in the same general area. It is possible that David Haldeman had already acted and sent the two detectives to Florida in an early attempt to capture Bowen or Hardin, and they were the two who would never return. In April 1877 David Haldeman wrote to the new Texas head of state Richard B. Hubbard and requested papers for the arrest of Bowen. Haldeman was obviously not satisfied with whatever efforts Governor Coke had made to bring the murderer of his son to justice. He mailed a copy of the indictment against Bowen to the governor and stated the $500 reward was insufficient, as few men would chance the arrest of such a dangerous fugitive for that amount, the reward not "sufficient to induce persons not personally interested" to bring Bowen back to justice. But he—David Haldeman, father of victim Thomas—now requested the authority to go to Florida himself and arrest Bowen. He concluded this communication to the governor by advising him that there were "two other indictments for willful murder & for committing a Rape in the same County."[25] Besides the Haldeman killing, there was the Robert Thomas killing and the rape of a black woman. The governor rightly rejected Haldeman's request, pointing out someone not so emotionally involved would be better suited for such a task. Hardin and Bowen could not have been aware of these actions taking place back in Texas.

A young Tom Tennille, son of George C. Tennille. *Courtesy the Jack Caffall Collection.*

In April 1877 "Mrs. Jane Swain" penned a letter to her uncle, Joshua Bowen, in which she asked which of the Taylors had been killed. That she was aware that one of them had died indicates they were somewhat aware of events in Gonzales and DeWitt Counties, although the death of Jim Taylor had occurred nearly sixteen months before. Although by 1877 the Sutton-Taylor feud was essentially confined to courtroom battles rather than shooting affrays, Uncle Joshua, answered that it was James Taylor "killed by Suttin [sic] Party," and that his cousin Billy Taylor had been captured a few days since and was in the Travis County Jail; he further pointed out that all of the Clements brothers were gone with the exception of Joe. Other news was that Thomas C. Tennille, son of George Culver Tennille killed back in July of 1874, had married Nancy Cobb.[26]

On May 9 Robert E. Hardin of Brenham, Washington County, wrote to the Swains. He had sad news to report: Rev. J. G. Hardin,[27] his brother, "had died last august after a short but painful sickness"; additional news concerned other family matters. R. E. Hardin had found when visiting Reverend Hardin's home that Jeff was still there, "and is a very good boy." Jefferson Davis Hardin had been born in 1861, so he was now about sixteen years of age. Elizabeth Hardin, now a widow, had recently sent R. E. a letter, saying they were all well; Jeff and Nannie "and little J. G. is all there is of the family now." J. G. was Joseph Gibson, born in May of 1874 in Comanche, the son of Joseph and Belle, only a few days prior to the killing of deputy sheriff Webb. Sister Mattie had gotten married the previous June, to "a very good looking gentleman by the name of Smith." His full name was William Bright Benjamin Smith, born March 4, 1848, in Huntsville, Alabama. He and Martha "Matt" Hardin, born April 19, 1857, in Polk County, Texas, were married in Limestone County on March 3, 1875.

R. E. continued with family news: Joe Clements was in the hog driving business, James Taylor was dead and Bill Taylor in jail awaiting his trial. "Times are dull here" and the "grasshopper made a raid" through their place last fall and this spring which made "every thing look gloomy[.]" But more importantly he wrote that there was "a great deal of murdering

William Berry Bright Smith, from the original tintype, a mere 1 × 2-½ inches in size. *Courtesy The John Wesley Hardin Papers, The Wittliff Collection, Texas State University*

stealing and mobing [*sic*] going on in the state which is quite a bad state of affairs[.]" But, Robert E. Hardin reckoned his nephew took "some of the Texas papers and get such general news as that." John Dixon's family was all well; the couple now had five children.[28] Of further interest, R. E. asked how the Swains had enjoyed the centennial. "We hear you went [although] none of us had the pleasure of attending this one [.]" Unintentionally R. E. now gave his nephew a moral teaching. Mrs. Jennie Swain, née Parks, "has been right sick but is getting well [.] She has quite a hard time trying to make a living [as] her husband drinks more than any thing else[.] they have no children [.] whiskey is the cause of many troubles in this life . . . may the God of mercies have mercy upon us all [and] Remember the advice of your dear departed Father."[29]

It would certainly be interesting to know just where Mr. and Mrs. Swain celebrated the centennial as probably any community of any size had a celebration. Perhaps the Swains as a family did not do much celebrating, as Jane was only weeks away from delivering her third child. Jane, but called Jennie as well as Callie, was born on July 15, 1877, probably in the Swain home in Pollard, Alabama. Jane now had three children to love and care for. Her first five years of marriage had been filled with stress, what with Wes's frequent absences and frequent difficulties with the law and others eager to capture or kill him. His drinking and the gunfight with Charles Webb had resulted in their being forced to leave Texas. Now Uncle Bob was freely giving advice about the dangers of too much alcohol consumption. And it would be of great interest to know if the Swains gave Uncle Bob's advice about drinking much thought. Could they not have realized that on so many occasions, the troubles Wes Hardin experienced were a result of his over consumption of alcohol?

Not long after his forced exit from Mobile, Hardin "concluded" that the saloon and liquor and cattle shipping business was not for him and formed a partnership with "an experienced logger" named Sheppard Hardy. This man, whom Hardin called "Shep," was born about 1837. In the 1870 census he is shown to be a native of Alabama and thirty-three years of age with a twenty-seven-year-old wife named Sarah. They were then living in Santa Rosa County, Florida, just south of Pollard, Alabama.[30]

Although Hardin's entry into a new business venture may have seemed like the perfect choice, events were happening back in Texas that Hardin and Bowen were both unaware of. Ironically Bowen himself was instrumental in bringing Texas law to the area, with dire results for both him and his brother-in-law. Contemporary Robert Warren Brooks was a "lumber marker" at the time and knew both men. While he may have been confused about the date he first met Bowen, he wrote of Brown Bowen many years later:

> Brown gathered around him a class of men like himself, among them Bob Hardy, Shep Hardy, and a lot of others, all of whom are now dead. When I went to Bluff Springs in 1872, there were four saloons in the burg, and Brown Bowen and his crowd were constant patrons of them. When sober, he was a friendly sort of man, but when drinking, which was often, he had an ugly temper, and was dangerous.

Brooks understood that Bowen made his living by stealing logs at the Bluff Springs Mill and then selling them elsewhere. The logs were mainly the property of the Moline Mill Company. As far as Brooks knew, Bowen "never killed any white man in this section, but several negroes were killed by him." Brooks remembered Bowen's "undoing": he went to Flomaton, only several miles from Pollard and tried to kill one of the Negroes then in the employ of Col. William Dudley Chipley, superintendent of the railroad. Chipley saw the angry Bowen chasing the employee with a pistol, intending to kill him. Fearlessly Chipley yanked the six-shooter out of Bowen's hands and beat him over the head with it.[31]

Hardin was also aware of this incident and dated the row as happening on July 19, 1877, but more likely it was August 19. He described the incident of Bowen going "on a spree and got into a row with Mr. Shipley [*sic*], the general manager of the railroad. He got the worst of the row and the next day came back to the junction [Pensacola Junction, Florida] vowing vengeance." In his rage Bowen claimed that "the peaceable John Swain" was not who he claimed to be in reality, but "the notorious John Wesley Hardin."[32] Brooks, in his version, also corroborated what Hardin wrote, saying that Bowen, with temper flaring, "swore vengeance against Chipley and intended to carry out his threats to kill him at the first opportunity."[33]

William Dudley Chipley circa 1865. *Author's Collection*

While Bowen was causing trouble in Florida, many lawmen in Texas were thirsting for the opportunity to capture or kill Hardin for the $4,000 reward, dead or alive. Ironically an accidental self-inflicted gunshot wound by a noted Texas Ranger resulted in lawmen coming into Escambia County. On May 29, 1877, John Barkley Armstrong, a veteran of two years' service with Capt. Leander Harvey McNelly's State Troops, while handling his own six-shooter in the Case Hotel in Goliad, "let it discharge." The ball entered "the pit of his stomach." It was a "dangerous and possible mortal wound" that kept Armstrong from doing any serious work as a Ranger; for a while he was even unable to mount a horse. Through June and July Armstrong gradually improved, and by early August was able to "limp along without his crutches."

During this time of relative idleness Armstrong concocted a plan to locate Hardin, the most wanted fugitive of Texas. He knew he needed to first determine where Hardin was, and he correctly surmised someone in Gonzales County would know. That had been Hardin's "home territory" and his wife's family lived there. As he would be recognized in Gonzales County, he needed someone who could ingratiate himself in the county and work undercover. Among the best detectives in the state was John Riley "Jack" Duncan of Dallas. Duncan was called in, and to give him what legal authority he needed, was sworn in as a private in Lt. Jesse Lee Hall's State Troops, on July 10, 1877. His only assignment was to work up the Hardin case.

Duncan, disguised as a day laborer, traveled to Gonzales, acting under the *alias* of Williams. Among others, he befriended Neill Bowen, Jane Hardin's father. He claimed to be interested in renting a storehouse on the Bowen property. Mr. Bowen delayed giving a definite answer, saying he would have to write to the owner, and wrote to "Mr. Swain." Duncan intercepted the letter and saw it was addressed to J. H. Swain in Alabama.

A slightly different version, but also involving an intercepted letter, was later given by Hardin himself. Bowen had written a letter to his father Neill, which he ended by saying his sister, Jane, sent her love to all. When Neill Bowen received this letter Duncan was staying at the Bowen home. He stole the letter, thus learning where Jane and Brown were; Duncan knew Hardin was no doubt close by. With this information Duncan now went to Gonzales and telegraphed the prearranged signal to Armstrong: "Come get your horse." Armstrong, with several other Rangers for show, quickly went to Gonzales and "arrested" Mr. Williams. They were back in Austin by August 17. Armstrong, still using his cane, began arrangements to go to Alabama, asking Adjutant General Steele to prepare the paperwork necessary to deliver Hardin, the true name, as well as Swain. Armstrong was so anxious to get on the road that he left without the papers, figuring he would get them in Montgomery, Alabama.

Man-hunters Armstrong and Duncan were on their way on August 18, heading into Hardin country. The pair arrived in Montgomery on August 20, and on the next day Armstrong sent the first of seven telegrams to Adjutant General Steele: "Arrived last night [.] Will wait here for papers [.] Duncan has gone ahead." Duncan arrived in Pollard, Alabama, located a few miles north of the state line. Again, playing the role of a transient, he contacted the local authority, by chance Neill McMillan, a deputy sheriff, and inquired about a fictional relative. Certainly unknown by Duncan was the fact that the McMillans were related to the Bowens. Deputy Neill McMillan was the son of the sheriff, Malcolm McMillan, and married to a cousin of Jane and Brown Bowen. During this conversation Duncan casually dropped the name of Swain, and was informed that Mr. Swain was then in Whiting, a community just north of Pollard. Duncan walked to Whiting, but now learned Mr. Swain was in Pensacola, Florida, on a gambling excursion. He then telegraphed Armstrong, still in Montgomery, to come to Whiting.

Now another fortuitous incident happened. Duncan met with railroad superintendent William Dudley Chipley, who had pistol-whipped Brown Bowen earlier that year. Chipley was a fifty-seven-year-old graduate of the Kentucky Military Institute and veteran of the Confederate Army, strong-willed and an entrepreneur who would eventually build two railroads. The town of Orange, Florida, would change its name to Chipley in his honor. Duncan confided to Chipley his real purpose, which resulted in Chipley being eager to contribute to their efforts to get Bowen out of the territory. He was the man who could provide transportation to the lawmen, as well as being personally interested in ridding the country of Bowen, as the ugly incident with that man was still fresh in Chipley's mind. He gladly provided a special engine to deliver Duncan and Armstrong, who had reached there on the morning of August 23, to

Pensacola. Once in Pensacola, the trio met with Escambia County Sheriff William H. Hutchinson. He had been elected sheriff in 1876, the first former Confederate to be so elected. He had a faithful deputy, a mysterious figure who appears only this once in the Hardin saga, A. J. Perdue.[34] Thus, on August 23, 1877, this group of determined men—Texas Rangers John B. Armstrong and John R. Duncan, railroad superintendent William D. Chipley, Sheriff W. H. Hutchinson and his deputy A. J. Perdue—descended on Pensacola ready to track down and capture or kill John Wesley Hardin, thus earning the reward offered for him, "dead or alive."

CHAPTER 13

"TEXAS, BY GOD!"

*"Jane I am in good hands now they treat me Better than you
have any Idea and assure me that I will not be mobed [sic] . . .
Jane Be in cheer and don't take trouble to Heart . . . But what I
have done in Texas was to Save my own Life [.]"*

J. H. Swain, August 25, 1877.

On the afternoon of August 23, 1877, Mr. John H. Swain was ready to leave Pensacola and return home to Jane and their three children. He was seldom alone on these gambling ventures, and this afternoon was no different: he was with several friends who together boarded the train, going into the smoker car. They may have been doing more than gambling, as they placed their shotguns above their heads in the baggage racks. Had they been hunting? What the other passengers did not know was that even with their shotguns out of reach, Jim Mann and John Swain had at least one pistol on their person; possibly Hardy and Campbell carried one as well, but not openly. The "peaceable Mr. Swain" and his companions, James Mann,[1] Shep Hardy[2] and Neil Campbell Jr.[3] now settled in for the train ride. As far as the community knew this quartet was of no significance to anyone, had never caused any trouble, and any gambling they did was more for enjoyment than any other reason. They chose this car as Mr. Swain had now taken up smoking a Meerschaum pipe, which he now readied to light up.[4] There may have been a few other passengers in this smoker; if there were his smoke would not be considered a bother by them.

As county sheriff, William H. Hutchinson[5] made it a practice to walk through the cars prior to the train's departure. He expected no trouble but

William Henry Hutchinson, Sheriff of Escambia County, Florida. *Author's Collection.*

if there were any "undesirables" present he would have them removed. This afternoon he entered the smoker, but none of the passengers thought anything of it as they knew this was a common practice of his.[6] And the quartet knew him, if not as a good friend, at least as a friendly acquaintance. Today Sheriff Hutchinson, known to many as "Hutch," entered the car but today his deputy A. J. Perdue was with him as well. Even this caused no concern to anyone.

The pair of lawmen addressed Mr. Swain. Hardin recalled that Perdue now asked him if he could not stay over in order that he could win some money back he had lost at the gambling tables. Hardin demurred, explaining that he would like to but not then as he had other business to attend to, adding, "Business before pleasure I can't stop over." After all, he had a wife and three small children waiting for him. Hutchinson and Perdue now exited the car, knowing that their target was there and off guard. Hardin was in the forward section of the car, facing the rear. He had his arms stretched out on the back of the seat, James "Jimmy" Mann next to him. Hardin had his pipe in his mouth, and all were relaxed.[7]

John Barkley Armstrong as he appeared in the 1870s. *Courtesy the Armstrong Family.*

Now the figure of Texas Ranger John B. Armstrong darkened the doorway and in his left hand he held his cane and in his right hand he held a Colt revolver with a seven-inch barrel. At the same time Armstrong entered from the rear, Hutchinson, Perdue and William D. Chipley entered the opposite end of the car, all four descending on the man with the Meerschaum pipe in his mouth. Almost immediately Hardin saw the Colt revolver, and knew this was no casual action. "Texas, by God!" he yelled out, later explaining that this "smelt of Texas business." With that recognition he attempted to draw his pistol, but now three men grabbed his arms and his legs, and he struggled. He attempted to draw his weapon but due to a flare up of an old wound he did not wear a gun belt and holster, but carried his weapon concealed under his shirt, suspended by a sort of shoulder holster. Violently he struggled, yelling out "Robbers! Protect me!" but with his arms and legs held down his struggles were useless.[8]

Artist R.J. Onderdonk's depiction of the capture of John Wesley Hardin. This first appeared in Hardin's autobiography. *The Life of John Wesley Hardin.*

James Mann reacted as if there were indeed robbers on board and whereas Hardin could not get his pistol in operation, Mann could. He fired once at Armstrong, narrowly missing his head. Armstrong returned the fire and shot Mann through the heart. Even though fatally shot, Mann was able to get off the train and onto the depot platform. Here other deputies had been stationed, and they fired at him as well. There Mann died, not knowing why the attack had occurred or who had killed him.[9]

Now Armstrong had reached the struggling group. Even if he had wanted to shoot Hardin it would have been too dangerous. He ordered Hardin to surrender, threatening to shoot if he did not, to which demand Hardin replied, "Blow away. You will never blow a more innocent man's out, or one that will care less." Another version of his response was "Shoot and be damned. I'd rather die than be arrested." [10] Hardin continued to fight, and to stop his struggles Armstrong hit him over the head with his heavy revolver, knocking him out. The reward had been for Hardin "dead or alive," but Armstrong wanted to take this prisoner back to Texas alive. He denied his true identity, maintaining his name was Swain.

Once "Swain" was subdued Armstrong pulled the bell cord to signal the conductor to start the train and pull out of the Pensacola depot. James Mann was left dead on the platform; Hardy, Campbell and "Mr. Swain" were in custody, the latter in irons. What Armstrong and the others perhaps only now realized, with them entering opposite ends of the car, they could have been shot by what is today called "friendly fire." And Hardin himself, once conscious, may have begun to realize that even if he had gotten his pistol out, he would have had no chance to survive with that number of lawmen acting against him. He had been in a capture or death situation, and now he was a prisoner; but he had been a prisoner before and had managed to escape. Why would this time be different?

After some miles the lawmen stopped the train and allowed Campbell and Hardy off, as there were no charges against them. Hutchinson and Perdue now were informed as to who Swain really was; Armstrong offered them $500 for their assistance. Just before Whiting, Alabama, the train stopped again to allow Chipley and Duncan off to search for Brown Bowen. They would meet Armstrong in Whiting, with or without Bowen.

On the next day, August 24, Armstrong and Duncan with their prisoner reached Montgomery, Alabama. The exhausted lawmen placed Hardin in the jail and then checked into a hotel to get some needed rest. On the twenty-fifth, at Verbena, Armstrong sent another telegram to Adjutant General Steele, in which he expressed confidence that all was well and they would soon get to Austin with the most wanted man in Texas: "It is all day now [.] on our way [.] papers O K[.]"[11] At Montgomery they had learned a mob waited, which intended to take their prisoner away; somehow Duncan had learned of this and had avoided this mob. At Decatur, Alabama, some 140 miles north of Verbena, they allowed the prisoner to write a letter to his wife. Armstrong apparently had obtained some stationery, in this case the letterhead of attorneys at law J. S. Clark and David P. Lewis, and, presumably, with the cuffs on, John Wesley Hardin wrote to Jane. At the top he scrawled a note to Allen Marion Mc-Millan[12], asking him: "I Hope [you] will consider Janes circumstances and Help Her all you can," in other words, help her with the three young children. His letter began:

> My Dear Wife and children this is the first time that I have had an opportunity of writing you a Letter Since I was arrested in pensacolia [*sic*]. Jane they Had me foul yes very foul [.] I was Sitting in the Smoking car Neal C [Campbell] & poor (Jimmie M) [Mann] By my Side with my arms Stratched [*sic*] on the Side when they co me in. 4 men grabed [*sic*] me one by each arm and one by each Leg so the[y] Stratched me locking and quick. But poor Jimmie he Broke to run out of the cars and was Shot dead by some of the crowd on the out Side [.]

Hardin, obviously aware that these Rangers wanted to take him back to Texas alive, attempted to assure Jane he would be safe and also to console her for her additional responsibilities in her raising the three children alone. He had to have known that he would have to stand at least one trial and that could take months. He continued:

> Jane I am in good Hands now they treat me Better than you have any Idea and assure me that I will not Be mobed [*sic*] and that when I get there that the Governor will Protect me from a mob and that I will hav[e] the Law [.] Jane bein [good] cheer and don't take trouble to Heart But look to the Bright Side [.] Jane I have not murded [*sic*] any Body Nor Robed [*sic*] any one But what I have done in Texas was to Save my Life [and] Jane time will Bring [*sic, bear*] me out[.]

He then explained to her that he had been able to have an attorney the previous day and attempted to be released on a writ of *habeas corpus* but the Rangers were able to show the proper papers for his arrest, convincing the judge he was indeed John Wesley Hardin, and thus was not released. His letter continued:

> Jane I got a rit of Habas corpus [*sic*] yesterday But fail[ed] to get out my trial was Set for tuesday but a requisition come for John Wesley Hardin Last Night. So they Say & Swore that I was the man J. W. Hardin that Killed Web[b] of Comanchie Texas [.] So they Had to give me up [.] Jane be cautious in writing me for they will examine your Letters before I see them & Direct your letters to Austin texas to J H Swain[.]

Now he attempted to give her further assurances that this particular trial would not last long, and she should feel confident that the day would come when they would be together again. He continued:

> Jane they can Never Hang me nor penitenchry [*sic*] me for Live [*sic, life*] by Law times are not like they was when we left Texas

[as] Mob law is played out [.] Jane I expect that it is a Good thing they caught me the way they did for they had 40 men withe the Shariffe and Deputie of pensicolia So you See I would have been a corps [*sic*] Now instead of Being a prisner if they Had not Stratched me as they did [.] Jane I had no Show to get my pistol if I Had I would Have Been Killed [as] my Hands were caught the first pass[.] Jane I am in Good Hopes yet— write to me at austin Texas [.]

And now he took the opportunity to explain to Jane why he was captured when he was:

Jane Brown's Bad conduct caused me to get caught in Pensicolia and all so his Last Letter to Texas Stating that his sister Joines Him in Sending Love to all [.] the Detective was Boarding at N B [Neill Bowen's] When the Letter come an[d] watched them put the Letter away and then Stole the Letter out N.B. thought the man Mr Williams to be a merchant wanting to rent the Store Hous [.]

And now Hardin knew full well who his captor was:

But His name is John Dunkan [*sic*] a State Detective of Texas [.] Jane B. [Brown] is the cause of my arrest. Jane go to your F [father] as Soon as possible and then You can come to See me if you wish do not Give up where there is a will there is a way [and] Remember 1874 & 1872 So Good By my Dear Wife (You Hav[e] ever Been True) remember me to the children and also to all my friends and do the Best You can [.] Tell you[r] connection your circumstances So Good By Dearest one [.][13]

He signed it "J. H. Swain." No doubt the "1874" and "1872" refers to the chaotic life they led following the Comanche tragedies; 1872 may refer to the crisis of Hardin being so severely wounded by Phil Sublett and the subsequent arrest and being jailed in Gonzales, and his escape.

Also on the twenty-fifth of August, the press issued a telegram date-lined Whiting, Alabama. It was reprinted not only in numerous Texas newspapers but also in the *Atlanta Constitution*, the *Chicago Tribune*, and the *New York Times* and no doubt many others. Of the extensive newspaper publicity Hardin received, this telegram received the greatest circulation.

> Whiting, Ala., August 24—To-day [*sic*] as the train was leaving Pensacola, Florida the sheriff, with a posse, boarded the cars to assist two Texas officials to arrest the notorious John Wesley Hardin, who is said to have committed twenty-seven murders, and for whose body four thousand dollars reward has been of-fered by an act of the Legislature of Texas. His last murder in Texas was the killing of the sheriff of Comanche County [*sic*]. He has lived in Florida for years as John Swain, and being re-lated to county officers, has escaped arrest. About twenty shots were fired in making the arrest. Hardin's companion, named Mann, who had a pistol in his hand, was killed.[14]

Although there were a few minor errors in this news report, the name of John Wesley Hardin of Texas was spread across the land. Armstrong, Duncan, Hutchinson, Perdue, Chipley—none was mentioned by name.

Hardin recalled that there was one opportunity for him to escape, but the sharp eyes of the detective from Dallas prevented it. He wrote that his guards "were kind to me, but they were most vigilant. By promising to be quiet I had caused them to relax somewhat, and they appeared anxious to treat me kindly, but they knew their life depended on how they used me." Hardin thought it was in Decatur where they stopped to change cars, got rooms and ordered meals. When their meal arrived Hardin asked that his cuffs be removed. "Armstrong," he wrote, "unlocked the jewelry and started to turn around, exposing his six-shooter to me, when Jack jerked

Jane Bowen Hardin's third child, Jane. *Courtesy the Robert G. McCubbin Collection.*

him around and pulled his pistol at the same time. 'Look out,' he said, 'John will kill us and escape.'" Hardin laughed at them both, ridiculing the idea, but he almost managed to get a pistol and perhaps would have shot one or both of the Rangers. This is what Hardin wrote.[15] Duncan recalled that it was somewhere in Arkansas that he saw Hardin had a knife up his sleeve, but "I took it out and threw it out of the car window. Then, John Wesley Hardin broke down and cried. We told him to behave himself and we would get along all right, and then he asked us if an attempt was made to lynch him would we give him a pistol to defend himself with." The answer was that he would be armed, and that he would not be mobbed.[16]

On August 27 the train carrying Hardin crossed into Texas and arrived in Austin the next day. Hardin was placed in the new Travis County jail, fortunately not the old one that had caused such a public outcry.

As Hardin was on the train rushing back to Texas he certainly was concerned for Jane and the children and their immediate welfare, but what of brother-in-law Brown Bowen? Hardin had no real idea of how much help Allen Marion McMillan could give his family, and he could not expect Brown to be of much help either; he also could not have known others were working on capturing Bowen. One wonders if his feelings against Brown were now stronger than his concern for Jane's welfare. One newspaper report provided an interesting word picture which may hold some facts, but portions are definitely fictitious. A Montgomery reporter described that a woman, "with a child six weeks old" had come up from Pollard on August 26 and "represented herself" as Mrs. Hardin. Some of what was written was accurate, that she was the daughter of a "gentleman" named Bowen, that she had married Hardin about six years before, they had three children, and that she was present when Webb was killed, meaning she was in Comanche, but not at the street when the killing took place. She told the reporter that she intended to get back to Texas "as soon as possible" but had little hope of seeing him again as he would probably be killed before he ever got to Texas. She also said two other men, "Dickerson and Taylor" were "engaged" in the shooting, which resulted in Webb's death. The reporter must have misunderstood her when he wrote that "both of whom were caught and hung by the Rangers" as it was only Dixon hung, along with his brother and Hardin's brother. Certainly Jane knew that so we must blame the reporter for this misinformation. "This woman," continued the reporter, "has the bearing and converses like a person of much more than ordinary nerve and courage. She boasts of being able to shoot and manage a horse as well as most men, and says things will be made extremely lively for Armstrong and Duncan . . . and also for some others who had a hand in the capture of Hardin." She may have actually made these threats, or the reporter may have added them for dramatic effect. Jane Hardin was described as "21 or 22 years of age" and "seems to be very well educated and speaks fluently, expressing her feelings with much force." Jane may have seemed "very well educated," but it is difficult to determine much about that aspect of her being; apparently no letters she wrote to her imprisoned husband have survived so it is impossible to comment with any degree of accuracy about her formal education. Probably it was no more than a rudimentary education, unlike her husband's whose father was a teacher as well as a minister. The reporter concluded with this amazing statement, that in Texas, "she has a good competency, consisting of a fine plantation well stocked, given her by her father on her marriage to Hardin." [17] Neill Bowen may have had some acreage to farm, but he had no plantation of any significance.

Armstrong and Duncan alone faced the responsibility of delivering their prisoner to the Travis County jail; what of the men who were involved in the capture who were left behind? Sheriff Hutchinson had a dead man lying on the train platform. Presumably the body was carried to the city morgue, or his home per the custom of the day, and the family notified. He also was obligated to give at least a big thank you to the twenty or more deputies he had arranged to be on the station platform to assist as needed, although for the most part they did nothing except several may have shot at Mann as he left the train car. Armstrong had shot him, but reportedly he had received numerous balls once outside of the train car. Hutchinson had been promised a portion of the reward, and he certainly obliged himself to give part of it to deputy Perdue, and perhaps divide some of it among the other deputies. William D. Chipley, the only one not a lawman involved in the capture, continued working with railroads, providing and improving transportation for the Florida Panhandle.[18] Hutchinson continued in law enforcement for one more term, was re-elected in 1880 but after the second term chose not to run again. His career was not nearly as full as Chipley's had been.[19]

Neither Hutchinson's name, nor that of Deputy Perdue, was mentioned in Hardin's autobiography, only the names of Armstrong and Duncan. As most of what has been written about Hardin is based on Hardin's *Life*, those two Florida officers have been largely ignored. Hutchinson's action, with Chipley and Perdue, of physically grabbing Hardin's arms and legs, guaranteed the success of the capture, preventing Hardin from getting his hands on his pistol. Hardin himself said he was at the point of getting his pistol when the men seized him, thus saving Armstrong's life.

Although there was a large reward offered for Hardin's capture, how much was divided up among those involved in the capture remains to be determined. Armstrong or Duncan may have promised the others $500, but they certainly did not have that with them when they arrived in Pensacola. Whatever oral arrangement or promise was made, and how much was actually paid, Hutchinson was not satisfied. On September 6, 1877, he left for Austin to discuss with Texas officials the disposition of the reward. The *Dallas Herald* reported his trip was for the purpose of arguing "his claims for a division of the reward offered by the state for the arrest of John Wesley Hardin." The *Herald* quoted a telegram it had received from Hutchinson: "I captured and forwarded John Wesley Hardin, the noted Texas outlaw. Please telegraph me amount of authoritative reward offered." The *Herald* indicated that Hutchinson was probably "left out" as Armstrong and Duncan had already drawn the $4,000 reward. If this was true, no official record of the reward being paid to anyone other than Armstrong and Duncan has been located.[20]

Years later, shortly after the August 19, 1895, death of Hardin, Hutchinson wrote a lengthy letter to the *Dallas Herald* in which he gave his account of the capture. He began his letter explaining that the official version as printed in the newspapers about Hardin's life and capture was "so strongly at variance with the actual arrest, that at the insistence of many friends" he was advised to furnish the real details. Hutchinson claimed that he met the Texas officers at the state line as they had "lost all trace of Hardin." He had then telegraphed his deputy A. J. Perdue, "who has since died, who was as brave a man as ever lived" and who notified him that their man was there in Pensacola. In this version Hutchinson claimed that he and Perdue entered the car together, and that the sheriff knew who Hardin was. Hutchinson brushed past Hardin, then "suddenly wheeled" and said, "I believe I want you." Hardin replied, "D –n you, take that" and struck Hutchinson "in the lower part of the abdomen with both heels, from the effect of which up to this date I have never recovered." As Hardin sprang up Hutchinson struck him "across the face with a pistol." He and Perdue then seized Hardin, and in the process discovered Hardin had a pistol concealed between his shirt and undershirt. Hutchinson grabbed the pistol, tearing the shirt, "and tossed it out into the car." Up to that point the struggle was Hardin against Hutchinson and Perdue alone, but needing more help, the sheriff called to Mr. John E. Callaghan[21] who quickly responded and together they subdued Hardin and tied his feet together with a rope. Then, still according to Hutchinson's version, J. W. Mann "becoming badly frightened" jumped up and attempted to escape through an open window, and "while in the position of leaping, was shot from the outside of the car." Then, and not until then, Armstrong and Duncan entered the car. With their prisoner, Armstrong and Duncan, with Hutchinson and Perdue, headed north. After a few miles the sheriff instructed his deputy to turn the prisoner over to the Texans at the state line, "which was carried out to the letter in an orderly and quiet manner, shaking hands in parting from Hardin and telling him he regretted the necessity of arresting him." At this point Hardin supposedly remarked: "I have killed twenty-seven men, and Hutch, you came near being the twenty-eighth."[22]

This is a remarkable version of the arrest, and it is strange that for eighteen years Hutchinson kept his anger within. Why did he not communicate this to the Dallas newspaper, or any Texan newspaper, within the weeks or months or the years following the capture? It would be very interesting to know what Hardin would have said in response to it. Hutchinson obviously believed Armstrong and Duncan cheated him. He admitted he knew nothing about the trip back to Texas, but "out of the promised rewards, aggregating several thousand dollars, I was the recipient of a paltry $500, which was given to those assisting me in the capture outside of Lieut. Armstrong and Duncan." How much accuracy there is in these lines is difficult to say, and one does suspect that by 1895 Hutchinson had brooded over his part in the capture and selfishly felt he ought to have received more of the reward than he did. Perhaps through the years his actual participation in the arrest became blurred to the point that in his mind he and Perdue alone accomplished what in reality was a combined accomplishment of the four. Even if one were to dismiss the entire Hutchinson version of what happened that August twenty-third, we do learn that deputy A. J. Perdue had passed on, no longer able in 1895 to give his version of what happened that day. Another question that now cannot be answered is that if Sheriff Hutchinson did know the real identity of the peaceable Mr. Swain, why did he not arrest him before the Texas officers came? If he had, he, and presumably his faithful deputy A. J. Perdue, would have had not only the reward but also the glory. The fact remains however that the wording of the reward stated that it was to be paid to whoever *delivered* Hardin inside the doors of the Travis County jail; this Armstrong and Duncan did, and Hutchinson did not.[23]

And what of Joshua Robert Brown Bowen? When he left Texas, thanks to Hardin and others liberating him from the Gonzales County jail, he fled to Santa Rosa County, Florida, some 600 miles east of Gonzales. He claimed he reached Florida in September 1873, which may be correct, as he claimed that he had nothing to do with the troubles between the Suttons and the Taylors. In Texas the cattle industry dominated; in his new home area of the Florida Panhandle the logging industry dominated. Along with partner Sheppard Hardy the pair developed their own "industry" on the Styx River; logging for them may have been honest labor, or at times they stole logs instead of cattle and horses.

But Bowen did find time to court Mary Catherine Mayo and they were married in 1875, although no license has been located. Born in September 1858, she was seventeen years old when she tied the knot with this Texas fugitive. One son was born to the couple, whom they named Neil, named after Brown's father, born in 1876. A wife and son did not change Bowen's life style: rumors circulated that he had killed several men in Texas as well as in Florida. Humorist Alexander Sweet of the Sweet &

Knox team of authors referred to a "fatal misunderstanding in Florida" but paraphrased Bowen in commenting on it: "Although he had killed several men in Florida, he did not feel the slightest compunction. His conscience only troubled him about his Texas misdeeds. What happened beyond the State line was wholly immaterial to him." Sweet knew how to turn a discussion of murder into a humorous comment, "This was the first time," he added dryly, "that I had heard of a man's conscience being affected by geographical boundary-lines." [24]

Bowen's undoing, which resulted in his and Hardin's capture was his row with Colonel Chipley. The *Pensacola Gazette* reported the argument, ending with Chipley taking Bowen's own pistol from him and then striking him over the head with it. Chipley described the incident of "knocking him down and continuing his moral and healthy exercise until my weapon was spoiled and his head too. Bowen yelled for mercy. . . ." [25] Chipley was a businessman to the core and five days following Hardin's capture he wrote Gov. Richard B. Hubbard of Texas urging that he offer a reward for Bowen, in order that he (Chipley) could cover his expenses if it was necessary to follow Bowen any distance. Chipley anticipated Bowen would attempt to lose himself in southern Florida. He concluded, "Bowen tried to assassinate me while on my depot platform [. I was] a perfect stranger to him. . . . I nearly killed him at the punishment I gave him." [26] Chipley concluded his letter pointing out that Lieutenant Armstrong had assured him that a reward would be forthcoming. In April that year the reward for Bowen was $350; on September 4 Governor Hubbard telegraphed Chipley that the reward was increased to $500, to be paid when the prisoner was delivered to the Gonzales County jail. Armstrong, in his August 24 telegram to Adjutant General Steele, had informed him "[I] Have arranged to have Bowen captured" which presumably meant he and Chipley, and perhaps Hutchinson as well, were looking for him. Bowen had good reason to fear for his own continued liberty.

Bowen did not remain a fugitive for long. The Montgomery newspaper reported, while the news of Hardin's arrest was still fresh, "One of Hardin's supposed confederates was arrested near Pensacola Junction

[September 17], and was sent to Texas in charge of Florida officials yesterday. He is the same man who made the attack on Col. W. D. Chipley several week[s] ago." [27] With Hardin and Bowen out of the country citizens of Escambia and Santa Rosa counties in the Florida Panhandle could feel more secure in their homes. Sheriff Hutchinson was still alert however, as on October 26 he arrested Henry Sutton, reportedly Bowen's father-in-law, along with a man identified only as McCall. They were described as "chums of John Wesley Hardin." These arrests disposed of "the gang which has so long bid raw defiance hereabouts." [28]

CHAPTER 14

HARDIN ON TRIAL

"I want justice. I want to be dealt with according to law. All I ask is legal protection against mobs."

John Wesley Hardin, August 28, 1877

rmstrong and Duncan arrived in Texas on August 27. From Longview Duncan sent a telegram to his brother S. W. S. Duncan informing him where they were and that they were "all safe" and that they would arrive in Austin the following day.[1] All along the way, once the news was out that Hardin the man-killer was on the train, people crowded the depots desperate to glimpse the notorious desperado. At Palestine, the county seat of Anderson County, a reporter provided a brief description for his readers. Working his way closer amongst the hundreds of people there he saw that Hardin was "heavily ironed with shackles and handcuffs." He also saw the Rangers; the trio had to disembark to change trains before they "took supper" there at the La Clede hotel on Spring Street, where proprietor James Denyven provided meals to travelers at all hours.[2] Someone in the throng called out, "What have you got there?" Aware only of guarding their $4,000 prisoner, neither Armstrong nor Duncan thought of an answer, but Hardin did and responded: "A panther." At supper they chanced to remove Hardin's handcuffs and he "ate quite heartily and unconcernedly, his manner being easy and indifferent." Hardin's attire even brought attention, "quite ordinary" to the reporter's eyes, "the Texas white wool hat with dark alpaca coat. His health is good and robust." A final word of assurance was that "there is no doubt of his identity."[3]

The train reached Austin the morning of August 28. The "large crowd" at the depot wanting to see the prisoner was disappointed, as Hardin was slipped out the rear of the train into a carriage with the curtains drawn.[4] He recalled the arrival in Austin with greater drama, relating that his "guards learned that there was a tremendous crowd at the depot" and therefore stopped the train and rode in a "hack for the jail." When the crowd at the depot learned of the trick the people "broke for the jail" and the hack "just did manage to get there first, and they carried me bodily into the jail; so when the crowd arrived, they failed to see the great curiosity." [5] While Sheriff Dennis Corwin[6] and his deputies dealt with how best to deal with the publicity, Hardin wrote to friends and relatives, perhaps requesting them to come and see him as he had been out of the state for over three years. He also was thinking about attorneys for his defense. As people applied to Sheriff Corwin to see Hardin, he realized there were numerous prisoners he knew, some as friends but some as enemies. Relatives included cousin Mannen Clements, charged with a Gonzales County killing; Bill Taylor was there, between court appearances on trial for the killing of Gabriel Webster Slaughter back in 1874; George Gladden and John Ringo were there as well, imprisoned for their activities during the Mason County "Hoo Doo" War; John Collins and Jefferson Ake were there as well, but perhaps most interesting among the eighty prisoners there were "several from DeWitt [County]," although not identified by name.[7] Hardin certainly recognized them as they were also participants in the bloody Sutton-Taylor Feud; these men were charged with the 1876 cold-blooded killing of Dr. Brassell and his son. Those DeWitt County prisoners were William D. Meador, Nicholas J. "Jake" Ryan, David Augustine, James Hester, Charles H. Heissig, Joseph Sitterle and William Cox. What Hardin and Cox may have said to each other, if they were within "talking" distance, may have been unprintable, as Hardin was involved in the shotgun ambush of Cox's father, James W. Cox.

Almost immediately the crowd of curious onlookers as well as the press discussed how many men the jail's most famous prisoner had killed. Of the nearly eighty prisoners confined, the *Galveston Daily News* announced that "many are considered as desperate characters as Hardin" and further commented: "No one can make a complete list of Hardin's victims, but the number will not probably fall short of twenty-three— eight in Kansas and the [Oklahoma] Territory and fifteen in Texas." To create a better picture of the man for those who could not see him in person, the *News* added: "He is about five feet ten inches high, 28 years old, stoutly built and intelligent." [8] He would not be 28 until 1881.

On August 28 the *News* reporter was able to have a lengthy conversation with the prisoner. His telegraphed report from Austin to Galveston was headlined "Interviewing the Man-Killer" and pointed out to all that Hardin was beginning to "realize the perils of his situation" and that was why he was "very cautious in replying to his questions." He began his report with Hardin's physical description: 25 years of age, "very stout and compactly built, weighing about 150 pounds, height five feet 10 inches, light hair and flaxen beard, and intelligent." Hardin revealed he had subscribed to the *News* while in Jacksonville, but had it sent to him as Swain, not Hardin. Proving that he was an intelligent man, in answer to the reporter's questions about various "troubles" he answered, "I don't think it would be proper for me to tell you about my killing anyone; but my first trouble was with the Yankees and the State Police." Had he forgotten about that first black man he had killed, Maje, or didn't he count a former slave?

In answer to suspected troubles in Kansas and the Indian Territory Hardin replied: "I had no trouble there." He then asked the reporter to read back what he had written, which displeased him; he said, "It might appear I said I have killed somebody. I don't want to deny, and I don't want to affirm I've killed anybody. . . . No, I never had any troubles except in Texas." Either Hardin had forgotten about the killings on the Newton Prairie and Juan Bideno and the troubles in Abilene—or else perhaps he had his own definition of what constituted a trouble. What happened in the Territory and Kansas was something else.

But now the reporter asked about Comanche, inquiring as to what he was doing there that day. "I was in the stock business, and had a herd of

800 cattle gone on to Kansas, and was on the way there in company with Jim Taylor, my wife having gone to Comanche where I had a father, J. G. Hardin, and my mother and a brother, Joe G. Hardin, who was afterward killed by a mob without any indictments against him anywhere. I went there on my business, and had no idea of any trouble." Like a man who was well aware that anything he said could ultimately be used against him, he pointed out that he had never had any type of a trial.

"But I have never had any showing in Texas. In the first place the Yankees and State police got after me and tried to arrest me without any warrants. I never yet got into any difficulty with legal officers; it was always mobs or Yankees, or State police." Obviously, at this point, Hardin did not consider Capt. John R. Waller a "legal officer"; nor State Police wearing a uniform and a badge, such as John Henry Hopkins Speights, as a legal officer. One wonders if he had forgotten Jeremiah Alexander Ferguson, one-time policeman, who had helped him escape from the trouble at Hemphill. To continue with the response, Hardin explained: "I was at Comanche about three weeks before the killing of Webb; was passing my time as pleasantly as possible, not expecting anything up to the hour of the Webb killing, and I think if I can get the protection that the law should give me I will come clear of killing Webb for he fired the first shot."

From the subject of Webb and Comanche the reporter inquired of trials. "I never stood a trial in my life; never had a fair showing. When the Legislature passed a law offering a reward for me I heard of it immediately. I never would have left Comanche except for fear of the mob—knowing that my brother and relatives had been hung by the mob. I have never feared the law and I do not fear it yet, and am perfectly willing to stand the law." If this reporter had asked him why he struggled so hard when the lawmen had arrested him, his answer no doubt would have been that he thought they were robbers ready to steal his gambling winnings.

Then the reporter followed through with more questions, which he described as "numerous and diversified." Hardin told of his movement from the time he left Comanche until he was arrested. He said he had learned of the $4,000 reward while he was in Gainesville, Florida; that after Comanche he went to Austin and then Gonzales. From Gonzales he went to New Iberia, Louisiana, accompanied by a friend whom he refused to identify. From New Iberia he then went to New Orleans where he met his wife, all the time traveling under the name of Walker. From New Orleans they went to Cedar Keys, Florida. "I went there for refuge from the mob." At this time he seriously thought of leaving the United States, perhaps locating in England, but instead they stopped in Gainesville where he bought out merchant Sam Burnett. At this point he recalled he went into the grocery and liquor business. Curiously, he added: "No, I never drank much."

At Gainesville he sold out the business and then moved to Jacksonville, "taking a drove of cattle, expecting to sell them to the butchers." But for a reason he did not explain to the *News* reporter, he said he "set up shop and went into the butcher business." He made no mention of the Haddock firm that he later discussed in his autobiography. He said he had "considerable money when I left Texas" but that he was forced to leave again after staying in Jacksonville from July 1875 to July 1876. He explained he was "forced to leave by detectives having found me out." Hardin "found out the detectives at the same time they found me out, and escaped before they could get papers from the Governor." He made no reference to them being killed.

By then Jane was spending time with relatives in the "eastern portion of Florida" while he went to Eufaula, Alabama, "and finding that my wife passed on with Gus Kennedy, I followed her to her kin folks" and remained there ever since.

But now an important question was posed, dealing with his whereabouts during recent killings in DeWitt County, during the Sutton-Taylor Feud. Hardin explained: "Sometimes I concluded I would come back and surrender, but was afraid of the mob, thinking I would not get the protection of the law. I never have been in Texas since 1874, and can prove it. I have not been anywhere except in Florida and Alabama, and I do not know anything about the murders they charge me with in that time. No, I was not back in De Witt county. I don't want to say anything about the

De Witt county murders. Never helped to break a jail in all my life, but I took legal process and got men out; but if a man was not a man of honor I never helped him at all." Had Hardin forgotten about the delivery of Brown Bowen from the Gonzales County jail, and also the burning of the jail when Eli was burned alive? Apparently so.

The reporter's questions were not recorded but almost invariably the question can be deduced from the answer Hardin gave. "I never had anything to do with horse thieves or robbers; I always avoided them. I had nothing to do with them in any shape or fashion. On the other hand, I have tried to bring them to justice. I could state instances, but don't feel disposed." What about William P. Longley, which brought about this response: "I don't know Longley or any of those parties; have no acquaintances of that kind. They have done all manner of crimes and laid them on to me; but I never had anything to do with them. I always went on my own hook." At this time "Bloody Bill" Longley was a prisoner in the Lee County jail in Giddings, east of Austin. Texas lawmen Milton Mast, sheriff of Nacogdoches County, his deputy William M. Burrows, and a constable of DeSoto Parish, Louisiana, had captured Longley on June 6, 1877. On September 11 Longley was sentenced to hang for one of his murders; he appealed and while waiting the result of the appeal was incarcerated in the more secure jail in Galveston.[9] Longley was never placed in the Travis County jail.

But did Hardin ever operate with a gang? "No, I never was leader of any band, and I never was with any large party, except to lead a party down in De Witt and Gonzales, and that difficulty was settled by both parties signing a pledge that they would let the matter alone and that neither party would take up arms only for legal purposes, which agreement I have kept up to the present hour. I quelled that trouble when I was at the head of one of the parties. I never helped mob any one; no one was killed when we made that agreement. The papers were signed peacefully, and no one was murdered." Here Hardin was referring to the peace treaty signed by numerous members of both feuding parties on August 12, 1873. Hardin signed this treaty but his name does not appear on the second treaty of January 3, 1874. He conveniently overlooked mentioning the plan to attack the Tumlinson home and burn out Captain Joe and whichever other Sutton followers may have been therein. The intent was to kill them as they ran from the burning house; but no one was "murdered" because the sheriff and a posse of citizens prevented that from happening and forced the two parties to sign a "peace treaty." Hardin easily provided selective answers to the reporter's questions.

Of the Pensacola capture what did he have to say? "When they arrested me the other day they kidnapped me and had no papers. No paper was shown me until we got to Montgomery. I [would have] got out on a writ of habeas corpus there, but the Judge had not nerve enough to stand by the law, so they kept on to Texas with me. I have never seen any indictment; don't know what the charges are. I think they want me for Comanche. They have said so. I am not afraid to go there, except from the mob. If I can get protection from the Governor against the mobs I am willing to go; more than willing to abide by the law."

A final question dealt with Senator John Stephens, who had backed the large reward for Hardin's capture. Had not Hardin threatened his life? "No, I never threatened Senator Stephens or any Representatives; never did it. When Stephens had the bill passed offering a reward for me, and was so scared of his life, I was not here in Austin, and would not have hurt him, for I did not know anything against him in particular. If I had wanted to hurt him I could have managed some plan to get at him. I never threatened him. They were all false reports, or else he had a guilty conscience." Following this statement Hardin provided a brief sketch of his life. He continued to stress what he wanted: "I want justice; I want to be dealt with according to law. All I ask is legal protection against mobs." He refused to discuss Helm's death, or the deaths of any "State Policemen and Yankee soldiers attributed to him—or to detail his connection with the feud in De Witt, or to admit any of the murders in Kansas and elsewhere, which it is so popularly believed he committed."

The reporter, pleased no doubt that he had been able to interview Hardin but perhaps disappointed that the "man-killer" had not been more forthright with him about certain accusations, was ready to conclude. He added rather ominously a statement that may have caused Senator Stephens to increase whatever security he may have had: "The county judge has given notice to the jailer that the county would not pay a cent for [additional] guards, and as escapes have been made from the same jail, it is not altogether improbable that Mr. Hardin will yet have a chance to get at the Senator from Comanche." [10]

Hardin soon had another relative in the jail—Joshua Robert Brown Bowen—recently captured in Florida. Florida officials, perhaps Col. W. D. Chipley himself with several deputies, delivered him to Austin on September 24. Chipley had arrested Bowen on September 17. Bowen was charged with the murder of Thomas Haldeman, although it was suspected he was guilty of several other murders as well. It was the Haldeman murder for which he was to be tried. [11]

Hardin was no model prisoner but he was sociable to reporters. Even at this stage of his confinement, with no attorneys as yet, he was attempting to provide a wrongly accused persona for public consumption. In mid-September another Austin reporter visited the jail. Sheriff Dennis Corwin courteously provided a tour of the facility, and the reporter concluded that "it matter not how many fiends we might have on the outside," there would be "no hope of getting out of that jail, nor out of the grasp of Sheriff Corwin." He interviewed Hardin, "briefly" and reported he was confined in the same "apartment or cage" with Bill Taylor and Jack Day, a relative of Taylor. Hardin again was talkative, pointing out that he had read several accounts of his capture and stated that all "were full of errors." He was aware of rumors that increased his reputation as a man-killer and bloody murderer. One rumor depicted him as often experiencing terrible dreams from which he would awake screaming from the torments. A St. Louis, Missouri, hotel clerk supposedly was now a cripple from having disturbed Hardin during one of his "spasms." This matter was apparently brought up by the *News* reporter, and Hardin denied ever being in Missouri. He further denied that he ever knew Bill Longley, which statement suggests the poker game he later described

William Taylor, slayer of Gabriel Webster Slaughter in 1874. *Author's Collection.*

in his *Life* was a total fiction; he stated that the civil officers in Florida were not entitled "to either credit or money for their aid in his late capture." This would suggest that Hardin implied only Armstrong and Duncan should receive any "credit or money." He also stated he was glad to hear of the governor's determination to send a strong escort with him to Comanche and that "he hoped to be protected from mob violence and wanted to have a fair, speedy trial." The trial, Hardin knew, would begin on the fourth Monday of September. The reporter concluded his report saying Hardin was "certainly as mild-mannered a man as any one we ever saw in such a fix" and hoped he and his "cagemates" would have "a quick and fair trial." [12]

Ranger John B. Armstrong had, on August 24, the day after he and Duncan and others captured Hardin, telegraphed Adjutant General Steele that he had "arranged" to have Bowen captured. Presumably this arrangement was with Colonel Chipley, as Chipley did make the arrest, although no details have yet surfaced. Their prisoner was turned over to Sheriff Corwin on September 24. Chipley received some attention in the press: "[Bowen] was arrested by Major Chipley, the same railroad man who held the train until Armstrong could get Hardin on it. There is a small reward for him." [13]

Hardin recalled he was kept in the Austin jail until late September. When all was readied to transport him to Comanche for trial he met N. O. Reynolds, lieutenant of Company E of the Frontier Battalion of Texas Rangers, who would deliver him to Comanche for trial. Hardin counted the guard as numbering thirty-five, which included Comanche County sheriff Frank Wilson and his several deputies. "The reason I was guarded by such a strong escort," Hardin explained later, "was because they were afraid that the brutal mob who had hung my relatives would hang me." [14] Hardin consistently spoke of dreading "the mob" as if the men who had lynched his brother Joe and the Dixon brothers were organized so well that now, over three years later, they could prove deadly again. He could not have forgotten the mob activity back in Florida, which resulted in the burning death of the prisoner Eli, and his own role in it. Hardin may have learned about the mob action in Mason County through reading the newspapers. There a mob broke into the county jail and took five men out intending to string them up to a convenient tree. The timely arrival of the sheriff interrupted this "neck-tie party" that did nevertheless leave two men dead from hanging and one shot to death. This had occurred in February 1875 and with Hardin's relatives corresponding with Mr. or Mrs. J. H. Swain he could easily have learned of it. [15]

While writing his autobiography Hardin remembered N. O. Reynolds, whose full name was Nelson Orcelus Reynolds, only recently named lieutenant commander of Company E of the Frontier Battalion. [16] During September Sheriff Corwin may have felt the pressure of such an important responsibility. He knew that there was no funding for additional guards, but fortunately Reynolds provided the help he needed. On September 3 he sent Corp. J. W. Warren with five Rangers to the new Travis County jail to give Sheriff Corwin additional help. This new county jail was considered to be one of the strongest in the state of Texas, but shortly after Hardin arrived the jailer discovered someone was trying to cut through the bars. They searched the cells but found no saw or knife. It is unknown how many cells, or "cages" there were, and there is no known image of the jail's interior. But Corporal Warren, the Rangers, Sheriff Corwin and his deputies prevented any prisoner from escaping.[17]

On September 19 Reynolds and his company loaded John Wesley Hardin into a buggy to begin the long 140-mile trek to Comanche. There was excitement all over Austin, and one of the Rangers, James B. Gillett, remembered his experience that day for years. He wrote:

> The rangers were drawn up just outside the jail, and [Private] Henry Thomas and myself were ordered to enter the prison and escort Hardin out. Heavily shackled and handcuffed, the prisoner walked very slowly between us. The boy who had sold fish and game on the streets of Austin was now guarding the most dangerous criminal in Texas; it was glory enough for me.[18]

A large crowd gathered at the jail to see Hardin, described by the *Statesman* as the "noted knight of the six-shooter," and he at first appeared nervous but then "became complacent and appeared pleasant," conversing with Sheriff Corwin and other guards. The departure from Austin proved uneventful, as it should have been with such a heavy guard. Reynolds' men, Sheriff Wilson of Comanche County, and an unknown number of deputies, the aggregate numbering thirty-five if we accept Hardin's count as accurate.

When the Rangers reached Lampasas on September 21, some sixty or more miles from Austin, people again gathered in the street to see him. The local newspaper, the *Lampasas Dispatch*, commented that more people had "rushed to see him than if he had been a rhinoceros, and he seemed not to be displeased with the eager attention shown him." [19] Quite possibly members of the two former feuding parties, the Horrells and the Higgins, were in the crowd to see the celebrity. Out on bond, some members of the two families were awaiting their own trials for acts committed prior to their peace treaty.

Hardin with his heavily armed escort arrived in Comanche on September 23, having averaged twenty-eight miles a day. Reporter Knix, sent to Comanche from Dallas to cover the trial, was ready with pen and paper. About 10:00 a.m. "the town was under some excitement, as well as interest, on hearing that John Wesley Hardin was coming to town." The news "spread like lightning, and in a few seconds everybody had left their employment to get a glimpse of him. Crowds had gathered along the streets where he had to pass, eagerly awaiting his arrival." [20]

To Hardin, the object of all this attention, the group presented a "military appearance" with him being in a buggy with Sheriff Wilson, with most of the company in front and the others bringing up the rear. Each night camp was prepared with guards rotating, and all that could reasonably be done to keep Hardin comfortable was done, even though he was kept shackled and cuffed. At Comanche the Rangers had to lift him from the buggy and carry him into the jail bodily, as he "was too heavily shackled to walk." [21]

Pvt. Mervyn Bathurst Davis, one of Reynolds' Rangers, provided an important description of delivering Hardin to Comanche and how he fared on the route. During the five days traveling between Austin and Comanche, Hardin "deported himself with the utmost decorum, evincing no restlessness, though his patience was sorely tried by the gaping crowds who gathered at the noon and evening camps to stare him in the face, with a curiosity that knew no sense of delicacy." Did he display anger or sullenness? To the contrary, Hardin was "quite communicative, talking freely of his terrible adventures, expressing regrets for what he termed his errors, and hopes for the future." If Hardin shared any of his "hopes for the future" Ranger Mervyn failed to record them. He did provide an accurate description, portraying him as "what the ladies would call a blonde, about five feet ten inches high; wears his whiskers in the French style, and is fairly educated in English and the common school branches." Hardin had received a number of wounds in those adventures, and suffered from one bullet wound in particular, perhaps the wound inflicted by Phil Sublett, or maybe Charles M. Webb.

Mervyn described the Comanche jail as "a small stone building thickly walled, heavily sealed on the inside with oak, containing an iron cage. He is also ironed and guarded by Rangers, who remain within the prison walls both day and by night." The company was camped on the yard just behind the jail, "so that the public may rest assured that there is no possibility of the prisoner's escape on the one hand or suffering by mob violence on the other." Hardin, the Rangers, as well as virtually everyone who was aware of the importance of this trial, were keenly aware of a mob near Comanche. One report stated that there were "a number of cattle men from the counties west of Comanche assembled and [which] uttered threats against the prisoner." Their "attitude was threatening in the extreme" but Lieutenant Reynolds made his presence known; when the mob learned that he and his company were "strongly posted" within the walls of the jail, and well knowing his determined bravery, they withdrew their forces without an offer of violence." [22]

Ranger Davis was more than just another Ranger in Reynolds' Company E, but also a poet who greatly appreciated nature and the world around him. He was aware of Hardin's killings, and knew how important his duty of guarding the prisoner was. In his letter of September 25, after reaching Comanche, he wrote:

But I have guarded this wild man, the report of whose bloody crimes has caused so much shuddering, whose name was a "bug bear" to the timid tourist in Texas. Yes, I have guarded him at midnight, when the moonlight was reflected on the dew drops on the prairie sedge, and in the tangled brush that skirts the cow house. Alone and standing guard among the sleeping rangers I

Mervyn Bathurst Davis, Texas Ranger and newspaper correspondent who guarded Hardin. *Courtesy Carol Davis Weiner.*

have gazed on the face of him I guarded, John Wesley Hardin, the gentlest sleeper of them all. Sometimes a troubled look disturbed his countenance for an instant; once he murmured "Johnny," his little son's name, but in the main his sleep was calmer than the moonlight stream flowing past me to the sea. If any demons ever haunted his bedchamber, they kept aloof of his bivouac. Were the irons on his limbs the potent charms that awed them, or, was it the cold blue gleam of the sentinel's Winchester? Perhaps some spiritualist can answer.[23]

On Tuesday, October 25, Hardin stood before Judge J. R. Fleming to be arraigned, charged with the murder of Charles M. Webb. The prosecution consisted of Messrs S. C. Buck, District Attorney; N. R. Lindsey, County Attorney; Honorable J. D. Stephens of Comanche and S. P. Burnes of Brownwood. Judge S. H. Renick of Waco; Abner Lipscomb of Brenham; Col. T. L. Nugent of Stephenville and Hon. W. S. J. Adams of Comanche were there for Hardin's defense. The attorneys spent half of the first day impaneling the jury, most of whom had not even been in Comanche County at the time of the Webb killing, although they were certainly aware of who Webb was and who Hardin was as well. There were at least eight witnesses for the prosecution, but the defense only called two. The Comanche County grand jury had originally indicted both Hardin and James Taylor for the Webb killing on October 31, 1874, but now the State entered a *nolle prosequi* as Taylor was dead. The new indictment was presented without Taylor's name. This was perhaps the first order of business for the court.

Testimony showed that the deputy sheriff of Brown County "while on a visit to Comanche, and while passing by a corner saloon," was "accosted" by Hardin in a "rude and insulting manner." Hardin was under the impression that Webb had a writ for his arrest, and led Webb to believe that he would not be arrested. Webb "seemed disposed to avoid any collision" and replied he had no warrant for him and turned to leave. Hardin continued to urge on the difficulty and "tantalizing him with attempting to leave" when Webb "turned abruptly" and placed his hand upon his pistol. At that same moment Hardin, Jim Taylor and one of the Dixons, the latter standing on either side of Webb, drew their pistols. Webb fired first, which report was followed "almost instantly" by the return fire of Hardin,

Taylor and Dixon. Webb then fell to his knees and managed to fire once again from that kneeling position. He was shot through the side of his head, as well as in the stomach. Testimony showed that Hardin's shot entered his stomach, and the head shot "doubtless coming from Taylor or Dixon." About twenty or thirty shots were fired "with such rapidity as to sound almost like a volley." This reported testimony showed that the State was attempting to prove a conspiracy to kill Webb, but failed. "[T] he position, action and character of the parties and the slight evidence adduced" indicated it was the intention of Hardin, Dixon and Taylor to kill Webb. The thinking was, that Webb, being an officer, would dare attempt to arrest them, therefore he should be removed; and he had earlier "incurred their displeasure" by arresting one of their friends, provided the additional motive to kill. The jury retired at 8:00 p.m.

The court room remained "packed with men deeply anxious to know the verdict" but order and quiet was maintained. "Order and quiet" was maintained because Lieutenant Reynolds' Rangers were at the doors and also "promenaded the aisles" with, as the reporter noted, "the flaming light of the candles gleaming upon their . . . pistols, and lending to the whole scene quite a warlike appearance." Hundreds of heads turned at each sound from the jury room, the spectators "breathless with attention." At 11:00 o'clock the jury returned with the verdict. They had found Hardin guilty of murder in the second degree and assessed his punishment at twenty-five years of confinement at hard labor. Hardin's counsel gave notice of appeal and the prisoner was taken back to jail. Once Hardin was at the entrance of the jail the judge allowed the people in the courtroom to leave. The judge reasonably feared the presence of the mob, as reporter "W" noted that had the verdict been one of acquittal, "it is confidently believed that Hardin would have been hung by a mob," and more remarkably W. added this statement: "the thirty Rangers to the contrary notwithstanding." A moral teaching concluded his report: in reviewing Hardin's career and the sudden end of his confederates for them "justice was swift and terrible," but for Hardin justice would now be "slow, but perhaps, not the less certain. He has by nature a bold and reckless, but not a bad disposition, and owes his ruin chiefly to whisky and bad associations. Let his history be a warning to young men, and his downfall a warning to caution all those who think Texas a safe asylum for cut-throats and desperadoes." [24]

"Cut-throats and desperadoes" may have been running rampant across the Texas plains, but many wanted to go stare at them in their cells where they were unable to commit further violent acts. Hardin was to remain incarcerated during the appeal process, and due to the inadequacy of the Comanche jail, or perhaps more because of the threatening presence of the mob, he was delivered back to the Travis County jail in Austin, protected by Rangers. In Austin on October 6, the curious citizens were not the only ones who wanted to visit the notorious prisoner in the county jail. Ranger Lt. Lee Hall and a squad of State Troops received orders to go to Austin and deliver the DeWitt County prisoners to Cuero for their trial. Accused of the double killing of Dr. Philip Brassell and his son in December 1876, they were in the Travis County jail due to the inadequacy of the DeWitt County facility. At least one of the Rangers wrote that while in Austin he had his "curiosity gratified" by meeting Hardin. As much a Ranger as a newspaper correspondent on occasion, he wrote about his visit and sent it to the *Galveston Daily News* for publication. This unidentified Ranger signed his letters "Total Wreck," presumably because he had covered many miles in the recent scouts, from Corpus Christi, Victoria, and on to Austin. Of his visit to the jail he wrote:

I found [Hardin] to be a great talker, though not near so boastful as the outlaw Longley, confined in your county jail for divers murders committed in various parts of the State.

Hardin speaks in high terms of his captor, and says he considered him a Texan of the old school, and was never treated better by any one in his life. His brother-in-law, Brown Bowen, recently sentenced to be hanged in Gonzales county, occupies the same call with him, and both seem to be in the best of spirits.[25]

While awaiting his appeal in the Travis County jail, Hardin had plenty of time to reflect on his life and career, renew acquaintances with friends and relatives, write letters, and also consider an escape from jail. Once the appeal was finalized, he would have to return to Comanche, to be either freed, face other murder charges, or else be on his way to the penitentiary.

CHAPTER 15

HUNTSVILLE AND PUNISHMENT

"I was carefully guarded by Lieut. N. O. Reynolds, who com-
manded twenty-five well armed brave men; but I knew the
power of the mob, the spirit that possessed them, and knew that
my life hung on a tread."

John Wesley Hardin

While waiting the result of his appeal, Brown Bowen was placed in the Travis County jail with Hardin, sent there from Gonzales. Confined together in the Travis County jail they could not avoid each other. On January 29, 1878, Hardin wrote to Jane, pointing out that friend Bill Taylor's conviction for killing Gabriel Webster Slaughter back in March of 1874 had been remanded; hence there was hope Taylor would be somehow acquitted of the deed, and be released from Galveston jail. Cousin Mannen Clements was to go to Gonzales for a bond hearing, and Hardin was confident he was "Sure to Get out Soon." He encouraged her to keep her spirits up, reminding her that where "there is a will there is a way and that the darkest hours are Just before day [.]" Of course Brown joined him "in Sending Love to all [.]"[1]

Hardin and Bowen may have kept their spirits up while waiting. Occasionally Bowen would play his fiddle; one song he seemed to enjoy was "Drunkard's Lamentation" and "Many other favorite tunes in His cell." Bowen now had gained weight in jail, Wes pointed out in this letter, but also: "[T]hey found him guilty of murder in the 1st degree for killing tom Halderman [*sic*] he has stood tryal [*sic*] and is Here for Safe Keeping."[2]

In the Travis County jail one never knew when new prisoners would be incarcerated. While Hardin endured his dreary existence in his cell, always contemplating escape, two members of the notorious Sam Bass gang were arrested by Texas Ranger Junius "June" Peak and men of Company B. The company of thirty men had accomplished good work in a relatively short time: mustered in on April 17, they already had two men cut off from Bass: Pipes and Herndon. These men were accused of participating with Bass in the robbery of the United States mails and sentenced to prison terms. Prior to sending them to Albany, New York, to serve their sentence, they spent some time in the Austin jail. A biographer of Bass obtained an account of a visit to the jail where they were.

> Passing through a hall walled in by solid masonry, the jailer unbolted a pair of heavy iron doors and he found himself in a large room filled with rows of iron cages. It was a hot day in July, and a July day in Austin is not to be described by any figure of speech which will not stand the test of white heat. The room was dark and not very well aired. The men were stripped to the waist and the perspiration was dripping from their bodies. The cages were of solid iron bars, the floor was sheeted with iron. There were no bedsteads in the cells, a blanket or quilt answered all sleeping purposes. From one to three occupants were in a cage. There were more than three-score prisoners in all.

Among the sixty prisoners was "the notorious John Wesley Hardin" described as "pert and saucy as ever and advanced to the front of his cage for a chat."

"This is a very bad place to come to," said he, "people better keep out of here. They say there is honor among thieves, but don't you believe it. There's not a word of truth in it. When they can't steal from anybody else, they steal from one another. . . . They tell lots of lies about me. They say I killed six or seven men for snoring, but it isn't true. I only killed one man for snoring."[3] On April 22, 1878, in his cell in the Travis County jail, Hardin picked up pen and paper and composed a letter, which appeared in Austin's *Weekly Gazette* newspaper. He had had ample time to review the recent happenings and time to see how Ranger N. O. Reynolds differed from Ranger John R. Waller, although he certainly knew they both answered to the same commander, Major John B. Jones. Hardin observed that Reynolds, upon arriving in Comanche and having placed him in the local jail, went out "to see what the situation was" as he termed it. Reynolds learned that there were 200 men about two miles from town whose sole purpose was to lynch the notorious prisoner. Upon returning Reynolds explained to him that if the mob attacked he would give Hardin pistols and he could, with the Rangers, defend himself until the mob either had him or had fled the scene. Reynolds had informed the vigilantes that this was "the situation" now, and in addition to arming Hardin he would arm the other ten or twelve prisoners in the jail as well. This was something Reynolds would have done; he was not only brave but nervy, and if the Rangers and the dozen armed prisoners were armed to save themselves from the action of the mob, it would even the odds. His men held him in great respect and knew his character; this revelation also was something which caused Hardin to hold him in high regard. But it didn't happen, as the 200 men obviously were afraid to attack this commander, so different from Waller, even though the numerical strength was clearly in their favor. Instead of an attack, a written communication was sent that stated that if the trial was postponed or else there was a change of venue, the mob would *demand* the prisoner.[4]

Hardin also now began to rationalize why he had been found guilty rather than being acquitted. He had announced ready for trial too quickly after arrival in Comanche because he "did not have the confidence in the Rangers I should have had," but surely his attorneys were aware of means to delay a trial. Further, he felt attorneys Renick, Nugent and Adams were afraid of the mob, "or some other unknown cause." Also his counsel allowed the State to "put in evidence my character to influence the jury" without raising any objection. And, like many defendants who are found guilty but claim innocence, Hardin believed the judge himself was "disqualified and biased."[5] With the guilty verdict he now had to wait until

September 1878 to hear the result of the appeal; he would spend that year in the Travis County jail.

In pondering these aspects of his trial and what might have been, Hardin still began his April 22 letter as a gentleman, thanking the editor of the *Gazette* for "your kindness to me on other occasions," which encouraged him to write and share with the public his views on the trial. The editor printed the letter in full with no editorial comment, unfortunately, as it would be interesting to know what "kindness" had been given "on other occasions." Hardin wrote:

> When I entered the public square of Comanche City I saw the faces of dozens of the same men who took part in hanging my brother Joe G. Hardin and my four cousins in 1874. Both my brother and my cousins were in the custody of Capt. Waller's company of Rangers at the same time they were mobbed, and I strongly suspect that the Rangers were directly or indirectly parties in this deed of violence. It was alleged at the time that my brother and cousins were parties to the killing of Charlie Webb, but at this day none in that county will deny that they were entirely innocent of the charge with the exception, perhaps, of one of the Dixon boys. Thus died five men, four of whom it is granted, even by those who slew them, were entirely innocent of crime. My brother and the two Dixon boys were hung and Anderson and Barekman were shot to death while asleep on their pallets in the jail. I was carefully guarded by Lieut. N. O. Reynolds, who commanded twenty five well armed brave men, but I knew the power of the mob, the spirit that possessed them, and knew that my life hung on a thread.

Whether or not the editor felt some or even most of this communication was false, he decided it was worthy to share Hardin's thoughts with his readers; he must have realized that the name of Hardin helped sell newspapers. The letter continued:

Accustomed to scenes of excitement from infancy, I read in the looks of the rangers, in everything that I saw from the grated windows of the prison, and on my trips to and from the jail to the courthouse, that a woeful death awaited me if once the mob obtained the mastery. Indeed it was hinted to me that if I obtained a continuance or a change of venue the beginning would be made of the bloody end. Therefore I went into trial knowing that I was prejudged and already harshly sentenced by the jury appointed to convict me of a crime I never committed.[6]

How Hardin had been led to believe Anderson and Barekman had been shot to death while *prisoners in the jail* is unknown; Waller's report indicated they were in the brush, hiding out, and had fired the first shots resulting in the return fire of the Rangers which killed them both. Had Reverend Hardin or Mrs. Hardin told this lie to their son?

Hardin also considered the cost of whatever had brought about the confrontation with Deputy Sheriff Charles M. Webb. Recalling the names of those who had lost their lives, he opined that "it is almost as bad to kill as to be killed": the Webb killing drove his father to an early grave; his mother was almost "distracted"; his brother Joe and cousins Tom and Bud Dixon were killed; his brother Joe's death left his widow with two "helpless babes"; Mrs. Anderson had lost her son and Mrs. Barekman had lost her husband, "to say nothing of the grief of countless others." In spite of all that sorrow and misery he now could itemize, did he not realize it was caused by his own action of killing Webb? Instead of admitting that his actions brought on the confrontation, he made this remarkable statement: "I do say, however, that the man who does not exercise the first law of nature—that of self preservation—is not worthy of living and breathing the breath of life."[7]

During this stressful period for Hardin, brother-in-law Brown Bowen was experiencing the workings of the Texas legal system as well. Following his 1877 arrest and delivery to the Travis County jail, Bowen had to work on his own defense. The Gonzales County jury had found him guilty of the murder of Thomas Haldeman in the first degree on October 18. Bowen could not claim self-defense in this matter, as the victim was asleep when killed. He claimed to have been "forced into trial without my witnesses, which cannot be denied. . . . The parties who have sworn my life away have committed cold-blooded murder; and they know it. . . . It is hard to think that I have to be cut off from my family and leave a disgrace on them and my people for another man's deeds."[8]

Martha E. Bowen, sister of Jane and Brown Bowen. Photograph by H.H. Morris, Galveston. *Courtesy The John Wesley Hardin Papers, The Wittliff Collection, Texas State University.*

Bowen was delivered back to Gonzales where on April 10, Judge Everett Lewis passed sentence. He was to be hanged by the neck until dead on May 17, 1878. Desperate now, his father Neill, and his sister Martha Elizabeth "Matt," found means to try and help. Two days before the scheduled execution his father and sister met with Governor Hubbard and showed petitions for clemency for Bowen. They also requested more time to gather witnesses, witnesses which he certainly should have had subpoenaed months before; after all, he had been in Florida where these witnesses resided. Why had he not been able to gather them in for his initial court appearances? But the *Galveston Daily News* reported the petitions were not "numerously signed, and not accompanied by any evidence justifying clemency." Governor Hubbard refused to intervene.[9] Bowen would hang.

Bowen believed, or at least attempted to convince everyone else, that Hardin had been the actual killer of Thomas Haldeman, and claimed that if he had his witnesses he could have proved his innocence. He believed his friends were intimidated through fear of Hardin, including the key witness who testified seeing him kill Haldeman. The *Gonzales Inquirer* editor, Carey J. Pilgrim, commented: "The popular verdict is that he had a fair trial, and his punishment is but just."[10]

On May 18 Hardin wrote a long letter to Jane on the letterhead of Sheriff Corwin complaining about his own situation. "I have been convicted by news paper reports and by the Lies of cowardley [*sic*] murder[er]s & assasins [*sic*] to predjidice [*sic*] the minds of the people and courts of the State of Texas against me but dear one I can bare it all." He told her that her father and her sister Matt had seen him on the fifteenth; Neill Bowen was "troubled all but to death," but he could do nothing. Hardin had explained to Neill that he could not make any kind of statement that would help his son. On the sixteenth Neill and Matt Bowen had returned to see him and to obtain the statement—which Hardin had said he could not make. The jailer explained to them Hardin had no statement for them, but ten minutes later he delivered a note from Matt: "Brother John you told me you would make a true Statement about my Brother oh god why

Didn't you oh my god my Poor Brother has to be Hung oh my god do Something for him on my account."

Hardin was not about to admit to anything at this point. He answered Matt's heart-wrenching note:

> Dear Sister my wil[l] is good. But Let every tub Stand on its own bottom [.] you Say for your sake. For your sake I would do anything honorable and I Know you would not ask me to do anything dishonorable [.] I cannot be made a Scape goat off [*sic*] and a true Statement wil[l] do your brother no good and a false one I cannot make . . . I am your Sympathizing Brother John W. Hardin.

John said he forgave "poor Brown" for his false reports and asked that God forgive him. According to Hardin's letter, based on the reporting from the Gonzales newspaper, Brown claimed to the very last that he was innocent of the crime and that Hardin had murdered Haldeman. He then fell seven feet and lived seven seconds (suggesting his neck was broken), witnessed by 4,500 people.[11] The *Gonzales Inquirer* devoted columns to the trial and execution of Brown Bowen. According to the *Inquirer*, Bowen "dropped a clear fall of seven feet." There were a few "convulsive shudders, slight working of the shoulders and limbs, and the body hung perfectly still. In about six minutes his pulse had ceased to beat." Obviously Hardin's information was not entirely accurate, but his concentration during this period must have been focused on his own situation. All he could have done to save Brown was to admit to the killing for which Brown was to hang. He now had a prison cell for a home, and began to consider how to change that environment, as well as writing letters.

His letters to Jane also recalled happier times when they were both carefree and enjoying being together as a family in Florida. In one letter he told her he was allowed to be in a cell by himself, which was much better than having to share—"this Hot weather which is much Better than being crouded [*sic*] with company"—which caused him to share a

Thomas Caffall, left, and Joshua Robert "Brown" Bowen. *Courtesy The John Wesley Hardin Papers, The Wittliff Collections, Texas State University.*

pleasant incident with her. "I had a nice treat to ice Cream to day by lieu-tenant Rundels [Reynolds] who taken me to comanchi [*sic*]" he wrote. "I think of our visits to the ice cream Salon [*sic*] in New Orleans [and] Jack-sonville [.]"[12] One wonders if Ranger Reynolds was in Austin delivering prisoners to the jail and for some reason felt like treating Hardin to ice cream. He certainly would not have treated all the prisoners, would he?

Hardin was fortunate in that he had not been captured a few years earlier as he then would have been placed inside the old Travis County jail.
If he had followed the happenings in Austin during his years in Florida
and Alabama he would have read the editorials of the *Democratic Statesman* concerning the facility. One described the building as "without air
or ventilation, infested with vermin, reeking with abominable stench and
crowded with a suffering mass of suffocating human beings . . . we say
the present condition should bring a blush of shame to the cheek of every
citizen in our county." It was further described as a "disgrace to the age
and a crime against humanity." By July 1876 the new jail was completed
and the prisoners were taken from the old to the new, into which Hardin
would be the most noted.[13]

Even while contemplating these matters Hardin plotted to escape. The
cells were made of "good material" with one set of cages on top of the
others, separated by sheet iron. Somehow he was able to make a key that
could unlock his cell door and put him in the "run-around"; he made one
to unlock that as well; so all that was left to do to escape was to climb up
to the window and saw through the bars. It had worked in the Gonzales
County jail, and perhaps would work in the Travis County jail. Unfortunately for Hardin some "trusties" found out about the escape plan and
told the guards. Hardin now had a guard inside the jail day and night,.
The escape plan had only reached the planning stage.[14]

Getting ready to return to Comanche for sentencing, others noted his
seemingly pleasant demeanor. He joked with members of his escort, he
alone riding in a wagon pulled by two horses and driven by a Ranger, and
surrounded by other Rangers; he may have boasted that he was the only
criminal in Texas who deserved such a large guard. Perhaps his pleasant
mood was brought about by having seen Jane for a few moments; she had
managed to get to Austin to see him again. The *Statesman* described her
as "a prepossessing lady of rather slight figure, and above the medium
height, showing traces of care and sorrow upon her face." She had the
three children with her. After leaving them and being placed in the wagon
Hardin wrote her a note, and "seemed perfectly resigned to his fate."[15]

Hardin may have been cordial to newspaper editors and selected others, but some believed his twenty-five years at hard labor were insufficient. A correspondent who signed his missives as "Yours Truly" noted his passing through Liberty Hill in Williamson County, northwest of Austin, while returning to Comanche on September 18. He wrote to the *Burnet Bulletin:*. "It is a shame that the boasted murderer of over a score of men should get but 25 years in the penitentiary, with a good possibility for escape." Hardin looked "considerably bleached by his long confinement," but was in good spirits, at least outwardly.[16]

At a camp near San Saba, the Rangers allowed Hardin to write a letter to Jane, in which he made no complaint about his guard, in fact pointing out that as he had "faired [*sic*] as they have in other words have had a good time." He anticipated their arrival at Comanche within a day or two; he would be there long enough only to receive his sentence and then head to the penitentiary. He anticipated he would be going through Austin or some other "railroad town" in early October. Now he was confident that the Rangers would protect him from any mob that might wish to challenge the escort. He advised her to write to him, sending letters to him in care of Superintendent Goree.[17]

After he received his sentence at Comanche, the Rangers again loaded him up in a buggy. Hardin was shackled to John Marston, a Comanche blacksmith convicted of attempted murder; the other two were Nat Mackey, charged with murder, chained to one Davenport, who was sentenced to a term of five years for theft of a horse. "Of course," Hardin wrote, "great crowds would flock from everywhere to see the notorious John Wesley Hardin, from the hoary-headed farmer to the little maid hardly in her teens."[18]

Davenport and Marston remain merely names, but Absalom James "Nat" Mackey proved to be a man who had his own experiences with mobs, and perhaps he and Hardin discussed this Texas phenomenon while they shared the miles to Fort Worth and Huntsville. In 1874 Mackey had killed a man named Jones, but no details have been found in the contemporary records. He also was suspected of horse theft, and often found shelter at the home of his father, James. In January, 1878, a mob of possibly thirty men came to the Mackey home, took "the old man" out and murdered him by hanging him to a tree. One report indicated there was no known reason for this, except that the father provided shelter to his son.[19] Another report indicated that he was suspected of "improper association with cattle and horse thieves."[20] Mackey was about five feet eight inches tall, "spare made, rather light complexion, quick spoken, is known as Nat Mackey."[21] He and Hardin had at least two things in common: they had both killed, and they both had lost loved ones to a mob.

The quartet of prisoners and their Ranger escort, including again Sheriff Frank Wilson, did not go to Austin from Comanche in spite of Hardin's wish, but instead traveled over 100 miles northeast to Fort Worth. His arrival there on October 3 had "thrown" the city "into a state of curious excitement" according to a *Fort Worth Democrat* reporter. The reporter was under the impression that Hardin himself had demanded such a heavy guard to protect him, and since Lieutenant Reynolds was in San Saba at the time, relatively close to Comanche, he was ordered to be his guardian. The reporter counted the guard as "twenty well mounted men, armed to the teeth with breech-loading Winchesters, six-shooters, etc." The Rangers rode into the St. Louis wagon yard on Weatherford Street and "took possession of a small frame house" in which the prisoner was placed with Mackey, Davenport and Marston. Rangers remained inside and outside of the house, protecting the quartet as well as preventing them from plotting an escape attempt. No one was allowed to communicate with the prisoners except "a few officers of the law and several newspaper men," one of whom was the *Democrat* man. He was "ushered in" and introduced to Hardin, "with whose general appearance he was most favorably impressed." Hardin was sitting up against the wall of the house, "Indian fashion" with his left leg shackled to the right leg of Mackey. The reporter learned that Mackey was going to Huntsville for sixteen years for killing a man at Hazel Dell "with a stone." Hardin, after learning the reporter's desire for an interview, "courteously invited him to a seat on a pallet of old coats and pants," which he accepted. He was made to feel "comfortable and easy," as though he was going to interview a minister of the gospel, "instead of a man who rumors and reports have it, has killed a regiment." Hardin, in spite of his situation, did impress the reporter. He was seen as "what any lady would describe as being a fine-looking fellow. His worn and shabby clothes did not distract a jot or tittle from his rather handsome face. [Hardin] has a fine well developed forehead, and a large brilliant, piercing, dove colored eye, which shows not only determination, but a world of bravery and daring recklessness, coupled with an equal amount of shrewdness and intelligence." Whereas a previous reporter had described his complexion as pale, the *Democrat* reporter saw his complexion as having "been tanned from his long journey in the sun." He continued gushing out his positive impression of the man-killer, pointing out his "pretty white set of teeth" which "completes the pen picture of our hero's face." Hardin, through the eyes of this reporter, stood about five feet, nine inches tall, weighing 160 pounds.[22]

Besides this reporter, there were plenty of other people who left their normal routine to see the gunfighter, turning out "like a Fourth of July picnic" as he recalled, boasting that he had to get out and shake hands for an hour "before my guard could get me through the crowd."[23]

After the Fort Worth adulation the next stop was at Palestine, 135 miles from Fort Worth, where crowds continued to wait and hope to see the prisoner. From Palestine, 80 miles south, the final stop for the prisoners, again Hardin was "astonished to see even the convicts in stripes gazing at me" once inside the prison walls. It was the fifth day of October 1878.

Did Superintendent Thomas J. Goree meet the notorious prisoner, curious as all the others had been? Thomas Jewett Goree was an Alabama native and Confederate veteran. Following the war's end he had practiced law in Huntsville and earned the respect of Governor Hubbard, who appointed Goree superintendent of the Texas State Penitentiary in 1877.[24] At the time he may have first met prisoner number 7109 Goree was forty-three; his most valuable prisoner was twenty-five.

A prison barber shaved Hardin "smooth" and cut his hair and weighed him in at 165 pounds. He was stripped and all scars and marks were entered into his file. His only occupation of any length of time had been as a cowboy, or stock raiser, as the butcher business was of such a short period; he was identified as a laborer. He was assigned to the wheelwright's shop,.

Early on, while his experience with Lieutenant Reynolds and his Rangers was still fresh in his mind, he wrote a letter to Jane, but failed to provide the date. From the context it appears that it was composed shortly after his arrival at Huntsville. "[A]s for my treatment Here I am treated Kindly and believe that I will have no Trouble in Getting along Here as I believe this prison is carried on by men who [are?] Just Honorable & even Benevolent," he began, and to express his belief in other words, stated, "if a man wil[l] only Do right he wil[l] be Treated right." He continued with the axiom that he intended to do right, because if one did wrong he then "must bear the consequences." As if surprised at the care given prisoners, he noted that there was more done than he had imagined: "if he got Sick He Has attention which I believe is good, at Least it is Said to Be." Further, as if he couldn't wait to advise brother Jefferson Davis how to behave himself, he advised Jane to tell the seventeen-year-old to "Shun the company of all Dishonerable [*sic*]" men, and if ever any "Dishonerable act is proposed Have nerve to Say no" because "that is what makes a man"; he should say no, and added "do it your Self." Perhaps Hardin was recalling how years before when in Abilene Ben Thompson had asked him to kill the city marshal, "Wild Bill" Hickok, and he had answered: "If Bill needs killing, why don't you kill him yourself?" Thompson supposedly had replied that he "would rather get someone else to do it."[25] This was only one of many lessons Hardin would attempt to teach his children through correspondence.

While Hardin began his prison life he may have learned about his contemporary man-killer, William Preston "Bloody Bill" Longley, who had boasted of killing many men but who in reality had killed far, far fewer than Hardin. Longley was waiting for the hangman's noose, set to die for a first degree murder. The two probably had never met, although they certainly knew each other by reputation. Years later, however, while writing his autobiography, Hardin described in great detail how he bested Longley in a poker game in Old Evergreen back in 1870. He certainly learned of Longley's upcoming execution, how on Friday, October 11, Lee County sheriff James Madison Brown would place the noose around his neck and spring the trap door. Sheriff Brown had hired about one hundred special guards to be on and around the gallows to protect him as well as the prisoner. Over 2,000 people were in Giddings that day to witness the hanging of the boastful killer. Facing the hangman's noose Longley admitted he knew the killing for which he was to hang was wrong, but he claimed it was done in self-defense. Longley believed he had not only a right but a duty to kill the man. Sheriff Brown, on the gallows looking over the crowd, just before the trap door opened, stated it was the first legal hanging in Lee County and he hoped it would be the last. Hardin claimed his killing of Charles M. Webb had been done in self-defense; he had to kill Webb to save his own life. Longley had learned Hardin had only received prison time for his killing while he was to be hanged; he naturally resented what he felt was a great wrong by the Texas justice system.[26]

Almost immediately Hardin began plotting an escape. He was well aware of "a heap of Judases and Benedict Arnolds in the world" and knew of "treachery" but learned where the armory was. He planned to tunnel underneath the carpenter shop, the offices of the superintendent and the director—about seventy-five yards of hard physical labor starting in the wheelwright's shop and ending in the armory. He picked "about seventy-five of the best men, mostly life and long-term men" to do the actual digging, they knowing of the actual plot. Others were "to blindly trust me to say the word and then follow me."[27] Once the tunnel was completed, they would wait until the guards were at supper after leaving their weapons in the armory, and then break in, and with the weapons take over the prison with the guards helpless and "liberate all who wished to go except the rape fiends."[28] It was an elaborate plan, knowing a good number of convicts had to be involved, and also realizing there were plenty who would betray any confidence to be issued a pardon or have their sentence reduced. Hardin recalled the work began about the first of November, tunneling through five brick walls each two feet thick. This work was "easily" done, according to him, although he may not have actually performed any of it. In spite of the careful planning several life convicts informed Superintendent Goree of the plan when it was nearly complete. Goree ordered Hardin to be arrested along with nine others, placing them in irons. Hardin of course denied any knowledge of the plan. Denial or not, it was widely reported that the attempt had been made. Someone revealed to a newspaper reporter what might have happened, stating that "several convicts employed in the wagon shop attempted to dig into the arsenal where a large number of Winchesters and 10,000 rounds of ammunition are stored. John Wesley Hardin was the leader, and but for the timely discovery of the plot would have been successful, about three hours more work would have let them into the arsenal. Hardin now takes his rations in the dark cell."[29] The "rations" consisted of bread and water for fifteen days. As further punishment prison officials ordered a ball and chain to be attached to his leg. Hardin suspected two "lifers" had informed on him, Bill Owens and Bill Terril, and he later believed they had been pardoned for their act of betrayal; in addition he believed there were three others whose sentence was reduced for their betrayal, although he gave no names. He later learned another convict, John Williams, had also betrayed him.[30]

While suffering this punishment he evaluated his escape plan and decided there had been too many involved; hence the next plot would involve far fewer numbers. He now somehow obtained or "manufactured" keys, and also found the means to remove his ball and chain. In late December 1878 he tested the homemade keys by having Williams—whom he still believed was trustworthy—try them out. He did and the keys worked perfectly. "I intended . . . to unlock my door and then all the other cells, muzzle the guard, unlock the main prison door and then gate after gate to freedom." He also had obtained "two good six-shooters" that a trusty had provided. Perhaps John Williams, whom Hardin believed was another convict like himself, was in reality the "trusty" from whom he obtained the six-shooters. A John Williams by 1880 was a guard in the prison, a thirty-two-year-old native Texan born in Washington County. The trusty in 1878 could easily have been made a guard by 1880.[31] But then the guards came and arrested him. He was searched, the keys found, and the bolt he had used to release the ball and chain. "[I]n short," number 7109 realized, "my cell mate had betrayed me and the game was up."[32]

In his autobiography Hardin placed the date of his giving the keys to John Williams to test as December 26. It was probably a week or more earlier, however, for in his letter to Jane dated December 28 he referred to the betrayal: "at times past Been thrown in with my enemies & Traitors" and after lengthy vows of love for her and statements of encouragement and hope, for her to be cheerful, he alludes to his break attempt. To Jane he wrote:

Sweet Jane you may Have Seen in the papers where I undertook to capture the armor[y] with 50 other convicts and that I am now receiving punishment for the same[.] Dear there was a brake [sic] contemplated Here Some time ago and it was Said they only Liked [sic, lacked] 2 hours work of Having the armor captured when the alarm was given & given By a convict or convicts and it is thought that in 2 Hours longer the convicts would of all Been released and as the work com[m]enced in my Shop of course they said Hardin was leader [.] Yes ever[y] thing would Have it Hardin was the one [.]

Hardin was then denying to Jane what he later admitted to doing in his autobiography, and he would not have said anything to Jane if she had not alluded to it in a letter to him. He continued:

So they put me in a dark cell for 5 days But you Bet the guards & convicts treated me well and I had all the candles extra grub tobaco [sic] and Beding [sic] I needed none of which a man is allow[ed] in a dark cell [.]

And he inferred that he would try again:

> Dear I in person Hant [haven't] tried to get out yet But you can
> rest easy if this place must Be Beat no telling what I might do
> in time to come [.]

This must have been one of the letters he was able to slip out through the
help of a guard, as he certainly knew that all letters written and received
would normally be examined by prison officials.

By January 1879 it became common knowledge that Hardin had received a severe punishment for his escape attempts, punishment which he
had not specifically mentioned in his letter to Jane. The *Brenham Weekly
Banner* of Washington County frequently copied items from other publications, and noted the *Huntsville Item* reported that Hardin "received 39
lashes a few days since." Then the reporter attempted to impress the readers with a bit of word play: "Hardin seems to have been impressed with
an idea that he was not an ordinary convict, as he received such marked
attention. He will probably get over it."[33]

CHAPTER 16

DREAMS OF A FUTURE

*"Dearest Be carefull with our Sweet Little children for the way
a twig is Bent the way it wil[l] Grow"*

John Wesley Hardin to Jane, July 27, 1879

How did John Wesley Hardin later describe this punishment of thirty-nine lashes? He only knew the pain of it being inflicted, not knowing or caring that the administration of lashes was a form of corporal punishment which harkened back centuries. Ancient Jewish punishment demanded that the maximum number of lashes allowed per infraction was forty, given in multiples of three, effectively making the maximum number at thirty-nine. The one left off was to show "compassion," although no prisoner ever felt there was any shown.

Hardin wrote that his cellmate had betrayed him. The night of the betrayal "about twenty officers" entered his cell and tied his hands and feet. Down upon the concrete floor, stretched to the extreme Hardin certainly knew what was going to transpire. Two men held the ropes which held his hands; two men held the ropes holding his feet. Then under-keeper Philip J. West[1] took the 29-inch long strap, 2-¼ inches wide, attached to a handle a foot in length. "He began to whip my naked body with this instrument. They were now flogging me and every lick left the imprint of every lash, of which there were four in this whip, consisting of thick pieces of harness leather." Hardin heard someone yell out, "Don't hit him in the same place so often."[2] According to his account the superintendent was also there, as witness to the punishment, who ended it after the thirty-ninth lash. Perhaps Hardin only glimpsed the instrument as having four straps of leather rather than three. He then was forced to walk in snow to another building, his back and sides "beaten into a jelly," and placed on a diet of bread and water. He refused to inform on those other convicts who had been involved in the failed escape plot. The punishment was the result of the "break" that Jane inquired about. He responded to her inquiries,

> I Have not done a days work in 6 weeks now Since the Break you Speak so much about. My Health Has not Been good at all Since the 1st of January [.] therefore I Have Been Keept [sic] in my cell [. I have] a good matrass [sic] plenty of covoring [sic] and plenty to eat and Drink and a doctor When ever I wished the latter only 3 time [s] and am on the mend at present.

He felt he was doing as well as could be expected. The superintendent had been very kind, and now he felt that was enough said about the attempted prison break. In this same letter he showed he cared deeply about others, asking about his "babes," asking her to kiss them for him, asking specifically how John Wesley Hardin Jr. was doing, sending to him the message that he was to be kind to little Jane and to mind his mother and grandmother. Apparently brother Joe's children were there as well, since Hardin asked how his nephew was getting along, and asking baby Mollie how she and "Budie" were getting along, "does he Bite yet?"[3]

About the first of February officials took Hardin out of his regular cell and placed him in a different one, perhaps in order to search it thoroughly. He was suffering from fever and "unable to work," either actually or in his mind. He was now placed in the wood shop, working satisfactorily but frequently arguing, "in a Row all the time with the guard."[4] Following the development of his children while he could only influence them through letters from prison was difficult enough, but there were some bright spots in his days. In a letter to Jane he told her of news that he thought would surprise her, as apparently he knew something she did not. "Jane Dear I expect to Surprise you a little[.] your Sister Mattie Has Married on[e] Oliver Odum So Chew on that for awhile."[5] It is curious that he had learned this important "social news" before Jane or possibly she already knew. Oliver Odum was also a Texan by birth, born in 1852, and married Martha E. Bowen December 30, 1878, in Gonzales County. Oliver Odum would not live long after his marriage into the Bowen family, as on June 22, 1881, he was shot and killed. No details of the killing ever appeared in the existing correspondence.[6] In the same letter to Jane he assured her that his health was still improving. Mannen Clements' influence appears as well, for Hardin shares with Jane that Mannen had told him to obey all commands of his keepers. He now resolved to "Strictly obey all orders and to Do right." Curiously the "Sup Says He wil Give me a fair Trial"[7] which suggests that Superintendent Goree had conversed with Hardin on the matter of the importance of obedience to prison rules.

Not having the letters of Jane remains a problem; apparently none of hers have survived, so one is left to attempt to reconstruct what she had written to him from his response to her. Apparently there was some discord between Jane and Elizabeth Hardin. In the letter of February 23, about two weeks after the letter in which Hardin assured her he would heretofore obey all orders, he begged Jane to get along with Ma Hardin, "treat her as a mother my Brothers and Sisters as you would your own they will and Do love you [;] they are our Best friend[s]." Occasionally the idea of them someday sharing their lives together with Jane is expressed in his writing.

> Jane Dearest we are both young and I think and Hope we may pass our Latter days together in perfect Hapiness [*sic*] then we can talk over our Hard Ship & trials of Life [.] Sweet Jane remember me often to our Sweet Little Babes which I Know you Do. Jane my Sweet wife I cannot find words to express my Love only think of time past and you wil[l] Know.[8]

While he assured Jane he would obey all orders, yet in this very letter he concluded by admitting the letter was written in haste, and he had to close as a "con" was coming, and it would be one of the rare "slipped" letters passed out and mailed by a guard who Hardin had bribed to obtain certain favors. Hardin identified the guard as J. C. Outlaw, but this name has not been found in Huntsville Penitentiary records.

As a prisoner Hardin had to rely on outside sources to provide him with news of his family and friends, and letters were the essential source. Those letters mainly touched on family issues, and him giving advice to Jane and through her his children. He wrote Jane that his sister Martha, or Matt as she was known, had now married a man named Bright Smith. He also advised that younger brother Jeff was farming, and he hoped he would have good luck in that occupation.[9] Jefferson Davis Hardin was born in 1861, thus he was now almost eighteen years of age. As yet no letters to the younger brothers have been unearthed, nor are there are any letters from Jeff or Gip preserved.

Mannen Clements was also having his problems with the law, but important for Wes Hardin was that he also informed him of news about various family members. One letter to Jane, with additional news from his wife Mollie Clements, preserved with Hardin's letters, informed her that the weather was "very dry here," that there was scarcely water for livestock, and there was hardly enough for people. Mannen unintentionally revealed why he was a favorite cousin of Wes as he expressed concern for the family members as well as younger brother Jeff Davis: "tell Jeff i admire his staying at home with his ma [and] tell him to Look at Wesses fate for example [.]"[10] Was young Jeff Davis Hardin already showing signs of the personality disorder which led to where his older brother was now? Mannen himself wasn't that much different from his cousin, but he was able to receive not guilty verdicts on the significant charges brought against him.[11]

In spite of the hardship Jane experienced raising her three children with her husband behind the prison bars of Huntsville, she perhaps found sufficient work sewing or watching other children to raise some money. In April 1879 Jane and the children were in Austin on their way to Richland Springs in San Saba County to visit the Clements family.

She intended to stay in Austin until the twentieth, then go on to San Saba County. "I hope you wil[l] injoy [*sic*] your Self there Knowing that you wil find Friends there that wil Look after your interest," he wrote, and added no doubt with pleasure that he had received "a letter from ma Stating how well you all Had gonton [*sic*] along But how much She lamented at your Departure." Further news, reminding one that the Sutton-Taylor Feud had not been forgotten, included the fact that Bill Templeton was there now in the penitentiary. William N. "Bill" Templeton was a major figure in the feuding days of the early 1870s. He signed both the treaty of peace of 1873 and of 1874. Hardin himself had signed the treaty of peace of 1873 as well as George C. Tennille, and all four of the Clements brothers. Templeton had signed on the other side, along with William Sutton, Gabriel Webster Slaughter, and Robert Addison "Add" Patterson, his step-brother.[12] Hardin's final note in this letter was for Mannen, to the effect that Templeton was there, "and Says The Sutton party no good But can git a man in But not out [.] tell Him ed Steadman who come Here for Braiking [*sic*] John Ringo and Sco[t] Cooley out of the Lampasas Jail died of Sickness on the 11th [.]"[13]

A later letter raises a question: was there yet another plot involving Mannen to get prisoner 7109 out of Huntsville? As Jane was visiting Mannen and Mollie Clements in San Saba County, Wes asks her to tell Mannen to try and come see him this summer or fall, stating "he might come as a guard with prisoners from his county which would Save expenses" which if arranged, might allow Mannen to get inside the prison, and then perhaps facilitate an escape.[14] But obviously if that was the plan it did not reach fruition.

In June prison officials assigned Hardin to work in the boot and shoe shop "at my own solicitation and soon became one of the best fitters and cutters they ever had." Perhaps. Again he began to realize just "how much of a traitor the average convict was to his fellow," which he should have realized some time before, perhaps while recovering from the thirty-nine lashes. Hardin identified the traitor involved in this plot as Jim Hall, who was imprisoned for his part in the murder of U.S. Marshal Harrington

Lee "Hal" Gosling. Hardin was misinformed, as it was Jim Pitts who murdered Marshal Gosling.[15] But once again, as Hardin and the others in the plot were "out into the prison yard" thirty "armed men arrested us" and placed the would-be escaping convicts in dark cells. Hardin affirmed this plot "was also given away" by a convict. Again, under-keeper Philip J. West, or someone with the authority to do so, administered punishment with the lash as before. Hardin wrote that the whipping was "not so cruelly as before." Hardin now, wisely, concluded that he "could make no play that the officers would not get on to," but also admitted that his "desire to escape was as strong as ever."[16] Hardin placed this escape plan and subsequent punishment as June 1879, but more likely it was in January 1880, as the official record of prison conduct for Hardin does not reference a punishment in June of 1879.

After this amount of time spent in Huntsville one might think that Hardin would have been forgotten as most other prisoners certainly were. But an unusual happening occurred in July of 1879, which placed Hardin's name again in the newspapers, not only in Gonzales County but throughout the state and even the pages of the *National Police Gazette*. The *Inquirer* headlined it on page two with bold type: "JOHN WESLEY HARDIN/ DENIES HAVING KILLED THOS. HALDERMAN/ His Own Statement." The *Inquirer* quoted a paragraph from the *Austin Statesman*:

> Brown Bowen, though hung, was not the murderer. John Wesley Hardin acknowledges that he committed the murder for which Bowen was executed. Bowen protested to the last that he was innocent, and his disappointment at Hardin not saving him from the gallows, it is said, caused him to succumb before death. He was overcome at the scaffold and had to be sustained while preparations for death were going on.[17]

Editor Pilgrim of the *Inquirer* noted that that paragraph, or similar ones, had been "going the rounds of the press" and as he had witnessed the execution of Bowen could accurately note that the statement that Bowen had succumbed was not true, calling it a "palpable error." He reminded his readers that Bowen, once upon the scaffold, called out to John Halde-man, the brother of the murdered Thomas, had some conversation with him which was not recorded, and ended by exclaiming, angrily, "You be-lieve a lie." Pilgrim did not stop there, but wrote to Hardin asking him for a statement for publication. Hardin responded to Editor Pilgrim on July 20; Pilgrim printed the letter in full, which was picked up by a number of other publications.

I am in receipt of your favor of the twelfth instant, and appreci-ate the same. I am enjoying good health and spirits, considering my unfortunate condition. Hope all in your county are enjoying the same with the exception of these bonds. You request me to inform you of the facts of a certain statement being published by many papers, alleging that I had confessed to having killed Thomas Halderman [sic], for which crime Brown Bowen was executed in Gonzales May 17, 1878. Every paper that has pub-lished the same has published a lie, which I fear was calculated to injure me and mine from the very beginning. Some of the papers say that a gentleman from San Antonio, who was just from Huntsville, claims that I made the same statement to him. I wonder what sort of a man it takes to compose the gentleman described by the paper? However, I suppose such gentlemen are easily found when selected from the old Jack Helm mob, which was never anything but a set of liars and coldblooded murder-ers. I wish to inform the public that the author of the state-ment is a liar instead of a gentleman. If I could have made the statement charged to me and have told the truth, I would have made it before Brown Bowen was executed; and if even now I was to say that I killed Thos. Halderman I would tell a false-hood, which I would consider equally as bad as the crime itself. All that I have to say in reference to the matter is, that Brown

Bowen was executed for a crime prompted by his own designs
and committed by himself. He was not convicted upon circum-
stantial evidence, but on the testimony of witnesses whose word
is and ever has been above reproach. The great book says "let
every tub stand on its own bottom."[18] That is my rule and I think
my load is heavy enough without being charged with a cold-
blooded murder I never committed. No one has ever suffered by
law for a crime committed by me, and I hope never will. A great
many papers describe me as and compare me with the most
diabolical murderer that ever roamed the state of Texas. They
sure are mistaken or the state of Texas has failed to do her duty,
or I would have met his fate on the scaffold. I never delayed trial
like a great many try to do, but went to trial on first application,
and the state proved that I never put my hand on my pistol until
deceased had fired the first shot. But I bow in humble submis-
sion to the decree and will wait the interference of a higher
court. I never have had nerve enough to take a man's life unless
I knew my own to be in jeopardy, and I trust and sincerely hope
that all who are laboring under this false impression will dispel
it. The press of the state has convicted me on false reports, and
I do hope that the papers, as well as the courts, will see the time
in the state of Texas when they will let truth and justice prevail,
and not be bowed down by a burden of prejudice.

He concluded this lengthy statement with a plea: "Please ask the press to
give me a rest unless they publish the truth."[19]

Hardin made no reference to this in any letter to Jane. Apparently
there was no need to say anything about it; that her brother had been
legally executed had placed a stress on the relationship between the Bowens and Hardin, and that is perhaps the reason why. As for Hardin's escape attempts and rumors of his punishment there is the official record,
which presumably recorded all of any consequence. Between the January 1880 punishment, and the next, in May 1881, there was the space of

fourteen months. This is no doubt correct, as Hardin wrote in a letter of June 3, 1881, that he had given up the idea of escaping.

> I failed to write you in my Degraded Stat[e] but it was Not for the want of faithfulness or Love but from Secretives motives purley [*sic*] for your good thoug [though] a man[y] a tear I have Shed in your Behalf and for our childrens Sake . . . it was only by the persuasion of my Respective and worthy superintendent that I again Began to write . . . for my part I have Long ago gave up any Disposition on my part to get out of Here by any other means than by Leagal [*sic*] process of Law as I believe I would be better off to Say nothing of those I Love Dearer than life if I was Dead than again to Become an outlaw [I] would rather Spend the Balance of my Life in a Dungeon than be the outlaw I might Be[.][20]

A month later, on a Sunday, "Locked up in my cell for the Night and by Spescial [*sic*] permition [*sic*] from my keeper," Hardin wrote that he was experiencing perfect happiness. He obviously had reflected a great deal on his life, and now began considering writing his life story, "the History of my life in full" in which he would tell the truth, and make his beloved Jane "the Heroine of your sex" within its pages. In this letter he also told her of some of the activities convicts were allowed to participate in. During the regular day he worked in the shoe and boot shop, but on Sundays there were other activities. One convict identified only as "John S." was secretary of the Moral and Christian Society and Hardin was secretary of the debating club. That particular evening the subject was "Whether women should have equal rights with men?" John S. spoke for women's rights, Hardin spoke against. John S. gave a fine closing speech but Hardin proved to be the better in his closing speech for the judges gave the victory nod to him. He was proud of his scoring another victory over John S.[21]

A recurring theme in the prison letters and then returned to in his published *Life*, which if he did not start writing in prison must have been started immediately after his release, is that he never had chosen the trail of an outlaw but was forced into it by circumstances beyond his control, i.e., the loss of the Confederacy, the emancipation of the Negro, the occupation of Federal troops. He still wrote of how happy he was and how his health was good, but always returned to the theme of being driven to outlawry. Did he ever wonder about the hundreds or thousands of other young men who had grown up in the same environment but had not become fugitives, forced to become outlaws? Never would he return to the life of the fugitive "unless circumstances demands it" he wrote,

> When I take a glimpse of the past and See how I Became an outlaw See How me & mine were driven from our homes our property Destroyed our relatives lives taken &C and See How often my life as it were hung upon a thread. And See to day that I am Still Spared makes me hope for some worthy purpose.[22]

At this point he claimed that he began reading "a good deal." He "took up" arithmetic and mathematics including Algebra and Geometry, and "the balance of my time I devote to history." But it was impossible to totally relax behind prison walls, as "One night" officers took him from his cell, "tied me and flogged me again for some imaginary crime" as well as administering the flogging to "thirty others for nothing." Hardin claimed total ignorance of why this was done, but thought punishment was administered "to scare me."[23]

It is impossible to determine if Hardin's recollections of punishments were real or imaginary. His official conduct record shows his punishments were in January 1879, January 9, 1880, May 1881, February 1883, July 28, 1883, February 1885, up to this time in his prison life. In all there would be eleven charges of misconduct, the character of which ranged from "Mutinous conduct to incite impudence," throwing food on the floor, laziness, gambling, and "Trying to incite convicts to Impudence." If Hardin's memory was accurate, and it appears to be fairly accurate as to events but not to dates (he recalled his capture was in July of

1877 rather than August 1877, for example), by early 1886 he had been punished six times, according to the record.

Hardin, as the son of a minister, had received an above average education for the times, as many of his fellow convicts certainly could neither read nor write. He also had kept informed of the events happening in the state by reading the *Galveston Daily News* and Austin's *Daily Democratic Statesman*. He improved his reading and writing abilities—at some point debating within whether to become an attorney or to enter the religious profession like his father—but there is no indication as to when a decision was made. At some point he decided to totally give up the idea of escaping and improve himself and perhaps receive an early pardon.

Benjamin McCulloch, Assistant Warden at Huntsville while Hardin was a prisoner there. *Norman W. Brown Collection.*

One historian attempted to provide an answer to this question. Journalist Lewis Nordyke in 1957 published his biography of Hardin. He wrote that a casual meeting between Hardin and Captain Ben McCulloch, a "one-time Texas Ranger" and acquaintance from the cattle trail to Abilene in 1871, resulted in the latter advising Hardin "to be good [and] cut about ten years off your time, and . . . give yourself a good education so when you get out you can make your mark."[24] Nordyke did not date this "casual meeting" nor provide a source, but there was an assistant superintendent of the prison, Benjamin Eustace McCulloch, the nephew of famed Confederate general, Ben McCulloch. This Ben McCulloch had attained the rank of captain during the war, so he could be legitimately called "Captain McCulloch" throughout the remainder of his life. He was assistant warden from 1883 to 1888 so indeed if Hardin's attitude changed drastically from plotting to escape to being on good behavior, it may have been in part from a meeting with this man McCulloch.[25]

During these years Hardin's attitude indeed did change. He certainly could reflect on what brought about those painful floggings, and after a period of no punishment he felt proud of that accomplishment. In late 1882 he wrote to Jane, then at Zedler's Mills in Gonzales County, reminding her that nothing "goes further to Aleviate my Sorrows" than receiving a letter from her, as she was the "one that I esteem above all others." He then allowed himself a bit of boasting: "Have Not Been punished this yr, 9 mo hast past this yr." He then realized that he was bragging which he disfavored, adding, "though I am not Braggin for Bragg Jeneraly meets with misfortune Before he reaches the woods."[26]

Whatever were the various reasons for Hardin to change his attitude about his circumstances, he did decide to follow the rules and improve his education. The change probably began earlier than he realized, and very gradually, as in one letter to Jane he revealed the anguish he was experiencing due to his inability to see her or communicate with her except through the infrequent letters. This letter does reveal his reading works of much higher quality than the *Police Gazette* or other similar works. He reveals he was reading among others the writings of Martin

Farquhar Tuppet, who published a collection of proverbs in 1850, which apparently was still a popular publication. In one letter he quotes, or almost quotes exactly suggesting he may have attempted to memorize it, by writing to Jane: "Solitary made a cincinatus Ripening the Hero & the patriot. It gave De Staell. Self knowledge it gave imperial Charles Religion for ambition That which Scipio Praised that which Alfred practised [sic] which fed the mind of Milton that which[h] fired Demonsthenese [sic] to Eloquence by all thing[s] Just & wise How truely [sic] Solitude thou art the fostering nurse of greatness."[27]

Mother Elizabeth Hardin was not the only family member finding life difficult without a husband beside her. Rev. J. G. Hardin's death on August 2, 1876, left her with child James Gibson, not quite two years old, at home. Now in 1882 she was living in Gainesville, Cooke County, "doing the best I can." Her daughter Nancy D., "Nannie," born March 31, 1866, had married William E. Casey on July 20, 1881, in Lamar County, but their marriage was in trouble. Mother Hardin wrote to daughter-in-law Jane that Nannie had left her husband for "he was any thing but a kind husband to her [.]"For a while after their marriage Mr. Casey and young Jeff Hardin "got along fine" but after the separation Jeff would have nothing to do with him. She accused Casey of saying improper things, or as she put it, "let his tongue runn" [sic], which Jeff "asked him" about. There was no gunplay fortunately, but mother wrote that "they had quite a Combat." She did not elaborate whether the combat was with words alone or with their fists. After several months passed Nannie Hardin Casey went back to her husband. Mr. Casey may have later appreciated the fact that Jeff Davis Hardin was not as headstrong and violence-prone as his older brother. But to his mother's dismay, son Jeff, then twenty-one years of age, went off and did not return home. In spite of this, she wrote that Jeff "was doing well," with his farming efforts at least. Jeff was proud of sister Nannie and in his mother's eyes he was a good, older brother to "little Gippie," now about seven years old. Other family news in this informative letter must have saddened Jane, as she now learned Martha Ann "Matt" and her husband, William Bright

Berry Smith, had lost their home to fire, losing everything in January 1882. Mother believed the fire was caused by a faulty stove pipe. The Smiths had now moved over to Fannin County. Better news was that son John was now reading the Bible in prison. Mother admonished Jane now "to teach your children the precepts of the Bible [and] may the good Lord bless you and them for ever and Save you all high up in heaven is the Prair [sic] of your troubled Mother [.]"[28]

A few months later mother and Nannie prepared a box of foodstuffs and sent it to John. This package contained a loaf of light bread, crackers, butter, pound cake, jellies, apples and peaches. Mrs. Hardin and Nannie wrote Jane to tell her what they had done, apparently quite proud of their accomplishment, but pointed out they had not yet received word from John that he had received this "box of nick nacks." John also inquired if John Wesley Jr. had received the boots he had made in the boot and shoe shop. John had earlier sent Jane the instructions on how to measure his son's foot properly, and John was wondering if the boots he made and sent had been received. John Jr. was then five years old and would not have known his father. John Wesley was also just as much a stranger to his youngest brother James Gibson, or Gippie or Gib, as he would be known. Mother added that if she could raise the money she would go and visit John in the fall and take "Gippie."[29]

Hardin claimed in numerous letters that his health was good, but mother Elizabeth nevertheless was concerned about her son's health at this time. She wrote to Jane that John had written to her that "his long confinement is begining [sic] to tell his weight only one hundred and forty lbs [.] poor boy I would take his place if I could." Other concerns were for other family members: Matt and Bright, who had lost their home to fire and had gone to Fannin County to live, now had moved to Lampasas Springs in Lampasas County.[30] Mother had not seen Jeff for some time, "Since I rote [sic] you last. I am nearly dead to see him." Perhaps Jane had inquired about how mother was doing, as she answered that she had plenty of milk and buttermilk, had her own cows, and a "splendid garden." Son Joseph's widow at least occasionally corresponded with her.

She had recently received a letter from Belle, and one from her daughter "little Dora" and son "Jodie," who had written to his uncle, John Wesley. She must have been overjoyed to learn that Belle, who had since been remarried to John Wood Pierce, had "professed religion" and had joined the Methodist Church, as had Pierce. As Wood Pierce was a professional gambler perhaps his joining the church was a positive influence from Arabelle Adams Hardin, Joe's widow. Like any typical grandmother, she expressed her love for John and Jane's children, "I am nearly dead to See Sweet little Mollie Johnnie and Jinnie [.] kiss them for me tell them Grand ma loves them dearly."[31]

The themes of the correspondence changed through the years. At times Hardin felt his health was good, but whether from old wounds or the results of inadequate medical attention at times it worsened. In a letter to Jane in early 1884 he complained of "much pain" and that he had been sick in bed from "my wounds." Prison doctors lanced them three times, and he expected the procedure would have to be repeated soon. He had not been able to work for over two months. But he admitted he was treated well; in fact Mrs. Goree, the superintendent's wife, and Mrs. McCulloch, the captain's wife, had paid him a visit on Christmas day, 1883.[32] Hardin may not have been the only prisoner to receive a visit from such distinguished ladies on that very special day. The superintendent's wife, born Elizabeth Thomas Nolley, worked with the prisoners in many capacities. She operated the prison Sunday school, learned Spanish so she could teach the Mexican-American prisoners, and attended every funeral in the prison. It may have been her influence, more than any other, which convinced Hardin to refrain from escape attempts and to study while in prison.[33]

In August 1885 John again asked for medical attention, writing a respective note to Captain McCulloch. He felt he was unfit for any type of work; not having any professional diagnosis he feared he may be suffering from cancer of the stomach, or Bright's Disease, or maybe heart disease. Whatever the problem was it gave him "much pain both mental & physicaly [sic] beyond Description." He requested to see Dr. Bush, and

asked the captain to inform the superintendent that he had become inca-
pacitated, and requested to be placed somewhere where he could "bear
my pain & Sufering [sic] unmolested" as he could not work.[34] Dr. Robert
H. Bush was a physician with many years of practice; living in Huntsville he may have been the official doctor for the penitentiary's inmates.[35]

Later that year John wrote again to Jane, now living at Sedan in Gonzales County, where old James Monroe "Doc" Bockius lived and now
could claim the title of postmaster. He had narrowly escaped the lynching
of Taylor, White and Tuggle in Clinton back in June of 1874 following the
Webb killing. He had married George C. Tennille's widow and they now
operated the post office at Sedan. The Sedan post office—established

Elizabeth Hardin Cobb, sister of John Wesley Hardin, and child. *Courtesy the
Wittliff Collection, Southwestern Writers Collections, Texas State University, San
Marcos.*

January 19, 1885—was modest in the extreme, as the mail was sorted and kept inside their home.[36] John had been keeping up with where family members were living. Sister Matt was then at Gatesville, Coryell County; Elizabeth was in Gainesville, Cooke County; Nannie and Gip were at Ennis in Ellis County. He did not know where his brother Jeff was, but now that he was married he thought he was living in Gatesville. Since mother had died, Nan was the only one who had written him. Almost as an afterthought he pointed out that he thought his health was improving, at least he hoped so. Apparently none of the family noted that his mother, Elizabeth Hardin, had died on May 28, 1885, at Ennis in Ellis County.[37]

Matt, writing to sister Jane in August 1886, told her about Bright and his having a good crop. She also noted that sister Nannie, who had been with them all winter and spring, had left for Ennis. Her letter contained both good news and bad. Sister Nannie in part represented the good news, as Matt supposed Nancy would "Jump the broom Stick before long [.] her fellow lives here but is in Arkansas now." Brother Gip had been to see them but he had left for Ennis as well. According to Matt the reason he went there was because they had a "fine" school there, "a real College." Matt advised that Gip would be there until his education was complete. Jeff, who had lost his wife "6 months after they were married" was then in Kansas with his cattle. Other sad news was that Matt had "hardly been able to be up in a month" and had such a "dreadful cough." She believed she had "consumption."[38]

The unidentified wife of Jeff who had died six months after marriage— and never identified in the surviving Hardin correspondence—was Mary Elizabeth "Mollie" Vinson. She was born about 1862, and she and Jeff were married in Henderson, Rusk County. After her death in 1885 Jeff married Ida Mae Croussore on October 24, 1887, in Lipscomb, Lipscomb County. After their divorce Jeff married Mary Taylor,[39] daughter of iconic Texas feud figure Creed Taylor, October 26, 1896, in Kimble County, Texas. Thus one can see that Hardin did not join the Taylor clan in their feud with the followers of William E. Sutton because of any relationship; Jefferson D. Hardin married Mary Taylor after the death of John Wesley.

Hardin revealed a glimpse into the relationship between warden and prisoner by a post script in a letter to Jane. He wrote that a virtuous and brave woman "has friends every where" and only the previous week Assistant Superintendent Captain McCulloch, "my chief boss" as Hardin referred to him, had told him that Jane "must be a noble excellent woman." This "high complement" filled his heart both "with joy and Sorrow."[40]

By the mid-1880s prisoner number 7109 was reading voraciously, whenever he could at least, spending hours in the official "library" where a prisoner could study law books and draft petitions for relief or clemency, or read the Bible and write letters. He learned from a conversation with his "chief boss" Captain McCulloch that in less than six years he would be released. Of course that depended on continued good behavior. Hardin told Jane that there was a law "that Shortens the Sentence of a man for meritorious conduct." He hoped that somehow the reduction of his twenty-five-year sentence would be even more than the six years, "but let us with patience wait hope and labor."

In the same letter Hardin spoke of the future, the time when he and Jane could both enjoy their lives together, how he could contribute as a family member, that with God's help he would have "purged" himself of all his "wicked intemperate ways." He told her that in sister Nan's last letter she had spoken so kindly of Jane, and told him of a dream in which she had seen Jane and that she "was as pretty and lovely as ever."[41] John Wesley Hardin could enjoy the packages of foodstuffs, and the letters from various family members as well as his children, but it was freedom and Jane that he now could only dream of and hope for.

CHAPTER 17

SEEING JANE AGAIN

"Dear child . . . common Sense and common intelligence of mankind wil[l] vindicate your father . . . there will be no Stigma attached to my name for the blood which I have Spilt is of that kind which can never Stain."

John Wesley Hardin to daughter Jane, July 14, 1889

t is evident from the Hardin correspondence beginning the second decade of his imprisonment that his studying showed results in greatly improved writing. His letters, although still far from grammatical and with occasional misspelled words, unfortunately are filled with axioms and proverbs, biblical quotes or paraphrases, and advice to his children. Rarely does he refer to his actions, which would have provided the historian details of his life. He continued to condemn the legal system that placed him in prison, his "unfair" trial, the appeal, the unjust imprisonment, and the legal murder of his brother and relatives. These were the things that were entirely unjust and actually criminal in his mind. At the same time he expressed pride in his achievements.

"Jane you Know I am an old warrior," he wrote in 1888, "born of battle and the wisest the bravest counseler [*sic*] I ever had except my father was myself. . . . I like advice but when it pertains to me." He continued with a broad overview of his accomplishments:

I belong to no man or Set of men[.] I belong to my Self to my god. his laws are right [.] It has been Said of me before I reached my majority that I had vanquished E. J. Davis's police from the red river to the rio grand from matamoris to Sabine Pass that I

had defeated the diabolical Burero [*sic*] agents and U S Soldiers
in many contests and that I had invaded a foreign State [Kansas]
and released from prison a relative a dear a true friend [Mannen
Clements] whose custodian was Wild Bill the Notorious the re-
doubtable Bill Heycoc of Abaline [*sic*] of whom no braver man
ever drew breath[.]

Hardin, having plenty of time to reflect on his youthful years and recalling the adventures of the Kansas towns of Newton and Abilene, recalled
the episode of meeting City Marshal Hickok and arranging the release
of cousin Clements, jailed for—as Hardin explained—the killing of the
Shadden brothers. He continued:

[A]s to the truth or falsity of these assertions I have nothing to
Say, except that I have ever been ready to stand tryal [*sic*] on
any or all of these charges where a fair and impartial investigation was vouchsafed. But never willing to place my life [and]
my liberty in the hands of a mob even if they wore the eupaulets
[*sic*] of the State [.]

He could not forget the killing of Charles M. Webb, and he still believed
he was justified in his act of killing him. "I . . . was not Sculking [*sic*]
from any law or hiding from any man when I Shot to death the would
be assassin on the 26the day of may 1874 Who desired [and] attempted
to rob me of [my life]."[1] It is not surprising that he continued to believe
the killing was in self-defense, and that he was found guilty not for that
particular killing but for the fact that he had killed so many other men.

As Hardin availed himself of the prison's library he determined there
was a possibility that his term could at least be shortened with the aid of
the legislature. On February 1, 1889, he and ninety-six other prisoners
signed their name to a petition. Hardin's name was the first to be inked;
only a few of the others' names have survived but they included Bill
Templeton, "Mit" Day, A. L. George, and John Tumlinson. No further

mention of this petition is recorded in Hardin's correspondence. Also during this time in spite of the improved writing ability of Hardin the letters are infrequent, sometimes with months in between. Of course there may have been numerous letters that did not survive.

On July 14, 1889, Hardin wrote a lengthy letter to his daughter Jane M., "Jennie," who he thought was mature enough to understand his position, in which he brought up the killing of Webb. He was convinced that killing Webb was "prompted" by the higher law, both "human and devine [sic]," of self-preservation. A man or woman who fails to obey "the mandates of this Supreme law is a poltroon and not worthy to be called an american." He recalled how he was forced to flee to save his own life, seeking "peace and happiness in a foreign State," living under an alias. This was necessary because "mob law reigned in the State of my nativity." Mob law had slain his relatives and friends and now "was aiming its venomous blows at my heart." He continued with the metaphor: he had been hunted "by the Sluth [sic] hounds of iniquity" and "forced from town to town, city to city: but like the noble elastic [elusive?] Stag chased by the hounds and the hunters from Swamp to Swamp from hill to valley is at last brought to bay by the dogs and Shot by the hunters" he was "at last brought to bay" and arrested. He was careful to point out, however, that he did not meekly surrender, but "not until I had exhausted every bit of the means within my power to free myself." To add insult to being captured, he expressed his conviction that "to the discredit of the officers and to the disgrace of the States interests" the arresting officers had no warrants or due processes of law. Further, the officers committed "another cold bloodied murder to accomplish their unlawful purpose." He did not identify James W. Mann by name in this letter, but he stressed that the young man "had not even a moments warning to prepare for eternity." Hardin firmly believed ultimately that he would be vindicated for "the blood which I have Spilt is of that kind which can never Stain." This explanation no doubt excused every one of his killings.[2] We have no idea as to whether his daughter believed that last statement about the blood not staining, or not.

To his son John Jr. he wrote a longer letter three months later. He began with "Noble boy brave and beloved son." His son had written him on September 4, "replete with interesting and joyful news [and] thank you for reviving my Slumbering but cherished hopes, for thrilling my Soul with delight bordering on the ecstatic." What thrilled his soul was the news that he and his two sisters were "quietly and bravely fighting this battle of life on as high a plane as possible" and that he—John Jr.—was "leading the little band Successfully against the great embattled walls of indolence of poverty. [o]f dissipation of bereavements of vice and crime." He regretted not being able to send his son and "lovely Sister" to school and provide for the wants and necessities of each of them, as well as those of their "estimable mother." As tuition for school was out of the question, now "education based upon the truth upon the bible is what each of you need now and will need in the future more than all else." Most important, each of them "must be brave honest and true." True to whom was the question not asked, and he, as the father, had the answer: "be true to yourselves be true to your god and you will be true to everybody else." Even if "poverty" would not permit receiving a "polished education," he had a plan: let "every day be a School day. . . . learn Something every day. [B]e inquisitive be modest, be gentle, but be brave, brave enough to Seek to ask information upon any Subject that you donot [*sic*] thoroughly understand [.] Every spare moment study the book you should have with you." In this letter to his children John Wesley Hardin revealed more the characteristics of a lay preacher than a prisoner, filling the page with guidelines for his son to become a model citizen. In their home at Sedan in Gonzales County, perhaps Jane read the letters as well, silently to herself, or aloud to all three? Or did she let her children open the letters addressed to them and read first? Unfortunately we know very little about Jane's child-rearing techniques. The family was poor, and it was a difficult task to raise the three children without a father to help, except whatever advice he could give in his limited correspondence. One must presume that Jane reinforced every notion within the home that her husband wrote about.

John Wesley Hardin Jr., from a photograph by Rice. Original on card board mount, 4-½ × 7 inches. *Courtesy The John Wesley Hardin Papers, The Wittliff Collection, Texas State University.*

John set aside the importance of studying to give his son some deadly advice. "I say if any man assail your rights your life or your character the laws of your country and the laws of god give you a perfect right to arrest to stop him and if need be to preserve these your dearest posessions [*sic*] you have a perfect right to kill."

A perfect right to kill . . . Did Jane ponder these lines with the children? Hardin as father may have paused momentarily in writing that last statement, but he added he hoped his son would "never have to exercise this inalienable right, but a man that will not fight for his rights and if need be bleed kill and die for them, will never have any possessions worthy of American yeomanry." That "tub" would stand on its own bottom, no doubt.

John Wesley Hardin Jr. definitely took his father's place as head of the household during this period of enforced separation. Naturally his mother Jane and his two sisters would "live virtuous lives" but he should be ready to shed his blood and die in their defense if necessary. Hardin Sr. believed there were "not devils enough in earth or hell to delude them or Seduce them from their virtuous path" but in the event "any lecherous treacherous Scoundrel," no matter what garb he may wear, would try to "assault the character and try to debauch the mind and hearts" of his sisters or mother—the advice was to "just quietly get your gun a double barrel [,] let it be a good gun have no other kind" and once the scoundrel was found "Shoot him down like you would a mad dog or a wild beast." Following the act he should go and surrender to the sheriff. Hardin advised his son not to fear the verdict "of a Texas jury" but in case he didn't "come out all right just lay the blame on me. I can Stand it."

Shoot him down like you would a mad dog or a wild beast . . .

John as father was not through in giving advice just yet and he returned to his letter. He continued this theme of how to live a righteous life with a thought he may have pondered many times. "Ah my son," he began," it is a Serious affair to kill a man, but to every man it is more Serious to be killed." He did not limit his fatherly advice to defending the virtues of his wife and daughters. He said nothing here about avoiding alcohol, but advised against using tobacco. "Don't use tobacco. I thank god and am proud to say that I was taught from infancy to abstain from its use in any of its many forms and now after many years of personal experience I can truthfully say that I donot [*sic*] believe its use is beneficial to health or necessary to manhood or womanhood or conducive to beauty or wealth whether chewed Smoked diped [*sic*] or Snuffed especially [.] "

In summary John asked his son to read the letter over and over again until he thoroughly understood what he had said. He then added for each of them an "affectionate adieu."[3]

While nothing seemed to have come from the petition signed earlier that year, one of the signers—Andrew L. George—was to receive wonderful news, no doubt totally unexpected by him, and perhaps providing a ray of hope for other prisoners. We know a great deal about George because, like Hardin, he wrote a memoir. George's father had died in 1865 when the boy was three years of age; then Mrs. George and her four children moved to Milam County and lived near Rockdale. For an unstated reason Mrs. George did not keep the children as a family unit, and Andrew was sent to live with relatives in DeWitt County. There he attended school in Yorktown. When eighteen he joined cattle drives and for several years lived the carefree life of a cowboy. He became tired of the "wild life" and in the fall of 1884 was in Lavaca County. He and two other young men attended a "Bohemian ball" which ended in a row; a man was killed and George was arrested, tried and convicted. On April 13, 1885, he was sentenced to be hanged on June 26 of that year. Gov. John Ireland "respited" him until August 6; on August 2 the governor commuted his sentence from death to life imprisonment. On August 20 he and Henry M. Sharp were delivered to Huntsville chained together by the neck. Arriving at the prison the guards removed the chains and he was locked in cell number 17 on row seven. The cell had two bunks, one above the other. The next day he was shaved, "all the hair was taken off our head and all the beard from our face." Breakfast consisted of "sour corn bread cooked the evening before, boiled bacon and black coffee." Then he was taken to the warden's office—Capt. William M. Roe then— and weighed, his description recorded, his "citizen's clothes" surrendered and he was dressed in the stripes of a convict. On the back of the shirt and trousers was his name "in large black letters" and under the name was a "red ball" about the size of a silver dollar, which indicated he was a prisoner for life. Captain Roe then took him to the third floor where there was a factory. On the way up they passed the paint shop and tailor shop. "In the latter," George wrote, "I saw for the first time the noted John Wesley Hardin."

Officers had delivered George to the prison with Henry M. Sharp, who had also been involved in the murder of the deceased, described by George simply as a "Bohemian."[4] Sharp suffered from ill health, and within four years of his imprisonment, in late September 1889, he was on his death bed. On September 28 Sharp prepared a death-bed statement in which he confessed to the murder of E. Konesick, the "Bohemian," back on October 1, 1884. He confessed that the killing was the result of an "altercation" between himself and Konesick, and that A. L. George had nothing to do with it. At the time of the killing George was in the adjacent bar-room, and had no connection with the murder. "I fired the pistol myself that killed Konesick," he said. He and George had merely stopped in the bar-room to get something to eat, where later Sharp and Konesick "got into the difficulty." Sharp's death bed confession exonerated George. Gov. L. S. Ross granted him a full pardon based on that confession. The seal of Texas was affixed to the pardon on January 22, 1890, and A. L. George was a free man. What he then did as an occupation is unknown but by 1895 his version of his experience was in print.[5] While in prison Hardin and other convicts certainly learned of George's good fortune; he and others thought there may be means for them to gain the same: what with good behavior and petitions from the outside, early release might be a possibility.

In April 1890 Hardin wrote to Jane and the children and expressed again how his heart was filled with love for them all. He had received an "anticipated intermissive and delectable letter" which, he said, "made me rapturous bordering on the ecstatic." He carried on in this vein, telling her that such "cheering messages" from her did more to keep him on the "path of rectitude and righteousness" than all the Federal soldiers, Bureau agents, carpetbaggers, scalawags, Gov. E. J. Davis's police force, Gov. Richard Hubbard's detectives, Gov. John Ireland's "torturing rack,"

Gov. L. S. Ross's "lenity humanity and magnanimity mixed." After reflecting on his life, he reminded her of the "13 years of Slavery Such as few men Survive" following the ten years of almost "incessant and tragic battle with yankie [*sic*] Soldiers" and he confidently assured Jane he was not conquered or cowed, nor had he sold his manhood to "any living creature"; furthermore he was "Square" with God, man and himself.[6]

Bringing his thoughts closer to reality he urged her to ignore any "wild tales" that she might hear, not to fear writing him any news or to make any inquiries about him. He had confidence in the penitentiary's assistant superintendent, Capt. J. G. Smither, advising Jane to mark her letters to him "private" and Captain Smither would "handle it himself." Hardin felt Smither was a "brave gallant man," and shared with him his belief that the officers and he were "in perfect harmony."[7]

Hardin either wrote fewer letters in the following years or they have not survived. In November, nearly half a year later he wrote expressing his wish to be a free man, "in about three years." He advised Jane to not lose all of her "former good looks." He had met former school mates and acquaintances although whether they were among the prisoners or among the people who visited the prison to see him is not clear. They all told him that he was "doing well" but "nevertheless I am sick all the time." More paternal advice followed on how she should raise the children. To John Wesley Jr. his advice, based on experience, was to not drink whisky, to avoid rowdies and not gamble, but to make an honest living for his mother and sisters. It was a veritable "Do as I say, not as I have done" lesson, from one who had learned life's lessons the hard way. All these admonitions to his children were the result of studying the Bible as well as his reading various law books in the prison library.

Could past offenses, if dealt with in the right way, help him to obtain a pardon? Most district clerks had more or less forgotten about charges that may have been on the docket in the early 1870s, but there was one in DeWitt County that was still current. It was the old matter of Hardin versus J. B. Morgan, a difficulty in which Morgan was killed. It had occurred on April 10, 1873, in Cuero. Hardin shot the man and quietly

John Wesley Hardin Jr. and sister Mollie, two of Hardin's three children. *Courtesy the Robert G. McCubbin Collection.*

left town, believing—as always—that he had acted in self-defense. On December 21, 1877, grand jury foreman J. D. Anderson and jury brought a true bill against "Wes Hardin," charging that amid the chaos of the Sutton-Taylor feud, he with force and arms "unlawfully feloniously Willfully and of his Malice aforethought" shot Morgan "in and upon the side back and breast" several mortal wounds, contrary to all law, both human and divine, and against the peace and dignity of the State. On December

21, 1891, District Clerk of DeWitt County C. C. Howerton provided a true and correct copy of the original bill of indictment for district attorney Asbury B. Davidson, acting as attorney for the Twenty-fourth Judicial District.[8] Hardin chose to plead guilty, gambling on the jury's decision to show mercy: a minimum of two years and a maximum of five. He and his Attorney William Seat Fly had discussed the odds and he chose to plead guilty to get the charge off the books, which would be the last. More importantly, perhaps Jane and the children would be able to be there as well so he could see them for the first time since 1878. He was taken from Huntsville to Cuero with high hopes.

Hardin was fortunate in obtaining the services of William Seat Fly. He was only two years older than the prisoner; he had also been a cattle drover as Hardin had been. In 1855 the Mississippi-born man with his family moved to Gonzales County where he began working as a common laborer in a hide and tallow factory. He began to study law at an early age, and ironically was admitted to the bar in 1873 in Gonzales, the same year that Hardin had killed Morgan in Cuero. Not only did Hardin gamble on the wisdom and experience of W. S. Fly to help him with his case, but Fly was placing his reputation on the line as well, as the Hardin appearance would prove to be a showcase with a court house full of spectators.

Why was the J. B. Morgan case a potential problem, being a matter of years before? William S. Fly was fearful that even with a pardon, Hardin could still be arrested for that murder if the charge remained on the books. Morgan's murder in Cuero was described by Hardin in 1895. He recalled that Morgan had initiated the fight, demanding that he treat him to a bottle of champagne. A short while later, outside the bar, Morgan challenged him. Hardin had to answer the challenge, and he wrote that his pistol ball struck Morgan "above the left eye." The indictment for murder did not occur until four years later, in 1877. He wrote that he pled guilty to manslaughter, "getting two years in the penitentiary for it."[9] Hardin may have realized the reason the indictment took four years, but the truth is that in the aftermath of the arrest and conviction of Brown

Bowen in 1877, Neill Bowen and perhaps others, tried to gain some favor or sympathy for his son by working against John Wesley. Two of the witnesses to the Morgan murder included Neill Bowen and Joe Sunday.

Hardin was a gambler, and he knew this action of pleading guilty in 1891 might go against him for the maximum, instead of the minimum. He did not describe his emotion when he, without shackles or chains, and Jane with the three children, met there in Cuero. Jane may have been haggard and tired and worn looking, but she certainly had applied whatever make-up she may have had to present herself as the woman her husband had remembered. To the three children, Mollie, Jane or "Jennie" and John Wesley Jr., their father was a stranger.[10] Others in the courtroom, besides the judge and jury members, included District Attorney Davidson, Fred Duderstadt, with whom Jane and family had lived for a few years, and of course William Seat Fly.[11] There were other friends such as members of the Duderstadt family present and it was standing-room only.

The arguments used by Attorney Davidson in that Cuero courtroom were not recorded. Certainly attorney Fly appealed to the sympathy and compassion of those DeWitt County jury members. The *Inquirer* of Gonzales had a reporter present and noted that Fly made "an earnest appeal before the court" on behalf of his client. Hardin, speaking in public for the first time in years, gave "a talk full of feeling."[12] Most everyone was sympathetic to the man, and the fact that Mrs. Hardin and the three children were there certainly had a positive effect that Attorney Fly worked to full advantage.

But not everyone agreed that the man-killer should receive sympathy. A correspondent from Runge, a small community southwest of Cuero in neighboring Karnes County, read with "quite a surprise" the sympathetic articles on behalf of Hardin, surprised at "the almost unanimous sympathy his speech created in the court room at his last trial." He wondered at the fact that "this man was once the terror of Cuero, DeWitt county, and West Texas, and large rewards offered for his capture." All was forgotten, "perhaps through his speech, gentlemanly appearance and declaring to be a reformed man." The Runge correspondent stated that nothing was "more detrimental to a town than those fighting characters who terrorize towns and whole counties, w[h]ere panic-stricken, business men close their stores to avoid difficulties with such men, and honest hard working farmers stayed away from towns and places of danger." A dead man can never return to life, no matter how much punishment the slayer receives, he stressed. "Runge" recalled that as a "small schoolboy" during Hardin's "best days" in DeWitt County, he could "remember well the deep seated dread and fear for this once famous out-law . . . and lots of men and newspapers did not dare to state the plain cold facts of the deeds of such men, fearing their revenge." He claimed he had nothing personal against Hardin, only that he wished to express his surprise at the reaction of so many.[13] To be a schoolboy during Hardin's "best days" would have placed him only a few years older than Hardin's oldest child.

The *Cuero Star* responded that the "true object of punishment" was to reform the criminal and transform him into a "peaceable man, a judicial citizen" and any further punishment would be cruel. The *Star* editor reminded his readers that since the prison officials—who had had him in their care for many years and had a large range of experience with human nature in general and the criminal in particular, as well as being men of "probity and honor"—pronounced Hardin "a thoroughly reformed man" and "requested clemency for him at the hands of our court," the *Star* was quite willing to accept their decision.

Hardin had won the gamble and he was sentenced to serve two years concurrently with the existing sentence. He was not taken back to Huntsville immediately. On January 4, 1892, he wrote to Jane telling her "Buck" Cobb had visited him but he was "Suffering intensely" from wounds, whether from old bullet wounds or complications from the floggings he had received he did not say. He also anticipated another visit from her within the next few days, and he noted that he would be there several days.[14]

Two days later, on January 6, he wrote to Judge Fly, from Fly's office in Gonzales, regarding petitions for his pardon. Fly responded he would circulate a petition in Gonzales and DeWitt counties "at once," believing he could get a thousand signatures in Gonzales County alone. In February he intended to go to Austin and present petitions to Governor Hogg "to get a full and free pardon." Attorney Fly expressed faith in Hardin's "integrity and manhood" and did not believe it was "displaced."[15]

Fly continued working for Hardin, but presumably it was out of friendship and his belief in Hardin's cause, as Hardin certainly could not have the funds to pay him. Friends of Hardin also may have contributed,. Fly wrote on May 18, 1892, now that Hardin was back in Huntsville, that he believed "getting the proof" about the Comanche case was a good one and "Will be of great benefit with the governor" in obtaining the pardon. Fly had recently attended the Sheriff's Association convention and had obtained signatures of "nearly all of them" on an application for pardon, through the courtesy of Gonzales County sheriff Richard M. Glover.[16] Fly advised him to get a lawyer in Huntsville to "fix up the papers for affidavits" in regard to Comanche.[17]

In his autobiography Hardin made no mention of Jane's health or how she was raising the children while he was in prison. By 1892 when he saw her, he may have realized she was not in the best of health. By August, with him back in his cell, Mollie, going on twenty years of age, wrote her father about her mother's condition. Her letter has not survived, but in John's reply is an indication her health was failing rapidly: "I cannot describe or explain on paper my deep and my Sincere solicitude for the health of your most estimable mother, my anxiety in regard to her feeble condition cannot be express[ed]. I only wish that it was possible for me to suffer in her Stead." He continued and expressed the hope that before the letter reached her (Mollie) that "my machless [sic] wife that my angelic wife will have regained her acoustom [sic] or normal health." In the same letter, writing to "Buck" Cobb, who was married to Hardin's younger sister Elizabeth,[18] he thanked him for his friendship and all that he had done for his wife and children. He expected to be pardoned by the middle of November, and that "the irrepressible Fly of Gonzales is in perfect political harmony with the democrats."[19]

A week later he wrote a letter to his son in which he quoted an item from the *Cuero Star* of July 18: "Mrs. J. W. Hardin had been very sick for the last three weeks but was able to be up again." In the *Cuero Bulletin* of July 26 a correspondent of Sedan wrote: "Mrs. Jane W. Hardin one of the most estimable ladies of our community had been very sick but that all had been done that could be done by many kind numerous friends and medical skill to restore her to health." That unnamed correspondent from Sedan probably was "Doc" Bockius. Hardin recognized that Jane might not survive much longer, but did not know what caused her to be "very sick." He stated that if "any Serious mishap" should happen to her or the children it would be a "calamity irretrievable and irreparable." Final advice to his son was "Keep away from bar rooms race tracks or any species of gambling or crime or vice."[20] He could not have forgotten that it was the combination of bar rooms, a race track and gambling that had led to the calamity in Comanche on the day he turned twenty-one.

CHAPTER 18

A FULL PARDON

"Enclosed I send you a full pardon from the Governor of Texas. There is time to retrieve a lost past. . . . The hand of every man will be extended to assist you in your upward course and I trust that the name of Hardin will in the future be associated with the performance of deeds that will ennoble his family and be a blessing to humanity."

William Seat Fly, to John Wesley Hardin

Following the brief visit with Jane and the children—strangers to him now, just as he was a stranger to them—prisoner 7109 returned to his cell. His feelings were mixed: euphoric at seeing and holding his family together, but seeing Jane no longer the beautiful woman he recalled, now worn, tired and dying. There are no further letters from him to Jane. A letter to his brother-in-law Joseph Benton "Buck" Cobb in mid-September reveals she was approaching death. He thanked Cobb "from the deepest deapths [*sic*] of my heart" for all he was doing, his taking her to various doctors for whatever assistance the medical profession could provide for what is believed to have been tuberculosis. He could only "hope and pray" that the "wise care and attention bestowed upon her by her friends relatives and medical advisers" along with her "courage prudence and patience" would soon restore her to her accustomed health. Further, he still believed he would be out in November—two months away—but in the meantime Cobb could "Say to her Softly" that all he wanted to do was to dedicate all his strength and efforts to her and "our lovely Children."[1]

This letter was directed to Cobb at Sedan. Certainly Mrs. Cobb—Elizabeth Hardin, Wes's sister—was there as well. Sedan was where former Hardin cowboy James Monroe "Doc" Bockius lived with his wife, Amanda Jane Bockius, widow of George C. Tennille. The Cobbs numbered among the many friends and relatives caring for the consumptive Jane Hardin.

On November 5 another letter from Cobb arrived. He admitted he had had some hopes for Jane's recovery, but this letter apparently was blunt enough that Hardin realized her death was only weeks, or maybe days, away. A line from Jane's letter to him, Hardin now quoted to Cobb, in which she practically admitted that she knew she was on her death bed:

John[,] it Seems So hard that we must be apart but that cannot be helped now, but to be away from my children is harder still under the circumstances and I am going to try to avoid this in the future. your loving your true wife until death Jane Hardin.[2]

It is unknown how Jane had managed to support herself and three children. Her diet was likely very poor, which contributed to the weakening of her immune system. Her diet may not have been that much better than her husband's in prison. Jane Bowen Hardin died November 8, 1892. She was taken to the Asher Cemetery in rural Karnes County where she was laid to rest, close to where her and brother Joshua Robert's grandmother was buried. A funeral card announcing her death was printed, which may have been distributed in various places in Gonzales, Karnes and DeWitt counties, and carried this comforting verse:

A precious one from us has gone,
A voice we loved is stilled;
A place is vacant in our home,
Which never can be filled.
God in his wisdom has recalled,
The boon His love had given;
And though the body slumbers here,
The soul is safe in Heaven.[3]

Even with Jane's death, the motivation to conduct himself so that he could obtain freedom prior to the final date of his sentence remained as strong as ever. Prior to her passing he had her as the optimum goal: sharing the remainder of their lives together. Now, without her, his children remained virtual strangers, but at least he could hope for a while he and they could be a real family. He may not have realized it yet but he would have little to no influence on them; after all, they were now young adults and their father had been in prison all during those growing up years.

Hardin now devoted his time to work on obtaining a pardon. He did not deal with this in his autobiography, but there are remaining letters and other documents that reveal his efforts; he had many friends working for him on the outside. In spite of all his good intentions to behave himself, an incident occurred that had the potential to do real harm to his pardon aspirations. From his description of the incident, in a letter to Captain Smither defending his actions, two prisoners had argued loudly in an altercation in the tailor shop where Hardin worked. Rowland, a black man, and Lynch, a white man, began fighting. Others attempted to separate the pair when Captain Kelly, a guard, "run up jumpt [*sic*] upon the Negro with both feet and Stompt [*sic*] him." In the excitement harsh words were uttered. Hardin claimed he refrained from mixing in, but from seeing Kelly jump on Rowland he said, "just let him jump on me." This phrase, regardless of how Hardin may have intended it or later attempted to placate Kelly, was heard, and possibly misunderstood by Kelly. He approached Hardin and demanded: "What have you got to do with it?" Hardin responded, "nothing unless it becomes personal let him jump on me." Captain Kelly, in this potentially violent situation, believed Hardin was challenging his authority. Hardin quickly grasped Kelly's intent and quickly shed any appearance of aggression, assuming meekness, in an apologizing tone, "I surrender to your authority [.] I don't mean you I would not hit you [.] I would not harm you for any thing [.] for god sake Capt don't do me violence."[4]

So claimed Hardin in his explanation to Assistant Superintendent Smither, who, one hopes, interviewed Captain Kelly and other witnesses to the altercation. Or he may have simply accepted Kelly's report, which would have put himself in the best light of course, and did little else. The lengthy document written by Hardin is undated, thus we can only presume the altercation happened in May of 1893. A newspaper article of September 1893 refers to "recent conduct" of Hardin "had the effect of extending his punishment sometime longer." This article explained that "some of the prisoners had a fight and one of the under keepers of the penitentiary went to stop it, but Hardin interfered" and because of that interference "about four years of the time that had been taken off of his sentence will go back and have to be served out."[5]

The certificate of prison conduct lists the final punishments, numbers ten and eleven, as being administered on May 12 and May 26, 1893. From the official record, the newspaper article and the undated document to Captain Smither, we must conclude that Hardin's attempt to separate Rowland and Lynch spiraled beyond his intentions until Captain Kelly believed he was an accomplice to the fight. Hardin claimed to have on an earlier occasion separated two other convicts, Jim White and Mit Day, from attempting to use deadly weapons, "blood Streaming from each. I did it with fairness[s] to both parties though one was my avowed enemy."[6] Was the May 12 punishment administered for the White-Day incident? Was the May 26 punishment for the Rowland-Lynch incident? Inadequate records fail to answer these questions, but within six months after Jane's death Hardin received punishment only two weeks apart. His most recent earlier punishment had been administered on August 26, 1885. He had behaved himself that many years. On October 29 Hardin wrote a brief note to Assistant Superintendent Smither requesting to know "when my time will be out providing my conduct remains excellent." He explained he wished to make application for pardon "since he was asked about that question many times." He finished the request with "Obediently and respectfully." Captain Smither responded immediately upon receiving the note, writing his response across Hardin's request: "If you continue to be have your self and you will go out at the proper time." Hardly a definitive answer, but better than no answer at all, or a "that depends."[7]

Hardin began the new year of 1894 by writing a lengthy and ver-
bose letter to Gov. James Stephen Hogg, reminding him of the events in
Comanche that resulted in the death of Charles Webb and the subsequent
deaths of his brother Joseph G. Hardin and cousins William and Thomas
Dixon. He admitted that at the time of his trial in 1877 he did not testify
in his own defense as he then was "not a competent witness." He now
had prepared a full account of the killing and stressed that from all the
evidence presented to the governor he believed that at worst he should
have been found guilty of manslaughter. He pointed out that the prejudice was so strong against him in Comanche that a company of Rangers
was provided by the governor to protect him from mob violence; that due
to the prejudice the trial should have been moved to a different county
from Comanche but was not; that a further example of prejudice against
him was that the state had offered the $4,000 reward for his capture but
had not appropriated a single dollar to apprehend any member of the
mob that had raided the Comanche County court house and taken out and
murdered his brother and cousins. Further, the men who had kidnapped
him in Florida and in so doing had shot to death a companion had done
so "without excuse and without warrant of law." Hardin requested that
if one is "acquainted with all the facts and circumstances in the case" he
should not be thought of "less worthy of citizenship than the individual
members of the mob" who murdered his brother and cousins.[8]

Hardin may have been so involved in his efforts to obtain a full pardon that he forgot about other family members, such as his brothers.
Younger brother James Barnett, but whose name was then changed to
James Gibson Hardin in memory of his father, "Gippie" as some family
members called him, but most often referred to as "Gip," had located in
Oklahoma. One of the few surviving letters from him came from Gainesville where J. B. Cobb and his wife Elizabeth, their sister and family
lived. Gip had intended to write William S. Fly that very week about
Hardin but if he did that letter has not survived; what he could have told
Fly is unknown, as he could only tell of what he had learned from others
later on as he was born in 1874. He was perhaps more of a stranger to

John Wesley than his own children. Gip told him how brother Jefferson Davis, known as "Bud" to family, but to all others as Jeff or J. D., was now in Perry, Indian Territory, and had asked him to join him, "and so I came." There Jeff had a saloon, a wagon yard and feed store and intended "to start up a meat market" soon. His business places were four blocks from the city square. The lots he had, in a year or two, "will be worth a great deal." Apparently Gip Hardin intended to become a worthy citizen of Oklahoma, although it then was officially still "Indian Territory." Sister Nancy D., "Nannie", was then in the small community of Whitt, northwest of Weatherford in Parker County. She had wanted Gip to locate there but he had refused, saying that there was "nothing but grass hoppers and dead grass out there" and he liked Perry "fine." In conclusion Gip reminded John that brother Jeff wanted to hear from him, that "he thinks [there] is no one like you." Obviously brother J. D. Hardin was a great admirer of his older brother.[9]

J. D. Hardin's second marriage was not an ideal union of two souls. Ida Mae left husband Jeff in Duncan, I.T. and with the children returned to her family in Kokomo, Indiana, for a while. Although she did not leave any recollections of her life as Mrs. Jeff Davis Hardin, she did leave a beautiful image of her with her children and an unidentified niece. After the Indiana visit she and the children moved to Colorado where on January 29, 1896, in La Junta, she married Manford Wilson Inskeep.

James Gibson Hardin, originally named James Barnett after several relatives but changed at some point to remember his father's name, in some ways was very similar to convict number 7109. He was raised with the best of intentions by loving parents. He received an excellent education, as had John, was naturally bright, and on May 12, 1892, graduated from high school at Ennis in Ellis County, Texas. Instead of getting into trouble with the law at an early age, he obtained a teaching position (which John also had for a short while). He definitely worked as a teacher in Junction, Kimble County, in March of 1896, but perhaps did some teaching prior to that responsibility. His future looked bright; he met and married a young lady named Pearl J. Turner, the sixteen-year-old daughter of Robert M. and Emma Scarborough Turner, both native born Texans. J. G. Hardin and Pearl J. Turner were married at Menard, Menard County, on January 19, 1898. They were not far from her father's home, Menard County being the county immediately north of Kimble County, but they were not married in her home suggesting an elopement. Perhaps the Turner parents did not approve of their daughter marrying a Hardin.

But in 1893 John Wesley was still in prison, J. D. was with Gip in Oklahoma, not yet having met Pearl J. Turner. Gip had earlier expressed the wish he could have met Wes when he was in Cuero for the Morgan manslaughter case, but it was impossible to make the trip. Perry, Oklahoma is situated nearly 300 miles north of Fort Worth. Why brothers Jeff and Gip chose Perry rather than some other location in Texas is unknown. A possibility is they were looking for free land. The "land run" opened at noon on September 16, 1893. Officials estimated that 100,000 men, women and children participated in the run. By nightfall of the first day numerous saloons were operating, although a saloon in those early days was not much more than two barrels with a board across them and perhaps a tent over the entire operation. Bartenders sold beer for one dollar a bottle.

The Hardin brothers could easily have been among the early entrepreneurs of the land rush, known as "Boomers." It would not be the first time a Hardin had operated a saloon. There is evidence that Jeff Davis Hardin had done so in Walsenburg, Huerfano County, Colorado, in the heart of a coal-mining district. At one time the population of Walsenburg numbered 20,000 residents. Robert Ford, the slayer of outlaw Jesse W. James operated a saloon there before moving on to Creede, Colorado, where he met his death in a gunfight. How long Jeff remained there in Walsenburg is unknown, but the Hardins' daughter Mattie Belle was born there on February 9, 1891.[10] One source states that Jeff Hardin and Ford both attempted to kill the other: they emptied their pistols at each other, standing at arm's length, but both survived, due to not only poor marksmanship but probably intoxication. Jeff Hardin was shot in the shoulder and hand, while Ford received a bullet wound in the foot. Both shootists were arrested and jailed; they paid their fine and then accepted the strong advice of the law to move on to greener pastures. Ford located in Creede and operated another saloon. Jeff packed up the family and moved on to the Indian Territory in a covered wagon.[11]

The Hardins, with Colorado behind them, spent some time in Duncan, Indian Territory, as their daughter Della Lillian was born there on December 14, 1893. One is forced to speculate on Jeff Davis Hardin and his troubles due to inadequate records, but Jeff may have gone on to Perry by September after establishing a home of sorts in Duncan. Jeff and Ida Mae Croussore had married on October 24, 1887, but now they divorced and she with the children moved back to Colorado. For years she refused to talk about the fact that she had been married to a Hardin. Her shame was such that she changed her name and that of her children to Davis. Thus, John Wesley Hardin, Mattie Belle Hardin and Della Lillian Hardin, children of Jeff Davis Hardin, became the Davis children. There was no problem in a legal name change; she simply became Mrs. Davis. None chose to challenge her.[12]

But concerns for brothers Gip and Jeff were secondary now. William Seat Fly worked diligently for his client, sending letters from good citizens and petitions signed numerously from various counties to the desk of Governor Hogg. Fly wrote to the governor in September regarding two petitions he had provided earlier that year: Hardin's was one and the other was for John Bratton, "a boy." Fly was eager "if possible" to receive the decision on both petitions. There were "several things" which "commend his application," and "he should be pardoned" as he had "hundreds of petitions in a number of counties and we have in addition to those filed several more petitions." A petition from Kimble County, for example, where several relatives and friends had years before moved to escape the violence of the Sutton-Taylor Feud, including Creed Taylor, carried the signature of William Clements, no relation to Hardin's cousins but a former Texas Ranger who had served with Lt. N. O. Reynolds and safely delivered Hardin to Comanche for trial in 1877. John Gibson and James Clements also signed this petition, as well as brother Joseph

Hardin Clements. On the same one is an indistinct signature that appears to be that of J. W. Turner, who would later have reason to regret meeting up with James Gibson Hardin.[13]

A similar printed application for pardon from Ellis County carried signatures of pillars of the community: J. B. Jones, Mayor of Ennis; R. N. Haynes, Justice of the Peace, Ellis County; W. J. McNeill, Ennis City Marshal; and W. P. Watt, sheriff of Ellis County. The signatures of law officials as well as common citizens finally resulted in what Hardin had hoped and no doubt prayed for, for years: a full pardon. His sentence, if fully served, would have ended on June 5, 1903. The petitions and letters all paid off as on February 17, 1894, prisoner number 7109 was released. At the base of his prison record is written that he had served concurrently a two-year term from DeWitt County for manslaughter, sentenced January 1, 1892. This was signed by then prison superintendent L. A. Whatley. The pardon read simply, in part, "I, J. S. Hogg . . . grant to said convict John Wesley Hardin full pardon . . . and restore him to full citizenship and the right of suffrage."[14]

The most feared gunman of Texas, the deadliest of the gunfighters of the 1870s, the man who defied the State Police of Gov. E. J. Davis, the Federal soldiers of occupation, the dangers of the cattle trail to Kansas, the most famous inmate of the Texas State Penitentiary, now was a free man who could vote, enter the legal profession, continue with his children in overseeing their education and growing up, and a widower much to his sadness. A rarity among convicts, he had studied well in his years behind bars, and now intended to become a worthy citizen to prove to all those who believed in him their faith had not been misplaced.

CHAPTER 19

ATTORNEY AT LAW, J. W. HARDIN

"Tell Wes to be a good man. And keep out of trouble."

Sheriff Thomas Bell to Richard M. Glover, April 14, 1894

One of the first people Hardin intended to meet in Gonzales was Richard M. Glover. They could hardly be called old friends, as Glover was still a boy when Hardin and the Clements brothers had been in Gonzales, driving cattle and feuding with the Sutton forces. Glover's older brother Edward had been with the Clements family and perhaps Richard developed an admiration for Hardin during those years. A decade younger than Hardin, he now was a highly respected citizen of Gonzales County. Born in 1862, his father had been killed on a battlefield in Mississippi. In 1887, "Dick" as he was popularly known, married Margaret A. "Maggie" Colley of Smiley Lake, Gonzales County. He ran for sheriff and on November 4, 1890 was elected; he was re-elected on November 8, 1892.[1]

In a letter to Hardin, Glover apologized for not meeting Hardin but explained that his sheriff's duties, as they did so often, prevented him from so doing. Hardin had already visited an "Aunt Elvira" and Glover assured John Wesley that the visit "did her a wonderful lot of good." Glover also related that he had received a letter from William M. "Buck" Walton, the well-known attorney, who assured Hardin of his "warmest friendship" and pledged to assist him at any time. Walton had written and published a biography of Hardin's former gambling acquaintance from the Kansas days, Ben Thompson.[2] Glover had no news of interest and invited Wes to come in for a visit. If during the day, then he should come to his office; if at night he should just ask anyone, as everyone knew where he lived.[3]

Another attorney at law also wrote to the newly released man, Barnett H. Gibbs of Dallas. He had read of Hardin's pardon in the *Galveston Daily News* and was "glad of it for however great your offense" Gibbs felt that Hardin had within him "the making of a useful man." Gibbs was aware of Hardin's intentions to become a lawyer and encouraged him: "Lawyers as a rule are generous and liberal in their views," he wrote, "and I dont think any of them will fail to appreciate your desire to make up the time you have lost in atoning for your offense against society."[4]

Other people from years past learned of Hardin's release and wrote letters of congratulation. There was one exception, however, as Thomas Bell, sheriff of Hill County, was aware that there was still an indictment against Hardin on the books in Hillsboro. Bell had been elected county sheriff on November 4, 1884, and again on November 2, 1886. Although someone else was elected in 1888, Bell was again elected on November 8, 1892.[5] Sheriff Bell wrote to Sheriff Glover that the indictment against Hardin dating from 1870 when Bradley was killed was still an active cause. Initially Bell had no idea whether or not the indictment would still stand, being that old, but he queried Glover about it. Bell claimed to have been in Hill County when the killing occurred, and was familiar with it. He supposed "there has been considerable change in [Hardin] since that time." Bell claimed to know all of Hardin's relatives in the county and they were "all fine people" and, according to Bell's viewpoint, the citizens thought that in general Hardin had "been punished enough." But still, Bell had a concern, and believed it would be best to keep the case open "untill [*sic*] he thoroughly proves by his conduct that he intends to keep out of trouble and not [cause] any one else trouble [.]"[6]

Glover was sympathetic to Hardin; his brother Edward had been frequently with him and Jim Taylor back in the days of the Sutton-Taylor troubles. Now Sheriff Glover actually sent the letter to "Dear Friend" Wes and underlined the words that described his feelings toward Bell: he seemed to have "a loose screw." It was ridiculous, felt Glover, for Bell to hold the old case over him, "as a kind of prize pole to make you do right." Glover admitted—perhaps aware of some of his own peculiarities—"we all have our peculiurauties [sic]." Glover said he would send Bell "another strong letter which I think will Completely knock his theory of holding this Case as a prize, out."[7] Bell responded two days later. He had visited the county attorney, who agreed the case against Hardin would be dismissed. Bell couldn't just let go with that, however, as if he had to have the last word, ending his communication that he trusted in Hardin's reformation and hoped that he might yet be a useful citizen."[8] Glover shared the letter with Hardin.

Now that Hardin was a free man people tended to use his name to further their own goals. R. W. Finley of Huntsville wrote him advising that he was to be a candidate for nomination to the office of Comptroller of Public Accounts. He had been appointed a clerk in the comptroller's office, was promoted to be chief bookkeeper, and after four years' experience was appointed financial agent of the Texas State Penitentiaries by Governor Hogg. He "respectfully and earnestly" solicited Hardin's support, and if elected he guaranteed his "best efforts" would be directed to the "wholesome economy" and "best interests of the taxpayers of Texas."[9] There is no evidence that Hardin responded to this letter, but Richard Watson Finley did achieve the goal he sought.

The friendship between Glover and Hardin ran deep. Glover had received his friend's letter of April 11 and was glad he was "still improving in health" and when he was "completely restored and ready for business" they would go on "hunting and fishing trips" together. Glover reminded him of the Democratic rally in Gonzales on April 21, with both Governor Hogg and his opponent George W. Clark as speakers. He invited Hardin to come to Gonzales to see them.[10]

Good news for Wes Hardin was abundant. Sheriff Glover called him a good friend; Tom Bell wrote to Glover on the fourteenth that District Court had adjourned and the case against him had been dismissed. "So there is nothing in Hill Co[unty] against him" wrote Bell. "Tell Wes to be a good man And Keep out of trouble."[11]

From Polk County, Ferdinand D. Bishop wrote, on letterhead of Sheriff T. J. Epperson, in response to Wes' letter of April 13, and said he would be "gladest in the World" to see him. He invited Wes to "Come over here" before settling down, advising that Polk County might be a good place to practice law. Bishop assured him that he had "a great many" friends there. Hardin probably did not know that on one of the petitions for pardon there were over 200 signers from Polk County, and one of them was that of F. D. Bishop. That same petition carried the name of Sheriff Epperson as well. When Bishop signed the petition he gave his

John Milam Taylor who remained a friend of Hardin from the days of the Sutton-Taylor Feud through his years in prison. *Courtesy the Robert G. McCubbin Collection.*

Fred Duderstadt who helped care for Hardin's children while he was in Hunts-ville. *Courtesy the Jack Caffall Collection.*

occupation as precinct constable. "Ferdy" Bishop as he was called did not give any hint to an additional occupation. By 1900 when the census taker called he gave his occupation as saloon keeper. In 1894 he was probably in the same occupation, and invited Wes to come and visit all his old friends in county seat Livingston. It was an open invitation for him to come and return to his old life style: frequenting saloons, gambling halls, drinking, all those habits which had so many times resulted in tragedy. Bishop, born in March of 1853, was only two months older than Wes Hardin and no doubt hoped to relive with him some scenes of their youth, at least over a bottle.[12]

Old friends from the days of the Sutton-Taylor feud of two decades before also wanted to see and visit with Wes. John Milam Taylor, who had narrowly averted death at the hands of a mob led by Capt. Joe Tumlinson, wrote, regretting that he was unable to get to Gonzales when Hogg and Clark were there to debate. He said he was "the same old John" that he always was, and was always glad to see old friends. His letter strongly hinted he was lonely: "I would like So much to see you and talk to you [as] it would remind me of olden times."[13] The letter was directed to Hardin at Sedan, Gonzales County, suggesting Hardin may have been staying with Doc Bockius, another old friend of the dangerous feuding days. John Milam Taylor was now in his sixties; born in 1835 he had served in his uncle Josiah Taylor's Company G, P.C. Woods Regiment, Texas Auxiliary Volunteers. He was wounded and returned home for a while but then enlisted in a company of Mounted Militiamen for Home Defense of DeWitt County, captained by another uncle, Joe Tumlinson. If Hardin and Taylor did have an opportunity to get together and talk about old times they certainly had a lot to discuss.[14]

Hardin was not entirely satisfied with the simple friendships of his life. Two letters from Thomas H. Lay of Seguin in neighboring Guadalupe County suggest Hardin may have considered raising horses, probably to develop a stable of racing horses. Lay complained in his letter about too much rain and not being able to get into the fields; others wrote Hardin about paying on the accounts he had. Gonzales dry-goods dealer J. P. Randle wrote him, pointing out that he wanted from his patrons "at least some payment" on their accounts; any payment "will be duly appreciated."[15] Certainly Randle knew who he was dealing with. Hardin at that date owed $114.12. He further drew Hardin's attention to the fact that "Mr. Glover does not feel that he can be responsible for the future increase of your acct." Apparently Hardin had been able to establish credit on Glover's recommendation. Hardin may have overlooked the bills he was accumulating, as he had been concentrating for his legal examination, as well as visiting old friends from his youth. The *Gonzales Inquirer* felt it was news worthy:

Mr. John Wesley Hardin was examined by a committee of the Gonzales bar this week and having passed a suitable examination in the principles of law, was granted a license by the court to practice in the district court and all inferior courts.[16]

Attorneys C. A. Burchard, W. W. Glass, B. R. Abernathy and H. A. Nixon examined Hardin's knowledge of law on July 21. T. H. Spooner, Judge of the 25th Judicial District, conducted the examination and the candidate received his license to practice law in the lower courts.[17]

John Wesley Hardin now had what could guarantee him respectability. No longer would he be referred to as a killer, or an ex-convict; he was a respectable man with a profession he would be proud of. He could set up an office overlooking the courthouse square in Gonzales, or anywhere else in Texas if he wanted to. As business increased he could employ a secretary to handle the daily paper work. Between clients he could even work on his autobiography, which he had been contemplating for some time. He did obtain an office in the newly erected three-story Peck & Fly Building, an impressive structure which remains a Gonzales landmark, and which is still standing today. The courthouse and jail was only a block or so across the square.[18]

But becoming an attorney was easier than developing a paying clientele. His clients were mainly poor people who often made their payment to him in livestock: a horse, cattle, or a wagon. He had enough idle time on his hands that he found he could become involved in the political life of Gonzales County. In November of that year there would be an election for various offices, one of which was for the position of county sheriff.

William E. Jones became the Democratic candidate. He had had a long career as sheriff: appointed as top county law officer on November 10, 1871, he served until November 8 of the following year. It was during this second term that Hardin and Jones first made each other's acquaintance: Jones as sheriff and Hardin as a young prisoner who was placed in the county jail. In 1872 Hardin made his escape, and claimed he had the help of Sheriff Jones. Jones focused on other pursuits until he ran again and was elected on November 4, 1884, and proved to be successful: he served now until November 4, 1890.[19] Then Richard M. Glover was elected on November 4, 1890, and again on November 8, 1892. By the end of that term Glover chose not to run again but left the field open to Jones and another candidate, Robert R. Coleman who ran on the Populist ticket. The man who claimed Jones had provided his means to escape from the jail in 1872, now chose to back his opponent, Robert R. Coleman, for sheriff. Some saw his act as a betrayal of the trust that should have remained between him and Jones.

Coleman also had had experience as a lawman, but as a deputy only. He was born in DeWitt County about 1858, the son of William H., a farmer, and Sarah B. Coleman.[20] Coleman and Ada Tully were married on September 8, 1883. He now wanted more than just farm work, and he worked for a number of years as a deputy alongside Richard B. Hudson. Coleman was too young to have participated in the feud, but Hudson had been a key player in several events back in the mid-1870s, claiming to have arrested Brown Bowen, as well as being in the posse that killed Jim Taylor and his two companions.

Hardin claimed he backed Coleman because he was aware of past events that an honorable sheriff should not have done, such as breaking a prisoner out of jail. He made this claim public in an effort to diminish Jones and to elevate Coleman. Hardin unwisely now neglected his fledgling law practice to place his energies in defeating Jones. He wrote cousin Jim Clements, then in Sterling County, Texas, asking for political ammunition: "Bill Jones by his treacherous conduct toward me has forced me to oppose him for the office of Sheriff and to favor R R Coleman. . . . Now I look upon him as a trator [*sic*] and a corrupt man . . . he has forced me to oppose him by trying to turn John Lackey against me [.]"John Lackey of course was the black man who had been wounded by Hardin when he and Special Policeman Green Paramore attempted to arrest him. Paramore was killed; Lackey severely wounded. Bringing up an incident of twenty years before, as well as what today would be "playing the race card" was taking place in the politics of Gonzales County in 1894. What "treacherous conduct" Jones had done, as perceived by Hardin, is unknown, other than helping Hardin himself escape. Lackey and Hardin had forgotten their past differences, but now Jones was using that old incident to attempt to control the Negro vote in Gonzales County. Hardin asked Clements that if he knew "anything that will reflect upon his Character as an officer please write me plainly, how about that trip of yours and his below if any &c." This mysterious trip may have occurred, or maybe only been contemplated, but Hardin believed Jones and cousin Mannen Clements had gone to Colorado County to kill the man who had killed Jones' brother-in-law. In Hardin's mind, in exchange for helping him out of jail, Clements had returned the favor by killing the Negro. It was beneficial to Hardin then, and now he was using it to defeat Jones. He concluded his letter to Clements with this unusual statement: "I am after him to defeat him for office and in case I fail will move [.]"[21]

The essential question of the 1894 Gonzales County sheriff's race centered on the integrity of William E. Jones. Was he in fact an accomplice in the escape of Hardin from the jail in 1872? If so, in Hardin's mind, he was a corrupt official, not worthy of continuing to hold the office. Coleman apparently had nothing in his background except honesty and integrity. Hardin claimed, and had it published in a local newspaper, that when he was delivered to the jail by the state police in 1872 Jones had informed him he would "turn me out" and "that it was all fixed for me to break jail." Jones gave him the necessary tools to use, a crow-bar, file, saws and grease, all in order to escape. And the reason he did this was so that he or Clements or someone in Hardin's circle could kill a man, a tit for tat proposition. It was an accusation made in print, which Jones could not simply ignore.[22] Some believed Hardin; others believed he should not bring this up as it amounted to an act of betrayal. He justified his action: "I have the courage to expose crime in high places, and I have done it not as Jones' tool, nor as Coleman's champion. But in vindication of myself." He was speaking as a champion of justice, holding only to the highest principles; and unintentionally revealing how his years of study while in prison had improved his ability to articulate his intentions.

William E. Jones answered his opponents' claims in the *Gonzales Inquirer*, the principal newspaper of the county. Jones stated that Hardin's claim was "a lie for the simple reason that my brother-in-law was not killed by a negro until the 19th day of Oct., 1873." The lie was obvious: the jail break was in 1872, and the "favor killing" happened over a year later. Jones was not through, as he obtained statements from three respected citizens who were also good friends of Hardin. They were Crawford Burnett, whom Hardin had worked for in 1871 as a cattle-drover, and brothers John and Fred Duderstadt. Jones claimed they had said they knew Jones as "an honest, faithful and fearless officer." Jones concluded his lengthy response to Hardin's accusations, by referring to "the judgement [sic] of the people among whom I have been reared" and to alert the people of "all campaign lies" which were withheld "till the eve of the election. Those given are false, so will be [proven] the others if Hardin's fertile imagination again gets into print."[23]

In response Coleman published a long letter in early November stating how "perfectly disgusted" he was with the "method of campaign in the sheriff's race [.]"Coleman stated that before either had announced their candidacy he had met with Jones to inquire on which ticket he (Jones) would run. Jones replied that he was uncertain, but he had "always been recognized as a democrat." Coleman claimed Jones told him that if he (Coleman) would run he would back him, as "he regarded me as the best deputy sheriff the county had ever had and the backbone of the sheriff's office." Coleman claimed that after the pair had announced that he again went to Jones asking that a "fair, friendly and courteous race" be run. Jones "readily agreed." Now Coleman claimed Jones was breaking the agreement, bringing up the old charges that Coleman had murdered a man in DeWitt County. He did not reveal that Coleman had been tried and acquitted on the charge. Coleman also claimed that Jones was spreading the lie that if he (Coleman) was elected he would make John Wesley Hardin a deputy, which Coleman now denied. "With Hardin's past record," Coleman wrote, "he thought he was a deadever [dead even?] in me and especially among the colored voters." This "damnable lie" Jones placed in the hands of his "criminal henchmen, both white and colored." He explained all the accusations Jones had circulated, that as a deputy he had to whip a "demented negro" in order "to control her"; he had shot a man but he was "an escaped convict and the law allowed an officer to shoot them when compelled to secure their arrest"; another shooting of a black man was because he had shot in self-defense. Coleman claimed that any action he had taken against blacks he would have done the same even if they had been white.[24]

Coleman was more than willing to let his background be opened for citizens of Gonzales County to see. He was proud of his experience as a deputy working alongside R. B. Hudson. "We have rooted out and indicted the conceded leaders of the thieves of Gonzales county," he claimed, "who were located in the town of Gonzales and who had been running their thieving for years, and too, right under W. E. Jones' nose whilst he was sheriff." Coleman pledged to the electorate he would rigidly enforce the laws, that he would have no deputy not acceptable to the people in the locality in which he would serve, and he would "endeavor to treat all, regardless of race and color, with courtesy and due respect."[25]

As election day approached some feared there might be violence, considering that Hardin might forget his past promises to be a peaceful citizen and revert to gunplay. Frank Kelso of Leesville wrote to Coleman that he and others were going to Wrightsboro to work up support from the Mexican voters. He also advised Coleman: "do not have any trouble if you can avoid it," and "you had better Keep your eyes open." He should caution Hardin to behave: "I would certainly hate to hear of his Being in Trouble again [.]"In Kelso's "private opinion" W. E. Jones would use "foul means to win." More significantly perhaps, he added, "if you are forced to Bulletts [*sic*] try and win & if it is left to Ballott [*sic*] you will win [.]"[26] J. F. Wingate, an old friend, was then living in Big Foot in Frio County. He had been following the events in Gonzales County, knew Hardin as he had also been in Huntsville penitentiary, but was released prior to Hardin's release. "[T]he last time we met it was at the Penitentiary," he wrote, "and bad enough I hated to leave you there in that dreadful place [.]"Wingate had lost a brother, Jack, by violence, and further sorrows weighed on him as his mother had died. He had lived in Trinity County as he pointed out that "Old John Gates" still lived there. It was at Gates' saloon and ten-pin alley where Phil Sublett had nearly killed Hardin years before. As to the sheriff's race, Wingate relayed to Hardin the fears of "Old Doc Hastings" who was a neighbor who feared "you are liable to get into Some trouble about the Sheriff election . . . I hope you will take no part and get into no trouble for sheriffs never did a great deal for you or myself [.]" Wingate continued to reminisce: "I have often thought of the escape you made at Trinity when you was wounded there [.]"[27] Wingate had been a fugitive for years. He was charged with murder in Trinity County in 1866 but was not indicted until 1874; his brother Ed was charged with assault to murder in Trinity County as well in September 1872.[28] One suspects Hardin and the Wingates were well acquainted with each other while in Trinity County, and in Huntsville Hardin at least developed some friendship with Frank. In addition to those expressing concern over what might happen during the heated election, Ben Bratton wrote to Hardin: "you have a great many friends out here but we are all uneasy about you for feare [*sic*] Jones will have some of his curs kill you some night [.]"[29]

Gonzales County citizens went to the polls on November 6 to elect the man who would become county sheriff. William E. Jones won; the man Hardin had backed, Robert R. Coleman, lost. And John Wesley Hardin, who had told many people that if Coleman lost he would move on, now prepared to head west. Two of his children, John Wesley and Jennie, had been staying with Mr. and Mrs. Glover and they had moved out, but Hardin did not hint at knowing why. Glover, who had not chosen to run but probably would have taken the office, now was winding up his affairs to move on as well to something else. He wrote that he now planned to go to San Antonio and look for a job working for Richard C. Ware, the U.S. Marshal of the Western District of Texas. He assured Wes that he had heard of no rumors that W. E. Jones planned to "work up" any old cases against him. He knew there would be "nothing in them save a little trouble for yourself and friends [.]"[30] This letter was addressed to his friend who was already in Junction City, Kimble County, in the Hill Country of Texas. Hardin had friends there; Creed Taylor and family were living there; the Clementses had lived there as well, some having moved out there to get away from the animosities of the Sutton-Taylor feud of the 1870s. Members of the James Madison Denson family were there. The large Denson family had been in Gonzales County in 1880, then consisting of head of household James Madison Denson and his wife Mary Jane Rebecca Clements Denson.[31] She had married first Wiley Kimbro but he lost his life in the war and left her with two sons, Wiley and Mannen. Following the death of her first husband she married James M. Denson and he raised them all together as his own. They had two sons together, John, twelve-years-old in 1880, and brother Green Hardin, eight-years-old, in that census.[32] Brothers John and Green would have an influence on John Wesley Hardin now that he had joined them in Kimble County, and later further west. Further, and Wes did not appreciate this until he was there, there was a young lady in Kimble County who would become infatuated with the gunfighter turned attorney who was now merely drifting. Her name was Carolyn "Callie" Lewis, and she was all of fifteen years of age.[33]

CHAPTER 20

TROUBLES IN PECOS

"There seems to be a feud existing between the Sheriff of that county & the city marshal of Pecos City, & some cittizens [sic] which is liable to terminate in trouble at any time, in fact I don't think it will be Settled So long as the present Sheriff holds office—if I have been correctly informed by some of the citizens."

Special Texas Ranger Baz L. Outlaw to Adj.
Gen. W. H. Mabry, September 6, 1893

How Callie Lewis and John Wesley Hardin met, were introduced, and became more than mere acquaintances is uncertain. For his first Christmas as a free man he may have been lonely, and he and his brother Jeff attended a dance in London, only a dozen or so miles from county seat Junction in Kimble County. There he met the spirited young lady named Carolyn Lewis but known as Callie by everyone. She was born in Burnet, Texas, on July 23, 1879, the daughter of Capt. Lemuel L. "Lyn" and Mary Elizabeth Boyce Lewis, known as Bettie.[1] From what we know about Callie Lewis she probably introduced herself to the man old enough to be her father, certainly a social *faux pas* at that time. His reputation certainly attracted her as he was, after all, *the* celebrity of the Hill Country.[2] However they first met there was a definite attraction between them. On December 30 Callie wrote to "Mr. Hardin"—not yet "Wes"—a note in which she revealed her outgoing personality, one which in the mind of Hardin gave her "spunk," but to her parents she was "forward." She wrote:

I guess you will be a little bit surprised to receive a note from me. Either that or think me Cheeky to address you first. [B]ut you told me if I wanted to see you to let you know so I will tell you I will Expect you new years [.] Come and I will be glad To see you.

She signed it "Your friend."

From December 30 to New Year's Eve was only a matter of hours. What transpired was the briefest of courtships. On January 8, 1895, W. G. Boyle,[3] Clerk of the County Court of Kimble County, issued a marriage license to Mr. John Wesley Hardin and Miss Callie Lewis. On the

Callie Lewis at the age of 15 years, from the original card board mounted portrait made by Iowa-born photographer William H. Curtis; studio located at 227-½ Houston Street, San Antonio. *Courtesy The John Wesley Hardin Papers, the Wittliff Collections, Texas State University.*

following day Fred Wahrmund,[4] Justice of the Peace of Precinct No. 6, united the pair in holy matrimony. London may have experienced somewhat of a shock when the news was made public. The newspapers were ecstatic, noting that London was "still in the swim." The reporter for the *Kimble County Citizen* continued with the great news, alerting the community that "[w]e now come to the front with one of the most romantic weddings of the season. . . ." Hardin needed no introduction to the public, but the reporter understated the obvious by saying he was "well known throughout the state." Miss Lewis was described as "a model young lady" who would be "greatly missed in our social order as she was the life of all social gatherings." Hardin was "a comparative stranger to us, [who] has the appearance of a nice gentleman and we bespeak for him many days of happiness and pleasure yet on earth and a home in heaven when he dies." The *Citizen* reported that Hardin would leave in the morning with his "beautiful and blushing bride" for Austin. He reportedly intended to make his home there "and write his life."[5]

Per the custom of the times citizens of Junction arranged for a ball to celebrate the wedding; friends and acquaintances could gather in friendship; the elite of the county were invited of course as well as the not-so-elite. The dance was to be held in the courthouse with a band that would begin the festivities with "Over the Waves" when the couple made their appearance. Who all was in attendance is unknown, but young John Spruill was. He was only seven years old in 1895, but in his later years he recalled Hardin as "a very nice guy. He laughed and had good manners, and a lot of people liked him." He added, "Course, there were some who didn't." Spruill believed that Hardin and his brother Jeff had come to London because they had cousins living there and wanted to settle down. "I was pretty small when he married this girl. . . . They were giving him a big blowout in Junction but he was too smart for them. He took off. That was the last time as far as I know that he was ever in London." Hardin made a favorable impression on young Spruill. "I don't think there's any doubt about it. I think he had more guts and nerve than anybody I ever seen or heard of. But a lot of people liked him. He had a good personality, friendly and I don't think he misused poor people. He just made it tough on the law. . . ."[6] But the couple did not appear at the ball and the disappointment for Junction society must have been great. Why would Mr. and Mrs. John Wesley Hardin not appear at the grand ball arranged just for them? Mr. and Mrs. Lewis, or Captain Lewis as his friends addressed him, were embarrassed but put on their best face for the sake of appearances.[7]

The Hardin couple may have gone on to Austin prior to the ball, but by the latter part of January the newlyweds were in Kerrville, county seat of Kerr County whose northern boundary line bordered the southern Kimble County line. There has been considerable speculation about the short-lived courtship. A rumor went around that Hardin won Callie in a poker game from Captain Lewis, or that Hardin forgave the gambling debts of Captain Lewis in exchange for the hand of his daughter. After the first glow of their wedding dissipated Callie began to realize that her celebrity husband did not live up to her fantasy. They were together in Kerrville in late January as Captain Lewis wrote to him, as "Dear Son and friend" advising him to tell Callie that her pets, a pig and a colt, were okay, and that Mrs. Lewis "Wants to Hear from you and Callie—tell us How you air plesed [are pleased] with the Trip"—apparently meaning the honeymoon to Austin. He further advised his son-in-law to keep Callie away from London. If she did come she would "Take the Blues" in three hours. Captain Lewis closed his letter with a loving, "Best Wishes to Both."[8]

Before the newlyweds could really become accustomed to each other, Callie became despondent. By early March they had separated, but to save face at least temporarily—to the unknowing public—it may have been nothing more than Hardin being away on business and during his absence Callie went home to her parents in London. She was down hearted; Mrs. Lewis allowed her to attend a dance with Green Denson but she did not dance. As her despondency continued, mother Bettie Lewis became perplexed: she wrote and advised Hardin not to send her any money for if she did she might simply leave—not knowing where she might go. What would she do and where would she go was the question, and mother explained that "she is wild." The other young people in the community were "mad" at her, Mrs. Lewis, because she would not allow her daughter to go to dances "like she did befor[e] she was mairred [*sic*]." Mother had told these angry friends that Callie was "a maird [married] woman and at hom[e] with her mama as the place for her while hire husbond [*sic*, her husband] is gone." Mrs. Lewis was ill at the time she wrote this letter, but she was able to conclude it by giving Hardin some hope for a happy marriage. She said she would be glad to see him "Some day" in the near future and she hoped to see him and Callie living happy with each other.[9] It proved to be a vain hope.

On the same day, March 4, Captain Lewis wrote to his son-in-law, addressing the letter to him at Pecos, Texas, some 200 miles west. Hardin had written him inquiring about Callie and the captain responded, in a letter that may have caused Hardin to appreciate the time he had spent studying in prison to improve his own vocabulary and writing skills, as his letters are notably superior. Lewis wrote in part: "Callie is just as you Left her—She is full of Hell—We Have Kept Her at Home—But the Devil is in Hear . . . and How She Will Com out is moor than I Can tell[.]"[10]

Almost three weeks later Captain Lewis again wrote to Hardin, in response to his letter inquiring about Callie, showing he still had some feelings for her. Captain Lewis apologized, saying he had delayed answering, "Wating to see if thir was Eney change in Callie [.] I See No change in Her She—Seems Just as you Left Her . . . you Said in your Letter you wanted me to Be plain in the matter [.] I Don't think she will Become Satisfied with you [.]" In the letters the name of Green Denson[11] appears occasionally as a friend who could influence Callie. Denson was a Hardin relative and in this letter Captain Lewis said he had not been around since he returned from Pecos, and that he could tell Wes "moore and can Do moore with Callie than all of us Put to gether—I Hope she will Becom[e] satisfied and make you a first class wife—But I am at my End—if Green Denson cant fix the matter Between you and Her we mite as well Let the matter sleep a while [.]"[12]

In spite of what Mr. and Mrs. Lewis wished for their daughter and son-in-law, and what Hardin may have hoped for, the pair never met again, and there was no divorce. Callie Hardin simply stayed in London with her parents and went on with her life. Callie Lewis Hardin for all intents and purposes again became Callie Lewis, not quite the young head-strong girl she had been before marriage to John Wesley Hardin.

Not having any reason to return to Kimble County, Hardin decided to stay for the time being in Pecos. He felt the pull of the old days, reminding him of such fast towns as Abilene, Kansas; that pull was stronger than whatever love he may have felt for his estranged wife. The difference now was that he was no longer a young drover pushing longhorns to market. He was a professional man, an attorney, one who would appear in a court of law and address a jury, defending a man wrongly accused of any number of crimes. Furthermore he had his autobiography to work on, the life story of a man who had consistently fought for what he believed in, defending his honor and his personal freedom, to the point of having to kill to save his own life. How much he had written by this time is unknowable, but it was common knowledge that the work was in progress. Newspapers had referred to his intent; Augustus G. Weston, the proprietor of the Two Brothers' Saloon of Kerrville, who knew him and no doubt shared a drink with the celebrity, wrote him inquiring how he was getting along "with your Book."[13] Later Jefferson Davis Hargis, a cowboy who had ridden the cattle trails but suffered from a severe winter up north and lost the use of his feet from freezing, wrote, saying: "when you get your life out I want you to give me all the Territory down here that I can possibly work [.] I believe I could sell 2000 [copies in Gonzales County.]"[14]

Why was Hardin in Pecos? Was it to escape from the unhappiness in Kimble County? He must have been depressed, his manliness insulted by whatever happened between him and his bride. The reliving of his youth while writing his life story was not enough. James Brown Miller, who had married Sallie Clements, the daughter of his cousin Mannen Clements, telegraphed Hardin to meet him at Sierra Blanca, some eighty miles

James Brown Miller and wife, Sallie Clements Miller and one of their children. *Courtesy Bill C. James Collection.*

east of El Paso. Miller, who was now considered a "cousin" by virtue of marriage to the daughter of a cousin, was at the time in Lordsburg, New Mexico. Miller wanted to meet with Hardin on the eighteenth of February. Although no details were provided Hardin was aware of the difficulties Miller was experiencing with a certain George A. "Bud" Frazer and as an attorney at law he felt he was needed; furthermore, it was a call from a relative, albeit distant, but a call nevertheless.[15]

James Brown Miller had lived a dangerous life in his twenty-nine years, dealing with accusations that he had murdered a number of people, not in order to save his own life like Hardin, but for money. His career was bloody indeed as after a killing he always avoided prison or execution by obtaining the best legal defense, or hiring witnesses to perjure themselves, or killing the leading witnesses. Hired assassin, yes, but on occasion he killed for revenge. On March 29, 1887, Mannen Clements and Joseph W. Townsend, a Runnels County deputy sheriff, argued in a local saloon; guns were drawn and Townsend killed Clements.[16] Shortly thereafter James Brown Miller ambushed Townsend, shooting him with a shotgun. Miller failed to kill Townsend, but the drastic wound cost Townsend his right arm. Less than a year later, on February 15, 1888, Miller and Sallie Clements—Mannen's daughter—were married. Rumors suggested that Sallie Clements became Miller's wife as a tangible reward for the attempted killing of Townsend, but of course that may have been only a rumor; or maybe Sallie Clements had enough "spunk" in her, like Callie Lewis, to offer herself to the man who attempted to avenge her father's death.

Miller later became a deputy sheriff in Reeves County, working under Sheriff George A. "Bud" Frazer. As a deputy he held a position of power which, in the mind of some, he abused. Barney Riggs, a former convict himself, now free after receiving a pardon, warned Sheriff Frazer that his deputy was a thief and a murderer. Frazer at that time did not accept the accusation. Barney Riggs, as tough a man as Hardin ever was, had married Annie Frazer, the sheriff's sister; Sheriff Frazer had married Mattie Riggs, Barney's sister, thus the close relationship.[17] The citizens had elected Frazer sheriff on November 4, 1890, and again on November 8, 1892.[18] James Brown Miller wanted that position, and if he could not obtain it at the polls he was well versed in other means. Since he was now a member of the Clements family he felt he could join Hardin in his circle of friends.

Although most of the colorful and dramatic events in the lives of such men as Miller and Hardin involved shootings and attempts to kill, their days were not entirely devoted to such macabre incidents. Occasionally such things as a birthday party allowed them to relax entirely. On May 14, 1894, Edward O. and Julia Lochausen celebrated the sixth birthday of their daughter Eda. Many of the Pecos residents were invited and many did attend. When most of the guests had left, two men arrived, men whom Mr. and Mrs. Lochausen knew by reputation but little Eda may have only seen at times. When she was elderly Eda remembered her birthday party and that J. B. Miller and J. W. Hardin were the two guests. She recalled that they arrived "after most of the guests had gone, and consumed a quantity of ice cream—a great rarity in that iceless country." If there was ice cream there certainly was cake as well. She shared her memories with historian C. L. Sonnichsen while he was researching the many feuds of Texas. She remembered that Hardin "was a handsome man, and as elegant in his manners as Miller. Probably never before had so much ruthlessness and so much refinement been seen together." One does not think of Hardin or Miller as being *refined*, but at least on this special occasion they could present themselves as debonair gentlemen of the town. For the sake of a little six-year-old girl they could play the hypocrites. But no doubt their weapons of choice were concealed. Little Eda Lochausen grew up and married a relative of the Clements clan.[19]

Miller never relied on his chances in a stand-up gunfight with his opponent. Facing an enemy entailed considerable risk: the pistol could misfire, or possibly get caught in the man's suspenders, or one could lose one's life simply by being outshot. Outnumbering your opponent would place the odds in your favor. On May 22, 1893, Sheriff Frazer was out of town on business, which provided an opportunity for Miller to enact his evil intention. He needed dependable associates to assure the success of his plot to kill. Miller could rely on Mannen Clements Jr. but he wanted one more gun. The third man he chose to help in the assassination plot was Martin Quilla Hardin, a Hardin relative although several generations in the past.[20] As far as known, Martin Hardin had never killed a man and from what we do know about the man he does not seem like an individual who would be drawn into an assassination plot. He came from a nest of Hardins, born in Savannah, Hardin County, Tennessee, on December 13, 1864, the son of Martin and Sarah Hardin. When her husband died Sarah Hardin was left with seven children to raise, the youngest being Martin, age five. Martin remained on the family farm until he was old enough to be out on his own and headed west. He may have actually worked with the Texas Rangers, but in spite of that claim no official record shows that he was ever sworn in as a Ranger. By the late 1880s or early 1890s he was in Pecos and became acquainted with Miller. He was considered a cousin of John Wesley Hardin, but if so the link went back at least to their great grandfathers being brothers. In their mind perhaps they were cousins, without a concern as to just how.

Miller convinced "Mannie" Clements and M. Q. Hardin to work with him in this plot to kill. They would create a disturbance at the train depot upon Sheriff Frazer's return from his trip. He would be off his guard and perhaps tired. During the disturbance shots would be fired and one of them would "accidentally" hit the sheriff. It might have been successful if kept secret, but Con Gibson, brother of the county clerk, overheard the plotting and alerted authorities. Texas Ranger Capt. John R. Hughes investigated the report and arrested the trio of would-be assassins without incident. The indictment stated that the three had plotted "with malice aforethought to then and there kill and murder G. A. Frazer."[21] They were released on bond and in October of 1893 were tried. Not surprisingly they were acquitted due to lack of convincing evidence. The three may have been relieved at the verdict, but Miller continued to hold a grudge against Frazer. Knowing of the plot to assassinate him, Sheriff Frazer decided to take the offensive and now foolishly attempted to kill Miller before he himself was killed. Why Frazer attempted this facing his adversary is unknown; obviously he was unaware of the metal plate Miller consistently wore under his coat, protecting him from all but a head shot. Frazer first attempted to kill Miller on April 12, 1894, but failed. He made a second attempt on December 26, 1894, but again his shots failed to kill. Miller did suffer wounds in the arm and wisely left town for his health, staying in Lordsburg, New Mexico, during his recuperation. Mr. and Mrs. Martin Q. Hardin operated a hotel there, and this provided a safe place for him while recovering. In this situation, Miller decided to use the legal system to defeat Frazer, using his tried and true method of assassination only as a last resort. Then he could become the Reeves County sheriff; at least that was the accepted belief among the citizens of Pecos.

In Lordsburg, 160 miles or more from El Paso and nearly 400 miles from Pecos where the troubles began, J. B. Miller recuperated from his wounds and contemplated revenge. Mannie Clements and M. Q. Hardin were with him. Being shot twice by Frazer was reason enough to plot the death of the former Reeves County sheriff. Perhaps unknown to Miller, Frazer himself was away from the trouble spot of Pecos. He knew full well the danger Miller presented as did the new county sheriff, Daniel Murphy.[22] He was fully aware of the potential trouble when the case of the *State of Texas vs. G. A. Frazer* was called with the two men and their followers ready to begin shooting at the slightest cause. Sheriff Murphy did not want to be alone when that came and wanted Texas Rangers to be there. On February 21, 1895, Sheriff Murphy wrote to Adj. Gen. W. H. Mabry pointing out to him that on March 4 the case would be called, and that since there had been two "shooting scrapes" between the two, and "as both parties have so many friends and as I am unable to keep down troble [*sic*] I would ask that you send me some rangers to remain here during Dist. Court." Murphy wisely preferred that men would not be acquainted with either Miller or Frazer and who would be entirely "disinterested."[23]

G. A. Frazer was also writing but he went a step above the adjutant general and wrote directly to Texas Gov. Charles A. Culberson. On February 24, from Eddy, Eddy County, New Mexico, he requested a detachment of Rangers be sent to Pecos to be there at the opening of District Court on March 4. "I deem my self in secure and unsafe" he wrote, as J. B. Miller would be there, and "he is a dangerous man." Frazer reminded the governor that Miller had been convicted of killing his brother-in-law; and further, Frazer pointed out, Miller had with him John Wesley Hardin "a man only out of the pen. A short time"; he also had his brother-in-law Clements and "a great many others" with him. Frazer explained he did not want any trouble but he knew if he and Miller did meet there would be trouble. "I left Pecos to keep from having any trouble," he said, omitting any mention of his two attempts to kill Miller, "and all I ask is that I be protected." Frazer stressed to the governor that he was sheriff four years and while sheriff "the trouble came up and it has been getting worse all the time . . . now it is a young war . . . and I want peace and Law and order." As a post script he added beneath his signature: "Now Dear Sir hoping You will see to this at once So I can be at court as I do not want to be run off from Justice or be murdered as I have a family to look for be side my self."[24]

Governor Culberson responded favorably to both the requests of Sheriff Murphy and G. A. Frazer by telegraphing and ordering Captain Hughes to "go yourself to Pecos City in command of detachment of 4 men [and] remain there during court." John R. Hughes, captain of Company D of the Frontier Battalion, had been a ranger since 1887. He began his long career that year as a private but with the death of his superior he was named commander of the company. He arrived at Pecos on March 3. When court opened he placed two men at the foot of the stairs leading to the second floor court room with orders to disarm everyone who started up the stairs except Sheriff Murphy and his deputy. Hughes was aware of the fear among the Pecos citizens, noting they were "badly scared and expecting trouble." He had made it clear to all from the time of his arrival that the first man who displayed a weapon would "be put in Jail at once." The case was called but as Hughes anticipated it was moved to El Paso as it was "impossible to get a Jury in this county as it is such a noted case." The Pecos citizens were pleased with Hughes' presence. He wrote Adjutant General Mabry that Frazer and his witnesses were leaving for El Paso the night of March 5. He would remain a day or so and then go to El Paso himself to be present there when the case was called.[25]

While defendant Frazer and Sheriff Murphy were satisfied that Ranger Hughes had prevented any further trouble in Pecos, James Brown Miller was securing his legal talent and this is why he contacted Hardin as mentioned before. He telegraphed Hardin to meet him at Sierra Blanca, then in El Paso County but today county seat of Hudspeth County, to meet and discuss legal strategy. The details of the prosecution have not been preserved but it must have been unnerving for George A. Frazer to receive the stares of two of the most notorious men of Texas, even if they were unarmed, at least in theory, while in the courtroom.

The trial of Frazer provided good copy for the newspapers of El Paso, but the decision of the jury was acquittal. The jurymen probably determined what Frazer had done was no different than what Miller would have done to him, and perhaps Miller's reputation acted in Frazer's favor. The citizens of Pecos, whether for or against Frazer or Miller, returned to their homes. Miller, who had earlier informed Hardin that he was "entirely broke," was confident that "the best citizens of Pecos" would make up a "reasonable fee" to pay him. Hardin had not taken the case just for the money however, but as a matter of honor: a relative by marriage had made the call, and as he was an honorable man he responded favorably.[26] For whatever services Hardin did for him, the "entirely broke" James B. Miller presented him with a valuable 1890 Elgin pocket watch and chain and a .38 Colt "Lightning" pistol in appreciation.[27] A jeweler had engraved "April 7, 1895 / J. W. Hardin From J. B. Miller" in the watch. On the back strap of the pistol only the initials "J. B. M. to J. W. H." appeared. How long Miller remained in El Paso is unknown, but besides presenting Hardin the watch and pistol the pair stopped at a photographer's studio for a formal portrait. They both dressed up for the special occasion, each wearing a white shirt, tie, three-piece suit, and looking quite satisfied with themselves. Or was this the normal daily attire for the professional killer that Miller was and the former convict who was now a respectable attorney at law?

As the legal system had failed to achieve what Miller wanted, he waited but finally took his revenge outside the court system, relying on a system that rarely failed. On September 14, 1896, Miller found his adversary Frazer playing cards in a saloon in Toyah, a village in Reeves County. Frazer should have suspected something when one of Miller's friends, William Earhart, carefully watched the game. Frazer had only time to glimpse Miller in the doorway with the shotgun in his hands before the first blast hit him in the body. He was close to death when the second blast hit him in the face. Frazer was armed, but he did not have time to reach his pistol. On October 3, less than a month after the Frazer killing, Earhart and John Denson attempted to kill Frazer's brother-in-law Barney Riggs in a Pecos saloon. This time they lost as Riggs killed them both. The death of Frazer had been avenged. James Brown Miller wisely left the area.[28]

CHAPTER 21

TROUBLES IN EL PASO

"[John Wesley Hardin is] a quiet, dignified peaceable man of business."

El Paso Daily Times, April 7, 1895

J ohn Wesley Hardin found El Paso much to his liking. In some ways it reminded him of the wild towns of his youth; El Paso now was a wild town of his middle age. The railroad had reached there in 1881 and by the time Hardin arrived the population had boomed to over ten thousand souls. That population was more Mexican than Anglo, but the latter held the power and influence.

Hardin's arrival was noted in the El Paso newspapers. The *Herald*, rushing to get the news into print, provided a two-sentence notice that contained two errors: "John Wesley Hardin, at one time one of the most noted characters in Texas, is in the city from Comanche County. It is reported that John Wesley is now studying law."[1] He had not been to Comanche County since 1878, and he was beyond "studying law" as he was already established as a bona fide attorney. After deciding he would make El Paso his home he opened his law office on the second floor of the Wells Fargo Building.[2] He had business cards printed, indicating his office was located at 200-½ El Paso Street. In contrast to the brief lines of the *Herald*, the *Times* provided a lengthy announcement, which no doubt was contributed by Mr. Hardin himself. This was not an unusual practice; although the publication termed it a "card," it amounted to nothing more than a self-serving advertisement. The announcement read:

Among the many leading citizens of Pecos City now in El Paso is John Wesley Hardin, Esq., a leading member of the Pecos City bar. In his young days, Mr. Hardin was as wild as the broad western plains upon which he was raised. But he was a generous, brave-hearted youth and got into no small amount of trouble for the sake of his friends, and soon gained a reputation for being quick tempered and a dead shot. In those days when one man insulted another, one of the two died then and there. Young Hardin, having a reputation for being a man who never took water, was picked out by every bad man who wanted to make a reputation, and there is where the "bad men" made a mistake, for the young westerner still survives many warm and tragic encounters. Forty-one years have steadied the impetuous cowboy down to a quiet, dignified peaceable man of business. Mr. Hardin is a modest gentleman of pleasant address, but underneath the modest dignity is a firmness that never yields except to reason and the law. He is a man who makes friends of all who come in close contact with him.[3]

El Paso was filled with notorious characters, or noted characters, depending on whether you stood for law and order or for a continuation of the reform movement, which was in the early stages when Hardin arrived. George A. Scarborough, the son of a preacher like John Wesley, was there; only he had followed the opposite path that Hardin had. After serving two terms as sheriff of Jones County, Texas, in the 1880s,[4] he became a deputy United States marshal working in El Paso. Born October 2, 1859, he was younger than Hardin by about six years, but he had accomplished a great deal; he had nerve, had killed men, and had valuable experience as a working lawman.[5]

Jefferson Davis Milton, born November 7, 1861, son of a governor of Florida, had an equally exciting career before arriving in El Paso where he was named Chief of Police on August 10, 1894. He and Scarborough

Jefferson D. Milton and George A. Scarborough. *Courtesy Western History Collections, University of Oklahoma Libraries.*

were friends; they had known each other back in 1878 before Milton had drifted to Walker County and—ironically—worked as a guard for the penitentiary, but whether he and Hardin ever met with the bars between them is not known. This work proved to be too tame for young Milton and to ensure more adventure he joined the Texas Rangers in 1880. He was nominally too young to join, but on July 27, 1880, he was mustered in after lying about his age.[6] On one occasion Milton and others arrested Hardin's cousin Mannen Clements in San Angelo, but no details have survived.[7] In El Paso Milton and Scarborough renewed their friendship from the earlier days and became solid citizens of the town, which was trying to shed its wild frontier image and become a city of the soon-to-be twentieth century. Instead of flimsy board saloons and muddy streets with no sidewalks, it had brick buildings of more than one story, and electric lights.

One other tough character had by now established himself in El Paso: John Selman Sr.; he had two sons, and all worked for the city as constables. Selman remains better known than either Milton or Scarborough today, mainly for the one defining act which ended the life of Hardin, but also because he had been a notorious desperado in Texas and New Mexico in the 1870s and 1880s. John Henry Selman was born in Madison County, Arkansas, on November 15, 1839; he was frequently referred to as "Old John" or "Uncle John" and apparently got along well with children. He was just old enough to be the father of John Wesley Hardin, and perhaps to the children of El Paso he appeared to be a grandfather figure. He was the son of Jeremiah Selman, who by 1858 had located the family in Grayson County, adjacent to Fannin County. By then the Hardins may

John Henry Selman, the slayer of John Wesley Hardin. *Courtesy The Western history Collections, University of Oklahoma Libraries.*

have already moved away so it is unlikely members of the Selman and Hardin family ever met there. John joined the Confederate Army in late 1861; he rose to the rank of Second Corporal and then deserted. Shortly thereafter he returned and served as a private, and then deserted again, for the second and last time. During the next two decades he became notorious, but he also worked as a rancher, and served under Shackelford County Sheriff John Larn as a deputy. In the 1880s he headed a gang of rustlers and murderers who rode and raped and rustled their way across Lincoln County, New Mexico Territory. By the late 1880s he was in El Paso along with his two sons, John Marion, called "Junior" and William, called "Bud." For a while he worked for the American Smelting and Refining Company. Perhaps not so strange, John Selman Sr., in spite of his lawless past, ran for constable of Precinct No. 1 in November 1892. He ran as an underdog but emerged victorious. On April 5, 1894, a drunken ex-Texas Ranger named Baz L. Outlaw shot to death a Ranger named Joe McKidrict outside a house of ill fame in El Paso. John Selman entered into the fray and mortally wounded Outlaw, but not before himself being seriously wounded in the leg. Another Outlaw shot was so close to his head that he was temporarily blinded by the blast. When the smoke cleared one man was dead and one was close to it, and Selman could not walk and could barely see, but he was alive. He would soon be back working.[8] Outlaw, still on his feet, was arrested by Francis M. "Frank" McMahan, who had also served as a Texas Ranger. Outlaw was dead within a few hours.

Frank McMahan had joined Company D of the Frontier Battalion on September 1, 1893, under Capt. John R. Hughes, then worked as a deputy under U.S. marshal Richard C. Ware and later served as a Ranger under Capt. John H. Rogers. He was the youngest of the tough men in El Paso: born July 9, 1870, in Saline County, Missouri, he was not yet twenty-five years of age.[9] Scarborough, Milton, the three Selmans and McMahan were representative of the law in El Paso. If they needed additional assistance Captain Hughes and his Rangers had their headquarters only a few miles away down in Ysleta.[10]

But these tough lawmen would not have been needed in El Paso if such a cauldron of men and women who flaunted the law had not become enamored with the city on the banks of the Rio Grande. If trouble developed in the *Paso del Norte*, one could cross the Rio Grande and lose himself in Juarez, Mexico. As Hardin and others walked the streets and gambled, others were working to enforce the laws against gambling, which in the minds of many attracted other forms of vice, such as prostitution. The numbers were against the lawmen, and those who would enforce the laws were in danger, in spite of their noted skill with their six-shooters. "I have every reason to believe, and do believe," wrote W. C. McGown, District Attorney of the 34th Judicial District of Texas, "that citizens whose only offense is an effort to enforce the laws of this state, are liable to attack at any moment, and their lives in constant danger from this lawless set of men, who have no interest in this community, except to violate its laws, and plunder its people." In his strongly worded appeal to Governor Culberson he requested Texas Rangers be sent to help enforce the laws.[11]

The arrival of John Wesley Hardin and James Brown Miller in El Paso meant two additional men for the El Paso lawmen to watch. Hardin may have served his time and was fully pardoned, and now was a reputable citizen, but still, no one knew what he might become in El Paso. With Miller and his crowd, and Frazer and his crowd, the potential for violence was almost tangible. Once the Frazer trial was complete and those who came had returned home, Hardin became aware of two additional hard cases: Vic Queen and Martin M'rose.[12] Queen was born to Elias and Martha Queen when they were in Arkansas in 1871. In 1880 the Queen family resided in Lampasas County and Victor was nine years old. In that year further south in the Lone Star State were the Sparks family, Burnet and John B. listed as heads of household, and laboring for them was eighteen-year-old Martin M'rose, born in Texas according to the census taker but his parents had been born in Poland. They were listed as stock raisers. Queen and M'rose a decade or more later were wanted by New Mexico Territory authorities for cattle and horse rustling. Hardin soon became involved in the doings of these two men, as an attorney as well as a man weakly holding on to his ideals of honor and integrity.

With the law getting closer and closer to their capture, they found refuge across the river in Mexico, but the Mexican *rurales* learned of their records and arrested them, Queen on March 26, 1895, and partner M'rose on April 6. M'rose was worth much more than Queen: the man who captured him could apply for the posted $5,000 reward. This attracted many lawmen and bounty hunters and detectives. The pair refused to stay in jail and escaped. Detective Beauregard Lee of Raton, New Mexico, was among the many hunting clues for M'rose's whereabouts when he observed Mrs. M'rose at the Mexican Central depot in Juarez. He wisely acquired passage on the same train, figuring that she would lead him to her husband. At Magdalena, Mexico, detective Lee "had the satisfaction of seeing her met by the redoubtable M'rose." But it was not a simple arrest: the lady would not go quietly; her husband was taken in as Lee was the quicker of the two. He also disarmed Mrs. M'rose, taking not only her pistol but also $1,880 from her. Now with two prisoners Lee returned and lodged the couple in the Juarez jail. Lee was eager to collect the reward offered by the Live Stock Association of southeastern New Mexico.[13]

Mrs. M'rose was allowed to leave Juarez to return to El Paso, but she wanted her husband out of the Mexican jail before extradition papers could be obtained and he was taken to New Mexico. Queen and M'rose had their own plan to avoid extradition and swore allegiance to the Mexican government. Mrs. M'rose, or Beulah as she was known, was aware of their intention. New Mexico authorities sent famous Texas Ranger George W. Baylor to meet with Chihuahua officials regarding the extradition matter, but he was delayed because the Supreme Court had not acted on the paper work. That was one report for the delay; another was that the absence of Governor Ahumada "has caused some delay in the extradition of [the] two noted New Mexico cattle thieves." Colonel Baylor anticipated they would be delivered to him "from the Juarez jail in a day or two."[14]

Helen B. M'Rose and child, from a photograph made in Juarez, Mexico. *Courtesy The John Wesley Hardin Papers, The Wittliff Collection, Texas State University.*

Colonel Baylor wanted the two men, but Mrs. M'rose was especially eager for her husband's safe return. She knew she needed an attorney to assist her, however, and went to the office on the second floor of the Wells Fargo Building and met with attorney Hardin. No legal notes were made apparently but there was more than a professional conversation between the two. Beulah by all accounts was an attractive woman. The one authentic photograph of her reveals a rather plain-looking woman, judging her by the standards of more than a century later, but perhaps the camera of the 1890s failed to bring out the beauty that others saw in her. Various historians have attempted to describe her. Lee Myers wrote:

"Beulah seems to have been quite an eyeful and John Wesley decided that he wanted her."[15] "After appraising the face and figure of the beauteous Beulah," Robert K. DeArment wrote, "[it was] lust at first sight, and the former prostitute was not accustomed to resisting ardor."[16] Leon Metz, the biographer of John Selman Sr., wrote simply that the woman was "a blond, blue-eyed prostitute called Helen Beulah."[17] Earlier Lewis Nordyke described her as "a bosomy blonde with heavy lips, blue eyes, and rouge-dabbed cheeks."[18]

Apparently the attraction was mutual and a romance began to flourish between attorney and client. Never mind that Hardin was legally married; never mind that Helen Beulah was married as well, although no marriage license has yet been discovered. They both must have realized that their affair could not be kept secret, and that Martin M'rose would somehow find out. In the meantime the lady had money, although it may have been rightfully her husband's money. So much for honor and integrity and the ideals Hardin had tried to teach his children.

Lawmen and attorneys from New Mexico were gathered in El Paso working to extradite M'rose and Queen. Of course the men in Juarez had friends who gathered, yet not knowing just how they could help. From Eddy and Lincoln counties in New Mexico those identified as allies of M'rose and Queen were Tom Fennessy, Sam Kaufman, and one known only as Lightfoot. These men sent word to Hardin that "he had better make himself scarce in Juarez."[19] They should have known better than make such a threat. Hardin of course could not let such talk pass without responding, but in lieu of sending a message through someone else he decided to deliver his response in person. The night of Sunday, April 21 Hardin was in Juarez and somehow met Fennessy, Lightfoot and others of the M'rose-Queen crowd. He was badly outnumbered and they "tried to bulldoze him and grew quite saucy in their talk." Hardin, outgunned, claimed he did not want to have "a row." This was important news, and the *Times* reporter learned of it, and with a hint of amusement described "Mr. Hardin" as "a spirited man and quick tempered, consequently the little Sabbath day collision did not sit well on his good natured stomach."[20] Hardin used discretion wisely—at least when out-gunned. If such an incident had happened during his pre-prison years he would have challenged these men, but Hardin was no longer the impetuous man of his youth.

The next night he and an unidentified friend were in Juarez and by chance met Police Chief J. D. Milton who was with an unidentified friend, but perhaps George Scarborough. They were not named in any of the newspaper reports, unfortunately. The quartet finished whatever business they had in Juarez and then decided to have a drink. A convenient saloon was found, and the four entered a private room to order refreshments. But with their entrance they discovered it was not such a private room, as there were five of M'rose's friends "in consultation" with Mrs. M'rose. The four faced the five, with a lady present. "To have backed out of the room would have looked like a retreat," explained the *Times*, "so the four friends entered, saluted and took seats." The conversation "became general" but the matter of Martin M'rose was brought up and "hot words" passed between Hardin and Tom Fennessy. "Both men jumped to their feet. In an instant Mr. Hardin had slapped Mr. Finnessy's [*sic*] face and had his gun at his breast." Fennessey's life was saved only by the quick action of Milton, who grabbed Hardin's pistol and prevented him from shooting. While Milton and Hardin were wrestling with the pistol, the other two, Scarborough and Hardin's friend, had drawn their weapons and covered the M'rose crowd. But Hardin's "blood was up" and remembering the occurrence of Sunday night, "he walked up to Lightfoot and gave him a slap in the face that could be heard a block." Milton, "as cool as if he had just stepped out of a bath" placed his back to the door and stated it was best to settle all accounts right then and there. The first occupants of the room, "though game themselves" quickly decided the matter should be dropped.[21] It would be interesting to know what Helen Beulah M'rose thought of Hardin at that point, seeing him in action although not firing a shot.

Before everyone had composed themselves following this near tragic encounter, Juarez police were on the scene. Hardin had slapped the face of two men and displayed his pistol in a threatening manner, but instead of any complaints made to the Juarez *policia*, Chief Milton "explained everything satisfactorily to Mayor Seijas and his officers," and everybody went home.[22] Milton had saved the day and now Hardin could return to his law office in the Wells Fargo Building. More likely he picked up a bottle from the Acme, or the Gem, or the Wigwam, and he and Helen Beulah retired for the evening in his room at the Herndon House.

Hardin was now, in spite of his best intentions, drinking more and more and gambling as well. Although he may have been as quick and accurate with a pistol as in his teen years, the combination of alcohol and age was wearing him down. That his law practice was suffering did not seem to trouble him outwardly. That he was not a good gambler (in spite of what his autobiography would have us believe) and a poor loser was evident. Jeff Milton resigned his position as Chief of Police on May 1 and Ed. M. Fink took over. The new city administration was in favor of loosely enforcing various ordinances against gambling, and the gaming houses reopened their game rooms that same night. The professional gamblers "jubilant at the loosening of municipal restraint" openly welcomed men to their games.[23] That evening Hardin found legal matters boring and chose to join the festive drinkers and gamblers.

At the Gem Saloon a "quiet game" was "moving along smoothly" when "a visitor to the city dropped into the game and commenced losing"; the visitor, whom everyone present must have known but whose identity was not given in the press initially, was Hardin. Phil Baker was the dealer that night and something was said that irritated Hardin. "Since you are trying to be so cute," Hardin responded, "just hand over the money I have lost here." He drew "a ferocious looking pistol" and placed the barrel "in the dealer's face" to emphasize his point. When the dealer had counted out $95 Hardin "raked it into his pocket" and "strolled leisurely out of the room." Hardin had lost and taken back his money at the point of a gun. Those who were present had made themselves scarce when Hardin drew his pistol, but one witness managed to stay close enough to observe what was happening. He compared the city then to a few years before when if anyone had tried to do what Hardin had done, he would not have "got out of the house alive." He noted that Hardin had done the same thing "the other night" although that did not make the El Paso press.[24]

Naturally what happened that evening with Hardin and dealer Phil Baker was the "all absorbing topic of conversation" on El Paso's streets the next day. The *Times* had not used Hardin's name in its reporting, which caused some people to consider it careless as a news source, claiming that if it was a serious newspaper it "would have given Mr. Hardin's pedigree." Hardin, in the eyes of the law, had on two successive nights, staged a robbery. Hardin, attorney though he was, perhaps thought he was only protecting his honor but El Paso law thought differently. He was aware of the talk and what the press said and decided to respond to it all. The *Times* published his statement in the issue of May 4.

> To the people of El Paso and to everyone to whom it may concern: I have noticed several articles in the TIMES and TRIBUNE reflecting on my character as a man. I wish to announce right now that in the past my only ambition has been to be a man and you bet I draw my own idea, and while I have not always come up to my standard, yet I have no kick to make against myself for default. My present and my future ambition is no higher than it has been in the past and I wish to say right now that whether in a gambling house or a saloon, and El Paso seems to be crowded with these places, my only aim is to acquit myself manly and bravely.

He must have paused then and attempted to justify his action in taking back his losses.

> And as to the Acme jack pot, I would not stand a hold out and got the pot without even threatening violence or drawing a gun. As to the Gem holdup on craps, after I had lost a considerable

sum I was grossly insulted by the dealer in a hoorah manner, hence I told him he could not win my money and hurrah me too, and that as he had undertook to hurrah me he could deliver me the money I had played and you bet he did it. And when he had counted out the $95 I said that is all I want, just my money and no more. He said all right Mr. Hardin, and when I left the room and had gotten half way down stairs I returned, hearing words of condemnation of my play. I said to everyone in the house and connected with the play, I understand from the reflective remarks that some of you disapprove my play. Now if this be so be men and get in line and show your manhood, to which no one made any reply, but others nodded that I was right and that they approved my play. Now some one has asked for my pedigree. Well, he is to gross to notice, but I wish to say right here, once and for all, that I admire pluck, push and virtue where ever found. Yet I contempt and despise a coward and assassin of character, whether he be a reporter, a journalist or a gambler.

Now he explains why he is in El Paso and what his intentions are.

And while I came to El Paso to prosecute Bud Frazier [*sic*] and did it on as high a plane as possible, I am here now to stay. I have bought an interest in the Wigwam saloon and you, who, whether in El Paso or elsewhere, that admire pluck, that desire fairplay, are cordially invited to call at the Wigwam where you will have everything done to make it pleasant for you. All are especially invited to our blowout on the evening of the 4th.

Now I have no apology to make to any one for my acts over a jack pot or a crap game, but solicit everybody's custom and guarantee fair play.[25]

The *Times* made no editorial comment on this lengthy statement, which was signed "John W. Hardin At the Wigwam."

Advertisement for the Wigwam Saloon of El Paso. *Advertisement from the* El Paso Evening Tribune, *June 13, 1895.*

Back in Gonzales, the county not big enough for both Hardin and the newly elected sheriff William E. Jones, the *Inquirer* printed the letter from Hardin, knowing that anything dealing with the former desperado would be of interest. Richard M. Glover read the article, and found reason to respond in a letter to Hardin. He was hoping his unsolicited advice would fall on accepting ears, reminding him "let me once more inform you to be cautious and guard well your every act and word. . . . We know your intentions to lead [an] honorable life and regret you are returning to old way of life." Glover advised him to "get right in the quiet practice of your chosen profession." He asked Hardin to write him a letter advising him of what was going on, hoping that such an act would cause Hardin to realize his former good intentions. "I believe however that you are more susceptible to temptation under certain influences than the ordinary man viz: whiskey cards and bad men. . . . Remember: that wherever we be that there is a God, Whether it be in a Saloon Gaming room or elsewhere and that He holds us accountable for all our acts and is ready and willing to remove all difficulties and troubles."[26] Glover was a friend indeed, and if he had been with Hardin during these months no doubt history would have been much different.

Attorney Hardin certainly realized his actions would not go unnoticed by the authorities. Operating a saloon on the ground floor while allowing open gambling on the second was one thing, but displaying a pistol to reclaim your losses was another. On May 6 Frank B. Simmons, the El Paso County sheriff, arrested Hardin on the charge of carrying a concealed weapon. He was taken before the Thirty-fourth District Court where he gave bond in the sum of $100.[27] Three days later Sheriff Simmons again went to Hardin, whether in his law office or in the Wigwam is not stated, and arrested him on the charge of robbery. In both instances Hardin meekly submitted to arrest. This time he "promptly" gave bond in the sum of $1,500 on his own recognizance with E. J. Symes and E. J. Bridges as sureties.[28]

On May 15 Hardin was in county court, charged with unlawfully carrying a pistol. The prosecution was by County Attorney Adrian D. Storms and J. R. Harper; Jay Good conducted the defense, "assisted by the defendant himself who is also a lawyer." A six-man jury was empanelled. First witness called was Charles F. Jones. He testified:

> I know defendant by sight. I saw him in the club room over the
> Gem saloon between 12 and 1 o'clock on the morning of May

2. I saw him display a gun and demand a certain amount of money. After getting the money he went out, but soon returned and challenged the people in the room to trot out if they did not like his play, and as no one trotted out I guess they liked the play. I was sitting at an other table watching a game.

Then some unintentional humor may have caused some laughter in the courtroom. Prosecutor Storms asked if Jones was playing at that game; he responded no, explaining he was broke. Storms then asked "Did you get broke there?" Jones, perhaps in all seriousness, responded: "No sir, I have been broke ever since Cleveland has been president of the United States. I was only there watching the game."

Phil Baker, the dealer who had supposedly hurrahed Hardin, also testified. "I know defendant by sight, saw him in the Gem club rooms on the occasion mentioned. I saw him with a pistol which he stuck in my face. It looked pretty large. He took it from his hip pocket." The defense maintained that Hardin's life was in danger and therefore he should have the right to carry a pistol. The friends of M'rose had made threats against him, had they not? Hardin believed that they would not hesitate to shoot him "should the opportunity present itself." The case would be continued the next day.[29]

The next afternoon, May 16, Hardin was surprised that the verdict brought in was of guilty for unlawfully carrying a pistol. His punishment was assessed at $25.00. Hardin "promptly" filed a motion for a new trial.[30] On June 1 Judge Hunter overruled Hardin's motion for a new trial; Hardin then gave notice of appeal.[31]

During these court appearances the affair between Hardin and Helen Beulah M'rose ceased to be a secret. It became general knowledge that she was staying north of the Rio Grande while her husband was forced to remain south of the river. Each time Hardin left the courtroom, she was there waiting. On one such occasion the fact that Hardin and she were elsewhere may have saved his life, as a visitor to El Paso came looking for him intending to kill him. On the night of May 23 Charles C. Perry of Roswell, New Mexico Territory, stormed into the Wigwam and announced he was looking for Hardin. He had a pistol in each hand and announced he intended to kill Hardin "before day." Fortunately the Wigwam's half-owner was not in, as he was out riding, probably with Mrs. M'rose, although that was not reported. George Gladden however, was there, one-time prisoner in the Travis County jail with Hardin back in the 1870s, who later served time in Huntsville, again with Hardin, until he too received a pardon.[32] Since Hardin was not there, and Perry wanted a fight, he challenged Gladden, who refused. Perry was becoming frustrated now, and in hopes of goading Gladden into a fight, Perry placed his two six-shooters on the bar and ordered Gladden to pick one. A final refusal to make the choice angered Perry sufficiently that he stalked out, leaving Gladden alone to ponder what had just transpired. Gladden then looked up his old associate and explained to him what he had missed. The next morning Attorney Hardin and Gladden appeared in Justice Harvey's court and filed charges against the lawman from Roswell. Hardin identified four charges: rudely displaying a pistol in the Wigwam; carrying a pistol; assault and battery upon George Gladden; and a warrant for peace bond. The *El Paso Herald* and *Times* both gave notice of this action, which in turn was printed in the *Gonzales Inquirer* which Richard M. Glover no doubt read. It is not known if he wrote another letter to Hardin concerning his actions in El Paso.[33] Perry was fined $5.00 on each charge and decided El Paso was not a city to his liking and left.

Hardin was half-owner of the Wigwam Saloon yet he certainly had not earned the money through his legal expertise. What he used to buy a half interest in the Wigwam, and the other money he spent liberally, was no doubt part of the money Mrs. M'rose had, which in turn belonged to her husband. He was aware of her adultery, and that provided a motivation to get across the river and be relatively safe from arrest. How badly he wanted to reconcile with Helen Beulah is open to question; but he definitely wanted to have at least one shot at John Wesley Hardin. To manage a safe crossing of the river M'rose established a relationship with George Scarborough. During the month of June he sent several messages across the river to him. On at least one occasion M'rose and Scarborough met in Juarez and "had a long chat" and attempted to arrange meetings with other unidentified parties. On June 29 M'rose planned to meet with Scarborough again, this time on the Mexican Central railroad bridge. He was still reluctant to consider crossing over to El Paso.

The pair did meet on the bridge; M'rose was alone, but Scarborough was not. He had two friends with him, out of sight: they were Jefferson D. Milton and Francis M. McMahan Scarborough was double-crossing M'rose, as his two associates were to order both him and M'rose to surrender and throw up their hands at a signal from Scarborough. Scarborough met the fugitive in the middle of the bridge, and, as he described the situation:

> He was waiting for me with a cocked revolver in his hand, and when I walked up to him he asked me to wait until he could uncock his gun, which he did with his back turned toward me. We sat down on the bridge and talked for about ten minutes. He remarked to me: "I'm d – n skittish about going across this river. They are watching for me on the other side."

Scarborough then told him he had better return to Juarez, that there was no reason he had to cross over. M'rose then asked if there were any others "hanging around this end of the bridge" and Scarborough answered that he did not see anyone when he went on the bridge. M'rose then jumped up and exclaimed: "By God, I'll go over with you" and the two men started walking toward the Texas side. Once on the Texas side M'rose jumped down on the embankment, Scarborough following him, keeping about six feet in front of him. Scarborough gave him one more chance to back out, telling him it was not too late to return to Juarez. Then, some twenty-five feet from where Milton and McMahan were hidden, Scarborough gave the signal. They called out "Hands up!" but instead of obeying, M'rose sprang to one side, and "as quick as a cat" faced Scarborough and drew his pistol, which he pointed at him. He realized he had been betrayed. At the sound of the click-click of M'rose's pistol being cocked ready to shoot, Scarborough fired. Then Milton and McMahan fired also and M'rose fell. "Of course I wanted to arrest M'rose," Scarborough related, "and there were plenty of other men after him, because there was a reward offered for him. I had been told he was a bad man, and he certainly died game." Deputy Sheriff Jones was quickly at the scene, and found the dead M'rose with his pistol close by his side, cocked. There was an empty shell inside, suggesting he may have managed to get off one shot. M'rose had "eight ugly wounds in his side and breast" some from pistol and some by buckshot. In his pocket was a sealed letter addressed: "Miss Beula M'rose, El Paso, Texas" which was opened at the inquest. The contents of this mysterious letter have not yet been revealed, leaving many historians curious. Scarborough received the credit for the kill. The body was taken to the Star Stable until the next morning for the inquest. After the inquest, undertaker Thomas Powell prepared the body for burial, but not before photographer J. C. Burge made at least one image of the dead man for posterity.[34]

J. D. Milton, as a Special Texas Ranger assigned to Captain Hughes' Company D, was required to make a monthly report. Whereas Scarborough's report was lengthy, Milton's was brief: "Attempted to arrest one Martin Mrose on 29th [.] Warrant was for Fugative [*sic*] from Justice from Eddy N.M. charge Theft of Cattle and horses [.] Mrose resisted and was killed [.]"[35] As the *Times* reported the killing, and Milton penned his letter to his superior, another notice appeared in the popular column "Around Town" of the *Times*: "John W. Hardin has sold his interest in the Wigwam saloon, and will devote himself to the task of writing his own biography." That was news. The editor added, "It will no doubt be an interesting book."[36]

Naturally the killing of Martin M'rose "was the talk of the town" over the next few days. Public opinion condemned the killing, probably considering it no different from the killing of Jesse James or Wild Bill Hickok. A reporter from the *Times* on Sunday heard only one person commend the action of the lawmen and.that one person was an officer. Justice Walter E. Howe presided over the preliminary hearing where

Scarborough, Milton and McMahan each gave their testimony as to what had happened. Here Milton's account was of greater length than what he had communicated to Adjutant General Mabry, as to be expected. Milton insisted that he and McMahan, as well as Scarborough, had yelled at M'rose to throw up his hands several times, but he refused. Milton said: "I thought he would kill Scarborough or some of us, and that was the reason I fired. I shot him once." Apparently first on the scene were two river guards, Thomas A. Bendy and Patrick Dwyer Sr. who brought lanterns and at that moment the investigation began. Justice Howe placed all three lawmen under $500 bond each for their appearance before a grand jury.[37] On Sunday afternoon, undertaker Thomas Powell of the Star Stables buried the earthly remains of Martin M'rose. Not a soul accompanied the hearse to Concordia Cemetery. John Wesley Hardin and Helen B. M'rose stood by at the freshly dug grave, waiting, waiting to say whatever final words came to them.[38]

CHAPTER 22

"I'LL MEET YOU SMOKING"

"Hardin threw his hand on his gun and I grabbed mine and went to shooting."

John Selman Sr., August 20, 1895

Various authors over the years have attempted to list the kills of John Wesley Hardin. Most have relied on Hardin's *Life* exclusively and accept what he wrote as accurate, not raising the question of whether the man Hardin shot was dead or merely wounded. Several of the gunfights in which he participated must be considered "group kills," in which two or more men participated. Examples include the killing of Cox and Christman, shot to death in an ambush by an unknown number of participants; Charles Webb died from gunfire from Hardin, Jim Taylor and one of the Dixon brothers, three to one, all four shooting. Hardin and Jim Taylor both shot to death Jack Helm. Should Hardin be credited with those kills alone?

Various historians have questioned if Hardin was involved in the killing of Martin M'rose. He certainly was not on that bridge or close to it the night M'rose and Scarborough faced each other, but was Hardin an accessory to the killing? The *El Paso Times* reported that M'rose "had made several threats that he would kill Hardin." Since it is not certain that M'rose and Hardin had ever met, we must deduce that the threat was to avenge his honor for Hardin having seduced Beulah M'rose.

The "old Hardin"—before the years spent in prison—would have gone to M'rose and challenged him to shoot it out if he had heard the threat. The death of one of them would have ended the matter. But prison had taught him such old effective ways could lead to imprisonment again, so Hardin found another way to deal with an enemy. M'rose desperately wanted his wife; lawmen desperately wanted the reward offered for him; and Hardin wanted him out of the way for his own reasons. Scarborough, Milton, McMahan and Hardin may have conspired to get Martin M'rose into a position of surrender, or kill or be killed. The lawmen could have easily claimed "self-defense" and J. D. Milton did have a warrant for his arrest. Historian Robert K. DeArment suggests that Hardin "must have been involved in the elimination" of Martin M'rose.[1] If the four could accomplish the capture or death of M'rose they could split the reward. Hardin would no longer wonder if Beulah would be faithful to him or go back to her husband and he could have access to her money. Placing Hardin directly in the conspiracy is beyond proving today, but all things considered, perhaps Martin M'rose should be added to the list of Hardin's kills. Historian Leon Metz in his popular *The Shooters* wrote: "The old Hardin would have looked up Morose and killed him. The new Hardin [after prison] decided to have him assassinated." Although Metz added, "the facts are vague and incomplete," he also included John Selman Sr. in this conspiracy to kill M'rose.[2] If the question arose among these men—Scarborough, Milton, McMahan, Selman and Hardin—four of whom were lawmen, and Hardin who was an attorney and could defend them if necessary, there would be no difficulty in their being acquitted.

With Martin M'rose dead, partner Victor Queen decided it was best to leave the troubles behind and return to Eddy County, New Mexico. There he lived out his years honorably, but also met death with his boots on. In December 1904 Queen and a deputy sheriff turned peace officer for the Burro Mountain Copper Company engaged in a shooting scrape with two other men in the town of Central. Queen was shot to death and his companion wounded. The gun fight took place in front of a saloon about 11:00 a.m. Queen was buried the next day in Memory Lane Cemetery in Silver City, New Mexico.[3]

Following their attendance at the burial of Martin M'rose, John Wesley Hardin and Helen Beulah M'rose may have found some consolation in each other's arms, but Hardin soon experienced additional mental stress. Hardin was sinking with his heavier drinking; he would soon face additional charges requiring him to be in the courtroom. Who he needed more than Beulah M'rose at his side now was a Richard M. Glover, to lift him up to the ideals that he had so strongly preached in the letters to his children.

On July 1, Hardin ought to have been in court but he wasn't. The newspapers gave no reason for his absence, but did report that the case against him for gambling was called for in the county court; since he failed to put in an appearance he forfeited his bond. Over the next few weeks an observant person would have realized that there was something troubling Hardin. It was probably a combination of certain factors: the reaction of the public to the way that Martin M'rose lost his life; troubles with Beulah, who was thought of as "Mrs. Hardin"; and how best to conclude his autobiography. These all could have played a part in his desperation. Beulah was having her problems as well, for on the night of August 1, while Hardin was possibly out of town searching for a publisher, she found comfort in the bottle, so much comfort that she began wandering San Antonio Street. She drunkenly challenged John Selman Jr. to a pistol shooting contest, and Selman arrested her for carrying the two .41 Colt pistols she had. After a few hours in jail, young Selman allowed her release but in court she was fined $50. Two days later Hardin returned and naturally became infuriated because Selman had arrested his woman.[5]

On August 7 the *Times* reported that he "had two pistols when he was arrested last night" but no details provided.[5] He and Beulah had had something much more serious than a "lover's spat" the night before. The couple both had rooms in the Herndon boarding house, and apparently the room they shared was not big enough for both of them. The *Times* indicated he became angry and started the fight when she went out "somewhere in the city" the previous night. Had he become so possessive he could not let her out of his sight? Had Hardin suspected she had gone to another man, and he felt jealous over this perceived slight? Whatever provoked Hardin's anger he became a man possessed, almost a different person. He forced her to get on her knees and pray for her life to be spared, "nearly the entire afternoon." She was frightened "nearly to death" and claimed that Hardin had threatened to kill her. She managed to escape from the room and run into the office of newspaperman Lowe of the *El Paso Tribune*, saying enough that Lowe understood Hardin was going to kill her. She managed to get to Justice Harvey's office and swear out a warrant for the arrest of Hardin. Harvey believed it was serious, what with the frantic Beulah M'rose standing before him, and ordered three policemen to go and arrest Hardin. The trio of lawmen, Capt. Frank Carr, Officer Joseph Chaudoin and John Selman Jr. found Hardin in the Acme Saloon wearing two pistols, and arrested him. Carr must have anticipated resistance from Hardin, but he accepted the arrest peacefully. In Justice Harvey's court Hardin was charged with threatening to kill Helen Beulah M'rose and for "frightening her nearly to death." Hardin was able to give a cash bond of $100 and did not have to spend the night in jail. This arrest of course caused much excitement on the streets, and many people expected to witness a killing soon. The *Times* reported that Hardin had taken "a number of drinks" and that he "expressed himself" that he was not pleased with Scarborough and "intimated that he would tell something about the killing of M'rose."[6]

Hardin supposedly apologized to Scarborough for his harsh language, but this did not satisfy Scarborough, who was already feeling the pressure the public was giving him and Milton for the manner of M'rose's death. Scarborough managed to corral Hardin and forced him to accompany him to the office of the *Times* and have a "card" placed in the issue of August 11. Hardin must have been deeply embarrassed with what he had to submit. The notice was addressed "To the Public" and read:

I have been informed on the night of the 6th, while under the influence of liquor, I made a talk about George Scarborough, stating that I had hired Scarborough to kill M'rose. I do not recollect making any such statement and if I did the statement was absolutely false and it was super induced by drink and frenzy.

The *Times* commented that the card was "published at the request of Mr. Scarborough, for whom it was written." Drink and frenzy! How low Hardin had fallen, from the wild, reckless youth in the early 1870s afraid of no man, to now threatening his woman and then being forced to admit to a lie in the press. That Scarborough forced him to make such a statement suggests he did indeed have something to do with the M'rose killing.

Perhaps for a change of pace, and associates, Hardin drifted over to Phenix, New Mexico, a wild town, which provided shelter for any number of gunmen, fugitives, loose women, and virtually any type of lowlife. Hardin had been there before when he defended cousin John Denson, so it was not a new setting. He found a game to wager on, and instead of winning big he lost, similar to what had happened in El Paso several times. Remembering how he recovered his losses there he simply scooped up his lost coins intending to show them how it was done. No one was impressed with his reputation, and the dealer, Richard Alonzo "Lon" Bass, was even less impressed. Just as brave as Hardin formerly had been, Bass simply pulled his pistol and stuck it into Hardin's face and forced him to return the pot. Hardin had done the same thing to dealer Phil Baker not long before and it had worked. This time, it was Hardin who had the pistol stuck in his face. He left on the evening train back for El Paso.[7] If Hardin had recalled any of his biblical teachings he may have thought of "How are the mighty fallen in the midst of the battle" from the book of Samuel.[8] Reverend Hardin may have, years before, preached a sermon on that very theme.

In spite of these actions indicating the shattering of all Hardin's ideals that he had clung to so consistently throughout his life, he still had some feelings for Beulah M'rose. It was about this time when Hardin was out of town that she was arrested by young John Selman. The *Times* reported that this action "greatly incensed Hardin" and made young Selman an enemy of Hardin. He was convinced that if he had been in town she would not have been arrested.[9]

Later he sent her to Phenix for an unspecified reason, but when she got to Deming she wired back a message: "I feel that you are in trouble and I'm coming back." She did return but left again shortly thereafter.[10]

John Marion Selman, known as John Selman Jr., who arrested Hardin's woman, as photographed by J.C. Burge. *Courtesy Leon C. Metz.*

They never saw each other again. Hardin was left alone in El Paso, having little money and few friends, abusing alcohol daily, and leaving his manuscript unfinished, but intending somehow to get it done and into print. Mrs. M'rose was accurate in her intuition that Hardin was "in trouble," but her brief return and then hasty departure did no good. With her gone Hardin shared some thoughts with his landlady, Miss Annie Williams, who had on more than one occasion gone to their room to get between them to stop their quarrelling. On one occasion she had told them that if they were going to kill each other then they should go outside her boarding house; she didn't want blood spilled under her roof. Hardin ought to have started his day with a good cup of coffee and worked on his manuscript, now that Beulah was out of the picture. Instead, he told Miss Williams that there were three more men to kill before he could satisfactorily complete his life story. She never shared the names of those three, if he had told her, but John Selman Jr. probably was one. John Selman Sr. learned of Hardin's anger over this and there was nearly a shooting between the pair. Old John claimed Hardin had insulted his family. The date is not certain but on one occasion, according to Selman, Hardin had made a "despicable fling at his family" and Selman challenged Hardin to shoot it out. Selman reached for his gun and told Hardin "then and there"

Louis H. Hubbard (right) who, as a boy, delivered a telegram to Hardin the night of his killing. At left is his brother Edward. *Courtesy Dr. George Hubbard.*

he must fight. Hardin lifted both hands and declared he was unarmed. Selman did not believe that of course but didn't shoot.[11] On that occasion Hardin realized he was at a distinct disadvantage and avoided the fight. He preferred to always have the advantage if there was to be a gunfight.

On Monday, August 19, Hardin set aside his writing materials and left his room and headed to the Acme Saloon bar. There, about 2:00 p.m., a young boy approached him with a telegram from an unknown sender. Louis H. Hubbard was working for Western Union then and the telegram had come in about an hour earlier. Perhaps it was from Beulah M'rose, or just as possible it was from his cousin Martin Q. Hardin in Lordsburg. It could equally have been from a prospective publisher. Years later the boy recalled the incident: "I was 11 years old working as a telegram delivery boy. The telegram for Hardin reached me about one p m (late). I delivered it to him about an hour later. He was in a saloon *beginning* to drink at that time . . . he put the glass down when I came up to him at a bar on San Antonio St. in El Paso, at that time a wide-open town. I saw him many times in saloons and gambling dens before that." Hardin tipped "Jack," as the boy was known, a dime and said to him: "Son, don't ever do this." Hubbard recalled that Hardin "loved night-life and was an habitué of the all-night saloons and gambling houses, and was usually still around when the *Times* came off the press. If I was the first to reach him with a paper he never turned me down. I always addressed him as 'Mr. Hardin.'"[12]

What all his actions were during the afternoon hours of August 19 is open to speculation, but he did not remain in the Acme the entire time. About 7:00 p.m. he and Constable John Selman met, close to the saloon entrance. Hardin spoke directly to Selman, insulting him and his family again. The conversation was rude and challenging.

"You've got a son that's a bastardly, cowardly s—of-a-b--!" was the insult from Hardin. As Selman had two sons, the father asked, "Which one?"

Hardin made it clear which one with his response: "John, the one that's on the police force. He pulled my woman when I was absent and robbed her of $50, which they wouldn't have done if I had been here."

Selman replied, "Hardin, there is no man on earth that can talk about my children like that without fighting, you cowardly s—of-a-b--!"

Hardin replied, "I am unarmed."

Selman wanted the fight and responded: "Go and get your gun. I am armed."

Hardin had to have the last word, and insultingly fired back: "I'll go and get a gun and when I meet you I'll meet you smoking, and make you—like a wolf around the block!"

But Hardin did not go and get his gun, because he was already armed with two pistols, concealed in his hip pockets. At that moment he did not want to fight. He then entered the Acme saloon and within moments had perhaps forgotten the abusive exchange with Constable Selman. He and Henry S. Brown began shaking dice.

Outside Constable Selman waited. Within moments his son John and Officer Frank Carr came along and they began to converse. Old John informed them both that he expected trouble when Hardin left the saloon. Concerned for his son more than for his own safety, Old John told young John to keep out of this trouble, and that he should merely continue walking his beat. Selman reiterated to Carr that he expected trouble with Hardin, but it was a personal matter between him and the man inside. Carr was by now well aware of the potential trouble between the two gunfighters but apparently did not advise Selman to leave and avoid the trouble, at least until another day. Selman sat down on a beer keg in front of the saloon, at that point intending to wait until Hardin exited. By now it may have been close to 8:00 p.m. Young Selman and Officer Carr went on about their business.

About 11:00 o'clock, Selman now having waited for several hours outside the saloon, E. L. Shackelford, an acquaintance, came along and wanted Selman to join him for a drink. Shackelford was in the brokerage business, and Selman had formerly worked for him. At first Selman answered, "No I do not want to go in there as Hardin is in there and I am afraid we will have trouble." But Shackelford was insistent, advising his friend that they could go in, have a drink but not get drunk, and avoid any contact with Hardin. Shackelford took Selman by the arm and led him in, going to the far end of the bar, away from where Hardin and Brown were shaking dice. Hardin became aware of the two men, and watched Selman very closely. "When Hardin thought my eye was off him he made a break for his gun in his hip-pocket and I immediately pulled my gun and began shooting" according to Selman's later statement. "I shot him in the head first as I had been informed he wore a steel breast plate." Selman did not know it then, but that first shot was all that was needed. He wanted to make doubly sure. "As I was about to shoot the

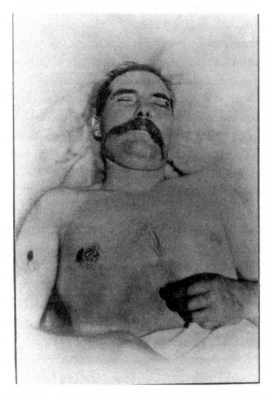

John Wesley Hardin after death, from the photograph made by El Paso photographer J.C. Burge. *Courtesy the Western History Collections, University of Oklahoma Libraries.*

second time some one ran against me and I think I missed him, but the other two shots were at his body and I think I hit him both times." Selman thus admitted firing four shots, now knowing for sure that the head shot had put Hardin down. Then young John entered, ran up to his father taking his arm, saying, "He's dead, don't shoot any more." Then father and son exited the Acme saloon. Old John was far from drunk, although he had had a drink with Shackelford, but he was "crazy-mad" at the way Hardin had insulted his family. Deputy Sheriff J. C. Jones accompanied them both to Old John's house. As a constable, Selman was not placed in jail but did consider himself under arrest. He concluded his statement with the *Herald* reporter at that point, stating that he would be willing to "stand any investigation over the matter. I am sorry I had to kill Hardin, but he had threatened mine and my son's life several times and I felt that it had come to that point whether he or I had to die."[13] This was Selman's version of how John Wesley Hardin met his violent death, made within hours after the shooting.

There were numerous people in the Acme when the shooting began and several gave their own statements as to what had happened. Selman had stated he and Shackelford were at the end of the bar when he saw Hardin go for his pistol. What did Shackelford state?

> When I came down the street this evening [August 19] I had understood from some parties that Mr. Hardin had made some threats against Mr. Selman who had formerly been in my employ and was a friend of mine and I came over to the Acme saloon where I met Mr. Selman. At the time I met Mr. Selman he was in the saloon with several other parties and was drinking with them. I told him I understood there was occasion for him to have trouble and having heard the character of the man with whom he would have trouble I advised him as a friend not to get under the influence of liquor. We walked out on the sidewalk and came back in to the saloon. I being some distance ahead of Mr. Selman, walking toward the back of the saloon. Then I

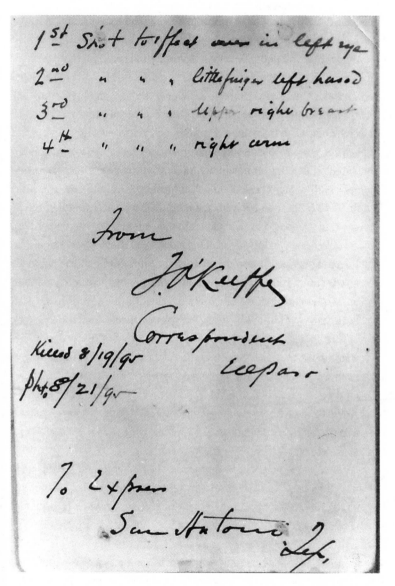

The reverse of the death photo used by the San Antonio Express reporter to note the bullet wounds. *Author's Collection.*

heard shots fired. I can't say who fired and did not see it. I did not turn around but left immediately. The room was full of powder smoke and I could not have seen anything anyhow.

The difference between Shackelford's and Selman's description is that the former claimed he met Selman in the saloon, not out on the street where Selman was sitting on a beer keg.

Henry S. Brown, with whom Hardin was shaking dice when the shots were fired, was as close to him as anyone. Brown was in the grocery business with a Mr. Lambert and had "dropped in" the Acme a little before 11:00 o'clock and Hardin had asked him to shake dice. As Brown remembered:

I agreed and shook first, he shook back and said he'd bet me a quarter on the side he could beat me. We both had our quarters up and he and I were shaking dice. I heard a shot fired, saw a flash and Mr. Hardin fell at my feet at my left side. I heard three or four shots fired [and] when the first shot was fired Mr. Hardin was against the bar facing it, as near as I can say, and as near as I can say his back was towards the direction the shot came from. I did not see him make any effort to get his six-shooter. The last words he spoke before the first shot was fired were "Four sixes to beat" and they were addressed to me.

R. B. Stevens was the proprietor of the Acme and of course he was also questioned by the *Herald* reporter. He told essentially the same story as the others: that he had heard there may be trouble between Hardin and Selman, that he came to the Acme that night and when he entered the saloon Selman was seated outside the door. Hardin was standing just inside the door at the bar shaking dice with Brown. He then went back into the "reading room" and sat down where he could see the bar. He then saw Shackelford and Selman walk in and take a drink. He then "understood" Shackelford say to Selman, "Come out now, you are drinking and I don't want you to have any trouble." They then went out together, and Stevens assumed at that point that there would be no trouble that night. He then relaxed and started talking with one "Shorty" Anderson.

Anderson's explanation of what happened was very specific as he claimed he saw Hardin go for his pistol.

> I watched the boys shaking dice in the glass. Pretty soon Shackelford and Selman came in—they had gone out and went to the bar and took a drink. I got up from the table then and walked about three feet from the inside doors. I saw Hardin turn and throw his hand back upon his hip, throw his coat back. Then I heard a pistol shot and he fell. I don't know who fired that pistol shot. I did not hear anything said when that shot was fired. Three or four shots were fired. When the smoke cleared up, I saw Hardin lying on the floor, and John Selman and his son in there.[14]

Numerous writers have claimed Hardin was so fast and accurate with his six-shooters that no one could beat him. Louis H. Hubbard, years after delivering those telegrams to Hardin, wrote of him: "He was the terror of every community he entered, and was reputed to be the quickest man on the draw of all the Southwestern desperadoes."[15] But on this occasion, he was not quick enough if we accept the statement of witness Shorty Anderson. Too late Hardin had finally come to the realization that speed was useless against a man who already had his gun out, cocked, and ready to fire.

CHAPTER 23

THE YOUNGEST BROTHER

*"Hardin was a born leader of men, whether for good or evil,
and had it not been for the unfortunate surroundings of his boyhood days, would undoubtedly have made a mark in civil life."*

Publishers Smith & Moore, 1896

Adrian D. Storms, the El Paso County Attorney, kept notebooks
concerning his business matters and on August 20 went to Thomas
Powell's funeral parlor with two friends, Maurice McKillegon and
Joseph Woodson, to look at the body of John Wesley Hardin. With a tape
measure he and Powell took measurements, and noted: "Bullet hole in
back of head was even in heighth [*sic*] with large cavity of right ear and
3 ¼ in[ch] from edge of rim of right ear. Bullet hole in left eye between
eye brow and edge of eye lid and at the extreme left of eye lid." Storms
sketched in his notebook the brow, the closed eye, and the bullet hole,
and continued: "Bullet hole just 9 in. from base of neck and about 1 ½
in. from back bone on right side . . . and just at right of right nipple where
Powell said drs. Said it went in. Another through right arm. Drs. Said it
went in back side. It was in back of arm 10 in. from point of elbo[w] and
on front side 8 ½ in. from front of elbo[w]." This he also sketched.[1]

Hardin was dead on the floor the night of August 19. The following day the corpse was delivered to the funeral parlor where Tom Powell cleaned it up prior to burial. While doing his work "a contraction of
the muscles" caused Hardin's arm to "swing around landing his fist in
Powell's back" as he leaned over the body. A surprised Powell "jumped
around" demanding to know who had struck him. Being alone he quickly
realized what had happened,.[2] On the same day photographer J. C. Burge

made at least one image of the deceased, showing the several bullet holes.³ From the photograph one can see that the fatal bullet entered the left eye and then went out the back of the head. The hole is small and neat. Unfortunately Burge did not photograph the back of the head. From examining the death photo and the testimony of witnesses it is clear that Hardin was facing Selman when he was shot. That one shot did the work; the others were added to make sure there was no reaction.

When Powell was finished with his work the deceased was placed in a casket with the words "At Rest" on the top. It was transported to Concordia Cemetery where he was buried, only a few feet away from the grave of Martin M'rose. Today one can visit this historic cemetery and stand before the two graves and ponder the ironies, that Hardin had allegedly hired assassins to kill M'rose while having an affair with the man's wife. Now they rest virtually side by side. M'rose's headstone, installed many years afterward, has an unusual but simple inscription: "Martin M'Rose/ Polish Cowboy/ Died at the Hands of Others/ June 29, 1895." Hardin's headstone informs the observer even less: "John Wesley Hardin/ May 26, 1853/ Aug. 19, 1895."⁴ But today Hardin's grave is covered by a cement slab to deter grave robbers. There are two concrete benches in front of the grave for the viewers to relax and ponder his life. On August 25, 1995, one century and six days after his death, a group from Central Texas traveled to El Paso intending to dig up whatever remains were found and bring them back, with the stated intention of burying Hardin in his "home country." A phone call to Leon C. Metz alerted friends in El Paso of what was to transpire, and amazingly during the night before the arrival of the would-be grave robbers the headstone was "stolen." El Paso police were notified of the grave robbery and when the Central Texas delegation arrived crime scene tape surrounded the final resting place of Hardin. The group returned home unhappy and without the remains of anybody. A legal battle lasted for months, resulting in the court's decision to leave Hardin buried where he was placed a century before. Today, besides the cement slab and the cage protecting the grave, is a state historical marker informing the viewer of the importance of John Wesley

Hardin. Students of Hardin's life and Texas Reconstruction history will find it of interest to study the account of how Hardin's grave was finally marked in 1965. C. L. Sonnichsen's essay, "The Grave of John Wesley Hardin" remains of great interest to scholars.[5]

With John Wesley Hardin dead and buried what he had left behind suddenly became very important. Even though a licensed attorney, he failed to prepare a will for disposal of his last effects. Surprisingly, he left a valuable collection, which became contested by the Hardin family and his one-time mistress, Helen Beulah M'rose. On August 21, the day after the burial, noted attorney at law T. T. Teel applied for letters of administration on the estate of John W. Hardin. A hearing would be held on September 2; all persons interested in the estate could appear and state their case. Teel was well-known throughout the southwest and many no doubt assumed he would obtain possession of the estate.[6]

Of greater interest is the application of Florida-born Joseph L. Whitmore for temporary letters of administration.[7] He provided history with a list of what Hardin had left behind. Much is of minor interest, such as the number of drawers, handkerchiefs, and so on. But some items are of extreme interest. For example, among other things in Hardin's possession were $94.85 in cash; a 165-page manuscript on the life of J. W. Hardin; one "dock" of old letters; one cabinet photograph of Mrs. M'rose and her child; three photographs of persons unknown; a book, *General Laws of Texas*; one photograph of Martin M'rose in death; one package of tintype pictures; one Colt pistol serial number 68837, .41 caliber; one Colt pistol serial number 84304, .38 caliber with white handles; one Colt pistol serial number 126-680, .45 caliber; one Elgin watch serial number 4069110; one bundle calling cards; one gold watch chain with jug charm; one Confederate $50 bill, serial number 74746; one opera glass case serial number 1233-19. In addition there were other law books, and one copy of *Rise and Fall of the Confederacy*. Whitmore added that also in the estate were two other pistols, a Smith & Wesson, .44 caliber, serial number 352 and a Colt pistol, .41 caliber, serial number 73728, but at the time of inventory the latter two were in possession of the county sheriff.

Helen B. "McRose," as her name is spelled in court records, also claimed the estate of her most recent lover. She was most interested in the history of his life, claiming "the manuscript was near its completion," composed both by Hardin and the applicant, "at the dictation of said Hardin." She further claimed that the manuscript was soon to be placed upon the market for sale "by said Hardin, and this applicant." Apparently the lovers planned to promote the book's sales together. The resultant funds were to be distributed as follows: one half to Helen M'rose; one half to Hardin after paying back to her $1,575.00 she claimed Hardin owed her. The document, typed on a lined sheet of paper, read: "I, John W. Hardin do hereby promise to pay to Helen M Rose, within a reasonable time, the

Pleamon S. Sowell who obtained the Hardin autobiography for publication. *Courtesy Roy B. Young Collection.*

Newspaper publisher John C. Moore of the firm of Smith and Moore. *Author's Collection.*

sum of $1575.00."[8] There is no doubt it was authentic, but if she hoped it would gain for her the estate she was mistaken. She estimated the value of the manuscript to be $2,000. She claimed that Whitmore had no right to the manuscript as Hardin was not indebted to him. Attorneys Patterson & Wallace represented her interests.[9]

Whitmore countered, through his attorney Peyton Edwards Sr., that the estate was worth only $1,000 and Hardin was indebted to "sundry persons" and that the petitioner was a relative of Hardin, and the three Hardin children had requested him to qualify as administrator of the estate. The spokesperson for the family was Hardin's daughter, Mollie E., now Mrs. Charles Billings. Whitmore was granted temporary administration

Frank P. Smith of the firm of Smith and Moore who published the John Wesley Hardin autobiography in Seguin, Texas. *Author's Collection.*

of the estate, taking charge of the effects "together with the manuscript of his biography and will save them for his son."[10]

Ultimately Whitmore won the contest for the estate, and the children obtained custody of the valuable manuscript.[11] How quickly the manuscript was delivered to the printers in Seguin, Guadalupe County, adjacent to Gonzales County, is unknown, but it appeared in print in 1896, due to the efforts of another who was working for the Hardin heirs as well: Pleamon S. Sowell. In the first edition of the manuscript a preface appeared, presumably written by one of the printers, Smith & Moore, which included this line: "To the Hon. P. S. Sowell, member of the Legislature from Guadalupe County, we are indebted for being able to publish this manuscript."[12] Although no records are known dealing with the publishing house of Smith & Moore, John C. Moore and Frank P. Smith were the publishers of the local Seguin newspaper. Sowell obtained permission for Hardin's *Life* to be published and chose a local firm to do so. Ireland-born John C. Moore immigrated to the United States in 1883, and within a few years had begun publishing the *Seguin Enterprise*. When Frank P. Smith joined him is uncertain.[13]

Years later J. Marvin Hunter reprinted the book and serialized it in his popular *Frontier Times* magazine in the September, October, November and December issues of 1925, which edition is now more rare than the 1896 edition. Years later T. A. Sowell, son of Pleamon Sowell, wrote J. Marvin Hunter expressing the following: "My father, Judge P. S. Sowell of Seguin, represented the Wes Hardin heirs and procured Hardin's personal effects through the courts at El Paso, among them being the MSS portraying his life adventures. It was written with an indelible pencil while in prison. This story was printed in booklets by the Sequin Enterprise and was sold for 50c." Mr. Sowell then added, in parenthesis: "I helped with the typesetting."[14] The exact number of copies made of the first edition is unknown. The original edition contained as frontispiece an engraving identified as Hardin, but it was quickly discovered that it was based on a photograph of his brother, Joseph G. Hardin, lynched in 1874. Then a smaller sheet was added with a photographic reprint tipped in of the famous portrait of John Wesley wearing a bow tie. Copies containing the tipped-in portrait are quite rare. According to bibliophile John H. Jenkins, after the first edition appeared Hardin's daughters objected and the book was withdrawn and stored in a San Antonio warehouse. The warehouse burned and only 400 copies were saved, which were sold "surreptitiously" to a San Antonio bookseller who sold them off one at a time.[15] Although the 1896 edition sold for only 50 cents, the bookseller sold them at prices ranging from $7.50 to $12.50. Today copies can be obtained through dealers on the Internet for a price amazingly high: a recent check found the price ranging from $200 to $850, depending on condition of course.

* * * * *

Surprisingly, sometime after Hardin's burial, a brother appeared in El Paso, intending to obtain the estate as well. In November, three months after the death and burial of Hardin, an article appeared in several newspapers reporting that his brother Gip Hardin had visited Waco, Texas, and let it be known that he was en route to El Paso to "secure the manuscript that Wesley Hardin wrote concerning his own life." Hardin claimed that the manuscript "rightfully belongs to him and he will have it or have a fight."[16] This item from Waco first appeared in the *San Antonio Express,* then in the *El Paso Times*; there it struck a nerve. The *Times* editor noted how the young Hardin "fires off his lip" in a "thoughtless manner," which would suggest he was related to "the late unlamented," reminding the readers how when John Wesley Hardin came to El Paso "he was going to make the officers take to the brush." The *Times* suggested it might be healthier for Hardin if he kept on going when he got to El Paso. Curiously, the *Times* reporter noted the character was "a humbug" as the real brother of John Wesley Hardin had been in the city several days. That could only be Jefferson Davis Hardin. Apparently neither surviving brother made a serious effort to gain control of the Hardin estate.

Gip was four days shy of reaching the age of twenty-one when Hardin was shot to death in the Acme saloon. Born August 15, 1874, at Mount Calm in Hill County, he was of an era when education was becoming more common; he completed high school on May 12, 1892, at Ennis, Ellis County. Whether he ever visited with his brother at Huntsville or Gonzales or in Kimble County is unknown, but in March of 1896 he held a teaching position at Junction, Texas. He likely had been at the Hardin-Lewis wedding, and no doubt knew the Lewis family. Gip married Pearl J. Turner on January 17, 1898.[17]

In spite of his reputation as the brother of John Wesley Hardin, Gip had avoided trouble. No incident has been found indicating he led a dangerous lifestyle that would parallel that of his older brother. But three months after his 1898 marriage, on March 28, a difficulty occurred that drastically changed his life. It was not caused by heavy drinking in a saloon as one might expect, but in a restaurant in Junction. A murder trial was taking place there; whether Gip had a particular interest in the trial is unknown but perhaps it was because of that trial he was in town that day. A number of people were dining in the Turman Hotel, and the trial was a topic of conversation among many, including those at the table where Gip was seated. Someone made a remark against the defendant, Allen Wesley Haley, who had been charged with the murder of a man named Edward Looney. Gip not only took offense but expressed his opinion with abusive language. Hotel owner John Turman did not allow this type of language and he told Gip to take it outside. Gip certainly knew Turman was also a deputy sheriff, and perhaps for this reason he did exit. Turman followed, then grabbed Hardin by the arm and announced he was under arrest. Hardin became angry, and responded that he would kill the next man who touched him. Turman and another man now attempted to subdue the angry Hardin, but he continued to resist. The situation escalated and Hardin drew a pistol. Not satisfied with simply threatening with his pistol, he shot Turman several times. Turman, although wounded, was able to draw his pistol and returned fire, shooting twice but missing both times. Turman died within minutes, forty years of age, with a wife and nine children to mourn his death. James Gibson Hardin now had killed a man. Did the thought cross his mind in those moments that his older brother had shot a man and became a wanted fugitive, and then spent years in prison? Did he realize that his brother had shot a deputy sheriff, which resulted in his spending years in Huntsville? Now Gip Hardin had killed a deputy sheriff as well.

The trial for A. W. Haley was now officially postponed so that Judge Allison could try Hardin. This clearly suggests a biased court; otherwise why not conclude one before beginning another? Some of the witnesses for the Haley trial were also witnesses who could have been called for the Hardin trial, but Judge Allison allowed them to depart, a further strange action if he wished to show impartiality. On March 29 Hardin stood before Judge Allison's bench charged with the murder of John Turman. Many considered the deceased a pillar of the community, one of the finest deputies Kimble County ever had. Hardin entered a plea of not guilty and his trial date was set for April 4. His attorneys made a motion to quash the murder charge, intending to make it a lesser degree but that was denied. The request for a change of venue was also denied. On April 5 a request for a continuance was made, but that too was denied. Hardin may have felt his case was beyond hope. Hardin believed he had a right to defend himself, even though the aggressor was a deputy. On April 5— the wheels of justice must have seemed to be in rapid movement—J. W. Wilson was elected jury foreman. The trial lasted three days and the jury brought back a verdict of murder in the second degree, the same verdict that brother John Wesley had received for the killing of Deputy Charles Webb. Oddly, whereas John Wesley had received a twenty-five-year sentence with numerous killings in his background, brother Gip received a sentence of thirty-five years with but one killing. If he were to serve the entire sentence he would be sixty years old when released, considered an old man in those days. He naturally gave notice of appeal and was given ten days to prepare the statements of fact. The judge stated that the sentence would be stayed while the court awaited the decision of the Court of Criminal Appeals. Hardin would not wait for that decision in the Kimble County jail as the judge was aware of potential mob violence if Hardin was kept in Junction. He ordered the prisoner to be confined elsewhere during the period, probably in Gillespie County. On March 29, 1899, a year after the death of Turman, Judge William Allison reconvened court in Junction. It was good news for Gip Hardin this time, as the court was ordered to conduct a new trial. He would be retried in Gillespie County during the September term. The judge provided a list of witnesses who were to give testimony as several people had ignored previous subpoenas and were now ordered to be located and ordered to comply. Gip Hardin was indeed a fortunate man; as he was found guilty only of manslaughter, a much less serious act than second degree murder. He would serve his sentence of three years in Huntsville State Penitentiary. During that time he was allowed to teach other convicts.[18]

While Gip served out his term, Pearl Turner Hardin remained in Junction with her parents. Once the walls of Huntsville were behind him and he was a free man Gip returned to Junction. Unfortunately the couple, like brother John and Callie, separated not long afterward. Once he left Pearl the trail of Gip Hardin is lost to documented history. What happened to the man? One story is that he found a job in the stockyards at Fort Worth. When World War I broke out he was hired to drive a herd of horses to Florida where they would be sent to European battlefields. One undocumented tale relates that on a ship off the coast of Florida, during a storm, Gip Hardin was crushed to death between two box cars, just as final an ending but not as dramatic as that of his more famous brother. That may be no more than an interesting piece of folklore, as no official record of his death has been found, nor has anyone yet produced a contemporary newspaper report confirming his death. The 1910 census—several years prior to any U.S. intervention in the war in Europe—shows Pearl as a widow with two children, Emma V., age nine, and Varda B., age six. She was working as a milliner and owned her own store. In those years living as "the widow Hardin" brought no shame, but being a divorced woman raised questions she did not want to have to answer. The end for Gip may have been off the coast of Florida during a storm, or after the separation he may have drifted elsewhere, changed his name, and died unknown, and been buried in a potter's field.

CHAPTER 24

END OF THE GUNFICHTERS

*"[Jeff Hardin] was at his place of business, when, it seems he
and John Snowden got into a dispute about an account.... [In]
a short time the shooting was heard."*

Dallas Morning News, October 12, 1901

Not surprisingly perhaps, brother Jefferson Davis Hardin experienced violence as well as his older brother. In 1874, at the age of thirteen, he was in Comanche when John Wesley killed Webb. Hardin barely mentioned him in his *Life*, a simple mention that he drove the wagon back to his father's farm. During the next thirteen years Jeff grew up. He lost his first wife, Mary Elizabeth Vinson, after only a few weeks of marriage. By the 1880s he was in Lipscomb County in the Texas Panhandle. The paper trail continues there with his marriage to Ida Mae Croussore, a young woman born on May 6, 1872, in Kokomo, Indiana, to William and Nancy Browning Croussore. How she arrived in Texas and when, and why she ended up in the isolated region of Lipscomb County remains a family mystery. Jeff Hardin and Ida Mae Croussore became husband and wife on October 24, 1887; he was twenty-six, she was fifteen.

Jeff Hardin became the first of the family to venture into the Texas Panhandle, Lipscomb being one of the least populated counties of the state. Located 128 miles northeast of Amarillo, it must have seemed like a genuine frontier. To the north and east was the border line of the Oklahoma Territory. The year Miss Ida Mae Croussore became Mrs. J. D. Hardin the Southern Pacific Railway reached the Panhandle. According to the 1880 Federal census only four ranches were located in Lipscomb

Jefferson Davis Hardin shortly before his death at the hands of John Snowden.
Note weapon. *Courtesy Jeff Hardin Collection.*

County, and it was not much different when the Hardins arrived a few
years later. In 1880 there were over 5,000 head of livestock but only
69 human beings. Of these sixty-nine, only nine were females. Of the
remaining sixty men one was black: twenty-year-old Henry Day, born in
Texas and working as a servant. Twenty-seven were from Mexico and the
balance were from various states and countries.[1]

For a fifteen-year-old girl, now a married woman, the actual remote-
ness and inner feeling of isolation may have been too stressful for her to
remain. It was a totally different world from Kokomo, Indiana. By 1889,

less than two years after their marriage, the Hardins moved to Mobeetie in Wheeler County, another small town sixty miles almost due south from Lipscomb. They had loaded their wagons and crossed the Canadian, the Washita and the Sweetwater rivers before seeing where their new home would be. In one way it was different from Lipscomb: there were 380 human beings according to the 1880 census, but many, if not most, were connected to Fort Elliott, one time the hub for hide hunters and soldiers

J.D. Hardin's second wife, Ida Mae Croussore Hardin, and children. Children from left are John Wesley Hardin, unnamed niece, daughter Mattie Belle; Ida Mae holding Della Lillian. The family later changed their name to Davis. *Courtesy Douglas Hitchcock.*

who eventually wiped out the vast buffalo herds as well as the raiding Comanche. When the Hardins arrived, the hunters were only a memory and the vast herds were now longhorn cattle; ranching was dominant.

On February 8, 1889, Mrs. Hardin gave birth to a son who was named John Wesley in honor of his uncle, then serving his eleventh year in Huntsville. With a newborn now, perhaps Jeff Hardin would truly settle down and plant roots. But sometime during the next two years for an unknown reason Jeff and Ida Mae packed up and moved across the New Mexico Territory and settled in Walsenburg, Colorado, again a totally different environment from the barrenness of the Panhandle. Walsenburg, the county seat of Huerfano County, was at an elevation of 6,000 feet. In lieu of raising cattle or sheep, men worked in the mines. Of course the miners were all hard-working men, and at the end of their shift they would be thirsty. Jeff Davis, choosing to serve thirsty customers rather than do the backbreaking work of the mines, operated a saloon in Walsenburg, and among other saloon owners was the notorious Robert Ford, a man who a decade earlier had gained national notoriety by shooting Jesse James in the back of the head. Perhaps Hardin and Ford, each having their own notoriety, cared little about the other's reason for fame: Ford, as "the dirty little coward who shot Mr. Howard" and Jeff, known as the younger brother of John Wesley Hardin.

Jeff and Ida Mae welcomed their second child, a girl they named Mattie Bell, on February 9, 1891. With a wife and two children depending on him, and an older brother serving a twenty-five-year-sentence for shooting a man in front of a saloon, Jeff ought to have considered the consequences of his actions. Part of the family lore is that Hardin opened up a saloon not far from that of Bob Ford. Allegedly the two men experienced a difficulty in Hardin's saloon, no one knowing what caused the shooting affray. An argument led to stronger words and then both drew their pistols. Inside a saloon, two men shooting at each other at close range, both men under the influence of liquor, should prove deadly. As each man fired he tried to slap the gun away from the other, resulting in wild shots only, neither taking time to deliberately aim. Both Ford and Hardin emptied their pistols but only wounded each other slightly. Ford received a bullet in the foot; Hardin a bullet in the shoulder. Presumably a hastily called doctor bandaged the wounds. The local law was pragmatic: both were ordered to leave Walsenburg and take up their business elsewhere. Bob Ford loaded up and established a new saloon in Creede, Colorado. He soon made another enemy who shot and killed him on June 8, 1892.

Not caring to challenge the law, Jeff and Ida loaded up the children and headed back east, some 500 miles later stopping in Duncan, Oklahoma Territory. On the route they may have stopped at their former home in Wheeler; at that point Duncan was only 200 miles further, and there Hardin opened another saloon. Here the third child arrived: Della Lillian Hardin was born on December 14, 1893. Hardin may have changed his location, but he did not change his ways. Having survived one recent gunfight, then trekking across 500 miles of difficult terrain, he ought to have changed his lifestyle. But he did not, and he seemed to become more and more involved in a reckless and at times violent group. According to family lore, Ida Mae at times was so fearful of her husband's associates that she would take the children and hide in a cornfield until the rowdy crowd left the premises or passed out. A responsible woman with three children could deal with this situation only so long, and she chose divorce. With her three children she left the territory and returned to Colorado. To further distance herself from the Hardin line she changed her name and her children's to Davis, and so the Hardin children remained Davis the remainder of their lives.

With only himself to be concerned with Jeff now chose to return to Junction in Kimble County. John Wesley was now out of Huntsville, and perhaps Jeff was present at his wedding to young Callie Lewis in nearby London. How long Jeff was there is unknown; he may have gone on to El Paso, but if he did he failed to receive newspaper publicity in either the *Times* or the *Herald*. Instead of a solid businessman, operating a saloon, Jeff Hardin was more of a drifter. Did he avoid publicity, being with his notorious brother, feeling annoyed as always being in the shadow of John Wesley Hardin?

In April 1895, Jeff was in San Marcos, Hays County just south of Austin, Texas. He found employment with the Judson Brothers who were digging an artesian well. Again an argument developed between Jeff and another worker, Ike Shrader (or Schroeder), which went beyond angry words. According to one report, a "serious affray" developed between Hardin, "brother of John Wesley Hardin" and Ike Shrader of San Antonio. Hardin, Shrader and two others became involved in the quarrel; Hardin gave Shrader a "serious stabbing." The wounded man was taken home and Hardin was placed in jail.[2] No further information has been learned of this event.

Hardin next appeared back in Junction where on December 26, 1896, he married Mary Jane Taylor, daughter of Texas hero Creed Taylor and his wife Lavinia Amanda Spencer Taylor. This marriage forged two families of significance in Texas history, the Hardin line and the Taylor line. Some historians have suggested that John Wesley Hardin had sided with the Taylors in their feud with the Sutton forces because he was related to that family, but that is incorrect. There was no blood relation, and the link did not occur until years after the shooting phase of the feud and then only with the marriage of Hardin's younger brother and Creed Taylor's daughter. Apparently Hardin avoided trouble in Kimble County, but then he became restless; in 1899 he and Mary packed up and moved to Kent County in West Texas. Jeff's first cousin, Benjamin Columbus Hardin, had previously settled there and that may have been the reason for choosing that location. Kent County was created in 1876 from Bexar and Young counties and named for Andrew Kent, one of the "Immortal Thirty-Two" from Gonzales who perished in the Alamo. In 1888 cattleman R. L. Rhomberg settled there and named a small settlement Clairemont, after a young woman named Clare (although the spelling is different) the daughter of a relative whom he admired. Few settlers came; the 1890 population was only 324 residents. In 1891 fence-cutters and farmers endangered lives and property over the open range and free-grass conflict. When Kent County was organized, Clairemont became the county seat. By 1900, 899 people lived in the county, and the Hardin family accounted for four of them, looking to the future and the new century.[3]

Jefferson Davis Hardin and his wife Mary Taylor Hardin and their children: Joseph Gibson and Cleburne, "Cleve," *circa* 1900. *Courtesy Jeff Hardin Collection.*

When census enumerator Larkin E. Skinner visited the Hardin household in 1900 he enumerated a family of four: head of household Jeff, his wife Mary, and their two children, Joseph G. and Cleburne. As a family man again Jeff perhaps had forgotten the difficulty in San Marcos,

Benjamin Columbus Hardin, son of Uncle Robert E. Hardin. *Courtesy Don Jay Collection.*

and certainly the difficulty in Walsenburg, Colorado. The two children born to him had helped erase some bad memories. Cousin Benjamin C. Hardin, born in 1834, was there in Kent County as well, with the respectable position of county surveyor. His son Benjamin Jr. assisted him in his surveying work. Benjamin C. had four lovely daughters to help with the housework, and perhaps helped to contribute to the social life of the community as well.

Four of the Benjamin C. Hardin daughters. Back row from left: Martha and Bertha; front row from left Fannie and Augusta "Gussie" who became Mrs. John L. Snowden. *Courtesy Don Jay Collection.*

Jeff's life now seemed to change as well. He began raising horses, perhaps to race, or to become a successful breeder. He bought a livery stable in Clairemont, even became a constable, enforcing the law instead of breaking it, and found additional work as a "scalper" for the huge O Bar O (Circle Bar) Ranch.[4]

Jeff Hardin's career is less well-known than that of his older brother. Numerous questions would be answered if he also had written his autobiography. One question that begs clarification is what happened during the winter of 1900–01. Jeff became involved in a difficulty in Fort

Worth, but few details are known. Historian Richard F. Selcer placed Hardin in Fort Worth in December where he held up a poker game at gunpoint "because he believed he had been cheated." Hardin was arrested by Officer John D. Nichols Jr. and Detective James W. Thomason.[5] Apparently he managed to avoid any jail time for this act which was no different from what his brother had done in El Paso a few years before. Whatever it was, after leaving Fort Worth he was "badly used up" by certain parties on the train between Fort Worth and Weatherford. As the latter town is less than twenty miles west of Fort Worth, presumably those who had an issue with Hardin got their work in very soon after leaving the depot. An important newspaper article provides some details of the incident. The passenger train from Fort Worth stopped at Colorado (today Colorado City), and Hardin "stepped off the train with his Winchester in hand" and related to the sheriff and others what had happened. Hardin told how shortly after boarding he was assaulted by several men who "crowded him and punched him around after the conductor had taken his gun. As soon as the gang that assailed him had finished their work they got off the train and were seen no more." Apparently the beaten Hardin could not identify any of his assailants, or chose not to, perhaps believing he could settle his own score without any interference from the law. Jeff had a bruise about the left ear and "is black about the right eye [and] is very sore from his treatment and necessarily angered because the cowards who clubbed in on him could not be found in time for a settlement." The reporter added that Hardin was "game and about the only way those toughs could handle him was to have caught him unaware and in over powering numbers."[6] Although there are still questions about the Fort Worth incident, Hardin managed to avoid jail time and then, back closer to his home country, quickly become involved in another tragic event.

On Monday, May 6, 1901, Jeff Hardin shot a man on a little creek in northern Scurry County. Hardin and John Snowden, a cousin by marriage to Jeff's second cousin, Gussie Hardin, were herding horses southward from Clairemont. They no doubt intended to water their horses at

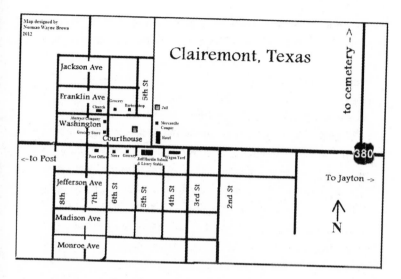

The townsite of Clairemont, Kent County, Texas. *Map courtesy Norman Wayne Brown.*

the little Ennis Creek, just inside Scurry County. In addition to their normal day to day activities, both Hardin and Snowden were "scalpers" for the O Bar O, generally known as the "Circle Bars." It was their job to look for and deal with cattle rustlers in this vast and open cattle country. Usually, when a scalper killed a rustler the law took little notice of it; there were no arrests and no investigation. Ranchers were aware of an earlier incident when eight men were killed following the theft of just one cow. Some were shot to death and one was dragged to death at the end of a rope.[7] Rustling was a serious matter for those assigned the task of weeding out thieves.

Due to unintentional errors in reporting, the facts of what happened initially were blurred. The editor of the *Colorado Clipper* in neighboring Mitchell County heard of the shooting incident at Ennis Creek and in spite of not getting the facts straight provided history with some details. The readers of the sad news learned that Jeff Hardin of Kent County had shot politician J. L. Stephenson. Perhaps the most grievous error was that the man shot was actually John S. Stevenson, a horse trader whose name was only similar to Stephenson's. The report in the *Clipper* continued:

> Particulars of the affair as near as can be learned are as follows: J. L. Stephenson is a horse buyer, and will be remembered as the man who spent some time here recently, disposing of a couple of Jacks which he kept at the Stokes Stable. He was up in that country purchasing horses. He and Jeff Hardin were drinking [watering] a number of horses and were riding close to one another. A dispute arose over some matter and a difficulty ensued, during which Hardin drew a six-shooter and fired at Stephenson, sending a 45-caliber bullet through his head. The ball entered just below the eye and passed entirely through the head, coming out at the back of the skull just above the ear. Reports say that Stephenson is dangerously wounded and that his recovery is doubtful. The wounded man was taken to Snyder and is under medical treatment. Hardin is in custody pending an examining trial.[8]

The newspapers of course attempted to provide correct information to their readers. The *Dallas Morning News*, albeit more than a week later, reported a follow-up item that had originated in Abilene. "News was received here yesterday of the fatal shooting of John S. Stevenson of this city at Snyder in Scurry County. No particulars are yet attainable."[9] Now the initials were changed from J. L. to John S. and the surname corrected to Stevenson. Casual readers may have assumed Stevenson's wound would prove to be fatal; in fact it became general knowledge that Hardin had indeed killed his man. They may have been surprised if they read the following letter which appeared in the Snyder newspaper, written at Abilene on May 17.

> During my recent stay in Snyder when severely wounded, the people extended to me and my daughter many kindnesses and

courtesies. We were strangers to the whole people, and are yet strangers to many persons who showed us great favors, and it would be impossible for us to personally acknowledge our indebtedness to each one who so kindly ministered to us in time of need. We, therefore, adopt this method of extending to each and every one our sincere and heartfelt thanks for their attention to us, in the trying ordeal through which we passed.

The letter writer continued:

Without intending to draw comparisons, for that would be well nigh impossible, we desire to specially extend our thanks to Mr. Beck, Justice of the Peace, and to Dr. Leslie, for the untiring efforts to make me comfortable.[10]

The letter was from J. S. Stevenson, and although still suffering from the effects of his head wound, he had recovered sufficiently to thank "one and all" of the people of Snyder.[11] Dr. Alonzo Chalmers Leslie obviously

Dr. Alonzo C. Leslie who provided excellent medical care to the man shot by Jefferson Davis Hardin. Courtesy *The Scurry County Museum Collection*

was a most capable doctor; the John S. Stevenson who many believed could not survive the head wound enjoyed life until his passing on June 9, 1930.[12]

Levi C. Darby,[13] the sheriff of Scurry County, arrested Jeff for the Stevenson shooting, pending an inquest plus further developments of Stevenson's condition. If Stevenson died from his wound there would be an inquest and possible charge of murder but Stevenson survived. At the time, Jeff Hardin likely told the sheriff that Stevenson was armed and he had to act to defend himself. Snowden said nothing. But what caused the shooting in the first place?

Don M. Jay, a Hardin descendant, related how Hardin and John Snowden were driving horses toward Ennis Creek Bridge, just inside the Scurry County line. They observed Stevenson whom they suspected of rustling Circle Bars cattle. Hardin confronted Stevenson at the bridge. There were words and perhaps threats uttered. Hardin drew his pistol and shot Stevenson in the face. The badly wounded man was placed in a wagon and transported to Snyder, thirteen miles away. He was taken to a doctor's house for treatment. At this early stage Hardin no doubt informed Scurry County Sheriff Levi C. Darby that Stevenson was armed and he had to defend himself. Snowden probably said nothing at this time.[14] It was an unfortunate incident to be sure, and to the Hardin family it was tragic: John Snowden's father-in-law was Benjamin Columbus Hardin and he was a first cousin of Jeff Hardin.

The final act of the tragedy came before the year's end. Hardin operated a livery stable which was legitimate enough, but he also had transformed part of it, the tack room, into a saloon. It was no different from his saloon in Duncan, Oklahoma, "a small, rough place, not only in clientele but aesthetically as well, having a bar, a table and four chairs on a dirt floor."[15] There, in that simple saloon, in great contrast to the elegant Acme of El Paso, the end came for Jefferson Davis Hardin.

The *Dallas Morning News* of October 12, 1901, carried a banner headline in bold: "KILLING OF JEFF HARDIN/ Brother of the Late John Wesley Hardin Shot to Death at Clairemont, in Kent County." Obviously

John L. Snowden, slayer of Jefferson Davis Hardin, seated right. In back are Will Snowden (left) and Bill Neely. Seated left is Will Rogers. *Courtesy Don Jay Collection*

the *News* determined it was necessary to point out where Clairemont was, but no one needed an introduction to the Hardin name. The report indicated that Hardin was killed on October 8, about 10:00 p.m. Reportedly he was in his place of business where he and John Snowden argued about an account. Before anything serious occurred other people entered

The Charles Oliver Fox Livery Stable in Clairemont, Texas, *circa* 1911. Jeff Hardin was killed in the smaller attached building on far right. Fox purchased the stable from Hardin's widow. From left: John Sampson, Mace Hunter, Will Rogers, Charles O. Fox, "Gee" McMeans, Jack Rogers, Maxie Williams, Willis Rogers, Dick Jay, Ed Underwood, Lee Byrd and Dick Sampson in buggy. Boys standing on roof are Gene Selmon and Burley Sampson. Two boys standing at right are unidentified. *Photo and identification courtesy Don Jay Collection.*

into the saloon and the argument ceased, but only temporarily. When the place emptied out John Snowden left as well, but Hardin called him back in. Three shots rang out within minutes; people entered and found Hardin dying, lying at the head of the counter. He was unable to speak. Hardin had received a bullet through the heart which passed out through the shoulder blade. A second bullet shattered his right leg; a third bullet passed through the left leg. Snowden had fired three shots, and all hit Hardin, causing death. The news from Clairemont stated that it was unknown if anyone had actually seen the shooting. Hardin's pistol was lying behind the counter. Had he drawn the weapon to shoot Snowden, or had Snowden placed it there, after he had shot Hardin? Officially there were no witnesses, so no one could say what actually transpired. Within the hour Snowden surrendered to Sheriff Norman N. Rodgers.[16] Snowden waived the examining trial and his bond was set at $5,000 which he "readily gave."[17]

Had Snowden killed an unarmed man? If there were only him and Hardin in that make-shift saloon he could easily have shot him to death, then drawn Hardin's pistol from a pocket or holster and placed it beside the body. There were rumors however that a witness had been there, who kept his mouth shut. George Underwood may have been the only witness to that murder: years later he told his children and grandchildren that he had actually seen the killing of Jeff Hardin.[18] Snowden, after firing the three shots and leaving Hardin prostrate on the floor, ran out of the saloon. He went to his father-in-law's house and told him what he had done. Benjamin C. Hardin told Snowden he had better leave the country for a while, that he could easily be the victim of a lynch mob. He went on to say that no one would believe Snowden had bested Hardin in a gun fight. Instead of fleeing, however, Snowden went to the sheriff and surrendered.[19] The ironic part of this tragedy was that Mary Taylor Hardin, now a widow, was carrying an unborn child. She soon left and went back to her parents' home where she delivered a third son from her marriage to Jeff. She named this son Jeff D. Hardin. In later years Mary told her children that Jeff's pistol was in the livery stable that night, and thus he was unarmed.[20] George Underwood could have clarified the situation, but he was fearful. If he told what he knew what would the Snowden family do to him? So he remained silent.[21] John Snowden was never tried for the killing of Jeff Hardin.

Following this difficulty resulting in the death of Jeff Hardin, in 1903 John Snowden loaded up the covered wagons and he and his wife, Augusta "Gussie" Hardin Snowden, her sister Nancy Francis "Fannie" and her husband Charles O. Fox, went to Colorado. They stopped at Cripple Creek where the men went to work in a gold mine. Gussie and her two boys perished in the influenza epidemic of 1918 in Teller County, Colorado, but her two daughters were spared. John was in Gila, Arizona,

Wedding portrait of Augusta "Gussie" Hardin and John L. Snowden, 1897. Photograph made at Clairemont, Kent County, Texas. *Courtesy Don Jay Collection.*

based on his World War I draft registration card, and when he learned of his family being ill he returned only to come down with the same illness. He was hospitalized but recovered and convalesced in his daughter's home.[22] In 1929 he was remarried, to a widow with four children, Hattie Collins.[23] John and Hattie Snowden moved to Houston, Texas, during the early 1940s and operated a laundry. Some years later and after the death of second wife Hattie, John Snowden moved to his daughter Billie Boley Snowden's residence in St. Petersburg, Florida. He died there on August 29, 1959, at the age of eighty-two.[24] Charles and Fannie Fox returned home to Texas after a year in Colorado and went back to ranching on the sprawling acreage of the 24 Ranch of Kent County, whose land extended from Clairemont, the county seat for almost thirty miles, to the western county line and to the south for twenty or more miles almost to the southern line. Charles Fox was a nephew of Martha A. "Matt" Garretson Brown, mistress of the 24 Ranch.[25]

With the last of the Hardin brothers gone—Joseph Gibson, John Wesley, Barnett Gibson and Jefferson Davis—and their slayers, John Selman and John Snowden as well, the age of the gunfighter had truly come to an end. The myths, legends, truths and partial truths would survive them. Some of the places where the Hardin brothers lived, fought and died were once prosperous locales; many have since become ghost towns with only a few remaining vestiges to remind historians what once was there. Moscow, where Rev. J. G. Hardin and his family once lived, today has a population of less than 200. Sumpter, in neighboring Trinity County, once the largest town in the county, today has only a cemetery and a historical marker to mark its existence. Old Evergreen, where Wes Hardin claimed to have bested Bill Longley in poker, also has a cemetery, a huge tree that gave the place its name and a historical marker. Clinton, once

Fannie Hardin Fox, wife of Charles O. Fox, with her horse, *circa* 1910. *Courtesy the Don Jay Collection.*

the county seat of DeWitt County, now consists of a cemetery, part of which is neat and occasionally used today, but part of which is fenced and overgrown with brush and small trees, as if to say to the world to leave it undisturbed. If any of the men who were killed in the Sutton-Taylor feud lie buried there, they have no grave markers. Mobeetie where the Jeff Hardin family lived for a short time today boasts of at least 100 souls, which is similar to London in Kimble County where Wes Hardin married girlish Callie Lewis. Clairemont, once the county seat of Kent County, is today a ghost town, with just enough remnants to prove it once existed. As ghost town historian T. Lindsay Baker observed on his last visit there in 1980, since Jayton replaced Clairemont as county seat, "the decline has been nearly complete."[26]

The visitors today can tour the site of what Clairemont used to be, observing an old red stone jailhouse sitting off in a mesquite thicket, and a one-story building with a historical marker explaining it was once the Kent County courthouse. Few outlaws, merchants, lawmen, cowboys, or gunfighters are remembered by the local people but visitors wonder about them with idle curiosity. Most people indicate a willingness to tell you what they know but few rarely do. They tend to leave the past alone. There is no one today to get inside Jeff Hardin's mind to determine his character. The descendants remaining from the Kent County saga say he was tough and mean and a bad man to cross. He did not mark up any known killings but he died by the gun, just like his big brother Wes.

If sufficiently brave, the visitor can continue up an old dirt road leading to the cemetery where Jeff Hardin and other early settlers of the area are buried. No homes or businesses remain; there is no signage indicating where the hotel, the livery stable, the church, the bank, post office, barber shop, blacksmith, wagon yard, and other mercantile stores were located. Nor is it known today where the saloons were located. Clairemont was named for a young girl named Clare; the last person known to have lived there was a girl named Manuelita. Who she may have married, or what became of her, is unknown.[27] Lots are still owned by various people but it is unlikely anyone would want to make their home there today. But back in the final years of the nineteenth century couples who had their wedding in Clairemont received a free town lot. Someone attempted to burn the courthouse but the fire was contained, saving the bottom floor. The identity of the arsonist is known by one living person but he was sworn to secrecy to never reveal the person's name. Some mysteries are best left alone.[28]

Just as towns disappear through the years, attitudes toward historical figures also change. John Wesley Hardin was considered a hero by some, fighting against Yankees and freedmen who refused to remain "in their place." But in spite of the admiration of some, in truth he had fearful issues within which brought out his violent nature. Other young men were too young to go off and fight Yankees; others were raised by enabling parents who refused to punish their sons for their illegal acts. But they did not go on to kill ten or twenty or thirty or more men and then justify their killings by claiming it was a case of kill or be killed. We can study psychological profiles but we still cannot explain fully what made Hardin the killing machine he became. Some considered him nothing more than a murderous outlaw, not worthy of anything more than being eradicated, a man with no virtues. Today, over a century and a quarter past his death, he is seen simply as an important historical personage whose reputation was created during the violent period following the American Civil War, a conflict seen by some as a continuous act of northern aggression, by others the necessary tragic conflict which preserved this nation, under God, one and indivisible. Hollywood has not found Hardin a marketable product, such as Billy the Kid or Jesse James. Only one motion picture featured him as the leading character, based loosely on his autobiography, entitled *The Lawless Breed*, which purported to portray the accurate story of Hardin. In spite of outstanding actors, Rock Hudson playing the role of Hardin, Julia Adams as his love interest, Hugh O'Brien and Lee Van Cleef, the motion picture did not receive rave reviews. In fact it was quickly forgotten. Some Hardin descendants claimed it was a great western, but other Hardin descendants felt quite differently. Fannie Hardin Fox, wife of Charles O. Fox, who could ride a horse as well as any man and who could probably shoot as well, attended a showing of *The Lawless Breed*. When a grandson questioned her about the motion picture she informed him that they were not related to *that* John Wesley Hardin. After all, she intoned, that Hardin was "just trash" and they were no kin to him. Historical figures such as Hardin, Bill Longley, Ben Thompson, Henry Ware, Jack Helm and Bill Sutton all evoke different responses in different people. We hope that honest historians will write history based on the available facts rather than presenting their agenda to change history.

APPENDIX

TEAGARDEN AND HARDIN

One of the fascinating aspects of Hardin's life is the fact that even though he was a hunted fugitive for much of his adulthood he befriended many lawmen, men whose sworn duty was to arrest him, such as state policemen, deputies, and county sheriffs. He seemed to have no problem in developing a relationship with a man of any profession. During his late prison years he was able to gain the help of many professionals to obtain his pardon. One of them was William Baker Teagarden, a man who attended school with him as a child and who remained his friend throughout his life.

Teagarden was born March 13, 1854, at Rusk, one of nine children of Oswin and Mahettible Baker Teagarden. He attended school with Hardin, then studied law and was admitted to the bar in 1885. He was extremely successful, representing the Southern Pacific Railway for thirty years. He married Fannie B. Walton on October 15, 1878, at Mineola, Texas. She died October 2, 1924; Teagarden died July 16, 1933, in San Antonio. Teagarden and Gonzales attorney William Seat Fly were instrumental in obtaining a full pardon for Hardin from Governor Hogg.

One of the more important letters preserved is the following written by Teagarden to Mrs. Charles Billings, the eldest daughter of John and Jane Hardin. It tells of their early years and also of how Teagarden perceived his long-time friend, even though he had many faults. It was typed on his letterhead, "W. B. Teagarden, Attorney at Law," from San Antonio, and addressed to Mrs. Charles Billings—"Dear Madam"—Nopal, Texas, and dated November 2, 1931.

> From newspaper notices of October 14th and 25th I was informed of the passing away of your sister, Mrs. Lyons, and your brother, John W. Hardin.

From the first notice I learned, for the first time, your identity and address, and while I know of your brother, I never could learn his address.

It is a sincere sadness to me that my procrastination and neglect have deprived them of reading what I shall write, and of hearing from one who knew your father better than anyone on this earth, not excepting his mother and father and brothers and sisters, or no man know the heart and soul of a person like the daily companion and implicitly trusted friend from childhood to manhood. We spent our time together in the woods, hunting and fishing, and in sports, when we were not required to be in school <u>or at Sunday school</u>.

Your grandfather, Reverend J. G. Hardin, was an educator, as well as a minister, and afterwards entered the practice of law. At about 1859 he established a large school at Sumpter, then the County cite [*sic:* seat] of Trinity County, and one of the largest towns in all East Texas, on the old beef trail to Alexandria. In that school John and I entered in the same class in the study of the alphabet, and under succeeding teachers we continued in the same class and at the same desk until we passed through the highest classes of the Seminary ten or eleven years later.

John, in all his actions in and out of school, was candid and honorable, <u>as he was throughout all his life</u>. He would sometimes perpetrate practical jokes, even on some of the teachers, but when the school room was called up to know who did it, John would promptly stand up, and braving the punishment, would confess that he did it.

When occasion required in our boyhood days, he protected me from harm from older boys many times, and on one occasion he stepped out into the aisle of the large school room, with open knife in his hand, and met the irate teacher coming with hickory in hand to whip me unjustly, and told him that he would kill him if he struck me with that stick. The teacher retreated and that was the end of it; he knew, and everybody in the school room knew, that John meant what he said. No two boys ever grew to manhood under more intimate relationship. It is therefore true that no one knew the inwardness of John's character as I did. There was not in his life or character a single sordid or dishonorable motive. All men who treated him fairly and decently were met more than halfway, but those who, by mistake or preference, treated him wrongfully or disrespectfully always had their challenges accepted, and they usually got what was coming to them.

It unfortunately happened that John became involved in a difficulty with a negro in Polk County while spending the holidays with his cousins in Polk County, and killed him. In those days it was not, under any circumstances, permissible for a negro to assault a white man, and death was always the penalty, and that was the result in that negro's case.

That was in Reconstruction times, and during the odious regime of E. J. Davis, the scalawag Governor of Texas. Davis had a kind of Ranger force called State police, filled with negroes, deserters from the Confederate service, carpet baggers, and scalawags, and in which no self-respecting man would take service. That force of odious constabulary, then in universal contempt of the people, was ordered to go after John, and a reward was offered for his capture, which increased as time passed. John made it a rule to never turn out of the road for them, and they always got the worst of the fight. The people of the country, except the carpet baggers and scalawags, applauded every time anybody killed one of the Davis police, and no one was ever indicted for it.

John had some troubles with gamblers and bullies, and first and last had to shoot two or three.

Any decent man could always get along with him without any trouble, and so could any man who would treat him fairly. He was always frank and honorable in all things, but he would not brook any kind of an insult from anybody. His sensitive, resentful disposition would not stand for it. The conditions stated caused all John's troubles.

John did not kill Webb in Comanche County, and was, in fact, innocent of that killing. Bud Dickson shot Webb, and the witness to the shooting did not in fact know one from the other, and Webb was really at fault, but at that time, under the law, John could not testify, and had no witnesses, and was convicted on his reputation.

It is a source of great satisfaction to me that the fates gave me opportunities to stand by his side and help him in some of his greatest dangers and perils, and that finally, when my friend and neighbor, James Stephen Hogg, became Governor, I was able to get him pardoned.

Many times I have rebuked lying blowhards for their false stories about John, and once or twice the magazines for publishing false and sensational stories about him, bought by them from irresponsible writers.

Some day I will take up the long-neglected duty, and write the true story of John's character.

You have no cause to be ashamed of your father's life and acts. His father and mother were as fine people as ever honored the citizenship of Texas, and so with the Dicksons, his aunt and uncle.

This letter has exceeded proper length, but my feelings and the subject prolonged it.

With assurances of my sincere sympathy in your bereavement, I remain,

Your friend,
W. B. Teagarden.

ENDNOTES

CHAPTER 1

[1]Marriage license preserved in Navarro County Clerk Records; copy provided by the late Ed Bartholomew.

[2]Her siblings were William A. Jr., born January 12, 1819; John Henry, born 1820; Alexander Joseph, born about 1824; B. F. (Benjamin Franklin?) born 1834; and Nancy Ann "Nannie," born 1835. All were born in Sullivan County, Indiana. Hardin Family Tree research provided by Norman W. Brown.

[3]Richard C. Marohn, *The Last Gunfighter: John Wesley Hardin* (College Station, TX: Creative Publishing, 1995), 3. Hereafter *The Last Gunfighter.*

[4]Revolutionary War veteran Colonel Joseph Hardin had married Jane Gibson in 1763. They became the parents of 12 children, one of whom was Benjamin P. Hardin, later a member of the Texas legislature. Born February 28, 1782, he married Martha Ann "Patsy" Barnett. Named after this family, Hardin County was created from portions of Liberty and Jefferson Counties. Benjamin and Martha Ann Barnett Hardin were the parents of Rev. James Gibson Hardin.

[5]Population figures from *The Texas Almanac, for 1857, with Statistics, Historical and Biographical Sketches, &c.,* 125. Facsimile edition by Glen's Sporting Goods, Irving, TX, 1986.

[6]"Abner Hugh Cook" in *The New Handbook of Texas*, by Kenneth Hatertepe, 310–12.

[7]The legal description is as follows: "at a small ash tree standing at the mouth of a small branch and on the North bank of Blair's Spring Branch; thence North 1475 varas a pin oak marked JGH standing on the south bank of Bois d'Arc Creek thence down sd. [said] creek with its meanders to the southeast corner of 13 acres sold by Linsey to Rt. McPhail; thence with the East line of sd. Original survey 1108 varas to the Northeast corner of W. Davenport's 37 ½ acres a chinquapin mkd [marked] X from which an other mkd D bears S 79 E 5 standing on Blair's Spring Branch; thence up and with the meanders of sd. Branch to the place of beginning."

⁸Land transactions of Fannin County; copies of deeds provided by Ronnie Atnip. Special Warranty Deeds recorded in Deed Books G and H, Fannin County Records. Additional information on locating the site of Reverend Hardin's home appears in a lengthy article by Jacqueline White, Lifestyle Editor of the *Bonham Daily Favorite*, Bonham, Texas, November 26, 1995: "142-Year-old Pecan Trees Pinpoint Hardin Family Farm." There are six photographs illustrating this article, one of which is incorrectly identified as depicting Rev. J. G. Hardin. The caption reads that the photograph was supplied by Ronnie Atnip but that is also incorrect. Interview with Mr. Atnip on February 7, 2012.

⁹Hardin, *The Life of John Wesley Hardin as Written by Himself*, 5. The first edition was printed by the firm of Smith and Moore of Seguin, Texas in 1896. The page references in this work are to the reprint by the University of Oklahoma Press, Norman, 1961 edition. Hereafter referred to as Hardin, *Life*.

¹⁰Information provided by Ronnie Atnip and Edward Southerland of page from scrapbooks of "Old Choc." The article was written January 25, 1896, but what newspaper it appeared in is not identified. Mr. Southerland, an independent historian, is a great-great-grandnephew of "Old Choc."

¹¹Marohn, *The Last Gunfighter*, 14.

¹²Hardin, *Life*, 5.

¹³Ballenger led his men to Virginia where the battles were raging; he was wounded and taken prisoner at the Battle of Antietam on September 17, 1862. Upon being freed during a prisoner exchange, he returned home disabled, resigning his position in April 1864. Information on Captain Ballenger courtesy John Luckey via e-mail of May 11, 2011.

¹⁴Hardin, *Life*, 5–6.

¹⁵John Wheat, *Postmasters and Post Offices of Texas, 1846–1930*. The Sumpter post office was discontinued on March 9, 1874. E-mail from James A. Mundie to author, May 6, 2011.

¹⁶Slave Schedule Census of Trinity County, Texas, 1860, 472.

¹⁷Census of Itawamba County, Mississippi, 1850, 348.

¹⁸Hardin, *Life*, 11. John F. Moore was elected on September 22, 1860; re-elected August 4, 1862 and served until August 1, 1864. See Sammy Tise, *Texas County Sheriffs*, 496, hereafter cited as Tise.

[19]Hardin, *Life*, 11.

[20]"Widow's Pension Application of Mrs. Elizabeth M. Ruff. For Use of Widows of Soldiers Who are in Indigent Circumstances."

[21]Hardin, *Life*, 7–8.

[22]Census of Burleson County, Texas, 1850, 437.

[23]Census of Trinity County, Texas, 1860, 329.

[24]Census of Collin County, Texas, 1880, 16. C. J. Slater had married Susan Castleberry on April 22, 1872. He was listed as 28 years of age, she 22. During the next eight years she gave birth to four children.

[25]Correspondence from John Luckey, Whitehorse, Texas.

[26]William Baker Teagarden to Mrs. Charles Billings, November 2, 1931. Teagarden then was a successful attorney-at-law in San Antonio and wrote the letter on occasion of learning of the death of John Wesley Hardin Jr.

[27]Marohn, *The Last Gunfighter*, 12.

[28]Claiborne C. Holshousen was born September 5, 1814, in Tennessee; he died April 25, 1889, in Polk County. His grave is marked but the lettering is greatly worn.

[29]William Barnett Jones was the son of Martin Alexander and Martha Ann Houlshousen Jones, born in 1848 in Polk County. By 1870 Barnett, as he was always called, was on his own, working as a farm hand for William Hardin. William and Ann Hardin, 63 and 59 years of age respectively, lived in Polk County and had extensive acreage. Their 1870 census household consisted of themselves and fourteen others, some relatives, some freed people. Barnett is listed as 20 years of age, with $400 worth of personal estate. One of the farm laborers was Nat "Houlhousand," a thirty-eight-year-old black man born in Louisiana. He and his wife Eliza had six children; the last listed in the household was Elizabeth Hardin, a fourteen-year-old black female "At home." Census of Polk County, Texas, 1860, 35, and 1870, 442. The following two households enumerated consisted of Hardins and Joneses, a mixture of black, mulatto and white people. Martha Jones, a thirty-eight-year-old white female, had three children, Martin, Clayborn and Elizabeth.

[30]Hardin, *Life*, 12.

[31]There is a Barnett Creek in the area today and one cannot help but wonder if this is where the incident with Maje took place.

[32]Ibid., 12–13; Lt. Charles Schmidt's official report is from Marohn, *The Last Gunfighter*, 19; and Leon C. Metz, *John Wesley Hardin: Dark Angel of Texas* (El Paso: Mangan Books Publishers, 1996), 14. Hereafter referred to as Metz, *Dark Angel*.

[33]Christopher Long, "Nogalus Prairie, Texas." This community, also known as Nogallis Prairie, is located thirteen miles northeast of county seat Groveton, in northeast Trinity County. Today it is a "dispersed rural community." See *The New Handbook of Texas*, vol. 4, 1026. Hardin's publishers, Smith & Moore of Seguin, Texas, misread Hardin's handwriting and printed the community as "Logallis Prairie." Some writers have followed this misspelling.

[34]Hardin, *Life*, 13–14.

[35]Frank M. Fly to Stan Line, April 19, 1961. Copy in Parsons' Collection.

[36]Census of Navarro County, Texas, 1870.

[37]Hardin, *Life*, 14.

[38]Ibid., 14.

[39]Aline Rothe, "Where Wes Hardin Started Running," *Frontier Times*, July 1972; and 1880 Trinity County, Texas Census, 329. The census shows the Davis family. Alexander Davis was head of household, 23 years of age and farming; his wife Sarah was 23 and the three children, James, 8, George, 6, and John, 3 were at home. One 26-year-old mulatto female resided there as well.

[40]Amanda Trammell Swink, quoted in Walter Clay Dixson, *Richland Crossing*, 207. She was the daughter of Lewis and Emiline "Sarah" Isenhour Trammell. She married James L. Swink on April 8, 1880, in Navarro County. Her death certificate indicates she had lived in Richland, Navarro County, for 65 years. She died August 12, 1962, and is buried in Richland Cemetery. Navarro County, Texas Census, 1860, 223; official certificate of death # 51386.

[41]Walter Clay Dixson, *Richland Crossing: A Portrait of Texas Pioneers* (Everman, TX: Peppermill Publishing, 1994), 208.

[42]Hardin, *Life*, 15–16.

[43]Hardin, *Life*, 16.

[44]"Report of Sheriff James A. Nelms" in Texas State Library and Archives. Nelms was appointed sheriff on July 7, 1870, and served until

June 1872. He was removed from office by the District Judge, with no reason given. See Tise, 389. On Sept. 23, 1878, Polk was killed but in the same gunfight he killed City Marshal Charles Powers. See Clifford R. Caldwell and Ron DeLord, *Texas Lawmen 1835–1899: The Good and the Bad* (Charleston, SC: The History Press, 2011), 242–43.

[45]Hardin was misinformed in believing that Dixon's mother, brother and sister had been killed by "Yankees." Simp's brother William "Billy" Dixon was killed during the Lee-Peacock feud, which took place in the four counties of Hunt, Collin, Fannin and Grayson, the "Four Corners" region, and his father as well. Both are buried in what is today known as the Sears-Doss Cemetery in rural Fannin County, near the site of the old Hardin home. The stones in that small untended cemetery mark the final resting place of three Dixons: William, born April 4, 1849, and who died March 6, 1868; the father, John Dixon, born October 20, 1808 and who died November 7, 1871, and the mother, "Suanna" as the stone cutter carved but on many other documents her name appears as Suzanna or Suzannah, identified as the wife of John H. Dixon, born February 14, 1823, and who died March 2, 1899. Obviously Simp's mother was not killed by "Yankees" in the feud between the followers of Robert Lee and Lewis Peacock, but died many years later. The visit to this cemetery was made possible through the efforts of Ronnie Atnip.

[46]Hardin, *Life*, 17.

[47]James M. Smallwood, Barry A. Crouch, and Larry Peacock, *Murder and Mayhem: The War of Reconstruction in Texas* (College Station: Texas A&M University Press, 2003), 130.

[48]Ibid. The squad leader was Sergeant Adam Desch. The 1870 McLennan County census shows him as a twenty-three-year-old soldier born in Bavaria. The report of Simpson's death appeared in the *McKinney Enquirer* of February 12 and was reprinted in the *Dallas Herald* of February 19, 1870. It was a fitting end to a desperado of the Reconstruction era; Wes would have felt pride in the manner of his passing. The stone marking Simp Dixon's grave was placed there in the 1940s, according to research by Ronnie Atnip. It reads incorrectly as "Sim Dixon/ 1872."

[49]Hardin, *Life*, 17.

CHAPTER 2

[1]Kenneth E. Austin, "Hill County," *The New Handbook of Texas*, vol. 3, 619–21.

[2]The Hill County Heritage Book Committee, *The History of Hill County, Texas*, Vol. 2 (Louisville, KY: Heritage Publishing Consultants, 2010), 43. Hardin served as sheriff less than a year, dying either in December 1862 or January 1863. See Hill County census, 1860, 85.

[3]Thomas Bowles was appointed sheriff on January 10, 1863, but resigned August 1, 1864. See Sammy Tise, *Texas County Sheriffs*, 258.

[4]Hill County census, 1870, 449. If this is the partner of Hardin, James B. Collins was 20 years old, from Mississippi, with a 17-year-old wife named Fanny and two children.

[5]Hardin, *Life*, 18.

[6]*Flake's Semi-Weekly Bulletin*, December 22, 1869.

[7]No further information has been definitely located about "Hamp" (Hamilton?) Davis nor Judge Moore. Thomas Ripley in his *They Died With their Boots On* called him Ed Moore but without any substantiation. See the Sydney, Australia, edition, 1936, 23.

[8]The Bradley household is found on the 1860 White County, Arkansas, census showing household # 59 as that of B. B. Bradley, a 40-year-old farmer with a 32-year-old wife, S. A, and six children, one of which is simply "B. Bradley," 18 years of age and also farming. This young man would later become the victim of Hardin. All members of the family were from North Carolina. 1860 White County, Arkansas Census of "Free Inhabitants in Gray township," 931. Hardin apparently learned Bradley had killed a man in Arkansas and had to flee as a fugitive, and then located in Hill County.

[9]Hardin, *Life*, 21.

[10]Article "John Wesley Hardin" from the *El Paso Daily Herald*, September 4, 1895. The same article, with very slight variations, appeared in the *Dallas Morning News*, August 31, 1895. Following Hardin's death numerous articles appeared about his career, some accurate and some less than accurate.

[11]Davidson's communication did not identify the sheriff by name, but the official election registers show that H. P. Harris was appointed sheriff on August 5, 1872. He was commissioned the same day and was qualified on August 19. He served until J. B. Cox assumed the office, qualifying on January 3, 1873. Thus the communication from Davidson's office landed in the hands of Sheriff H. P. Harris. Donaly E. Brice, Texas State Library and Archives, to Parsons, June 7, 2011.

[12]Barry A. Crouch, "Captain Thomas Williams: The Path of Duty," in *The Human Tradition in Texas*, ed. Ty Cashion and Jesus de la Teja (Wilmington, DE: Scholarly Resources, No. 9), 71–86. A valuable treatment on the varied aspects of Reconstruction in Texas is *Still the Arena of Civil War: Violence and Turmoil in Reconstruction Texas 1865–1874*, ed. Kenneth W. Howell (Denton: University of North Texas Press, 2012).

[13]Pinoak, no longer in existence save for a small cemetery, was in eastern Milam County, four miles northwest of the community of Gause on Farm-to-Market Road 2095, then not far from the Washington County line.

[14]Dorothy Dixon Stanley and Annie Maud Knittel Avis, *History of Burton*, entry entitled "Union Hill" (No publisher, no date), 1.

[15]*New York Clipper*, February 12, 1870. The *Clipper*, focusing on entertainment, became well known in 1853 and continued until 1924 when it was absorbed into today's *Variety* magazine.

[16]Charles Askins, *Texans, Guns and History* (New York: Winchester Press, 1970), 101. Comstock may indeed have been the man's name, as highly respected historian Frederick Nolan identifies him thus in his *The Wild West: History, Myth and the Making of America* (Edison, NJ: no press, 2004). Nolan writes that Comstock "mistook [Hardin] for a 'rube' and tried to enmesh Wes in a badger game," 98.

[17]Marohn, *The Last Gunfighter*, 25.

[18]Washington County, Texas Census, 1870, 3.

[19]Hardin, *Life*, 25.

[20]Ibid.

[21]*Flake's Semi-Weekly Bulletin*, July 2, 1870, printed in Galveston, Texas.

[22]"An Act to Establish a State Police and Provide the Regulation and Government of the State," Austin, July 4, 1870, 2.

[23]This is probably P. Rushing, a 70-year-old widow residing there with her two sons. See Navarro County census, 1870, 79.

[24]"Ant Prude" was Prudence Jane Anderson, a sister of Alexander Hamilton Anderson who was married to James Thomas Patrick on June 15, 1870, by Rev. J. G. Hardin. The feud between the Anderson and the Love families began in 1855 in a dispute over neighboring land holdings worth twenty-five cents an acre. William M. Love shot Dr. William Nicks Anderson on February 9, 1855; Anderson died the following day after identifying his slayer as Love. His widow, mother of four and pregnant at the time of her husband's death, vowed to raise her unborn son to someday kill Love. The baby was born July 6, 1855, and given the lengthy name of Doctor James Thomas Lee Buchanan Anderson, but generally called Jim. William Love was shot and killed on May 19, 1873 as reported in the *Sherman Patriot* and reprinted in the *Clarksville Standard* of June 7, 1873. A witness identified Alexander H. "Ham" Anderson and Alexander Henry "Alec" Barekman as the slayers, but Jim Anderson may also have been involved. Following the slaying Ham Anderson and Alec Barekman drifted to Lincoln County, New Mexico Territory, where they remained several months before returning to Texas and joining John Wesley Hardin.

[25][Mary] Elizabeth Hardin to "My dear brother," August 27, 1870. Original in the R. B. Dixson Collection, Texas State Library and Archives.

[26]Hardin, *Life*, 25–28.

[27]Ibid., 28.

[28]Ibid.

[29]Karen R. Thompson and Jane H. DiGesualdo, *Historical Round Rock, Texas* (Austin: Eakin Press, 1985), 121–22, 460–61.

[30]Hardin, *Life*, 29.

[31]State Police Captain M. P. Hunnicutt had recommended Hoffman to Adjutant General Davidson, advising him that Hoffman had served in the Federal army during the war and was "a man of property & has Suffered persecution on account of his political beliefs." Hunnicutt to Davidson, July 11, 1870, original in Texas State Archives. Prior to becoming a policeman Hoffman had operated a livery stable in Waco, McLennan County, Texas, 1870, 53.

CHAPTER 3

[1] James Davidson, *An Act to Establish a State Police and Provide for the Legislation and Government of the Same*, Adjutant General's General Orders No. 1., July 4, 1870, 1–2.

[2] Ibid., 5.

[3] Hardin, *Life,* 29.

[4] Ibid., 30.

[5] E. T. Stakes was commissioned a police lieutenant on October 16, 1870, and resigned on December 17, 1871. Barry A. Crouch and Donaly E. Brice, *The Governor's Hounds: The Texas State Police, 1870–1873* (Austin: University of Texas Press, 2011), 291. The 1870 Milam County census shows him as Elisha *Stokes*, 42 years of age, born in Alabama, 278. No occupation is given.

[6] Hardin, *Life*, 31.

[7] James Smalley was born about 1846 in Mississippi. In 1870 he was living in Harrison County. He was commissioned a state policeman on October 18, 1870. See Crouch and Brice, *The Governor's Hounds*, 290.

[8] Hardin, *Life,* 31.

[9] *Flake's Daily Bulletin*, Saturday February 4, 1871, citing a report from the *Fairfield Ledger* of January 28, 1871.

[10] Hardin, *Life*, 33.

[11] The Dallas article was headlined "John Wesley Harding" (strangely misspelling his last name) and appeared in the issue of Saturday morning August 25, 1877. Strange that editor J. L. Bartow misspelled the prisoner's name as he was well aware of the stories about him. In the same column of "Local Jottings" appeared this: "What will our frontier papers do now for sensations, since John Wesley Hardin is arrested?" This Dallas article was reprinted in the *Memphis* (Tennessee) *Weekly Public Ledger* of September 4, 1877 with a sub-headline, "The Captured Outlaw for Whom the Rewards Aggregate $20,000." It probably appeared in numerous newspapers, increasing Hardin's notoriety. The latest copy of this article we have found appeared in the Georgetown *Colorado Miner* issue of November 17, 1877.

[12] Karon Mac Smith, "Archibald Greene Cone and Sally Cocke" in *The History of Gonzales County* by Gonzales County Historical Commission, 1986, 259. The 1870 Wilson County census shows household #

384 as that of James Cone with his wife and six children; household # 385 William Cone and his wife and seven children; and household # 386 Greene Cone with his wife and two children. 1870 Gonzales County, Texas Census, 483.

[13]The first Emanuel Clements (born in 1813 in Kentucky), along with Benjamin Hardin, had migrated to Texas prior to 1836. He married Martha Balch Hardin on July 30, 1836, in Marshall, Mississippi. She was the daughter of Benjamin and Martha B. Hardin. They had eleven children. In his *Life* Hardin mentioned that Mary Jane Clements, one of those eleven, was married to James Madison Denson and Minerva her sister was married to Ferdinand Jackson "Ferd" Brown. Actually this was Mary Jane's second husband. Her first husband, Wiley Kimbro had died in 1862.

[14]From Gonzales to Red River crossing was 326 miles; from Red River to the Kansas line was 230; from the Kansas line to Abilene was 121, for a total of 677 miles. Gary Kraisinger to Parsons, June 26, 2011.

[15]See "Two Early Texas Cattlemen: The John Duderstadts," an unpublished manuscript by Harold D. Jobes, presented at the Spring meeting of the Edwards Plateau Historical Association at Harper, Texas, May 5, 2012. Copy in author's possession.

[16]Fannin County, Texas Census, 1860, 242. The future Mrs. Joseph G. Hardin was eleven years old in 1860. Her name here was spelled "Arabel" but she was known as Belle most of her life. Their post office was Honey Grove.

[17]Hardin, *Life*, 34.

[18]A Robert King, 47 years of age and black, resided in neighboring DeWitt County in 1870 and is perhaps the man Hardin refers to here. DeWitt County census, 1870, 227. Their post office was Clinton.

[19]Carroll was born about 1843, the son of Jacob and Sarah Carroll; by 1860 the family resided in Gonzales County. Little is known of his life outside the writing of Hardin. There is a Columbus Carroll buried in the Fort Stanton Military Cemetery, Lincoln County, New Mexico. Fort Stanton at one time was a hospital for consumptives, so it is probable that Carroll went there for health reasons. The burial records suggest a death date of October 25, 1905. There is a Carroll

Family cemetery in Gonzales County but Columbus is not listed as being interred there.

[20]R. T. Mellard, "The Latch String is on the Outside" in *The Trail Drivers of Texas*. Crawford Burnett was born April 19, 1835, and lived in Gonzales County much of his life. He died there January 12, 1915; Burnett is buried in the Pilgrim Cemetery near Smiley in rural Gonzales County. R. T. Mellard began his career as a cowboy in 1870. That year he "got acquainted with Mr. Crawford Burnett, a better man Texas never produced," 597. According to *The Trail Drivers of Texas*, Burnett was "one of the first to drive herds to Kansas in the late '60's and has the credit of driving the last herd out of Gonzales county [1887] to the northern markets," 796.

[21]Hardin, *Life*, 35.

[22]Hardin, *Life*, 37–38.

[23]Ibid.

[24]*Kerrville Mountain Sun*, February 24, 1938.

CHAPTER 4

[1]*Life*, 38.

[2]William G. Cutler, *History of the State of Kansas* (Chicago: A. T. Andreas, 1883).

[3]Hardin's version of the fight on the Newton prairie is in *Life*, 38–42.

[4]The *Wichita Tribune*, Thursday, June 1, 1871.

[5]The *Kerrville Mountain Sun*, February 24, 1938.

[6]Waldo E. Koop, "Enter John Wesley Hardin: A Dim Trail to Abilene," *The Prairie Scout* 2 (Abilene: The Kansas Corral of the Westerners, 1974).

[7]John Duderstadt, Fred's brother, related to his son that the cowboys with Hardin and Clements did bury the Mexicans. Interview with John Duderstadt Jr. by Harold D. Jobes, recorded in "Two Early Texas Cattlemen: The John Duderstadts." Unpublished manuscript, copy in author's possession.

[8]Stuart N. Lake, *Wyatt Earp Frontier Marshal* (Boston: Houghton Mifflin Company, 1931), 106.

[9]The *Topeka Commonwealth*, May 11, 1871.

[10]George C. Anderson, "Touring Kansas and Colorado in 1871: The Journal of George C. Anderson," *Kansas Historical Quarterly* 22, no. 3 (Autumn 1956): 215.

[11]Joseph G. McCoy, *Cattle Trade of the West and Southwest* (Readex Microprint Corp., 1966), 44.

[12]History remembers Mrs. Lou M. Gore although she and her husband J. W. Gore operated the establishment jointly. The Dickinson County census shows J. W. Gore, 39, as "Hotel Keeper" with $17,000 in real estate property and $5,000 in personal estate. Mrs. Gore is listed as "Keeping House." Dickinson County census, enumerated July 29, 1870.

[13]*The Trail Drivers of Texas*, 454.

[14]In his photo album, beneath this white-hatted man-killer, Hardin scrawled that it was made in Abilene in 1871. The 1870 Dickinson County census reveals there were at least three photographers there in Abilene that year. There was Frank Gray, age 20, and Samuel Howell, age 26, both from Ohio. Their names may be slightly misspelled due to the poor quality of the census image. The third was J. M. Honigan, or Harrigan, 25, from New York. Dickinson County, Kansas census, 1870, 5 and 14.

[15]The *Abilene Chronicle*, June 8, 1871.

[16]Ibid., June 22, 1871.

[17]City ordinances published in the *Abilene Chronicle* issue of June 28, 1871. They had been approved on June 24, at a time when Hardin and his fellow drovers had been in Abilene long enough to know them.

[18]The *Junction City Union*, August 19, 1871. Junction City, the county seat of Geary County, is some twenty miles east of Abilene.

[19]Joe Parker, the "noted desperado," remains elusive. At his death in 1875 he was described as "well known in northern and Western Texas." A report reaching Lavaca County told how he had been "overtaken and killed" in the eastern part of Collin County by a sheriff of that county. See *Herald and Planter*, Hallettsville, Texas, January 7, 1875.

[20]G. B. Ray, *Murder at the Corners* (San Antonio: The Naylor Company, 1957), 96.

[21]James M. Smallwood, Barry A. Crouch, and Larry Peacock, *Murder and Mayhem: The War of Reconstruction in Texas* (College Station: Texas A&M University Press, 2003), 38.

[22]Oliver Wolcott Wheeler was born March 26, 1830, in Stonington, Connecticut. After a harrowing youth, contracting tuberculosis and then a tropical fever in Panama, he ultimately found health and success. By 1874 he was a well-known figure in the western cattle business. Wheeler died February 17, 1890. See McCoy's *Cattle Trade of the West and Southwest*, 257–69.

[23]*Abilene Chronicle*, July 13, 1871.

[24]Hardin, *Life*, 44–45.

[25]Unpublished manuscript, excerpt from memoir of A. I. "Babe" Moye, no date, courtesy Bernice M. Dobbins, Conroe, Texas. Moye also contributed an article to *The Trail Drivers of Texas*. In Abilene he said he "met up with John Wesley Hardin, Buffalo Bill Thompson [brother of Ben Thompson], Manny Clements and Gip Clements, and we went over to the gambling house. It did not take the gamblers there long to relieve me of all the money I possessed. Wild Bill Hickok told me that the best way to beat the game was to let it alone. I took his advice and have been beating the game ever since." "Buried a Cowboy in a Lonely Grave on the Prairie" by Moye, *The Trail Drivers of Texas*, 455–59.

[26]John Wesley Hardin to his wife Jane, from Huntsville, June 24, 1888. The originals of these many Hardin letters and accompanying photographs are in the Wittliff Collection, Southwestern Writers Collection, Texas State University, San Marcos.

[27]Hugh Anderson was one of the sons of Walter P. and Susan Bailey Anderson, born on November 25, 1851, in DeWitt County, Texas. Of interest is that his sister, Mary Florence, married William P. "Buck" Taylor who was killed in the early years of the Taylor-Sutton Feud in which Hardin became a major player. Anderson was in Kansas with Hardin and he remained there some time after Hardin and the others had returned to Texas. He would have been forgotten had he not become a leading figure in the Newton gun battle on August 20, 1871. In this melee Anderson killed a man named Mike McCluskey, in retaliation for McCluskey's killing of a man named William Bailey some time before. Anderson lived out his adventurous life and died at the age of sixty-two in Lincoln County, New Mexico. He was struck by lightning on June 9, 1914. DeWitt County, Texas Census, 1860 shows the Anderson

family; Bill O'Neal, *Encyclopedia of Western Gunfighters* (Norman: University of Oklahoma Press, 1979), 24–25; Douglas W. Ellison, "The West's Bloodiest Duel—Never Happened!" *Journal* of the Wild West History Association 1, no. 5 (October 2008): 17–30. One wonders if the William Bailey who avenged his friend's death was somehow kin to Susan Bailey Anderson, Hugh's mother; could this have somehow been an incident in the long-lasting Sutton-Taylor Feud?

[28]The Bideno chase and killing is in *Life*, 46–50.

[29]The description of the killing of Bideno, whose identification is given only by Hardin, appears in the *Oxford Times*, July 13, 1871.

[30]Hardin, *Life*, 50.

[31]The *Kansas Daily Commonwealth* (Topeka), July 11, 1871.

[32]It would be interesting to know more about Tuttle, especially with his misadventures in Newton. Perry Chauncey Tuttle was born in Beloit, Wisconsin in 1845. By 1860 the Tuttle family was in Shawnee County, Kansas, where father Charles C. worked as a landlord in Topeka. When the war came, Perry enlisted in the 11th Regiment of Kansas Volunteers, Company E, on August 19, 1862. He was mustered out on August 7, 1865. By 1870 he was still in Topeka operating a livery stable. When he left Topeka to operate a business in Newton is unknown, but perhaps the troubles with the "Texas Rangers" were too much as by 1880 he had moved away from Kansas and was living in Humboldt County, Iowa, operating a saloon. Tuttle died October 26, 1898, and is buried in Graceland, Creston Union, Iowa. His grave is marked with a Grand Army of the Republic marker.

[33]Hardin, *Life*, 51.

[34]Reprinted in the *Kansas City Daily Commonwealth*, July 20, 1871.

[35]The *Kansas State Record*, July 26, 1871.

[36]The *San Antonio Daily Express*, June 13, 1876.

[37]Hardin, *Life*, 58.

[38]The *Abilene Chronicle*, August 10, 1871.

[39]Ibid.

[40]The *Salina Weekly Journal*, August 10, 1871.

[41]The *Abilene Chronicle*, August 17, 1871.

[42]Hardin, *Life*, 60.

[43]Ibid., 60-61.

[44]Edith Connelley Ross, "The Bloody Benders," *Quarterly* of the Kansas State Historical Society 17 (1926).

[45]Robert N. Mullin interview and article by Chuck Parsons, "A Texas Gunfighter and the Kansas Murder Family," *Real West* 23, no. 171 (July 1980).

[46]The story of the Benders has remained a popular subject due to its violence as well as its mysterious aspects. Besides the early work of Ross (1926) and Fern Morrow Wood (1993), more recently Phyllis de la Garza researched the Kansas family and published her results in *Death for Dinner: The Benders of (Old) Kansas* (Honolulu: Talei Publishers, 2005).

[47]Fern Morrow Wood, *The Benders: Keeper of the Devil's Inn* (Chelsea, MI: BookCrafters, 1993).

[48][Thomas E. Hogg] *Life and Adventures of Sam Bass the Notorious Union Pacific and Texas Train Robber* (Dallas: Dallas Commercial Steam Print, 1878), 68–69.

CHAPTER 5

[1]Hardin, *Life*, 61.

[2]Barry A. Crouch and Donaly E. Brice in *The Governor's Hounds*, explain the different responsibilities of the special and regular state policemen. The specials composed "a force created . . . to oversee political activities, to make certain all voters were fairly registered, to maintain order at the polls in counties where they might be necessary to ensure an honest election, and to prevent a local crisis," 92. The regular State Police had statewide authority.

[3]For two recent studies of the Sutton-Taylor difficulties, although with contrasting interpretations, see James M. Smallwood, *The Feud That Wasn't: The Taylor Ring, Bill Sutton, John Wesley Hardin, and Violence in Texas* (College Station: Texas A&M University Press, 2008); and Chuck Parsons, *The Sutton-Taylor Feud: The Deadliest Blood Feud in Texas* (Denton: University of North Texas Press, 2009).

[4]Gonzales County, Texas Census, 1870, 13 (Lackey) and 67 (Paramore). Interestingly the 1870 census lists the post office of both Lackey and

Paramore as Belmont, a small community a dozen miles from county seat Gonzales. Lackey later moved to Gonzales town where he established his residence and continued work as a blacksmith. When John Lackey died has not been determined unfortunately. When his wife died she received a lengthy obituary in the *Gonzales Inquirer*.

[5]Hardin, *Life*, 62.

[6]Mark Odintz, "Smiley, Texas" in *The New Handbook of Texas*, vol. 5, 1088.

[7]A thorough discussion of this incident appears in Dennis McCown, "A Shooting, Much Exaggerated," Wild West History Association *Journal* 4, no. 5 (October 2011): 39–44.

[8]The item first appeared in an undated *San Antonio Herald* and reprinted in *Flake's Semi-Weekly Bulletin*, October 13, 1871.

[9]Hardin, *Life*, 63.

[10]Ibid.

[11]George Culver Tennille at this time was a wealthy stock raiser and farmer in DeWitt County. Born in 1826, he was 44 years old. His second wife, Amanda Jane Billings, was 30, and the children living at home were: Anne C., 13; Thomas C., 11; Henriette, 10; Harriet M., 8; Nancy, 8. In the same household was his son-in-law Joseph Clements, 22, and his wife, daughter Sarah J., 15. A stock hand also lived there, one Benito Silgera, 27 years old and a native of Mexico. See 1870 Gonzales County census, 269.

[12]See # 1357 and #1556 in Gonzales County marriage Book B; John Gipson Clements and Elizabeth Celea Evans were married November 4, 1875, #2055 recorded in Book B1.

[13]Hardin, *Life*, 64.

[14]Marriage license archived in the Gonzales County Courthouse.

[15]Hardin, *Life*, 64.

[16]DeWitt County, Texas census, 1860, 487; and for 1870, 213.

[17]Crouch and Brice, *The Governor's Hounds*, 261.

[18]Karen S. Parrish, "Banquete, Texas," *The New Handbook of Texas*, vol. 1, 373.

[19]Hardin, *Life*, 65.

[20]Ibid.

[21]Harper as sheriff from *Texas County Sheriffs*, Sammy Tise, 447. Family
   information from Southeast Texas Regional Gedcom Project, accessed
   October 11, 2011. Harper was born January 15, 1813, in Dickinson
   County, Mississippi, and had married Julia Ann Lane, a Georgia lady
   born in 1817. By 1860 they were in Sabine County, Texas, with their
   six children. In 1860 his family consisted of his wife and six children,
   of whom Hardin mentions Jesse, John and Billy in his memoir. These
   three were not listed in the household in 1870, so they were "on their
   own."

[22]Hardin, *Life*, 65.

[23]Ibid., 66.

[24]Ibid.

[25]Hardin wrote: "I learned afterwards that Judge O. M. Roberts was the
   man appealed to." Oran Milo Roberts had a distinguished career in the
   legal field as well as the political field. Born in South Carolina in 1815,
   by 1841 he was in San Augustine, Texas, and had opened a law office.
   In January 1874 he was appointed Chief Justice of the Texas Supreme
   Court, and it was at this point that Speights made his appeal, although
   no documentation of such an appeal has been found. Of course Speights' appeal may have been nothing more than a desperate verbal cry
   for protection. Roberts was elected governor in 1878 and served two
   terms, and was also the first president of the Texas State Historical
   Association. He died May 19, 1898, and is buried in the Texas State
   Cemetery. See Ford Dixon, "Oran Milo Roberts," *New Handbook of
   Texas*, vol. 5, 611–12 and research by Donaly E. Brice.

[26]William "Billy" Harper's older sister Gracie Berintha was born in
   1838. Billy was born in 1853, the same year as Hardin, so there was a
   difference of fifteen years in their age.

[27]Hardin, *Life*, 66–67.

[28]A summary of Speights's report, dated August 21, 1872, appears in
   "Ledger of Letters Received in the Adjutant General Papers," 401-702,
   89, Texas State Archives.

[29]Crouch and Brice, *The Governor's Hounds*, 291.

[30]Widow's Pension Application # 26250 for widow of Civil War veteran
   J. A. Ferguson. His widow, Nancy Jane Griffin, died June 7, 1928.

[31]"Accusations Against Wesley Hardin," *Austin Daily Democratic States-man*, August 30, 1877.

[32]Crouch and Brice, *The Governor's Hounds*, 291.

[33]The (Lampasas) *Weekly Dispatch*, October 31, 1871.

[34]John Wesley Hardin to Jane Hardin, June 24, 1888, from Huntsville State Penitentiary. The "Hardin Letters" are archived today in the Wittliff Collection, Southwestern Writers Collections, Texas State University, San Marcos. An important work for historians who may not be able to examine the letters personally remains *The Letters of John Wesley Hardin*, trans. and comp. Roy and Jo Ann Stamps (Austin: Eakin Press, 2001).

CHAPTER 6

[1]Hardin, *Life*, 68.

[2]The "bull-dog" Hardin claimed to have carried at this particular time was probably a Hammond single-shot pocket-pistol with a 4-inch barrel, produced from 1866 to 1868. Manufactured in calibers of various sizes, the most common was the .44, and this may be the one Hardin carried as a hide-out weapon. They were accurate only at close range. See Joseph G. Rosa, *Guns of the American West* (New York: Crown Publishers, 1985), 76.

[3]Hardin, *Life*, 70. This verbosity seems most unlikely for a young man who has just received a blast from a shotgun. No doubt he felt that at the time, but the expression may have come only while writing the memoir.

[4]1870 Polk County, Texas Census, 474.

[5]William B. "Billy" Teagarden was the son of Oswin and Mahettible Baker Teagarden, and was born March 13, 1854, at Rusk, Cherokee County. He was a boyhood friend of Hardin and remained so throughout his life, helping him now in his hour of need as well as years later when Hardin was attempting to obtain a pardon. Billy "received his preliminary education in private schools and studied law during vacations and after school in the offices of friends." He was admitted to the bar in Wood County in 1875 and entered into private practice. Teagarden died July 16, 1933, and is buried in Mission Park Cemetery

in San Antonio. His lengthy obituary appears in the *San Antonio Daily Express*, July 17, 1933.

[6]W. M. Waddell and others to Gov. E. J. Davis, September 30, 1872. Governor's Papers, Box 301-81, Folder 260.

[7]Hardin, *Life*, 74.

[8]The "Waddell letter" was signed by the following: William M. Waddell, a revenue collector from North Carolina living in Palestine, Anderson County; R. J. Blair, a farmer living in Houston County; John Blair, a Justice of the Peace, also living in Houston County; L. W. Cooper who may be Lemuel Cooper, a farmer living in Rusk County; Myamin Priest, an Attorney at Law, or his son, Myamin D. Priest, also an attorney at law, living in Cherokee County. Anderson County Census, 59; Houston County, 301 and 306; Rusk County, and Cherokee County, 193. H. W. Moore also signed but he was not found on the 1870 census.

[9]Ellen J. Reagan to Parsons, April 30, 1969. The information about the Reagan family is in letters from Ellen Reagan, granddaughter of Sheriff Reagan, May 14, April 17 and April 30, 1969. Reagan's wife, who helped care for the wounded Hardin, was Martha Black Reagan who was born August 19, 1819, and died May 29, 1886. Sheriff Reagan was born in Tennessee in 1820. The Reagans are buried in Cedar Hill Cemetery on the edge of Rusk, just off Farm to Market 241 south. It is the oldest large cemetery in the county.

[10]Hardin, *Life*, 75.

[11]Dr. Thomas Young Jameson was born in Alabama on September 21, 1827, and before the Civil War was living in Cherokee County. He married Mary Cornila and had several children. He died on September 9, 1888, and is buried in Cedar Hill Cemetery in Rusk, beneath a tall monument. His marker points out that he was a veteran of the Confederate States Army.

[12]The *Austin Daily Democratic Statesman*, July 10, 1874, in an article entitled "The Jail." By the time Hardin was captured and placed in the Travis County jail in August 1877 the county had built a new facility.

[13]Zimpelman was elected sheriff on June 25, 1866, but was removed from office by General J. J. Reynolds on November 1, 1867, by Special Order # 195. He was elected a second time on December 3, 1869,

re-elected on December 2, 1873, and served until February 15, 1876. Tise, 494.

¹⁴The *Galveston Daily News*, November 21, 1872, reprinting an item from Austin's *Lone Star Ranger*.

¹⁵The *San Antonio Herald*, November 26, 1872.

¹⁶Adj. Gen. Frank Britton would later send Williams to Lampasas County to enforce the law forbidding wearing weapons within the city limits, which was being defied by the Horrell party. Williams and a squad of police arrived there on March 14, 1873, and were ambushed by the Horrells. Williams and two privates were instantly killed and one was mortally wounded. Williams was buried in the Texas State Cemetery in Austin. His small grave marker is within the shadow of Gov. E. J. Davis' huge monument. A brief biographical sketch appears in Barry A. Crouch, "Captain Thomas Williams: The Path of Duty," in *The Human Tradition*, no. 9, ed. Ty Cashion and Jesus F. de la Teja (Wilmington, DE: Scholarly Resources, 2001), 71–86.

¹⁷Hardin, *Life*, 76.

¹⁸William E. Jones was appointed sheriff on November 10, 1871, and served until November 8, 1872; he was elected again on November 4, 1884, re-elected November 2, 1886 and November 6, 1888 and served until November 4, 1890. After a period out of office he was again elected on November 6, 1894, and served until November 3, 1896. Tise, 209.

¹⁹William E. Jones to Adj. Gen. F. L. Britton, November 1, 1872. Letters Received, Ledger 401-620, Texas State Archives.

²⁰Henry Orsay to Sheriff Jones, November 11, 1872.

²¹Adj. Gen. F.L. Britton to Jones, November 27, 1872.

²²Thomas G. Patton to Adj. Gen. F. L. Britton, January 14, 1873, in Letters Received, 660.

²³Details and this dialogue from the testimony are preserved in the appeals court record. "Bowen vs the State" in *Texas Court of Appeals Reports* (Galveston, TX, 1878), 628.

²⁴The notice of the peace treaty appeared in the *Star* of January 9, 1874. The treaty with all signatories is included in Parsons' *The Sutton-Taylor Feud*, 289–90.

²⁵Proclamation for Reward in Governors Papers, Texas State Library.

[26]*Report of Adjutant General of the State*, 1873, 122.

[27]The *New York Times*, September 10, 1873.

CHAPTER 7

[1]*The Governor's Hounds:* Davis, 262; Helm, 271; Tumlinson, 294.

[2]This detail of Bowen's version of the killing is from the *Gonzales Inquirer*, May 18, 1878.

[3]Hardin, *Life*, 78.

[4]Ibid., 79.

[5]Ibid., 80.

[6]F. L. Britton, *Report of the Adjutant General of the State of Texas for the Year 1873* (Austin: Cardwell & Walker, Printers, 1874), 116.

[7]Ibid., 118.

[8]Ibid., 122–23. Samuel T. Robb served in the Texas House of Representatives for the 13th Legislature (January 14–June 4, 1873) representing District 2 (Angelina, Shelby, Nacogdoches, Sabine, Trinity and San Augustine counties). He was a native of Ohio, born in 1823 and appointed post master of newly established office of Trinity on February 28, 1872. He died July 24, 1908, and is buried in Trinity Cedar Grove Cemetery. Donaly E. Brice to Parsons, October 26, 2011. In the 1870 Federal Census for Trinity County Robb was household number 3. John Gates was household number 1 while the Teagarden family was number 2. It was a close gathering of people who figured in Hardin's life.

[9]Britton, *Report of the Adjutant General . . . 1873*, 122.

[10]Ibid., 125.

[11]Hardin, *Life*, 80.

[12]William Steele's report to Gov. Richard Coke is in Letter Press Ledger 401-621 dated July 10, 1874, 297.

[13]Jack Hays Day, *The Sutton Taylor Feud* (San Antonio: Sid Murray & Son, Printers, 1937), 16.

[14]Ibid., The *San Antonio Daily Herald*, June 20, 1873.

[15]Hardin, *Life*, 82.

[16]Jack Hays Day, 18–19.

[17]Hardin, *Life*, 82.

[18]Undated article in the *Victoria Advocate* reprinted in *The Texas Vendetta; or, Sutton-Taylor Feud* by Victor M. Rose, 30.

[19]They were married August 22, 1867. DeWitt County Marriage Record Book A, license # 680, 221. Cox's second marriage was on August 22, 1872. Book D, license # 1139, 44.

[20]Marjorie Burnett Hyatt, "Littleberry Wright Family" in *The History of DeWitt County, Texas*, 830.

[21]*San Antonio Daily Express*, July 25, 1873.

[22]Newspapers headlined the event, "Assassination of Jack Helm." Available accounts include the *Gonzales Index* report reprinted in the *Bastrop Advertiser* of August 2; the *Fayette County New Era* of La Grange, August 8, and the *San Antonio Daily Express*, August 9, 1873. The wide coverage of the killing emphasizes the belief that Helm was perhaps as notorious an individual as Hardin himself.

[23]Hardin, *Life*, 84.

[24]David George, "Jack Helm Meets John Wesley Hardin," *The Texas Gun Collector*, Spring, 2003, 48–49. The weapon was recently examined by this writer; the attached card informs the viewer that Hardin later loaned or gave the weapon to J. C. Jones, who became Gonzales County sheriff for one term, 1880–1882.

[25]L. B. Wright to Gov. E. J. Davis, July 24, 1873.

CHAPTER 8

[1]Adj. Gen. James Davidson to Joe Tumlinson, April 29, 1871, in Letterpress Book 401-1032, page 32. Tumlinson had written to Davidson that he could not "comply with orders" and was discharged. Unfortunately we have only Davidson's reply, not Tumlinson's original letter revealing what orders he could not comply with.

[2]DeWitt County, Texas Census, 1870, 255, shows Joseph Tumlinson as a 59-year-old "Stock Raiser" from Tennessee. His wife Elizabeth is shown to be forty-one and keeping house while their one child then was Peter, fourteen years of age. Their post office was Clinton. His military service is discussed in "Joseph Tumlinson" by Samuel Tumlinson in *The New Handbook of Texas*, vol. 6, 587.

[3]Hardin, *Life*, 84.

[4]James Francis Blair first served as sheriff from June 25, 1866, until February 15, 1869. Then after the death of Jack Helm he acted as sheriff until the appointment of William J. Weisiger. Tise, 157.

[5]Hardin, *Life*, 85.

[6]Peter Creed obviously was named after first-wife Johanna Taylor's brother, Creed, who according to some students of the feud, acted as a virtual crime ring leader, although with no solid basis for the claim.

[7]Christopher Columbus Simmons lived an exciting life, not only due to his Civil War experiences, but also to his service in the Texas State Police and aligning himself with the Sutton forces afterwards. He died in 1918 in the Confederate Home in Austin and is buried in the Texas State Cemetery, one of the very few former State Policemen buried there.

[8]*Daily Houston Telegraph*, August 20, 1873, citing a report from the *Gonzales Inquirer*.

[9]Jack Hays Day, *The Sutton Taylor Feud*, 40. The White brothers, Joseph Priestly "Doc" and Daniel Jefferson were sons of James Knox and Elizabeth McCullough White. See "Captain James Knox White Family" by White descendant Nantie P. Lee in *The History of DeWitt County, Texas*, 815.

[10]Hardin, *Life*, 85.

[11]The *Cuero Weekly Star*, January 9, 1874.

[12]Robert Clow was in his mid-sixties when he was traveling. Apparently he was on his way home to Austin when he stopped in Cuero. What his occupation was in 1874 is uncertain, but by 1880 he was a clerk in the Comptroller's office in Austin. The Pennsylvania-born clerk was married to Elizabeth, age fifty-five, and living at home with three unmarried daughters. Travis County 1880 Census, 205.

[13]The *Austin Daily Democratic Statesman,* January 22, 1874, in the "Texas News and Comments" column.

[14]The registration ledgers of the Ellsworth Hotel have been preserved and microfilmed, now archived in the Kansas State Historical Society of Topeka. Also see Chuck Parsons' "Eyewitness to Cowtown Violence," *Real West* 23, no. 169 (April 1980): 36–39, 49.

[15]*Austin Daily Democratic Statesman*, February 27, 1874.

[16]Ibid., February 28, 1874.

CHAPTER 9

[1]Hardin, *Life*, 87

[2]The *Austin Daily Democratic Statesman*, March 15, citing a letter dated March 11, 1874, written by an apparent eye-witness.

[3]Sutton had a Smith & Wesson pistol, serial number 21418, which he had purchased in Ellsworth, Kansas, in 1873. John Meador later testified to this fact, claiming he was with Sutton when he bought it.

[4]*Austin Daily Democratic Statesman*, March 15, 1874.

[5]Laura Sutton's reward notice appeared in the *Victoria Advocate* of June 4, 1874, and no doubt numerous other newspapers as well.

[6]Hardin, *Life*, 88.

[7] Ibid.

[8]Joseph G. Hardin served as postmaster from April 18, 1872 until April 1873. See Homer Stephen, *The Frontier Postmasters* (Dublin, TX: The Dublin Progress, 1952), 36.

[9]Dora Dean Hardin died as Mrs. Henderson on November 7, 1951, in Coleman, Coleman County, Texas. She is buried in the Coleman City Cemetery. Joseph Gibson Hardin Jr., born May 24, 1874, died June 22, 1927. He married Ada Louise Currie (July 27, 1878–January 2, 1939). Both are buried in Evergreen Cemetery in Ballinger, Texas.

[10] Hardin, *Life*, 90.

[11]The census shows a Charles Webb, with no initial given, as age 26, a white male born in Tennessee with no occupation shown, but it's not possible to say that this is the Charles M. Webb who was shot by Hardin. He was a boarder in the house of F. N. Hammon and family. Dallas County census, page 415, enumerated September 9, 1870.

[12]J. H. Gideon was elected sheriff of Brown County on December 2, 1873, and served until February 15, 1876. Tise, 70.

[13] Ibid., 90–91.

[14]J. P. Lipscomb to John Wesley Hardin, in an undated letter, but probably written in October or November 1877. Joseph P. Lipscomb appears in the census of Tarrant County for 1870 and 1880 as a merchant, not as an attorney as one might expect of one who intends to help defend a

man in a court of law. By 1880 he and his wife Fannie Elizabeth had a family of four children. Tarrant County, Texas census, 1870, 530; 1880 census, 142.

[15]No Gouldstones have been found in this area during the 1870s. Who was meant was no doubt Samuel Sullivan Gholson, noted stock raiser and Texas Ranger. S. S. Gholson is found in the 1870 Federal census of Coleman County, with post office at San Saba. S. S. Gholson, 29 years old and a native of Texas, is head of household with his wife Mary, 25, and two children. Their occupation was listed as "Driving Cattle." See Coleman County census of 1870, 307, and Donna Gholson Cook, *Gholson Road: Revolutionaries and Texas Rangers* (NP: 1st Books, 2004).

[16]Hardin, *Life*, 90.

[17]Henry James Ware was born October 19, 1844, in Quebec, Canada, the son of James and Catherine Nicholson Ware. When he arrived in Comanche is unknown, but he must have been there at least a year or so prior to Hardin's arrival in 1874. He later was in Val Verde County where he became a substantial figure in the community of Del Rio. On occasion he served as a deputy sheriff and made some arrests of importance. Ware died May 25, 1931, and is buried in the Del Rio Cemetery. Official death record of Val Verde County, # 26156.

[18]This version of what led to Webb's death is from Hardin's *Life*, 91–93. It of course presents Webb as the aggressor, attempting to get the drop on Hardin, even attempting to shoot him in the back.

[19]The *Houston Daily Telegraph*, June 3, 1874.

[20] Hardin, *Life*, 94–95.

[21] The *Houston Daily Telegraph*, June 3, 1874, a report from Comanche provided by a Brown County official.

[22] Ibid. This lengthy Houston report appears to be a mingling of reports from Bell County as well as from Beeman's observations, which may have appeared initially in the Comanche newspaper. Unfortunately early files of the *Comanche Chief* were lost.

CHAPTER 10

[1]John R. Waller served as sheriff from August 5, 1860, to August 4, 1862. Tise, 176. He may have resigned as sheriff to enlist in Company A of Evans' 15th Texas Regiment in the Civil War as the pension application

of his widow indicated he had served for the three years from 1862 "until the end of the War." According to the application, Waller died October 28, 1908. Pension Form B, number 33370. The burial place of John R. Waller is unknown.

[2]Waller to Major John B. Jones, May 30, 1874.

[3]J. G. Hardin Jr. died on June 22, 1929, in Eastland, Texas, and was buried in Ballinger, Runnels County, Texas. His wife was Ada Currie, the daughter of Joseph B. and Annie Elizabeth Browning Currie. In 1900 the family was living in Concho County, Texas; he was raising stock and she was tending house. Their children were Pauline A., born in April 1896; William M., born in December 1898; and Jay D., born in December 1899. Ada C. Hardin died on January 2, 1939 in Seymour, Baylor County, Texas.

[4]Hardin, *Life*, 98.

[5]The Taylor letters are preserved in the Texas State Library. William M. Green's memoir appears in *Frontier Times* 1, no. 8 (May, 1924): 3–6.

[6]William M. Green's account, "Breaking up the Lawless Element in Texas." Green was born in January 1854 in Tyler County, Texas. By 1861 he was an orphan but he does not indicate with whom he lived until his majority. Available service records show Green enlisted on May 25, 1874, in Company A of the Frontier Battalion and was honorably discharged on December 23, 1874. Green was the founder of the Texas Ex-Rangers Association. He was elected to the position of major commander at Weatherford in 1920, which he held until his death in Colorado City, Texas, on December 23, 1930. *Frontier Times* 8, no. 5 (February 1931): 207.

[7]Comanche County, Texas Census, 1870, shows a William Stone, aged 53, who was a dry goods merchant. He and his wife were from Alabama, and neither could read nor write. This presumably is the man Hardin identified as his cousins' betrayer. On the same census page are the names of an Andrew L. Stone, raising stock, and a Rodman Stone, also raising stock. Between their households is a James W. Milligan, stock raiser, who may be the same Milligan who was with the group who attempted to recover Joe Hardin's cattle in Brown County. Peter Gravis, minister of the gospel, who supposedly preached the funeral service for Joseph G. Hardin, is also enumerated on this page. If there

was such a sermon, perhaps the two Dixon brothers were laid out as well prior to their hasty burial.

8John L. Taylor to Harriet Smither, April 29, 1937.

9William M. Green. "Breaking Up the Lawless Element in Texas," 4.

10Capt. John R. Waller to Gov. Richard Coke, June 6, 1874.

11Capt. John R. Waller, Record of Scouts, Comanche, June 30, 1874. Waller's muster roll shows the aggregate of Company A was seventy-six men.

12*Austin Daily Democratic Statesman*, June 17, 1874, reprinting an article from the *Denison News*.

13*Austin Daily Democratic Statesman*, June 28, 1874, reprinting an article from the *Comanche Chief.*

14Hardin, *Life*, 101.

CHAPTER 11

1Major John B. Jones to Capt. John R. Waller, Special Orders No. 6, June 3, 1874, from Headquarters of the Frontier Battalion in Austin. A complete biography of the Ranger commander is Rick Miller, *Texas Ranger John B. Jones and the Frontier Battalion, 1874–1881* (Denton: University of North Texas Press, 2012).

2J. D. Stephens to Gov. Richard Coke, June 10, 1874.

3William J. Maltby was captain of Company E of the Frontier Battalion from May 5, to December 9, 1874. He authored a very disappointing autobiography, written in the third person, entitled *Captain Jeff or Frontier Life in Texas with the Texas Rangers*, which fails to mention John Wesley Hardin in spite of his being stationed in Brown County in 1874 and referring to Hardin in at least one of his letters to Major Jones. The memoir focuses mainly on his experiences hunting Indians. Maltby was born December 17, 1829, in Sangamore County, Illinois, the son of Orlanzo and Rebecca Maltby, and died June 27, 1908, in Callahan County, Texas. He is buried in Belle Plaine Cemetery, Callahan County. There is a Texas State Historical Marker at his gravestone. James A. Mundie Jr., et al., *Texas Burial Sites of Civil War Notables: A Biographical and Pictorial Field Guide* (Hillsboro: Hill College Press, 2002), 188.

[4]W. J. Maltby to Maj. John B. Jones, June 7, 1874.

[5]Ibid.

[6]Hardin, *Life*, 104

[7]Ibid., 103.

[8]Major Jones to Adj. Gen. William Steele, written from Comanche, dated July 1, 1874.

[9]Hardin, *Life*, 106.

[10]Comanche County, Texas Census, 1880, 132.

[11]Hardin, *Life*, 110.

[12]*Austin Daily Democratic Statesman*, June 16, 1874.

[13]*San Antonio Daily Express*, June 19, 1874.

[14]Hardin, *Life*, 107.

[15]Ibid., 108.

[16]The name of Sgt. J. V. Atkinson remains basically a name on a muster roll. From available documents in the Adjutant General's Papers he served from May 25 to November 7, 1874. His $40 per month was reduced on his final day due to the $20 deducted for his weapon which he apparently kept and for a total of $128 in cash which had previously been advanced. His final pay was "For Services as Corpl in Co. 'A' front. Bat Texas State Troops" and he received $89.30.

[17]C. L. Sonnichsen, *I'll Die Before I'll Run: The Story of the Great Feuds of Texas* (New York: Harper & Brothers, 1951), 57–58.

[18]*San Antonio Daily Express*, July 4, 1874.

[19]*San Antonio Daily Herald*, June 1874. Reprinted without date in *The Taylor Party* by Eddie Day Truitt, 230.

[20]Information on Tip Davis from interview with Juanita Davis Woods, August 30, 2011, and family papers including the S. T. Davis obituary notices from the *Gonzales Inquirer*, April 10 and 24, 1919. Were Hardin and Davis good friends because of their mutual connection to George C. Tennille? George Culver Tennille Sr. married Sarah Davis on January 6, 1820, in Missouri. Sarah Davis was a sister of Jesse Kincheloe Davis, the father of Tip. If correct George Tennille Jr. and Tip Davis were cousins. Juanita Davis Woods is a granddaughter of S. T. Davis. Also, Hardin, *Life*, 108.

[21]Charles Langhammer was elected sheriff on December 2, 1873, re-elected February 15, 1876, and served until November 5, 1878. See Tise, 24. In 1870 he is shown as a 25-year-old merchant with post office at Cat Spring, born in Bohemia. He and his wife Matilda, born in Texas, then had one child. Austin County census, 1870, 344–45.

[22]Hardin, *Life*, 110.

[23]Ibid.

[24]Duley Parks and his wife Nancy were both natives of Tennessee, he a 58-year-old, she a decade younger. In 1870 their children were: Willie W., an 18-year-old; Elvira J. (Jennie), 21; Laura, 13; Maud, 10; and Pearl, seven years old. Elvira J. was born January 16, 1848; known to all as Jennie E., she was married to Harry Swain.

[25]Washington County census, 1880, 129.

[26]L. H. McNelly to Adj. Gen. William Steele, August 31, 1874.

[27]Letter from T. C. Robinson written September 18 and printed in the *Statesman* of September 24, 1874. Robinson was obviously exaggerating in what he wrote about Hardin. Thomas Stell, DeWitt County sheriff in the years following the feud, wrote of Hardin, "Several times in past years I have seen statements in print as to how 'Wes' Hardin was wont to come to Cuero, order the merchants to close their stores, ride into the saloons flourishing his six shooters and terrorizing the inhabitants for hours at a time . . . in defiance of the citizens of Cuero. . . . I say emphatically there is no truth in such statements and the only time that 'Wes' Hardin ever displayed any violence in Cuero was when he killed Morgan in 1874 [*sic*, 1872]." From "The Taylor-Sutton Feud," copy of an unpublished manuscript in author's collection, original in the C. L. Sonnichsen Collection, Box 1 FF 109, Special Collections, University of Texas at El Paso. Thomas M. Stell was elected sheriff of DeWitt County on November 8, 1892, and was re-elected six times, serving until November 6, 1906. Tise, 157. Born in 1856, Stell lived in the county during the feud and knew many of the participants. He died on July 3, 1939, in Cuero and is buried there in Hillside Cemetery. There is a State Historical Marker at his grave. *The History of DeWitt County, Texas*, no author.

CHAPTER 12

[1]Today the Florida town of "Cedar Keys" is Cedar Key. When the town dropped the letter "s" is unknown.

[2]1870 Alachua County, Florida census. Samuel W. Burnett and wife Rosanna, 45; children Samuel J., 21; daughter Tabula, 19; and Jeff Davis (aged nine years), 17 ; 1880 Alachua County Census, 101, shows Samuel J. Burnett as 32 years old, and mayor of the town. He had a wife and two children then.

[3]Hardin, *Life*, 110.

[4]The 1870 and the 1880 census for DeWitt County both show Bill Mc-Cullough as living in the residence of George Washington Davis, listed as a stepson. McCullough lived from May 5, 1837, until March 15, 1884. He and his wife are both buried in the Davis Cemetery in rural DeWitt County. See 1870 DeWitt County Census, 236; 1880 DeWitt County Census, 415; and see Patsy Goebel and Karen McWhorter, *Cemetery Records of DeWitt County, Texas,* vol. 1 (Privately printed, Cuero, Texas, 1986), 23.

[5]1870 Alachua County Census shows Wilson as a hotel keeper; in 1880 he is identified as a landlord. Wilson was born about 1816, and resided in the community of Newmansville. 1860 census, 91; 1870, 15. By 1880 he had passed on as the census shows Rafaila Wilson as a widow.

[6]Hardin, *Life*, 110–11. The 1880 Alachua County Census shows James D. Cromwell, as a 40-year-old dentist, born in North Carolina, 89.

[7]Hardin, *Life*, 111. The 1870 Alachua County Census shows 17-year-old black man named Eli Williams, who may have been the unfortunate Eli, 14.

[8]Hardin, *Life*, 111.

[9]*Jacksonville City Directory*, 1876–1877.

[10]Ibid., 89.

[11]*State Police Ledger*, "Report of Arrests," Call # 401-1001, Texas State Archives, 275–79.

[12]Minutes of District Court, DeWitt County, Vol. E, cause # 563 against "Geo C Tennell."

[13]This was perhaps Augustine K. Kenedy, born about 1848 in Florida, the son of Henry and mother's name unknown. Clay County, Florida census of 1860, 155.

[14]Hardin, *Life*, 112

[15]*Victoria Advocate*, September 8, 1877.

[16]*Galveston Daily News*, August 28, 1877.

[17]Hardin, *Life*, 112

[18]The Stephens reward was introduced and read on January 14 and 15, and approved on January 20, 1877. When Hardin escaped from the Gonzales County jail in 1872 Sheriff Jones offered $100 reward for his capture. Hardin now had a $4,000 reward, five years later. Texas had never before offered such a large reward for a single individual.

[19]*Dallas Daily Herald*, November 7 and 9, 1875.

[20]*Mobile Register*, November 11, 1876, cited in A. J. Wright's article, "A Gunfighter's Southern Vacation," NOLA *Quarterly* 7, no. 3 (Autumn, 1982): 12–18.

[21]The wounded policeman, William A. Ryan, was still in 1880 a Mobile Police Sergeant. Ryan, born in Alabama about 1845, was residing in the Fourth Ward with his wife Hannah, 24 years old, and two-year-old son, William A. Jr., according to the 1880 census. Residing with them was a 12-year-old daughter Nellie, attending school, probably a daughter from a previous marriage. Mobile County, Alabama census of 1880.

[22]*Mobile Register*, November 10 and 11, 1876, cited in A. J. Wright.

[23]Ibid., November 12, 1876.

[24]William R. Friend to Governor Coke, March 23, 1875.

[25]David Haldeman to Governor Hubbard, April -- , 1877.

[26]Joshua Bowen to Jane Hardin Swain, May 6, 1877.

[27]Rev. James G. Hardin died on August 2, 1876, in Red River County. Unfortunately his actual grave site has been lost.

[28]The John Dixon Hardin family, by 1880, included six children: Robert, 9; Dudley, 8; J. N., 7; Jennie, 5; John, 3 and G. L., one year old. Their household in 1880 was number 688 with the Henry Clay Swain family living in household number 689. 1880 Waller County, Texas Census, 397.

[29]R. E. Hardin to J. H. Swain, May 9, 1877.

[30]1870 Santa Rosa County, Florida Census, 560.

[31]R. W. Brooks article, "Oldtimer Tells of Desperado in this Section," *Atmore Advance* newspaper of Atmore, Alabama, October 15, 1931.

This is the first of three articles by Brooks about desperadoes in that section of Florida in the 1870s. The subjects of them were Bowen, then Bob Hardy (October 22) and Hardin (October 29). Brooks was a native of Alabama. The Escambia County census of 1880 shows him as a 27-year-old "Lumber marker" by trade, with wife Ellen and a daughter. In 1920 he was a resident of Escambia County, Alabama, just across the Alabama-Florida state line, then 67 years old living with wife Ellen, a decade younger. His occupation then was shown as Minister of the Gospel. He also enumerated the census for that year. Escambia County, Florida Census, 1880, 105; Escambia County, Alabama Census, 1920.

[32]Hardin, *Life*, 115.

[33]R. W. Brooks, "Oldtimer Tells of Desperado in this Section," *Atmore Advance*, October 15, 1931.

[34]A. J. Perdue remains a mysterious figure. He first appears in the Hardin biography as the deputy of Sheriff W. H. Hutchinson in 1877. The regular column "Alabama News" featured in the Columbus, Mississippi, *Daily Enquirer* of November 14, 1878, announced that on November 11, he, of Pensacola, Florida, married Mrs. Sallie L. Whiting, of Montgomery, Alabama. He continued working in law enforcement, mainly in Alabama. In 1880 the Montgomery County, Alabama census (page 172) shows him as a deputy U.S. Marshal, age twenty-five, boarding with his wife Sallie and then a nine-month-old daughter, "Mattie." The city directories continued to carry his name, but the 1895 Montgomery directory lists Sallie L. Perdue as a widow. No exact date has been found for the death of Andrew J. (Jackson?) Perdue but his widow passed on June 3, 1911. W. H. Hutchinson, in an interview not long after the death of Hardin in 1895, referred to his deputy, A. J. Perdue, as having died prior to 1895.

CHAPTER 13

[1]James W. Mann was born in Santa Rosa County, Florida, although there are discrepancies in the census. He was the son of James W. and Mary Elizabeth Mann; in 1860 he is shown to be one year old. A decade later the family still resided in Santa Rosa County but he was then shown to be

14 years old, suggesting a birth year of 1856. Hardin wrote that when he was killed in August, 1877, he was 19 years of age which may be closest to accuracy. Santa Rosa County, Florida, 1860 and 1870 census.

[2]Sheppard Hardy appears in the 1870 Santa Rosa County, Florida, census as a 33-year-old laborer with a 27-year-old wife, Sarah. In 1880 he is found in Baldwin County, Alabama, still a laborer but now with eight children ranging in age from 21 years down to two years. All were born in Florida.

[3]Neil Campbell Jr. was also a laborer, identified occupation being "logger" in the 1880 Santa Rosa County, Florida Census. In 1880 he is shown to be 25 years old, his wife Amazone, 20 years old, with a one-year-old son. Neil Campbell Jr. lived from 1854 to 1922. His wife lived from 1860 to 1935; her headstone identifies her as Anna Campbell. Apparently Campbell had no trouble with the law even though he was considered an associate of Hardin.

[4]Hardin, *Life*, 117.

[5]William Henry Hutchinson was born in Prattville, Autauga County, Alabama, on June 7, 1845, the son of Thomas Walton and Ann Fralick Hutchinson, but was raised in the neighborhood of Montgomery, Alabama. On March 6, 1862, he enlisted in Company K of the 1st Alabama Regiment in Prattville for three years. In his pension application he claimed to have been at Island No. 10 in March 1862, later at the siege of Port Hudson and "surrendered" on July 9, 1863. He was among those paroled and perhaps after this parole he served as a "secret scout" under General J. H. Clanton. At war's end he returned home where he worked in his father's store. In 1868 the family moved to Pensacola and opened a mercantile store on South Palafax Street. He married Miss Alice Stanley McKenzie on October 1, 1868, and ran for sheriff of Escambia County in 1876. After his first wife's death he married Ila Temple Merritt. Hutchinson died on January 14, 1911. See Hutchinson's Application for Pension # 3695; Widow's Application for Pension; obituaries from the *Pensacola Journal*, January 15, 1911, and *Pensacola News*, January 14, 1911; unpublished biographical sketch by Lola Lee Daniell Bruington. Copy in author's possession.

[6]Leon Metz expressed it best in his *John Wesley Hardin: Dark Angel of Texas* (El Paso: Mangan Books, 1996): "Sheriff Hutchinson, nonchalantly strolled through, throwing off drunks and undesirables while mentally evaluating Hardin and his friends." 168.

[7]Sources do not agree on how the quartet was seated. On the news of Hardin's death in 1895 Jack Duncan granted a lengthy interview in which he stated Hardin was seated by himself and Mann was in the seat ahead of him. *Galveston Daily News*, August 23, 1895.

[8]Hardin, *Life*, 117.

[9]*Montgomery Daily Advertiser and Mail*, August 28, 1877.

[10]Hardin, *Life*, 118. The latter version is from the *Austin Daily Democratic Statesman*, August 29, 1877.

[11]Telegram from Lt. J. B. Armstrong to Adj. Gen. William Steele, August 25, 1877.

[12]Allen Marion McMillan was the son of Malcom and Mary Jane McCaskill McMillan, born March 28, 1843. By 1880 he was probate judge of Escambia County, Alabama. He died May 31, 1896. Escambia County, Alabama census, 1880, 235; and Cemetery Inventory of Coon Hill Cemetery, Santa Rosa County, Florida.

[13]"J. H. Swain" to Jane, August 25, 1877.

[14]*Denison Daily News*, August 26, 1877. Reprint from the *Dallas Daily Commercial*.

[15]Hardin, *Life*, 121.

[16]*Galveston Daily News*, August 23, 1895.

[17]*Montgomery Daily Advertiser and Mail*, August 28, 1877.

[18]William Dudley Chipley, native of Georgia, was born June 6, 1840, the son of a prominent physician and Baptist minister. He received a superior education, attending the Kentucky Military Institute and in 1858 graduating from Transylvania University in Lexington, Kentucky. He joined Company C of the 9th Kentucky Infantry in 1861; by 1863 he was a 1st Lieutenant. He was wounded in the Battle of Shiloh, and was again wounded and captured by General Sherman's army at the Battle of Peachtree Creek at Atlanta. He spent the rest of the war as a prisoner. In 1876 he moved to Pensacola and took charge of the Pensacola Railroad, and with his success and vision by the 1880s he was general land

contractor for the Louisville and Nashville Railroad. He continued in public life, was elected mayor of Pensacola, and in 1894 to the Florida State Senate. He lived a full and exciting and purposeful life, dying on December 1, 1897. On the public square in Pensacola is an obelisk erected in his honor;.

[19]He married in 1868, but their first child died the following year. In 1882 his wife died and he was remarried on February 20, 1884, in his home town of Prattville, Alabama to Miss Ila Temple Merritt, and on December 15, 1884, their daughter Lily Kathleen was born. In his later years he became active in local politics, serving on the Board of Public Works, the United Confederate Veterans, and the International Order of Odd Fellows. On September 27, 1906, a hurricane wiped out his fishing business, leaving him nearly destitute. Hutchinson died at his home on January 14, 1911.

[20]*Austin Daily Democratic Statesman*, September 7, 1877, reprinting undated article from *Dallas Daily Herald*.

[21]John E. Callaghan was a lumber merchant in Pensacola, 45 years old with a wife and two children. Escambia County, Florida, census, 1880.

[22]*El Paso Daily Times*, September 8, 1895.

[23]For full biographical treatments of Hutchinson and Duncan, see *The Capture of John Wesley Hardin* by Parsons, and *Bounty Hunter* by Rick Miller.

[24]Alexander Sweet, *On a Mexican Mustang through Texas, From the Gulf to the Rio Grande* (Hartford, CT: S. S. Scranton & Co., 1883), 426–27.

[25]*Pensacola Gazette*, reprinted from the *Montgomery Advertiser and Mail*, August 26, 1877.

[26]W. D. Chipley to Gov. R. B. Hubbard, August 28, 1877.

[27]*Montgomery Daily Advertiser and Mail*, September 19, 1877.

[28]Ibid., October 28, 1877. To our knowledge Henry Sutton was not a relative of William E. Sutton of the Sutton-Taylor feud.

CHAPTER 14

[1]*Dallas Herald*, August 28, 1877.

[2]The advertisement appears in the *Athens Courier* of Anderson County, Texas, February 9, 1876. Denyven was from Scotland, but when he

arrived in the United States in unknown. The Palestine City Directory and the Anderson County census for 1880 are extremely fragile and partially illegible.

3*Galveston Daily News*, August 28, citing a report from Palestine, August 27, 1877.

4Ibid., August 29, citing special telegraphic news from Austin, August 28, 1877.

5Hardin, *Life*, 122.

6Dennis Corwin was elected sheriff of Travis County on February 15, 1876, was re-elected November 5, 1878, and served until November 2, 1880. See Tise, 494.

7Hardin, *Life*, 127. For background on these individuals see Rick Miller, *Sam Bass and Gang* (Austin: State House Press, 1999); Dave Johnson, *The Mason County "Hoo Doo" War, 1874–1902* (Denton: University of North Texas Press, 2006); and Johnson, *John Ringo: King of the Cowboys, His Life and Times From the Hoo Doo War to Tombstone*, 2nd rev. ed. (Denton: University of North Texas Press, 2008) and Rick Miller, *Bloody Bill Longley: The Mythology of a Gunfighter* (Denton: University of North Texas Press, 2011). Miller, in his Longley biography, describes Charles Jefferson Haley Ake as wanted for horse and cattle theft, and "no less a scoundrel than his brother," 109–10. It is impossible to determine who this John Collins was, unless it was the one involved in the Hill County killing of Benjamin B. Bradley back in 1870.

8*Galveston Daily News,* August 29, 1877, citing special telegraphic report from Austin, August 28, 1877.

9Rick Miller, *Bloody Bill Longley.*

10*Galveston Daily News*, August 31, 1877. The interview took place on August 28.

11*Montgomery Daily Advertiser and Mail*, September 19; and the *San Antonio Daily Express*, September 27, 1877, contain brief articles about Bowen's delivery to the Austin jail.

12*The Texas Capital*, Austin, September 16, 1877.

13*San Antonio Daily Express*, September 27, citing a report from Austin dated September 24, 1877.

14Hardin, *Life*, 122.

[15]Dave Johnson, *The Mason County "Hoo Doo" War, 1874–1902*.

[16]Reynolds was born in Pennsylvania on November 21, 1846. He and the family had moved to Illinois by the time the war broke out but Reynolds did not become a soldier until the latter days. After the war he returned to Illinois, then drifted until he ended up in Texas. In San Marcos, Hays County, Reynolds tried running a boot shop and for a short while served as a guard under Sheriff Zachariah P. Bugg. In 1874 he enlisted in Capt. Cicero R. Perry's Company D. Reynolds quickly rose to the rank of sergeant and then in July 1877, amidst the turmoil of the Horrell-Higgins Feud, he gathered a small squad and in the middle of a stormy night managed to sneak into the Horrell "household" and arrest them without bloodshed. Major John B. Jones arrested the Higgins party and with Jones' persuasive powers the leaders of the two groups signed a peace treaty. In contrast to the peace treaties signed by Sutton-Taylor feudists, which were easily broken, the Horrells and the Higgins men actually kept the peace. Besides the accolades he received for this noteworthy accomplishment, Reynolds was named lieutenant commander of the newly reorganized Company E. He made out his first muster and pay roll on September 1; his first assignment of any significance was to deliver John Wesley Hardin from Austin to Comanche for trial. Reynolds' life and career is detailed in *Texas Ranger N. O. Reynolds: The Intrepid*, by Chuck Parsons and Donaly E. Brice.

[17]*Galveston Daily News*, September 11, citing a special telegram from Austin dated September 10, 1877.

[18]James B. Gillett, *Six Years with the Texas Rangers*, 125–26.

[19]*Lampasas Dispatch*, September 27, 1877.

[20]*Dallas Weekly Herald*, September 29, citing a report written September 26, 1877.

[21]Hardin, *Life*, 122–23.

[22]*San Antonio Daily Express*, October 14, 1877, in "State Items" column.

[23]This letter by "Mervyn," as he signed his communications, was written in Comanche on September 25, printed in the *Galveston Daily News* of October 3 and reprinted in the *Galveston Weekly News* of October 8, 1877. The complete letters with annotations by this author,"' Mervyn'

A Poetical Correspondent," were published in the *Brand Book* of the English Westerners Society, Winter 1988–1989, pages 1–9.

[24]The summary of the trial is from the *Weatherford Exponent*, October 13, 1877, and "Hardin v. The State" in 4 *Texas Court of Appeals Reports*, Austin 1878, 355–72.

[25]*Galveston Daily News*, December 26, contributed by "Total Wreck" written from Cuero on December 21, 1877. Of the seven men arrested for the Brassell killings, only one was ultimately convicted: David Augustine. He was quickly pardoned by Gov. J. S. Hogg. Who was Total Wreck? His identity remains unknown. The letter in full appears in an article, "Rangers in Lockhart" (Caldwell County, Texas) with annotations by this author, published in *The Plum Creek Almanac* 22, no. 2 (Fall 2004): 136–39.

CHAPTER 15

[1]John Wesley Hardin to Jane Hardin, January 29, 1878.

[2]Undated letter from Hardin to Jane Hardin.

[3][Thomas E. Hogg], *Life and Adventures of Sam Bass: The Notorious Union Pacific and Texas Train Robber* (Dallas: Dallas Commercial Steam Print, 1878), 68–69. According to the definitive biography of Bass, this 1878 biography was written by Thomas E. Hogg but his name does not appear in the published work. Rick Miller, *Sam Bass and Gang* (Austin: State House Press, 1999, 351). Hardin remembered Sam Pipes and Albert G. Herndon when writing his own life story. The two were pardoned in 1886.

[4]Hardin, *Life*, 123

[5]Ibid., 124.

[6]*Austin Daily State Gazette*, April 27, 1878. This letter was written on April 22, 1878.

[7]Hardin, *Life*, 125.

[8]*Gonzales Daily Inquirer*, May 11, 1878

[9]*Galveston Daily News*, May 17, 1878.

[10]Ibid.

[11]J. W. Hardin to Jane Hardin, May 18, 1878.

[12]John W. Hardin to "My Dear wife" dated June 6, 1878, written from the Austin jail.

[13] *Austin Daily Democratic Statesman*, July 10, 1874, and July 26, 1876.

[14] Hardin, *Life*, 125–26.

[15] *San Antonio Daily Express*, September 20, citing an article from the *Daily Democratic Statesman* of Austin. This same article later appeared in the *San Antonio Weekly Express* of September 26, 1878.

[16] *Burnet County Bulletin*, September 28, 1878.

[17] John Wesley Hardin to Jane, "My Dear wife," written from San Saba, September 24, 1878.

[18] Hardin, *Life*, 126.

[19] *Dallas Weekly Herald*, February 2, 1878.

[20] *Galveston Daily News*, February 6, 1878.

[21] [William Steele], *A List of Fugitives from Justice* (Austin: 1878), 14, 174. There was a reward of $250 for Mackey's capture.

[22] *Fort Worth Democrat*, October 4, 1878.

[23] Hardin, *Life*, 127

[24] Langston James Goree V. and Deborah Bloys Hardin, "Thomas Jewett Goree" in *New Handbook of Texas*, Vol. 3, 252.

[25] Hardin, *Life*, 44.

[26] See Rick Miller, *Bloody Bill Longley: The Mythology of a Gunfighter*, 2nd rev. ed. (Denton: University of North Texas Press, 2011).

[27] Hardin, *Life*, 127.

[28] Ibid., 128.

[29] *Brenham Weekly Banner*, December 27, 1878.

[30] Hardin, *Life*, 128–29.

[31] The 1850 Washington County, Texas census shows a John Williams as living in the household of R. and Henrietta Harris.

[32] Hardin, *Life*, 129

[33] *Brenham Weekly Banner*, January 31, 1879, citing a report from the *Huntsville Item*.

CHAPTER 16

[1] Philip J. West is identified as an "under keeper," a Missouri native, thirty-six years of age, in the 1880 Walker County census.

[2] Hardin, *Life*, 130

[3] John Wesley Hardin to Jane Hardin, January 26, 1879.

[4] Hardin, *Life*, 130.

⁵John Wesley Hardin to Jane, February 9, 1879.

⁶Oliver Odum was shot and killed by Randolph House, although the reason has not been determined. Odum is buried in the Bethel Cemetery near Weesatche, Goliad County. His grave is marked.

⁷Ibid., March 2, 1879. The Odums initially lived on the Frank Asher place. The Ashers and Bowens were fairly close as Nancy Bowen, the grandmother of Jane, Martha and Brown, who had died August 5, 1875, was buried in the Asher Cemetery.

⁸John Wesley Hardin to Jane, February 23, 1879.

⁹Ibid., March 2, 1879.

¹⁰Mannen and wife Mollie Clements to Jane Hardin, March 23, 1879. At the time Clements was living near Richland Springs in San Saba County. Clements married Mary Ann "Mollie" Robinson in Gonzales County on June 3, 1866, according to the pension file she prepared, based on his service as a Confederate soldier. Pension file # A-16644.

¹¹The only serious work on Mannen Clements remains Robert W. Stephens' biography, *Mannen Clements: Texas Gunfighter*, a limited edition of 250 signed and numbered copies, privately printed, 1996.

¹²Walker County, Texas Census, 1880, shows Bill Templeton as a 28-year-old prisoner, native of Texas, with no other information given other than he was a white male. The final fate of William Templeton is unknown.

¹³John Wesley Hardin to Jane, April 13, 1879.

¹⁴John Wesley Hardin to Jane, April 20, 1879.

¹⁵See *Texas Lawmen 1835–1899: The Good and the Bad* by Clifford R. Caldwell and Ron DeLord, 381-82 for details on this killing.

¹⁶Hardin, *Life*, 130–31.

¹⁷*Gonzales Inquirer*, July 26, 1879.

¹⁸Presumably Hardin means the Bible with the term "the great book"; however, the proverb he quotes is more likely from John Bunyon's 1678 publication, *The Pilgrim's Progress*: "Every fat [tub] must stand on his [its own] bottom" meaning every man must strive for independence and self-reliance, not depending on others.

[19]This statement from Hardin also appeared in the August 16, 1879, issue of the *National Police Gazette*.

[20]John Wesley Hardin to Jane, June 3, 1881.

[21]Ibid., July 3, 1881.

[22]Ibid., February 26, 1882.

[23]Hardin, *Life*, 131.

[24]Lewis Nordyke, *John Wesley Hardin: Texas Gunman* (New York: William Morrow & Company, 1957), 217.

[25]Benjamin Eustace McCulloch was born at Peach Creek in Gonzales County January 16, 1845, and died November 1, 1916, at Buda in Hays County. He is buried in Oakwood Cemetery in Austin. During the war he served as captain of Company K of George W. Baylor's Texas Cavalry. After his work at Huntsville he became superintendent of the House of Correction and Reformatory at Gatesville, Texas. When he left Huntsville he was followed by James G. Smither whom Hardin would also know. *Biennial Reports of the Directory & Superintendent of the Texas State Penitentiary, December 1, 1878–October 31, 1880.*

[26]John Wesley Hardin to Jane, October 1, 1882.

[27]Ibid., September 25, 1881. The exact quotation reads: "Solitude made a Cincinnatus ripening the hero and the patriot/ And taught De Stael self-knowledge, even in the damp Bastille;/ It fostered the piety of Jerome, nurtured the labours of Augustine,/ And gave Imperial Charles religion for ambition;/ That which Scipio praised, that which Alfred practiced, which found Demosthenes to eloquence, and fed the mind of Milton,/ Which quickened zeal, nurtured genius, found out the secret things of science . . ." From *The Complete Poetical Works of Martin Farquhar Tuppet, Esq.* Series 2 (Hartford: Silas Andrus & Son, 1850), 224.

[28]Elizabeth Hardin to Jane Hardin, May 25, 1882. What happened to W. E. Casey is unknown, but later Nannie married John H. Mosteller on June 24, 1887. Nan died on January 18, 1953, in Fort Worth. Texas Death Certificate for Nancy D. Mosteller, # 32948. The death certificate also gives her date of birth as October 10, 1870, which conflicts with some other sources.

[29]Elizabeth Hardin to Jane Hardin, August 13, 1882. John had instructed Jane how to measure his son's foot in his letter to her of February 26, 1882.

[30]In 1880 William Bright Berry and Martha Ann Smith were living in Denton, Denton County, north of the Dallas-Fort Worth area. Then he was thirty-two and farming; Martha was twenty-three and keeping house; they had one child, a two-year-old named Lillian. They would have seven more children.

[31]Elizabeth Hardin to Jane Hardin, August 13, 1882. Jane was then living at Rancho, Gonzales County.

[32]John Wesley Hardin to Jane Hardin, January 6, 1884.

[33]Langston James Goree V. and Deborah Bloys Hardin, "Elizabeth Thomas Nolley Goree" in *The New Handbook of Texas*, vol. 3, 251–52.

[34]John Wesley Hardin to Captain McCulloch, August 26, 1885.

[35]The 1880 Walker County Census shows Robert H. Bush as a 45-year-old physician from Virginia.

[36]Chuck Parsons, "James Monroe 'Doc' Bockius," *Newsletter* of the National Association and Center for Outlaw and Lawman History 2, no. 4 (Spring, 1977): 9–12.

[37]John Wesley Hardin to Jane Hardin, November 22, 1885. Just as Reverend Hardin's final resting place is unknown, so is Elizabeth Dixon Hardin's.

[38]Mattie Hardin Smith to Jane Hardin, August 3, 1886. N. C. Griffin was the first postmaster of Sedan, followed by Bockius on January 19, 1885. The post office was discontinued on December 31, 1909, and the mail was delivered to Rancho. During the early 1900s much of the population of Rancho moved to nearby Nixon, with businesses following. Today there is nothing left of Rancho. Records do not show a postmaster after Bockius; presumably he remained in that position until the office was abolished. Bockius died in 1909 and is buried in the Billings Cemetery in Gonzales County. Jim Wheat, *Postmasters and Post Offices of Texas, 1846–1936.*

[39]Mary Taylor was born June 4, 1877, and died January 2, 1959, in Phoenix, Arizona.

[40]John Wesley Hardin to Jane, January 22, 1888.

[41]Ibid., February 5, 1888.

CHAPTER 17

[1] John Wesley Hardin to Jane, June 24, 1888.

[2] John Wesley Hardin to Miss Jane M. Hardin, July 14, 1889.

[3] John Wesley Hardin to John Wesley Hardin Jr., October 20, 1889.

[4] The 1880 Colorado County, Texas census lists H. M. Sharp as a white male, 28 years old, a farmer born in North Carolina. He had a wife and a one-year-old child.

[5] A. L. George, *The Texas Convict Sketches of the Penitentiary, Convict Farms and Railroads Together with Poems* (Self-published, September 1895. Facsimile edition by Vikon Publishing Co., Dallas, Texas 1983). The mention of Hardin appears on page 11.

[6] John Wesley Hardin to Jane, April 6, 1890.

[7] The assistant superintendent now was James Gabriel Smither. His father was born in Virginia, mother in South Carolina; he was born in Texas. J. G. Smither died in 1922.

[8] "Asbury Bascom Davidson" by Carolyn Hyman in *The New Handbook of Texas*, vol. 2, 521. He had moved from Gonzales to Cuero in the early 1880s, then served as a state senator and then was elected lieutenant-governor and served from 1906–1912. Davidson died February 4, 1920, and is buried among many other DeWitt County notables in the Hillside Cemetery in Cuero.

[9] Hardin, *Life*, 80.

[10] Mary Elizabeth, called Mollie, was born February 6, 1873; John Wesley Jr. was born August 3, 1875 and Jane, or "Jennie" was born July 15, 1877.

[11] *Galveston Daily News*, January 4, 1892.

[12] *Gonzales Inquirer*, January 7, 1892.

[13] Ibid., February 11, 1892.

[14] John Wesley Hardin to Jane Hardin, January 4, 1892.

[15] William S. Fly to John Wesley Hardin, January 8, 1892.

[16] The Petition to Gov. J. S. Hogg was from members of the Sheriffs Association, "believing that John W. Hardin has been punished sufficiently and the law has been vindicated and they would respectfully ask that he be pardoned." Among the signatures of lesser known sheriffs were those of several whose name is well known among Texas historians: D. A. T. Walton of Bee County, vice president of the association; R. M.

Love of Limestone County, president; R. E. White of Travis County, treasurer; John J. Seale of Karnes County; Thomas M. Stell of DeWitt County; John T. Olive of Williamson County and D. S. Ake, constable of Williamson County, and Richard M. Glover of Gonzales County. Obviously there were quite a few sheriffs who either did not attend the convention or else chose not to sign. It was dated May 18, 1892, and sent to Governor Hogg.

17 William S. Fly to John Wesley Hardin, May 18, 1892.

18 Elizabeth Hardin Cobb, born June 23, 1855, lived a long life, dying on October 28, 1930.

19 John Wesley Hardin to Mollie Hardin, August 21, 1892.

20 John Wesley Hardin to John Wesley Hardin Jr., August 28, 1892.

CHAPTER 18

1 John Wesley Hardin to J. B. Cobb, September 11, 1892. James Benton "Buck" Cobb is buried in the Griffin Cemetery, not far from the Asher Cemetery where Jane Bowen Hardin is buried.

2 Ibid., November 6, 1892.

3 Original bereavement card in the Wittliff Collection, Southwestern Writers Collections, Texas State University, San Marcos.

4 John Wesley Hardin to Assistant Superintendent J. G. Smither, undated.

5 *Gonzales Daily Inquirer*, September 7, 1893.

6 John Wesley Hardin to Assistant Superintendent J. G. Smither, undated.

7 Ibid., October 29, 1893.

8 John Wesley Hardin to Gov. James Stephen Hogg, January 1, 1894.

9 James Gibson Hardin to John Wesley Hardin, January 28, 1894.

10 Her death certificate reflects the date and location of her birth; it also indicates her name change to Davis.

11 Interview by N. W. Brown with Doug Hitchcock, whose wife Barbara Slade Hitchcock is a great-granddaughter of Ida Mae Croussore Hardin; and Larry J. Woods, "John Wesley Hardin's Deadly Brother," *Wild West*, February 2006, 58–59, 66.

12 N. W. Brown, "In the Shadow of John Wesley Hardin," *Journal* of the Wild West History Association 4, no. 4 (August 2011): 10–16.

13 Application for Pardon from Kimble County, filed February 10, 1892.

¹⁴Pardon document in the Wittliff Collection, Southwestern Writers Collections, Texas State University, San Marcos.

CHAPTER 19

¹Following that term William E. Jones, a former friend of Hardin, was elected, but after one term Glover was re-elected on November 3, 1896; he was again elected in 1898 and again in 1900. On June 14, 1901, he was killed in an attempt to arrest Gregorio Cortez. Frank Merriam Fly completed his term. See Tise, *Texas County Sheriffs*. Of interest is that Richard M. Glover was a brother of Ed Glover. Edward J. Glover, Jim Taylor and Ed Harris were at Powder Horn in Calhoun County, Texas, together and had their photograph made in the early 1870s. A biographical sketch of Richard Glover by Carol J. Archer appears in *The History of Gonzales County, Texas* by the Gonzales County Historical Commission (Dallas: Curtis Media Company, 1986), 317–18.

²William M. Walton, *Life and Adventures of Ben Thompson, the Famous Texan*. See the commentary on this biography in John H. Jenkins, *Basic Texas Books: An Annotated Bibliography of Selected Works for a Research Library* (1983; Rev. ed., Austin: Texas State Historical Association, 1988), 555–58.

³R. M. Glover to John Wesley Hardin, February 28, 1894.

⁴Barnett Gibbs to John Wesley Hardin, February --, 1894.

⁵Bell was elected a second time in 1892 and remained in office until November 6, 1900. See Tise, 258.

⁶Sheriff Thomas Bell to R. M. Glover, March 27, 1894.

⁷R. M. Glover to John Wesley Hardin, March 28, 1894.

⁸Ibid.

⁹R. M. Finley to John Wesley Hardin, April --, 1894. A biographical sketch of Finley had appeared in *Personnel of the Texas State Government* by Lewis E. Daniell, 1892.

¹⁰Ibid., April 13, 1894. The victory of Hogg effectively ended Clark's political career.

¹¹Thomas Bell to R. M. Glover, April 14, 1894.

¹²By 1900 Bishop was providing for his large family, a wife who had birthed ten children, all living, with six still at home. Polk County, Texas Census,

1900. A few households prior to that of the Bishops was that of the Gibson family. Their servant was a 34-year-old black man named George W. Holshousen, born in 1866. He was probably a relative of "Maje."

[13]John M. Taylor to John Wesley Hardin, April 28, 1894.

[14]John Milam Taylor died March 5, 1906. One obituary described him as "one of the landmarks of this county"; his death was "at an advanced age after an eventful and very useful life." He was buried with Masonic honors in the Taylor Cemetery near Nordheim, DeWitt County. *Cuero Daily Record*, March 6, 1906.

[15]J. P. Randle to John Wesley Hardin, August 4, 1894.

[16]*Gonzales Inquirer*, July 26, 1894.

[17]Marohn, *The Last Gunfighter*, 181. The original document, an application to be examined, is in a private collection.

[18]A recent visit to the Peck & Fly building, in February 2012, revealed a "thrift store" on the ground floor; apartments on the second floor where Hardin once had his office, and meeting areas for the Masonic order on the third. A plaque on the outside wall indicates the construction of the building was in 1891. With the remodeling of the second floor into apartments all evidence of former offices there was lost.

[19]Tise, 209.

[20]By the time of the 1870 DeWitt County census the Coleman family consisted of the parents, their ten children and one grandchild. Robert, child number seven, was the first to be born in Texas; the others were all North Carolinians. Twelve years old then, young Coleman was listed as a farmer working for his father.

[21]John Wesley Hardin to Jim Clements in Sterling City, October 4, 1894.

[22]*Drag Net*, October 23, 1894. The *Drag Net* was a short-lived newspaper of Gonzales County. Few copies remain. Clipping in the Wittliff Collection, Southwestern Writers Collections, Texas State University, San Marcos.

[23]*Gonzales Inquirer*, October 25, 1894.

[24]Ibid., November 2, 1894.

[25]Ibid.

[26]Frank Kelso to Robert R. Coleman, October 20, 1894.

[27]J. F. Wingate to John Wesley Hardin, October 21, 1894.

²⁸[Steele, William, Compiler] *A List of Fugitives from Justice* (1878; Facsimile edition by State House Press, Austin, 1977), 132.
²⁹Ben Bratton to John Wesley Hardin, October 22, 1894.
³⁰R. M. Glover to John Wesley Hardin, December 1, 1894.
³¹Gonzales County Census, 1880.
³²Ibid., and Kimble County Census, 1900.
³³Callie Lewis was born on July 23, 1879. She was about 15 and a half years old when she met up with the 41-year-old Hardin.

CHAPTER 20

¹Kimble County, Texas Census, 1800. The census shows Lewis' occupation as farming and raising stock. He was 33 and his wife was 23 and keeping house. Callie was less than a year old in 1880. Her death certificate incorrectly shows her birth date as July 23, 1882. After Hardin was killed, she married Perry Allen Baze, a physician, in 1898. Their first child, son Seth L., was born in March 1899. By 1910, when Callie was 32, the couple had left Kimble County and located in Mason County. Dr. Baze is shown to be a physician, general practice. By 1920 they were still in Mason County. In 1930, the last available census, physician P. A. Baze and "Bessie" had two children living at home, J. P. an eight-year-old son and daughter Betty, two years old. Son Seth L. Baze is elsewhere in the town of Mason working as a merchant. He had a wife and one son. Callie Lewis Hardin Baze died of "coronary insufficiency & congestive heart failure" as determined by the medical doctor who saw her last alive on September 30, 1963. Kimble County, Texas Census, 1880; and Mason County Census, 1900, 1910, 1920, 1930. She was best known by the name of Callie, although her death certificate and headstone shows her name as Carolyn. The small stone marking her grave in Mission Burial Park in San Antonio, shows her as "Carolyn L. Baze / July 23, 1882 / Sept. 30, 1963." The informant for the death certificate was Billy Baze who may have honestly believed she had been born in 1882. Dr. Perry Allen Baze, born in 1877, died in 1959 and is buried in the Gooch Cemetery in Mason.
²Lewis Nordyke, *John Wesley Hardin: Texas Gunman* (New York: William Morrow & Company, 1957), 258.

[3]Kimble County, Texas census, 1880. The 1900 census shows the New York native still working as a county clerk.

[4]Kimble County, Texas census, 1900, shows Wahrmund as a 42-year-old farmer with a wife and six children at home.

[5]The license remains in the Kimble County Courthouse. The details about the wedding appeared in an undated *Kimble County Citizen,* which was then sent to the newspaper to Hardin's last home. It was printed in the *Gonzales Inquirer,* January 31, 1895.

[6]"Outlaw's Wedding Early Memory for London Man" by Don Hendrix, in *San Angelo Standard-Times,* October 3, 1971.

[7]Nordyke, 259–60; and an undated clipping from an unidentified newspaper in authors' collection.

[8]Capt. L. L. Lewis to John Wesley Hardin, January 23, 1895.

[9]Bettie Lewis to John Wesley Hardin, March 4, 1895.

[10]Capt. L. L. Lewis to John Wesley Hardin, March 4, 1895.

[11]The Densons were kin to the Clementses. Mary Jane Rebecca Clements, sister of Mannen, Gip, Jim and Joe, and Wiley W. Kimbrough/Kimbro obtained their marriage license on January 21, 1860, in Gonzales and were married the following day. Marriage Book A, Gonzales County, license # 607. W. W. was killed in the war; widow M. J. R. Kimbrough then married James Madison Denson. In 1880 they were living in Gonzales County; step-sons Mannen and Wiley Kimbro were then 19 and 18 respectively, and the Denson children were Martha, 14; John, 12; Elmira, 10; Green, eight; Eugene, six and Minerva, three years old. By 1900 James M. Denson, now 61, and Mary Jane Rebecca, 58, were living in Kimble County, with four children. Gonzales County, Texas Census, 1880, and Kimble County, Texas Census, 1900. The 1880 Gonzales County Census spelled their name *Kimbro*, but a descendant in the twentieth century spelled the family name *Kimbrough*.

[12]Capt. L. L. Lewis to John Wesley Hardin, March 23, 1895.

[13]A. G. Weston to John Wesley Hardin, February 5, 1895. Augustus G. Weston was still operating a saloon as late as 1900. He was born in 1867 in Texas. The 1900 Kerr County, Texas census shows him as a 32-year-old saloon keeper with a wife and one daughter living in Kerrville.

[14]J. D. Hargis to John Wesley Hardin, July 28, 1895. Jefferson Davis Hargis, the son of William K. and Esther Jane Glover Hargis, was born

September 8, 1861. He was a familiar sight in the 1890s, hobbling around the jail helping in whatever means he could his cousin, Sheriff Richard M. Glover, the good friend of Hardin. The Gonzales County Historical Commission, *The History of Gonzales County, Texas* (Dallas: Curtis Media Corporation, 1986), 334. Hargis died July 10, 1920, in the Bexar County Home for Aged in San Antonio. The official death certificate, Bexar County # 21445, stated he was widowed, although the Gonzales County history entry states he was a lifelong bachelor. Also see "Notes on the Hargis Family" by Johnnie Lea Moffit, an unpublished collection of Hargis family material available in the Gonzales County Historical Archives. Hargis was not a lifelong bachelor as some in the family believed. By 1900 he and his family were residents of Eddy County, New Mexico. Hulda A. was listed as his wife, born in Texas in February 1863; his son Virgil B. was born in New Mexico in January 1900. In 1910 the family, now consisting only of J. D. and son Virgil B., resided in Socorro County, New Mexico. A decade later Hargis and his son resided in San Antonio, Texas.

[15]The telegram appears as an illustration in Leon Metz' biography, *John Wesley Hardin: Dark Angel of Texas*, 220.

[16]Mannen Clements was buried in the Cox Cemetery in rural McCulloch County, north of county seat Brady. The original stone, now very worn and nearly illegible, shows his life spanned from February 26, 1845, to March 29, 1887. In 1995 Robert W. Stephens and Chuck Parsons placed a new flat stone at his grave, the legend reading: "Mannen Clements/Feb. 26, 1845/ Mar. 29, 1887/ Border's Texas Cavalry/C.S.A." The only biography of Clements remains Stephens' *Mannen Clements: Texas Gunfighter*, privately printed, 1996.

[17]Bill C. James, *Barney Riggs: A West Texas Gunman* (Carrollton, TX: privately printed, 1982). A more recent study is *Barney K. Riggs: The Yuma and Pecos Avenger* by Ellis Lindsey and Gene Riggs (XLibris Corporation, 2002).

[18]Tise, 436.

[19]Eda Lochausen married Rankin Byars Kimbrough. Her obituary in the *El Paso Herald-Post* of January 17, 1961, announced she had passed the previous day. She was described as a "member of a pioneer West Texas ranching family. Her husband was a well-known El Paso banker

and businessman. Her father was an early day cattleman; her mother, Julia Ardoin Lochausen, was a direct descendant of Dr. Anson Jones, the last president of Texas as a Republic. Eda received her education at Mulholland School in San Antonio and attended Madame de Jarnets Finishing School in New York City. She later studied voice abroad where she resided for many years." The woman whose world was so refined and grand and so drastically different from her pioneer home in Pecos, could not forget that afternoon when she was six years old and among the guests were James Brown Miller and John Wesley Hardin. C. L. Sonnichsen, *Ten Texas Feuds* (Albuquerque: University of New Mexico Press, 1957, 1971), 205. And the *El Paso Herald-Post*, January 17, 1961.

[20]Hardin County, Tennessee census, 1860 and 1870. Martin Hardin was born about 1826 in Tennessee. His first wife was Martha Bills, but he was married a second time to Sarah G., maiden name unknown, by 1850. Martin Q.' s obituary shows he was a highly respected member of the community in which he had lived. The *Lordsburg Liberal* praised him as a pioneer of the county, and notes that at an unspecified date he "got the western fever about [the] time he attained his majority, when we find him a Texas ranger, one of the bravest of the brave." When he went to New Mexico Territory, "he was appointed deputy U.S. marshal, an office which he held for many years, in fact he has been a natural peace officer most of his life." Hardin was named postmaster by President Wilson "and did everything in his power to serve his constituents well and faithfully." He must have left Reeves County, Texas, area shortly after the unsuccessful murder plot as in 1896 he married Arminda Ellen Conner. The couple had two children: Herbert Quilla and Millard. At his death on January 28, 1933, the *Liberal* described him as a "Pioneer Leader"; the Heather funeral home was "packed to its doors" and "could hold only a fraction of those who came from far and wide to pay a last tribute of love to our pioneer citizen." See *Lordsburg Liberal*, February 3, 1933. Martin Quilla Hardin was buried in the Mountain View Cemetery in Lordsburg, New Mexico. His grave is marked.

[21]Bill Leftwich, *Tracks Along the Pecos* (Pecos, TX: The Pecos Press, 1957), 48. Leftwich quotes portions of the court document, case # 150.

²²Daniel Murphy served one term, elected on November 6, 1894, and serving until November 3, 1896. Tise, 436.

²³Daniel Murphy to Adj. Gen. W. H. Mabry, February 21, 1895.

²⁴G. A. Frazer to Gov. Charles A. Culberson, February 24, 1895. The community of Eddy, New Mexico is now known as Carlsbad.

²⁵Capt. John R. Hughes to Adjutant General Mabry, March 5, and March 7, 1895.

²⁶J. B. Miller to John Wesley Hardin, undated but January 1895.

²⁷The serial number of the watch is 4069110; the serial number of the Colt is 84304. The presentation was made on April 7, 1895. A photograph of both items appears in Bill C. James' biography of Miller, *Mysterious Killer: James Brown Miller 1861–1909* (No place: privately printed, 1976), no pagination. The photo of the watch and pistol also appears in *The Last Gunfighter* by Richard C. Marohn, 216. Miller continued his career as a hired killer until his own death in 1909 at the hands of a lynch mob in Ada, Oklahoma. For the last killing and subsequent lynching see Parsons, *James Brown Miller and Death in Oklahoma: Was Justice Denied in Ada?* (Gonzales, TX: Reese's Print Shop, 2009 and 2011).

²⁸The saloon is today a museum.

CHAPTER 21

¹*El Paso Herald*, March 30, 1895.

²This historic three-story building that Hardin had used for his office from April 1895 until his death, burned during the night of April 19, 2012. On the twentieth a number of items were found on Hardin's grave: several dollars in change, a few bullet casings, and a 14-inch wooden cross. All these items were gathered up and preserved "in the growing collection" of items left on Hardin's grave. See *Grave Concerns*, the *Newsletter* of Concordia Heritage Association, May, 2012. Dorothy Elder, editor, in answer to the authors' query as to the possible cause of the fire, responded: "I don't know but I do know they were using it for storage which made it a risk." Elder to Parsons, July 2, 2012.

³*El Paso Daily Times*, April 7, 1895.

[4]George A. Scarborough was elected sheriff on November 4, 1884, was re-elected November 2, 1886 and served until November 6, 1888. Tise, 293.

[5]*Historical and Biographical Record of the Cattle Industry and the Cattlemen of Texas and Adjacent Territory* (Facsimile edition, New York: Antiquarian Press, 1959), 371–72. Originally published by Woodward & Tierman Printing Co. in St. Louis in 1895. The complete life of Scarborough is in Robert K. DeArment's *George Scarborough: The Life and Death of a Lawman on the Closing Frontier* (Norman: University of Oklahoma Press, 1992). Scarborough was appointed a deputy U.S. marshal working under Richard C. Ware, the U.S. Marshal for the Western District of Texas.

[6]Milton's Texas Ranger Service record shows this date of enlistment in Capt. Ira Long's Company of the Frontier Battalion.

[7]J. Evetts Haley, *Jeff Milton: A Good Man with a Gun* (Norman: University of Oklahoma Press, 1948), 39.

[8]The best work on Selman remains Leon Claire Metz, *John Selman: Texas Gunfighter* (New York: Hastings House, Publishers, 1966; repr. University of Oklahoma Press, 1980, under the title *John Selman, Gunfighter)*.

[9]No full biography of McMahan has yet appeared, except a brief article by Doug Dukes, "Frank McMahan in Custody," *Journal* of the Wild West History Association 8, no. 4 (August 2009): 36–39. See also his Ranger Service Records. McMahan later married Alice Hunter, the sister of noted newspaperman and book printer, J. Marvin Hunter. McMahan died March 6, 1940. A bit of irony is that J. Marvin claimed that he had met John Wesley Hardin when he was working in his father's print shop in Mason. It is known that Hardin was working on his autobiography while in Kimble County and apparently Hardin went to Mason to inquire about the cost of printing his book. John Hunter had started the Mason newspaper in 1892, but in late 1894 or early 1895 when Hardin visited he did not have the equipment for such a publication. J. Marvin Hunter remembered meeting Hardin years later.

[10]In addition to the early biography of Hughes, *Border Boss: Captain John R. Hughes—Texas Ranger* by Jack Martin (San Antonio: The Naylor Company, 1942; repr. State House Press in 1990) see Chuck

Parsons, *Captain John R. Hughes: Lone Star Ranger* (Denton: University of North Texas Press, 2011).

[11]W. C. McGown to Gov. Charles A. Culberson, July 31, 1895.

[12]Victor Queen was born on September 5, 1871, in Arkansas. Shortly after his birth the family migrated to Lampasas, Texas. As a young man Vic rode off and joined his uncle Kep Queen, then a member of the Cornett-Whitley gang of train and bank robbers. How long Vic Queen was a gang member is unknown but at some point he left the gang and traveled to New Mexico Territory. It was there that he met and became friends with Martin M'rose. Queen died December 11, 1904, in Silver City, New Mexico. See "Who Was That Outlaw?" by Linda Kirkpatrick, *Texas Escapes,* August 10, 2010. M'rose was the more notorious of the pair. He was "a young Silesian from the San Antonio area who became an outlaw in the Pecos River valley of New Mexico and far west Texas." Did the pair meet up in Live Oak County? That is where M'rose was when the census taker enumerated him in 1880, his occupation given as stock raiser. By the 1890s he had left Texas and developed a cattle and horse raising operation which to him was quite successful. He was also a wanted man with a reward for his capture. Queen's partner's name is seen in a great variety of ways. The El Paso newspapers usually spelled it "Morose" or "M'rose" but occasionally "M'Rose." T. Lindsay Baker spelled the name "Mroz" in his book *The Polish Texans* (San Antonio: The Texan Institute of Cultures, 1982).

[13]*El Paso Times*, May 12, 1895.

[14]Ibid., April 21, 1895.

[15]Lee Myers, "Two Lives of Sin Had Impact on Southwest," *El Paso Sunday Magazine*, November 10, 1963.

[16]DeArment, *George Scarborough*, 98.

[17]Metz, *John Selman: Texas Gunfighter*, 162–63.

[18]Nordyke. *John Wesley Hardin: Texas Gunman*, 265.

[19]*El Paso Times*, April 24, 1895.

[20]Ibid.

[21]Ibid.

[22]Ibid.

[23]DeArment, *George Scarborough*, 113.

[24]*El Paso Times*, May 2, 1895.

[25]Ibid., May 4, 1895.

[26]Richard M. Glover to John Wesley Hardin, May 18, 1895.

[27]*El Paso Times*, May 7, 1895.

[28]Ibid., May 10, 1895.

[29]Ibid., May 16, 1895.

[30]Ibid., May 17, 1895.

[31]Ibid., June 2, 1895.

[32]The only work on this noted individual remains "G. W. Gladden—Hard Luck Warrior" by Dave Johnson in the *Quarterly* of the National Association and Center for Outlaw and Lawman History (NOLA) 15, no. 3 (July–September, 1991): 1–6.

[33]*El Paso Herald*, May 24, 1895; and *Gonzales Inquirer*, June 6, 1895.

[34]*El Paso Times*, June 30, 1895.

[35]J. D. Milton, Special Ranger, to W. H. Mabry, Adj. Gen. State of Texas, June 30, 1895. This brief report was penned on letterhead of Sheriff Frank B. Simmons.

[36]*El Paso Times*, June 30, 1895.

[37]Ibid., July 3, 1895.

[38]Ibid.

CHAPTER 22

[1]DeArment, *George Scarborough*, 110.

[2]Leon Claire Metz, *The Shooters* (El Paso: Mangan Books, 1976), 261.

[3]Lee Myers, correspondence to Parsons, September 26 and November 18, 1970, and undated *Silver City Enterprise*, December 1904.

[4]The *El Paso Times* and *El Paso Herald* of August 2, 1895 describe the incident. Whether Hardin learned of it through the newspaper or from Beulah herself is not divulged. DeArment suggests that Hardin was out of town because he was searching for a publisher of his manuscript, 121.

[5]*El Paso Times*, August 7, 1895.

[6]Ibid.

[7]*Eddy Current*, August 15, 1895. See also Bob Alexander, *Lawmen, Outlaws and S.O.Bs. Gunfighters of the Old Southwest,* vol. 2 (Silver City,

NM: High-Lonesome Books, 2007), 103; and *Deadly Dozen: Twelve Forgotten Gunfighters of the Old West* by Robert K. DeArment (Norman: University of Oklahoma Press, 2003), 176–77. Richard Alonzo "Lon" Bass was no relative to Texas outlaw Sam Bass. In 1880 he resided in Frio County, Texas, with his wife Cordelia and their three children. Bass was born about 1856. He met his fate in a gunfight with an Arizona Ranger, Bill Webb, on February 8, 1903.

[8]From King James Version, 2 Samuel, 1, 25.

[9]*El Paso Times*, August 20, 1895; Metz, *Dark Angel of Texas*, 257.

[10]Metz, Ibid.

[11]*El Paso Herald*, August 22, 1895.

[12]Correspondence to Parsons from Dr. L. H. Hubbard, President Emeritus, Texas Woman's University, Denton, Texas, December 29, 1972. Original in author's collection. And Louis H. Hubbard, "A Boy's Impression of El Paso in the 1890's," *Password* (Official Publication of the El Paso County Historical Society) 11, no. 3 (Fall 1966): 98.

[13]John Selman's version of killing Hardin is from the *El Paso Herald*, August 20, 1895.

[14]The statements from Selman, Brown, Shackelford and Anderson are all from the *El Paso Herald*, August 20, 1895.

[15]Hubbard, "A Boy's Impression of El Paso in the 1890's," 98. Hubbard recalled that if he received a telegram for Hardin in the morning he would take it to his room; if it was received in the afternoon he found Hardin in one of the several saloons he frequented. Hubbard, in the fall of 1899, entered as a freshman in the University of Texas. He later became president of Texas Woman's University in Denton. He died on July 13, 1973, and is buried in Oakwood Cemetery in Austin. His simple headstone shows only his full name and the dates of his life: 1882–1973.

CHAPTER 23

[1]From the scrapbook of Attorney Adrian D. Storms in the Special Collections, University of Texas-El Paso Library. This is a combination of drawings and notes and clippings from various El Paso newspapers.

[2]*Daily Herald* (Brownsville, Texas), September 6, 1895, reprinting an item from the *El Paso Daily Times*. For various reasons Hardin's name was kept alive for some months after the killing.

[3]*El Paso Daily Times*, August 21, 1895, in the popular column "Around Town." Commented the *Times:* "The city was as quiet as a country church yard last night. The police had nothing to do."

[4]Martha Deen Underwood and Hamilton Underwood, *Concordia El Paso Walking Tour* (El Paso: El Paso Regency Printing Co., no date), 49–51.

[5]C. L. Sonnichsen. *The Grave of John Wesley Hardin: Three Essays on Grassroots History* (College Station: Texas A&M University Press, 1979.) The other two essays are "Blood on the Typewriter" and "The Pattern of Texas Feuds." Also see "The Great Attempted Body Snatching Caper," the afterword, in Metz' *John Wesley Hardin: Dark Angel of Texas*, 287–93.

[6]Application for Letters of Administration of T. T. Teel, dated August 21, 1895, number 260. El Paso County Court Records.

[7]In 1900 Whitmore was residing in El Paso with wife Bobbie, who was a Hardin relative, hence the Hardin children acquiring his services to represent them. El Paso County census, 1900.

[8]A photograph of this unusual document, once in this author's possession, appears in Richard Marohn's *The Last Gunfighter*, 223.

[9]"Application for Letters of Administration of Helen B. McRose," El Paso Court Records. Curiously she later claimed the manuscript, the watch, one of the revolvers and two rings (not listed in the estate papers) were worth an astronomical $10,000. This in the *El Paso Times* of August 30, 1895.

[10]*El Paso Daily Times*, August 22, 1895.

[11]"Application for Temporary Letters of Administration of J. L. Whitmore," number 261, El Paso County Court Records.

[12]*The Life of John Wesley Hardin, As Written by Himself* (Norman: University of Oklahoma Press, 1961), 4.

[13]Whereas John C. Moore was born in Ireland, Smith was a local boy, born in Guadalupe County in 1861, and perhaps remained in that county his lifetime. He married Miss Cora Walker in 1891 and they had one child. He was part owner and business manager of the *Seguin Enterprise*. An obituary described him as "honest and correct, filling the duties of citizenship with fidelity." The *Seguin Enterprise*, August 19, 1898.

[14]Letter from T. A. Sowell to J. Marvin Hunter in *Frontier Times*, May 1935, 368.

[15]John H. Jenkins, *Basic Texas Books: An Annotated Bibliography of Selected Works for a Research Library* (Austin: Jenkins Publishing Co., 1983), 222.

[16]*El Paso Daily Times*, November 10, 1895.

[17]The Kimble County 1900 census shows Robert M. Turner as 42, wife Emma as 37, living with their six children in household number 158. Two households below is that of Pearl Hardin, living alone, 19 years of age. She was born in April 1881. The census taker obviously erred in placing Pearl in a separate household.

[18]1900 Walker County census shows Hardin: 25 years old, married, teacher.

CHAPTER 24

[1]Lipscomb County 1880 census; "Lipscomb County" by Donald R. Abbe in *New Handbook of Texas*, vol. 4, 215–17.

[2]*Houston Daily News*, April 9, 1895. The stabbing occurred on April 7. A search of Hays County District Court records failed to provide further information on this affair. Apparently it did not result in any legal action.

[3]William R. Hunt, "Kent County" in *New Handbook of Texas*, vol. 3, 1073–74.

[4]Hardin as constable in Kent County is from the *Dallas Morning News*, May 19, 1901. The expression "scalper" refers in this context to a man hired by a rancher to protect his herds from rustlers. Modern readers may be more accustomed to the term "Range Detective" or "Bounty Hunter" but that is probably a creation of Hollywood.

[5]Richard F. Selcer and Kevin S. Foster, *Written in Blood: The History of Fort Worth's Fallen Lawmen Volume I, 1881–1909* (Denton: University of North Texas Press, 2010), 190. Selcer cites the *Fort Worth Register* of December 16, 1900.

[6]This is originally from the *Coming West* newspaper, date of March 21, 1901. It was the only publication in Scurry County during that time. It was reprinted in the *Colorado Clipper* of Colorado City of May 8,

1901. This was the newspaper of the day when the county seat was simply Colorado. It was later changed to Colorado City, the seat of Mitchell County, Texas.

[7]Personal interview with Don M. Jay by Norman W. Brown, May --, 2011. The incident was related to Jay by his grandparents.

[8]*Colorado Clipper*, May 8, 1901.

[9]*Dallas Morning News*, May 19, 1901.

[10]This was Alonzo C. Leslie, a 39-year-old physician from Virginia. In 1900 he and his wife had been married nine years but had no children. Apparently he arrived in Scurry County at the turn of the century and chose to remain. In 1930 he was still practicing medicine, listed as such by the census. His death record indicates he died on April 1, 1943, in Snyder, at the age of 82. The record further indicates he was buried the following day in the Snyder Cemetery. J. P. Beck was also the proprietor of a hardware store in Snyder and provided some type of service to Mr. Stevenson during his recovery at Dr. Leslie's home.

[11]*Coming West*, May 23, 1901. This was a short-lived newspaper of Scurry County.

[12]Death certificate of John S. Stevenson.

[13]Tennessee-born Levi C. Darby was elected on November 6, 1900, and served until November 4, 1902. See Tise, 460; Scurry County Census, 1900.

[14]The various versions result from interviews with Don M. Jay, direct Hardin descendant, and author-historian of Kent County.

[15]The description of the saloon is from Don M. Jay.

[16]Norman N. Rodgers was a native of New Orleans, Louisiana. His family first came to Parker County, Texas, and when he was twelve years old his mother sent him off to become a cowboy. He made his first cattle drive to Johnson County, Arkansas, that year. Rodgers and his friend James B. Gillett joined the Frontier Battalion of Texas Rangers in 1875 but Rodgers went back to working cattle until he was elected sheriff of Kent County. He was first elected November 6, 1894, and was re-elected four times, serving Kent County until November 4, 1902. From Rodgers' unpublished autobiography in family scrapbook and Tise, *Texas County Sheriffs*, 303.

[17]*Dallas Morning News*, October 12, 1901.

[18]Personal communication from D'Lynn Williams to Norman W. Brown, October --, 2011. The description came down to Williams through Ned Underwood, grandson of George W. Underwood, who may have witnessed the killing of Hardin, but refused to admit that possibly out of fear of retaliation. And personal interview with Don M. Jay.

[19]Ibid.

[20]Personal interview with Jeff Hardin, grandson of Jeff Davis Hardin, and Norman W. Brown, December 5, 2011. Hardin heard the story from his grandmother Mary Taylor Hardin Blount.

[21]Personal communication from D'Lynn Williams to Norman W. Brown, October --, 2011.

[22]*Cripple Creek Times*, November 19, 1918. The daughter's name was Mrs. Frank Helms.

[23]Teller County, Colorado census, 1930, shows Snowden, 52 years old, and his wife Hattie, 37 years old, and four stepchildren ranging in age from nineteen to six years of age.

[24]Personal communication from Ken Kyser of Margate, Florida, to Norman Huppert Sr., of Enterprise, Alabama. Mr. Huppert went to Cripple Creek, Colorado, in May 2012 and researched local sources for Snowden's movements. He then provided copies of his research to Norman W. Brown.

[25]Interview with Don M. Jay.

[26]T. Lindsay Baker, *Ghost Towns of Texas* (Norman: University of Oklahoma Press, 1986), 54.

[27]Jewell G. Pritchett and Erma Barfoot Black, *Kent County and Its People* (Rotan, TX: Self-published, 1983), 49.

[28]Personal observations by Norman W. Brown.

SELECTED BIBLIOGRAPHY

PRIMARY SOURCES

Adjutant General Records: Letters Received and Letters Sent, 1870–1872. Texas State Library and Archives, Austin. Texas State Police Ledgers, 1870–1873.

Biennial Reports of the Director & Superintendent of the Texas State Penitentiary, December 1, 1878–October 31, 1880. In Texas State Library and Archives.

Bruington, Lola Lee Daniell. "W. H. Hutchinson." Unpublished manuscript.

Cemetery Inventory of Coon Hill Cemetery, Santa Rosa, Florida.

Cemetery Records of Santa Rosa County, Florida.

Clements, Mary Ann Robinson. Pension Application.

Clow, Robert J. Notebook. Archives in the Briscoe Center for American History, Austin.

Davis, Gov. E. J. Papers in Texas State Library and Archives.

DeWitt County Marriage Records. Books A, D.

Ellsworth Hotel Registers, The Grand Central Hotel. Microfilm copy in author's collection.

El Paso County Court Records.

Fannin County Deed Records, copies provided courtesy Ronnie Atnip, Bonham, Texas

Ferguson, Nancy Jane Griffin. Widow's Pension Application.

Florida Death Index, 1877–1998, Vol. 2.

Gonzales County Marriage Record Books. Books A, B, and B1.

Green, William M. Texas Ranger Service Records. Texas State Library and Archives, Austin.

Hardin, John Wesley. Petitions for Pardon.

Hardin, John Wesley. *The Life of John Wesley Hardin As Written By Himself.* With introduction by Robert G. McCubbin. Norman: University of Oklahoma, 1960.

Hardin Letters in the Witliff Collection, Alkek Library, Southwestern Writers Collections, Texas State University, San Marcos.

Hutchinson, Mrs. Ida Temple Merritt. Widow's Pension Application.

Hutchinson, William H. Pension Application.

Jacksonville, Florida City Directory, 1876–1877.

Jones, Major John B. Correspondence to John R. Waller, June 3, 1874.

Moffit, Johnnie Lea. "Notes on the Hargis Family." Scrapbook archived in the Gonzales County Archives.

Moye, A. B. Autobiographical sketch; manuscript copy in possession of author.

Navarro County, Texas County Clerk Records.

Palestine, Texas City Directory.

R. B. Dixon Collection, Texas State Library and Archives, Austin.
Ruff, Mrs. Elizabeth M. Widow's Pension Application.
Scrapbooks of "Old Choc" copies provided courtesy Ronnie Atnip, Bonham, Texas.
Stell, Thomas M. "The Taylor-Sutton Feud." Manuscript in C. L. Sonnichsen
    Collection, University of Texas–El Paso. Copy in author's collection.
Taylor, John L. Correspondence to Harriet Smither, April 29, 1937.
Waller, Mrs. John R. Widow's Application for Pension.

FEDERAL CENSUS—TEXAS COUNTIES

Anderson, 1870, 1880
Austin, 1870
Burleson, 1850
Cherokee, 1870
Coleman, 1870
Collin, 1880
Colorado, 1880
Comanche, 1870
Concho, 1900
DeWitt, 1860, 1870,
    1880
El Paso, 1900, 1920
Wilson, 1870

Fannin, 1860
Gonzales, 1870
Harrison, 1870
Hill, 1860, 1870
Houston, 1870
Kent, 1900
Kerr, 1900
Kimble, 1900
Lipscomb, 1880
McLennan, 1870
Milam, 1870
Navarro, 1860, 1870

Polk, 1870, 1900
Rusk, 1870
Tarrant, 1870, 1880
Travis, 1880
Trinity, 1860 (Slave
    and Free), 1870,
    1880
Walker, 1880, 1900
Waller, 1880
Washington, 1870,
    1880

ALABAMA COUNTIES

Baldwin, 1880

Escambia, 1880

Mobile, 1850

ARKANSAS COUNTIES

White, 1860

COLORADO COUNTIES

Teller, 1930

FLORIDA COUNTIES

Alachua, 1870, 1880

Escambia, 1880

Santa Rosa, 1860,
    1870, 1880

MISSISSIPPI COUNTIES

Itawamba, 1850

NEW MEXICO COUNTIES

Eddy, 1900   Socorro, 1910

TENNESSEE

Hardin, 1960, 1870

INTERVIEWS

Ronnie Atnip with Parsons, February 7, 2012
Douglas Hitchcock with Brown, various dates
Don M. Jay with Brown, various dates
Juanita Davis Woods with Parsons, August 30, 2011

PERSONAL CORRESPONDENCE

Donaly E. Brice to Parsons, June 7, 2011; October 26, 2011
Dorothy Elder to Parsons, July 3, 2012
Dr. L. H. Hubbard to Parsons, December 29, 1972
Gary Kraisinger to Parsons, June 26, 2011
John Luckey to Parsons, May 11, 2011 and undated
James A. Mundie to Parsons, May 6, 2011
Lee Myers to Parsons, September 26, November 18, 1970
Ellen J. Reagan to Parsons, April 17, April 30, May 14, 1969
Michael K. Simmons to Parsons, April 15 and undated, 2012
D'Lynn Williams to Brown, October --, 2011

NEWSPAPERS

TEXAS

Athens Courier
Austin Daily Democratic
    Statesman
Bastrop Advertiser
Colorado Clipper
Coming West (Snyder)
Cuero Daily Record
Cuero Weekly Star
Bonham Daily Favorite
Brenham Weekly Banner

Brownsville Daily Herald
Burnet County Bulletin
Clarksville Standard
Daily State Gazette (Austin)
Dallas Daily Herald
Dallas Morning News
Drag Net (Gonzales)
El Paso Daily Times
El Paso Daily Herald
El Paso Herald-Post

Fayette County New Era
   (La Grange)
Flake's Semi-Weekly Bulletin
   (Galveston)
Fort Worth Democrat
Galveston Daily News
Gonzales Inquirer
Houston Daily News
Houston Daily Telegraph

Kerrville Mountain Sun
Lampasas Weekly Dispatch
San Antonio Daily Express
San Antonio Daily Herald
Seguin Enterprise
Texas Capital
Victoria Advocate
Weatherford Exponent

ALABAMA

Atmore Advance

Mobile Register

*Montgomery Daily
   Advertiser and
   Mail*

FLORIDA

Pensacola Journal

Pensacola News

KANSAS

Abilene Chronicle
Junction City
Kansas City Daily

Commonwealth
Kansas State Record
Oxford Times

*Salina Weekly
   Journal*

NEW MEXICO

Eddy Current

Lordsburg Liberal

*Silver City
   Enterprise*

NEW YORK

*National Police
   Gazette*

New York Clipper

New York Times

TENNESSEE

Memphis Weekly Public Ledger

BOOKS, PAMPHLETS, AND ARTICLES

Abbe, Donald R. "Lipscomb County" in *The New Handbook of Texas*.

Alexander, Bob. *Lawmen, Outlaws and S.O.Bs: Gunfighters of the Old Southwest*. Vol. 2. Silver City, NM: High-Lonesome Books, 2007.

Anderson, George C. "Touring Kansas and Colorado in 1871: The Journal of George C. Anderson." *Quarterly* of the Kansas State Historical Society. Autumn, 1956.

[Anonymous] *The Texas Almanac for 1857, with Statistics, Historical and Biographical Sketches, &c*. Irving, TX: Glen's Sporting Goods, Inc., 1986; facsimile edition.

Archer, Carol J. "Richard Glover" in *The History of Gonzales County*. Dallas: Curtis Media Corp., 1986.

Askins, Charles. *Texans, Guns and History*. New York: Winchester Press, 1970.

Baker, T. Lindsay. *Ghost Towns of Texas*. Norman: University of Oklahoma Press, 1986.

———. *The Polish Texans*. San Antonio: Institute of Texan Cultures, 1982.

Bowden, Jesse Earle, and William S. Cummins. *Texas Desperado in Florida: The Capture of Outlaw John Wesley Hardin in Pensacola, 1877*. Pensacola: The Pensacola Historical Society, 2002.

Brown, Norman W. "In the Shadow of John Wesley Hardin." The *Journal* of the Wild West History Association 4, no. 4 (August, 2011).

Caldwell, Clifford R., and Ron DeLord. *Texas Lawmen 1835–1899: The Good and the Bad*. Charleston, SC: The History Press, 2011.

Cook, Donna Gholson. *Gholson Road: Revolutionaries and Texas Rangers*. N.p.: 1st Books, n.d.

Crouch, Barry A., and Donaly E. Brice. *The Governor's Hounds: The Texas State Police, 1870–1873*. Austin: University of Texas Press, 2011.

———. "Captain Thomas Williams: The Path of Duty." In *The Human Tradition*. No. 9. Edited by Ty Cashion and Jesus de la Teja.

Cutler, William G. *History of the State of Kansas*.

Daniell, Lewis. *Personnel of the Texas State Government*. 1892.

Day, Jack Hays. *The Sutton-Taylor Feud*. San Antonio: Sid Murray & Son, privately printed, 1937.

DeArment, Robert K. *George Scarborough: The Life and Death of a Lawman on the Closing Frontier*. Norman: University of Oklahoma Press, 1992.

———. *Deadly Dozen: Twelve Forgotten Gunfighters of the Old West*. Norman: University of Oklahoma Press, 2003.

DeWitt County Historical Commission. *The History of DeWitt County, Texas*. Dallas: Curtis Media Corp., 1991.

Dixson, Walter Clay. *Richland Crossing: A Portrait of Texas Pioneers*. Everman, TX: Peppermill Publishing Company, 1994.

Dukes, Doug. "Frank McMahan in Custody" in the *Journal* of the Wild West History Association 2, no. 4 (August 2009).

Elder, Dorothy. *Grave Concerns* (The Official Publication of the Concordia Cemetery Association), May, 2012.

Ellison, Douglas W. "The West's Bloodiest Duel – Never Happened!" in the *Journal* of the Wild West History Association 1, no. 5 (October, 2008).

Garza, Phyllis de la. *Death for Dinner: The Benders of (Old) Kansas.* Honolulu: Talei Publishers, 2005.

George, A. L. *The Texas Convict: Sketches of the Penitentiary, Convict Farm and Railroads Together with Poems.* Self-published, 1895; facsimile edition by Vikon Publishing Co., Dallas, 1983.

George, David. "Jack Helm Meets John Wesley Hardin." *The Texas Gun Collector.* Spring, 2003.

Gillett, James B. *Six Years with the Texas Rangers.* New Haven: Yale University Press, 1963.

Goebel, Patsy and Karen McWhorter. *Cemetery Records of DeWitt County.* Vols. 1–3. Cuero, TX: Privately printed, 1986.

Green, William M. "Breaking Up the Lawless Element in Texas" in *Frontier Times*, May 1924.

Haley, J. Evetts. *Jeff Milton: A Good Man With A Gun.* Norman: University of Oklahoma Press, 1948.

Hill County Heritage Book Committee. *The History of Hill County, Texas.* 2 vols. Louisville, KY: Heritage Publishing Consultants, Inc., 2010.

[Hogg, Thomas E.] *Life and Adventures of Sam Bass: The Notorious Union Pacific and Texas Train Robber.* Dallas: Dallas Commercial Steam Print, 1878. Facsimile edition.

Hubbard, Louis B. "A Boy's Impression of El Paso in the 1890's" in *Password.* El Paso County Historical Society, Fall 1966.

Hunt, William R. "Kent County" in *The New Handbook of Texas.* Austin: The Texas State Historical Association, 1996.

Hyatt, Marjorie Burnett. "Littleberry Wright Family" in *The History of DeWitt County, Texas.* Dallas: Curtis Media Corp., 1991.

Hyman, Carolyn. "Asbury Bascom Davidson." In *The New Handbook of Texas.* Austin: Texas State Historical Association, 1996.

James, Bill C. *Mysterious Killer: James Brown Miller 1861–1909.* N.p., 1976.

———. *Barney Riggs: A West Texas Gunman.* Carrollton, TX: Privately printed, 1982.

Jenkins, John H. *Basic Texas Books: An Annotated Bibliography of Selected Works for a Research Library.* Rev. ed. Austin: Texas State Historical Association, 1988.

Johnson, Dave. "G. W. Gladden—Hard Luck Warrior." *Quarterly* of the National Association for Outlaw and Lawman History (NOLA), July–September 1991.

———. *The Mason County "Hoo Doo" War, 1874–1902.* Denton: University of North Texas Press, 2006.

Johnson, Dave. *John Ringo: King of the Cowboys. His Life and Times From Hoo Doo War to Tombstone.* 2nd. rev. ed. Denton: University of North Texas Press, 2008.

Kirkpatrick, Linda. "Who Was That Outlaw?" in *Texas Escapes*, August 10, 2010 column.

Koop, Waldo E. "Enter John Wesley Hardin: A Dim Trail to Abilene." *The Prairie Scout* 2. Abilene: The Kansas Corral of the Westerners, 1974.

Lake, Stuart N. *Wyatt Earp Frontier Marshal*. Boston: Houghton Mifflin Co., 1931.

Langston, James Goree V, and Deborah Bloys Hardin. "Thomas Jewett Goree" in *The New Handbook of Texas*. Austin: Texas State Historical Association, 1996.

Lee, Nantie P. "Captain James Knox White Family." *The History of DeWitt County, Texas*. Dallas: Curtis Media Corp., 1991.

Leftwich, Bill. *Tracks Along the Pecos*. Pecos, TX: The Pecos Press, 1957.

Lindsey, Ellis and Gene Riggs. *Barney K. Riggs: The Yuma and Pecos Avenger*. XLibris Corp, 2002.

McCown, Dennis. "Two Women" in the *Quarterly* of the National Association for Outlaw and Lawman History (NOLA) 23, no. 2 (April–June 1999): 20–25.

———. "In Search of Martin Mrose" in the *Quarterly* of the National Association for Outlaw and Lawman History (NOLA) 24 [23], no. 4 (October–December 1999): 18–30.

———. "Broken Heart, Broken Dreams" in the *Quarterly* of the National Association For Outlaw and Lawman History (NOLA) 27, no. 4 (October–December 2003): 1, 5–13.

———. "A Shooting Much Exaggerated" in the *Journal* of the Wild West History Association, October, 2011.

McCoy, Joseph G. *Historic Sketches of the Cattle Trade of the West and Southwest*. Facsimile edition by Readex Microprint Corp., 1964.

Marohn, Richard C. *The Last Gunfighter: John Wesley Hardin*. College Station, TX: Creative Publishing Company, 1995.

Mellard, R. T. "The Latch String is on the Outside." *The Trail Drivers of Texas*. Austin: University of Texas Press, 1986.

Metz, Leon Claire. *The Shooters*. El Paso: Mangan Books, 1976.

———. *John Selman: Texas Gunfighter*. New York: Hastings, 1960; repr. as *John Selman Gunfighter* by Norman: University of Oklahoma Press, 1980.

Metz, Leon. *John Wesley Hardin: Dark Angel of Texas*. El Paso: Mangan Books, 1996.

Miller, Rick. *Bounty Hunter*. College Station, TX: Creative Publishing Co., 1988.

———. *Sam Bass and Gang*. Austin: State House Press, 1999.

———. *Blood Bill Longley: The Mythology of a Gunfighter*. Denton: University of North Texas Press, 2011.

Mundie, James A., et al. *Texas Burial Sites of Civil War Notables: A Biographical and Pictorial Field Guide*. Hillsboro, TX: Hill College Press, 2002.

Myers, Lee. "Two Lives of Sin Had Impact on Southwest." *El Paso Sunday Magazine*, November 10, 1963.

Nolan, Frederick. *The Wild West: History, Myth and The Making of America.* Edison, NJ: Chartwell Books, 2004.

Nordyke, Lewis. *John Wesley Hardin: Texas Gunman.* New York: William Morrow & Co., 1957.

O'Neal, Bill. *Encyclopedia of Western Gunfighters.* Norman: University of Oklahoma Press, 1979.

Parrish, Karen S. "Banquete" in *The New Handbook of Texas.*

Parsons, Chuck. *The Sutton-Taylor Feud: The Deadliest Blood Feud in Texas.* Denton: The University of North Texas Press, 2009.

———. *Captain John R. Hughes: Lone Star Ranger.* Denton: University of North Texas Press, 2011.

———. "A Texas Gunfighter and the Kansas Murder Family." *Real West,* July 1980.

———. "Eyewitness to Cowtown Violence." *Real West,* April 1980.

———. *James Brown Miller and Death in Oklahoma: Was Justice Denied in Ada?* Gonzales: Reese's Print Shop, 2009, 2011.

———. "The DeWitt County Feud." In *The History of DeWitt County, Texas.* Dallas: Curtis Media Corp., 1991.

———. *The Capture of John Wesley Hardin.* College Station, TX: Creative Publishing Company, 1978.

———. "' Mervyn' A Poetical Correspondent." The *Brand Book* of the English Westerners Society, 1988–1989.

———. "Rangers in Lockhart." *The Plum Creek Almanac.* Fall, 2004.

———. "James Monroe 'Doc' Bockius." In *Newsletter* of the National Association for Outlaw and Lawman History (NOLA), Spring, 1977.

Ponder, Jerry. "John Wesley Hardin's Widow, Callie Lewis Hardin." In the *Quarterly* of the National Association for Outlaw and Lawman History 29, no. 4 (October–December 2005): 32–37.

Pritchett, Jewell S. and Erma Barfoot Black. *Kent County and Its People.* Rotan, TX: Self-published, 1983.

Ray, G. B. *Murder at the Corners.* San Antonio: The Naylor Company, 1957.

Ripley, Thomas. *They Died With Their Boots On.* Sydney Australia Edition, 1936.

Rosa, Joseph G. *Guns of the American West.* New York: Crown Publishers, Inc., 1985.

Rose, Victor M. *The Texas Vendetta; or, The Sutton-Taylor Feud.* N.p.: J. J. Little & Co., 1880. Facsimile repr., Houston: The Frontier Press of Texas, 1956.

Ross, Edith Connelley. "The Bloody Benders." In the *Quarterly* of The Kansas State Historical Society; repr., Vol. 17, 1926–1928.

Rothe, Aline. "Where Wes Hardin Started Running." *Frontier Times.*

Selcer, Richard F., and Kevin S. Foster. *Written in Blood: The History of Fort Worth's Fallen Lawmen. Vol. 1.* Denton: University of North Texas Press, 2010.

Smallwood, James M., Barry A. Crouch and Larry Peacock. *Murder and Mayhem: The War of Reconstruction in Texas*. College Station: Texas A&M University Press, 2003.

———. *The Feud That Wasn't: The Taylor Ring, Bill Sutton, John Wesley Hardin, and Violence in Texas*. College Station: Texas A&M University Press, 2008.

Smith, Karon Mac. "Archibald Greene Cone and Sally Cocke" in *The History of Gonzales County*. Gonzales County Historical Commission. Dallas: Curtis Media Corporation, 1986.

Sonnichsen, C. L. *I'll Die Before I'll Run: The Story of the Great Feuds of Texas*. New York: Harper & Brothers, 1951.

———. *Ten Texas Feuds*. Albuquerque: University of New Mexico Press, 1957, 1971

———. *The Grave of John Wesley Hardin: Three Essays on Grassroots History*. College Station: Texas A&M University Press, 1979.

Stamps, Roy and Jo Ann. *The Letters of John Wesley Hardin*. Austin: Eakin Press, 2001.

Stanley, Dorothy Dixon, and Annie Maud Knittel Avis. *History of Burton*. N.p., n.d.

[Steele, William] *A List of Fugitives from Justice*. Facsimile repr., Austin: State House Press, 1957.

Stephen, Homer. *The Frontier Postmasters*. Dublin, TX: The Dublin Progress, 1952.

Stephens, Robert R. *Mannen Clements: Texas Gunfighter*. Privately printed, 1996.

Sweet, Alexander. *On a Mexican Mustang through Texas, From the Gulf to the Rio Grande*. Hartford: S. S. Scranton & Co., 1883.

Thompson, Karen R., and Jane H. DiGesualdo. *Historical Round Rock*. Austin: Eakin Press, 1985.

Tise, Sammy. *Texas County Sheriffs*. Albuquerque, NM: Oakwood Printing, 1989.

Truitt, Eddie Day. *The Taylor Party*. Wortham, TX: Privately printed, 1992.

Tyler, Ron, General Editor. *The New Handbook of Texas*. Austin: Texas State Historical Association, 1996.

Underwood, Martha Deen and Hamilton Underwood. *Concordia El Paso Walking Tour*. El Paso: Regency Printing Co., n.d.

Walton, William A. *Life and Adventures of Ben Thompson, the Famous Texan*. Repr., Houston: The Frontier Press of Texas, 1954.

Wheat, John. *Postmasters & Post Offices of Texas, 1846–1930*.

Wood, Fern Morrow. *The Benders: Keepers of the Devil's Den*. Chelsea, MI: BookCrafters, 1993.

Woods, Larry J. "John Wesley Hardin's Deadly Brother." *Wild West*, February, 2006.

Wright, A. J. "A Gunfighter's Southern Vacation." The *Quarterly* of the National Association and Center for Outlaw and Lawman History. Autumn 1982.

INDEX

Italicized page numbers refer to illustrations.

481